# KIRTIPUR: AN URBAN COMMUNITY IN NEPAL
## its people, town planning, architecture and arts

# KIRTIPUR: AN URBAN COMMUNITY IN NEPAL

## its people, town planning, architecture and arts


Editors

**MEHRDAD SHOKOOHY**
(PROJECT DIRECTOR)

**and**

**NATALIE H. SHOKOOHY**

Contributors

| | |
|---|---|
| **MARC BARANI** | **RAMENDRA RAJ SHARMA** |
| **PADAM B. CHHETRI** | **MEHRDAD SHOKOOHY** |
| **ROBIN LALL CHITRAKAR** | **NATALIE H. SHOKOOHY** |
| **CHRIS MIERS** | **SUKRA SAGAR SHRESTHA** |
| **SHANKER M. PRADHAN** | **UTTAM SAGAR SHRESTHA** |
| **GAURI NATH RIMAL** | **SUDARSHAN RAJ TIWARI** |



**ARAXUS**

Monographs on Art Archæology and Architecture

**South Asian Series**

**London**

**1994**

First published in Great Britain 1994

ISBN 1 870606 02 7

British Library Cataloguing-in-Publication Data
A catalogue record of this book is available from the British Library.

**Designed, published and produced by Araxus Books, 130 St. Julian's Farm Road, London SE27 0RR, England.**

Printed by J. W. Arrowsmith Ltd, Bristol.

# TABLE OF CONTENTS


| | | Page |
|---|---|---|
| **Mehrdad Shokoohy** | *Introduction* | 1 |
| **Gauri Nath Rimal** | *Private and public involvement in conservation policy development* | 9 |
| **Mehrdad Shokoohy** | *History* | 13 |
| **Mehrdad Shokoohy** | *The Newars, the people of Kirtipur* | 21 |
| **Sukra Sagar Shrestha** | *Social life and festivals* | 29 |
| **Mehrdad Shokoohy** | *Urban fabric* | 35 |
| **Chris Miers** | *The Newari house* | 49 |
| **Ramendra Raj Sharma** | *Traditional houses of Kirtipur, their types and their building materials* | 57 |
| **Marc Barani** | *The residential unit - symbolic organization* | 63 |
| **Sukra Sagar Shrestha** | *Historic public buildings* | 75 |
| **Sudarshan Raj Tiwari** | *Tiered temples of Kirtipur, a study of their form and proportion* | 123 |
| **Natalie H. Shokoohy** | *Buddhist monasteries* | 131 |
| **Padam B. Chhetri** | *Kathmandu Valley Land Use Plan and Kirtipur* | 147 |
| **Shanker M. Pradhan** | *Land use and population survey* | 151 |
| **Uttam Sagar Shrestha** | *Land use changes in Kirtipur* | 155 |
| **Uttam Sagar Shrestha** | *Road transport and communications* | 167 |
| **Robin Lall Chitrakar** | *Water supply and sanitation* | 177 |
| **Mehrdad Shokoohy** | *Tourism and its effects on Kirtipur* | 185 |
| **Sukra Sagar Shrestha** | *Art and antiquities* | 189 |
| **Appendices** | | |
| Appendix A | *Inscriptions of Kirtipur* | 207 |
| Appendix B | *National Museum Kathmandu, images from Chilañcho Vihār* | 240 |
| Appendix C | *National Museum Kathmandu, objects from Mūl Bhagvānsthān, Chilañcho Mahāvihār* | 241 |
| **Glossary** | | 242 |
| **Bibliography** | | 247 |
| **Index** | | 251 |

## EDITORIAL NOTE

The method of transliteration of Sanskrit and Nepali words follows Monier Williams's *Sanskrit-English Dictionary* (Oxford, 1893) with slight modifications. A similar method has been employed for Newari words as written in the Devanagari script, rather than using a separate system to indicate Newari pronunciation. Common Anglicized words and geographical names are given without diacritical marks, in the form in modern administrative use.

Photographs and drawings by the individual contributors are acknowledged in the relevant captions. All other photographs are by Mehrdad Shokoohy, and all other drawings are based on the surveys of Mehrdad Shokoohy and Ian Thomson and produced by the Kirtipur team at the University of Greenwich.

# INTRODUCTION

MEHRDAD SHOKOOHY

Kirtipur, meaning the city of glory, is a small town in the Kathmandu Valley, about five kilometres south-east of the capital, Kathmandu. Kirtipur, also known as Kipu and Kyapu, is one of the oldest settlements in the valley, and is recorded as an ancient capital of Nepal. The town, inhabited by Newars, the earliest population group of the valley, occupies the top of a steep rocky hill, a location very different from the other main towns of the valley, as Kathmandu (formerly Kantipur or Kapu) and Patan (Lalitpur or Lalitpatan) are both on the plain, while Bhaktapur (Bhadgaon or Bhatgaon) is laid out on gently sloping ground at the top of a hill, and its steeper southern side. In ancient times Kirtipur was a stronghold, probably fortified, and the historical records show that up to the 18th century the control of Kirtipur was a key to maintaining power in the valley.

Today scanty traces of the ancient fortifications and parts of the later town walls still stand, and the mediaeval fabric of the town has survived with little change. Kirtipur's location on the hill top was not always an advantage for the population. The difficulty of transporting goods there, and the lack of easy access to the town restricted its development. While the other three main towns of the valley prospered, each growing to become the capital of a small regional kingdom, Kirtipur remained relatively small, with its boundaries virtually unchanged.

## MODERN CHANGES

In the past three decades changes in the way of life, as well as the introduction of motor vehicles to the valley have dramatically affected the urban fabric of Kathmandu, Patan, and to a certain extent Bhaktapur. Not only are the towns expanding beyond their old boundaries, but in the older quarters many narrow lanes are used by motor vehicles. These lanes are often not wide enough for man and motor car to pass side by side, and priority is not as a rule given to the former. During the last two decades in these towns some conservation projects have been undertaken to save the traditional squares and their buildings. In Kirtipur, although there have been no such conservation schemes, the stepped lanes have so far prevented motor vehicles from being taken into the town. The ancient layout of the open and built up areas has remained unchanged, the lanes are pedestrian, while the *ṭol* or urban square accommodates the daily activities of the neighbourhood, varying from domestic chores to drying crops.

With the rapid development of Kathmandu, and the proximity of the capital to Kirtipur, the town has come under increasing pressure for modern development. Kirtipur is a farming town. During the 1960s the rice paddies to the south-east of the town were chosen as the site for Tribhuvan University, and were compulsorily purchased from their owners. With the University came a new metalled road, and bus transport to the edge of the town. Kathmandu itself has expanded to such an extent that its outskirts are now very close to Kirtipur. The rising prices for building plots in Kathmandu and the nearby town of Patan have also made Kirtipur attractive for cheap residential development, and apart from students and some employees of the University, people of the lower income brackets from outside Kirtipur rent accommodation and shops in a new area called Naya Bāzār (new market), which has developed in the last decade without any planning at the foot of the hill to the south-east of Kirtipur. The impact of this area, accessible by public transport and already filled with four and five storeyed houses, is increasingly felt in the old town. It is of course unrealistic to stop the development of new areas around Kirtipur, but if

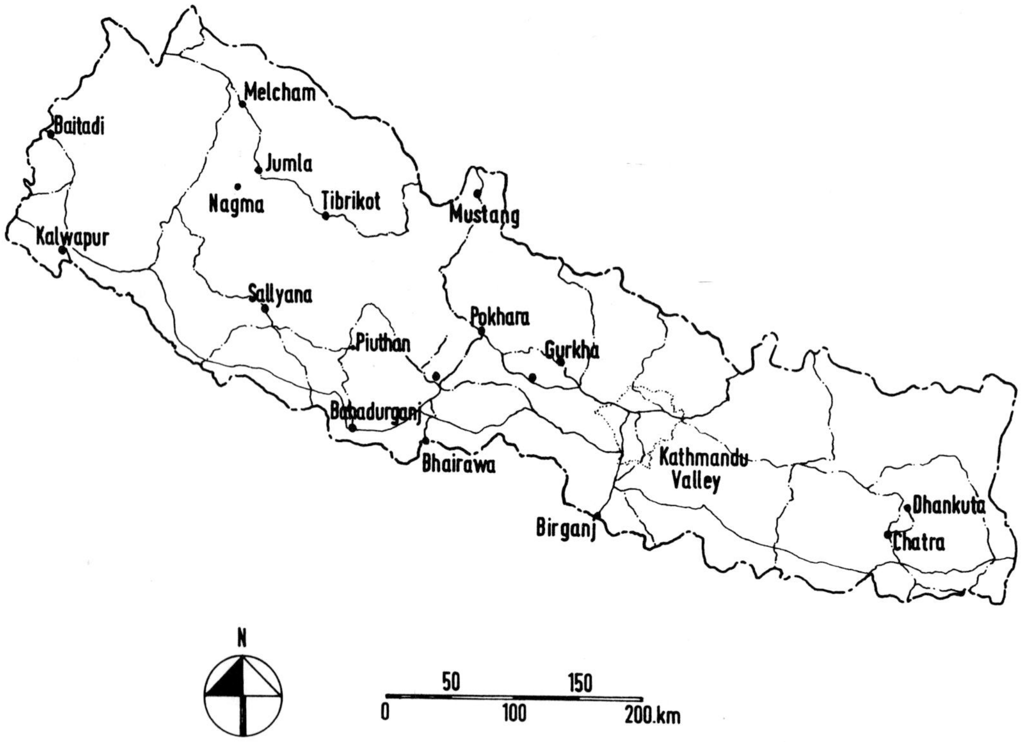


Figure 1 Map of Nepal.

the growth of Naya Bāzār is not supervised it may be destined to develop to a large unplanned township without the appropriate infrastructure.

In the time between a United Nations survey of Kirtipur in 1972 and our surveys in 1986-90 many new houses have also been built in the old town itself, but so far the new buildings are mainly infill, apart from some houses in the southern outskirts of the town where there is an asphalted motorable road. In general the present development has tended to remain in the areas near the motorable roads, but in the absence of a properly implemented plan the motor car is likely to be introduced to the parts of the old town which, while potentially convertible to motorable roads, are not necessarily suitable for accommodating such vehicles. Not only is the urban fabric of Kirtipur in danger of disfigurement, but together with it a way of life.

## STUDY OF THE TOWN

With the rapidly changing face of Kirtipur it is a matter of importance to the people of the town, and specialists elsewhere to have an up-to date and accurate account of the town, looking into its historical past and its present condition in some detail. The present volume is the result of a survey which was carried out as a background study for a conservation plan for Kirtipur. The Master Plan for conservation, described below, is under preparation.

During the background study a large amount of information was collected covering a wide range of subjects from history, urban studies and social life to architecture, the arts, archaeology and epigraphy. These studies not only provide the grounds for the plans for conservation, but also contain information of interest to those involved in South Asian and Himalayan studies, as well as those concerned with development and conservation issues in the developing world. The background studies were therefore prepared in the form of a monograph, presented here.

## NEEDS FOR CONSERVATION

The Government of Nepal has already recognised the need for the conservation of the cultural heritage of the town. In the *Physical Development Plan for the Kathmandu Valley*[1] Kirtipur is noted as a semi-rural town with a strong cottage industry (weaving), but dependent on Kathmandu for both commerce and employment. The *Plan* also mentioned that 'the future of Kirtipur is uncertain. Aside from changes in the organization of its cottage industries, one main hope lies in maximising the employment opportunities at the University for the villagers'. However, the University campus has had little effect on

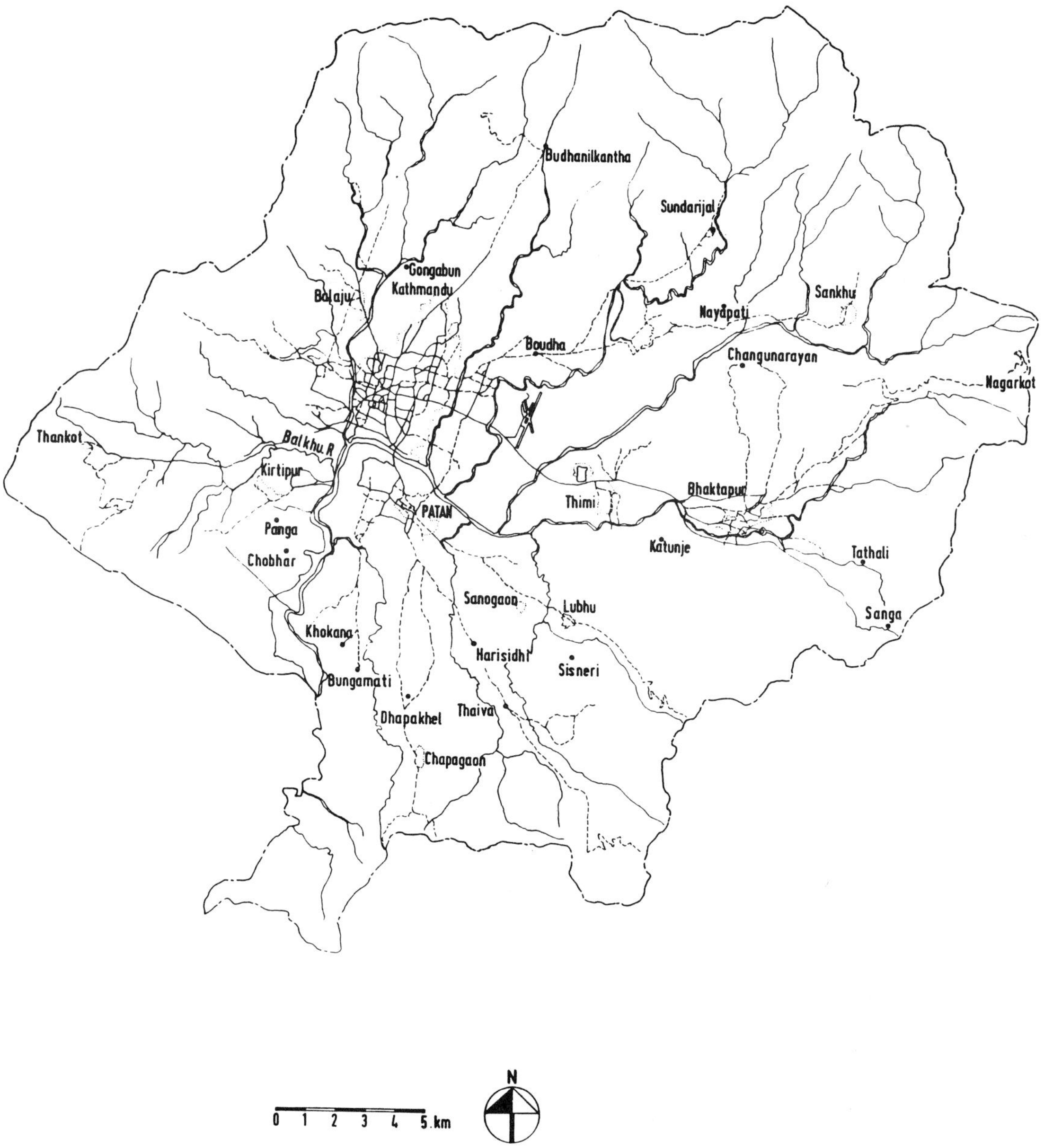


Figure 2 Map of the Kathmandu Valley.

Figure 3 East west section through the Kathmandu Valley looking north and showing Kirtipur as a small hill west of the centre.

employment in Kirtipur, and, with the growth of Kathmandu in the last twenty years, the economic dependence of Kirtipur on Kathmandu has increased even further. The *Plan* also recognized the historical and cultural importance of the temples of Kirtipur, particularly the 16th century Bāgh Bhairav, and the main Buddhist stupa.

The protection of the urban fabric of Kirtipur, as well as its individual monuments is also within the policies of the Government of Nepal for the Kathmandu Valley. The *Protective Inventory*[2] records Kirtipur as a unique site and proposes: 'The location of the settlement on a widely visible hillock above the central plains of the valley

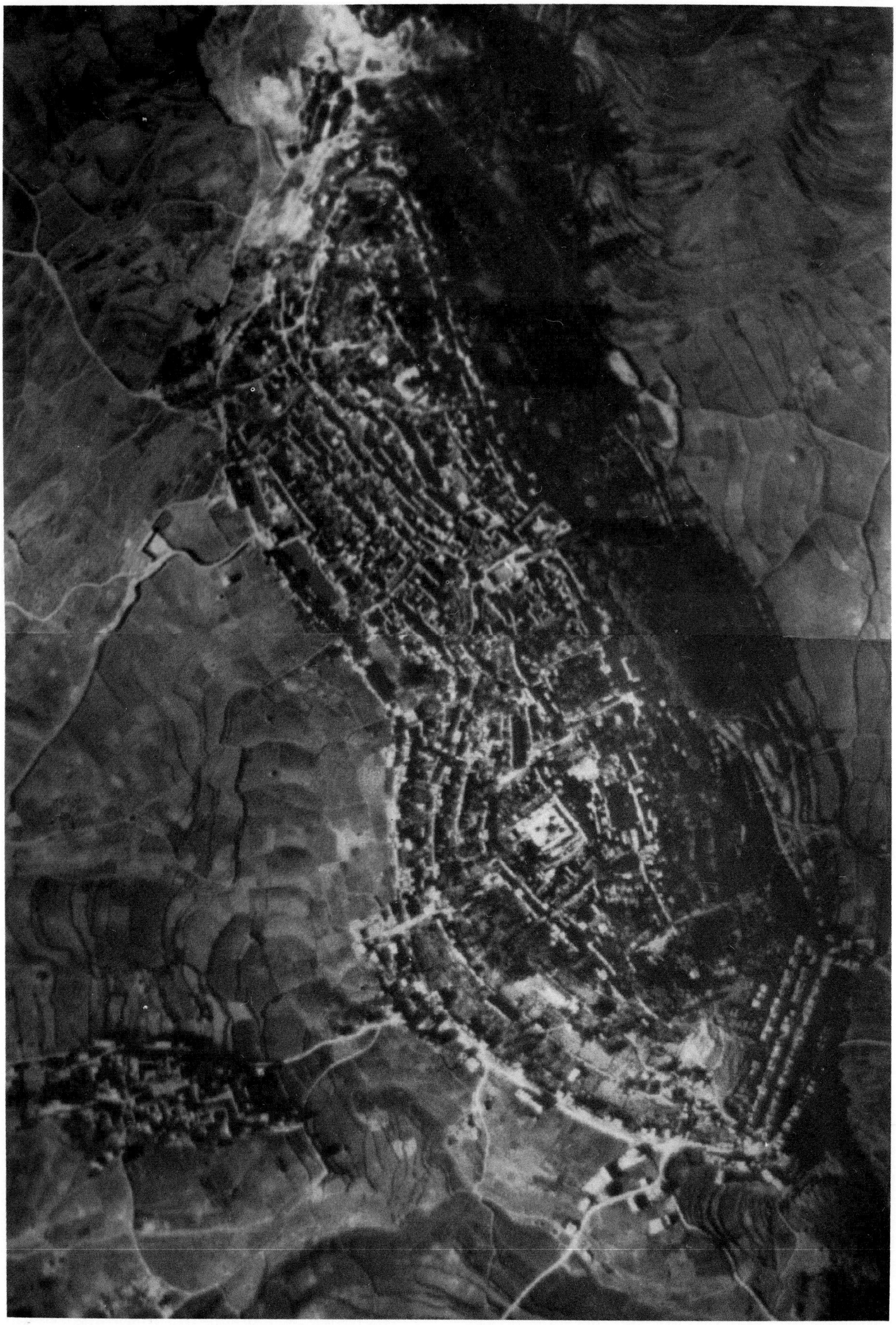

Plate 1 Aerial photograph of Kirtipur, January 1985.

Figure 4 Kirtipur town plan showing the built areas.

demands particular attention being paid to its skyline and vistas. The entire hill range is therefore to be considered as a protected area. No developments of any kind are to be permitted which might endanger the view of this historic district'. The *Protective Inventory* lists 12 classified, and four other religious edifices in Kirtipur.

The need for the conservation of Kirtipur has also been recognized by the United Nations (UNESCO) as early as 1974, and again in 1977 in the *Master Plan for the Cultural Heritage of the Kathmandu Valley.*[3] In the *Master Plan*, Kirtipur and its surroundings were designated as a 'Rural

Plate 2 General view of Kirtipur from the south-west, showing Labhā Pukhū in the foreground.

Preservation District, Category A', and the immediate conservation of the town was highly recommended.

## EARLIER DEVELOPMENT PROJECTS

The development of the town has so far remained limited to the provision of basic amenities. Almost all houses have an electricity supply. In 1975 there were 3 primary schools, a secondary school, and a high school. There are now two more primary schools. The town has a police station, two banks and a post office, as well as a health centre which works on a very limited basis. While a project has been carried out to provide fresh piped water, the supply is inadequate and the shortage of water is still a serious problem. In 1986 there were 36 public taps in the streets and half a dozen private taps. The supply is intermittent, and runs only for a total of six hours each day.

The most successful single development project for Kirtipur has perhaps been the provision of low cost latrines for all households. The project was started in 1981 by the Government's Department of Water Supply and Sewerage with the aid of the United Nations Global Project, and was carried out in less than five years. Prior to the scheme there were very few private latrines in Kirtipur, and people used open spaces, streets and lanes, making them a serious public health hazard. By 1986 we were informed that over 90% of households had their own latrine. The streets are still far from clean, as children and some adults have not yet adapted fully to using the new amenity.

In spite of the recogition of the need for a conservation programme both by the Government of Nepal and the United Nations no specific plan has yet been produced for Kirtipur. Between 1979 and 1982 two teams of graduates in architecture and other disciplines from Bristol University carried out research work in Kirtipur over a period of 18 months. The groups were funded by UNESCO, the British Government's Overseas Development Administration, Bristol University, and other British institutions. The results of their work[4] were published in two reports in 1980 and 1982, which include summaries of their surveys on the social structure, religion, housing and local economy of the town. They also made a number of valuable recommendations, particularly with regard to the preservation of the culture of Kirtipur, but their studies remained theoretical and they failed to produce any specific project. As a result the funding organizations withdrew their support, and the research work was discontinued. No other attempt has since been made to produce a general planning scheme for Kirtipur.

## SURVEYS AND STUDIES

Early in this century a detailed survey map of the Kathmandu Valley (scale 7/8 inch to a mile, 1:73,000 approx.) was published by Lévi,[5] specially produced for him by Stanford's Geographical Establishment, London. In spite of the early date of the map it is still one of the best and most accurate maps of the region. This map appears to be the basis for some later commercial maps published in Nepal[6] with additional information such as the location of the airport, and showing the asphalted roads, which follow the outline of earlier tracks already marked in Levi's map. A more recent map of the valley has been prepared by the Department of Housing and Physical Planning, HMG Nepal, and is given in the *Physical Development Plan for the Kathmandu Valley*. The map is more up to date, but is on a smaller scale (1:120,000), and is less detailed. Another recent survey of the valley has been published by the Association for Comparative Alpine Research,[7] in two sets of larger scale maps of 1:10,000 and 1:50,000.

There are also two even larger scale maps of Kirtipur, one on a scale of 1:4,500 made by the Department of Housing and Physical Planning, and included in the *Physical Development Plan* (p. 67). The map is somewhat sketchy, but is apparently based on a mid-1960's aerial photograph and shows the individual buildings. The map is useful as comparative material for establishing the development of built-up areas during the last quarter of this century.[8] The latest, and most complete survey map of Kirtipur was made as part of a detailed 1:2,000 survey of the Kathmandu Metropolitan Area by the United Nations Development Programme[9] in 1972. This map was used as the basis for our site survey of the town in 1986, when its information was updated and the newly constructed buildings marked in. The same map is also the basis for the maps used by government departments in Nepal and given in the 1980 report of the Bristol University group. In the present report detailed site plans of some of the areas of the town are also given, based on surveys carried out by the contributors or the project team, and our land use study is based on unpublished aerial photographs provided by the Government of Nepal.

In addition to the reports and surveys already mentioned there are also a number of architectural, sociological and economic studies concerned specifically with the town. These studies can be divided into two categories: those written as theses or dissertations,[10] and those carried out by professional bodies on behalf of HMG Nepal.[11] These reports provide valuable information on the social structure of Kirtipur, and the facts and figures given in the reports for the Government of Nepal may be regarded as officially confirmed statistics, and have been used in the present work, as well as information from the independent surveys.

## THE PRESENT STUDY

The preliminary studies for a conservation project were initiated in 1985, encouraged from the first by Mr Gauri Nath Rimal, the then Additional Secretary to the National Planning Commission, and now Secretary to the Ministry of Water Resources and Power, HMG Nepal. In 1986 the project was set up in the School of Architecture and Landscape of Thames Polytechnic, now the University of Greenwich, and in 1988 the Government of Nepal accepted in principle our outline proposals for the conservation of Kirtipur. A number of specialists from the Ministry of Housing and other government institutions have participated in the background studies. We should also mention the enthusiastic response to the proposals by the people of Kirtipur, who provided practical guide-lines and valuable advice. A major part of the present study has been carried out by members of the Kirtipur community.

As part of the background study the UNDP 1972 survey map was updated, and surveys were carried out, including measured drawings of individual buildings, and almost all the important monuments of the town. A photographic record of the town was made, and an archive of photographs and colour slides was prepared for future reference. A number of students from the School of Architecture took part in carrying out the site surveys and preparing the drawings, and we are particularly grateful for the help given by Richard Barriteau, Mark Stokes and Ian Thomson, as well as Allen Poole who helped with printing the photographs and Bahram Leissi who was in overall charge of the production of the final drawings.

### *The conservation project*

The historical heritage of Kirtipur, while recognized by a few specialists in Nepal and elsewhere, has remained relatively unknown. The richness of the architecture of the Kathmandu Valley, however, has long attracted attention, and has been studied in some detail. These studies are mainly concerned with the buildings of Kathmandu, Patan and Bhaktapur. Kirtipur has usually been ignored, or mentioned only briefly, sometimes with supporting photographs.[12]

Kathmandu, Patan and Bhaktapur have also benefited from conservation projects. In Kathmandu and Patan the Royal Palaces and the main ceremonial Darbār Squares with their rich temples and other public and religious buildings have been restored and maintained.[13] Apart from these squares, which constitute the heart of the towns, many other individual buildings of historic value have been restored in other quarters of these towns. These projects were mostly carried out with the assistance of foreign aid and United Nations funds. The then Federal Republic of Germany funded and supervised an extensive conservation project in Bhaktapur,[14] which included the restoration of its Darbār Square as well as buildings in other streets and squares of the town, assistance with the restoration of private dwellings which were of historical and cultural interest, renovation and construction of drainage and sewerage systems, and many other activities. The German team still continues its work, which includes another conservation scheme, this time in the town of Gorkha outside the Kathmandu Valley. Kirtipur's share, however, with the exception of the Low Cost Latrine Project, has been limited to the restoration of a few temples and religious buildings, mainly by the efforts of the townspeople, and sometimes with limited funds from the Government of Nepal.

In the present volume we do not intend to discuss proposals for the conservation of the town, but it should be noted that any project of this nature has to consider not only the physical environment of Kirtipur, but also the social conditions of its community. The main aim of such projects should be to preserve the cultural heritage of the town, while incorporating proposals for the development of the town to suit it to modern life. In Kirtipur, which is rapidly changing from a mediaeval town to a modern satellite of Kathmandu, it is sometimes difficult to draw the line between a conservation plan and a development plan, and in many cases the aims of one become the goals of the other. Improvements in housing, public spaces, infrastructure, and amenities may also be regarded as steps towards further development.

## NOTES

1 *Physical Development Plan for the Kathmandu Valley*, HMG Nepal, Kathmandu, 1969, 66, 150.

2 *A Protective Inventory*, Anton Schroll & Co. for HMG Nepal, 2 Vols., Vienna, 1975, 118-9, 261-5.

3 UNDP Report no. FMR/CC/CH/77/216 (UNDP) NEP/74/003, UNESCO, Paris, 1977.

4 E. P. Davies et al., *Kirtipur, A Newar Community in Nepal, Development in Debate*, Bristol, 1979-80; *Expatriate Assisted Community Development as a Possibility in Kirtipur*, Kathmandu, 1982.

5 Sylvain Lévi, *Le Népal*, I, Paris, 1905, Appendix.

6 For example *Map of Kathmandu Valley, Kathmandu, and Patan*, Kathmandu, 1981.

7 *Kathmandu Valley Maps*, Association for Comparative Alpine Research, Munich, 1977.

8 The same map has been reproduced in F. P. Hosken, *The Kathmandu Valley Towns*, New York & Tokyo, 1974, 309.

9 *Kathmandu Metropolitan Area*, UNDP (SF)-Project 0025 (Nepal), Kathmandu Water Supply and Sewerage Project, Aermap, Firenze (Binnie and Partners, London), 1972, Sheets 28 and 35.

10 A number of these studies are included in our bibliography, but the most important is Reinhard Herdick, *Kirtipur, Stadtgestalt, Prinzipien der Raumordnung und gesellschaftliche Funktionen einer Newar-Stadt*, (Doctoral Dissertation, Technische Universität, Aachen, 1982) published Munich-Cologne-London, 1988.

11 Nepal Red Cross, *Community Basic Service, Kirtipur Survey*, 1980; *Report on Evaluation Study of the Kirtipur Demonstration Project in Low-cost Sanitation*, Prepared for the Department of Water Supply and Sewerage, Ministry of Water Resources, HMG Nepal, Development Research and Communication Group, Kathmandu, 1982; *Nepal, Master Plan Report on Low-cost Waterseal Latrine Project in Eight Urban and Semi-Urban Communities in Nepal*, UNDP Interregional Project INT/81/047, The Technology Advisory Group, Kathmandu, June 1985.

12 For example see H. A. Oldfield, *Sketches from Nepal*, 2 vols., London, 1880, I, reprinted New Delhi, 1974, 125-31; P. Brown, *Picturesque Nepal*, London, 1912, 81-3; P. Landon, *Nepal*, 1928, I, 17 and 63; F. P. Hosken, op. cit., gives a number of photographs from Kirtipur, mostly showing the architecture; D. L. Snellgrove, Shrines and temples of Nepal, *Arts asiatiques*, VIII, 1961, i, 2, 9; ii, 99-100, 106, figs. 6-7, 17, 25; R. Bernier, *The Nepalese Pagoda: origins and style*, New Delhi, 1979, pls. 40, 42, 63.

13 J. Sanday, *The Hanuman Dhoka Royal Palace Kathmandu, Building Conservation and Local Traditional Crafts*, (AARP), London, 1974; J. Sanday, *Les monuments de la vallée de Katmandou*, (UNESCO), Paris, 1980; J. Sanday, *Kathmandu Valley: Nepalese Historic Monuments in need of Preservation*, (UNESCO), Paris, 1982.

14 See Alex Künzle & Giovanni Scheibler, *Bhaktapur: mittelalterliche Stadt in Nepal*, Zurich, 1977; Bhaktapur Development Project, *Bhaktapur Town Development Plan*, 3rd revision, Heidelberg, 1979; Ute Müller, *Land Acquisition for Public Purposes in Nepal*, Town Implementation Office, Bhaktapur, 1981.

# PRIVATE AND PUBLIC INVOLVEMENT IN CONSERVATION POLICY DEVELOPMENT

GAURI NATH RIMAL

In the past the built environment in Nepal, with its palaces, monuments and temples, as well as squares and open places for religious and secular use was created through the joint efforts of the rulers and their subjects. The rulers built edifices and monuments to glorious deeds, using craftsmen and the local communities as free sources of labour, but the people were not in a position to question the importance or necessity of such buildings. In general the accepted principals laid down in the book of building or *Vāstu Śastra* were followed. From very early times the rulers also made careful and elaborate arrangements for the future upkeep and restoration of monuments and the architectural environment through endowments and gifts of land.

## THE GŪṬHĪ SYSTEM

The *gūṭhīs* or guilds, associations comprising members of the community, were usually responsible for the work to be carried out under these endowments, which included the upkeep of the physical environment and the organization of festivals related to the principal deities or *kula devatā* of the community. The proceeds from donated lands were intended to provide a steady flow of funds for financing the continuation of the traditions of daily worship and periodic festivals, as well as the repair and preservation of monuments, temples, water tanks, bridges, rest houses and public utilities. At the call of the headman, the members of a community had to give their labour free of charge, and work carried out in connection with the endowments had to be done according to the principals laid down in the *Vedas* and *Āgam* (the sacred Hindu texts and treatises on sacred science). There is little documentation on the nature of the actual restoration carried out, or the form, scale or shapes to be used, but it can be said with certainty that the continuation of function was always assumed, and it seems that vernacular architecture was built on established patterns. The *gūṭhī* system ensured that the whole community was aware of its responsibility for taking part in the maintenance of its religious and secular architectural heritage.

The religious merit or *puṇya* to be derived from such an act of co-operation has been enumerated on many inscriptions on stone and metal. Such inscriptions extol virtue, and promise rewards in terms of fulfilment and enjoyment of marital life, freedom from disease, health and welfare for the community, fertility, and attainment of heaven. At the same time curses are pronounced on those who desecrate or tamper with religious objects or endowments.

The unique man made environment of the Kathmandu valley and its townships and settlements was also a result of the people's respect for the unwritten codes of an agrarian society. These included building settlements such as Kirtipur on non-irrigated higher plateau land; surrounding settlements with endowment land protected from other kinds of development; holding the forests as sacred; protecting communal property; delineating boundaries; and keeping the arable land exclusively for agriculture. The traditions were followed through consensus and thus no need for coercive legislation was felt. The system depended on the people's awareness, and ability to participate and co-operate with each other.

### *Erosion of the gūṭhī system in the 19th century*

The old system gradually started breaking down under the influence of European ideas of progress, and building practices changed drastically with the introduction of the neo-classical architectural style by the ruling Rānā family during the mid-19th century. Large neo-classical palaces with gardens were introduced into the traditional setting of Kathmandu, and the nobility followed the example of the rulers by building their houses with gardens, putting down the roots

Plate 3 General view of the northern part of Kirtipur from the east, showing the Bāgh Bhairav temple on the left and the Umā Maheśvara temple on the right.

of suburbanisation in the Kathmandu Valley. The *gūṭhī* system declined, and consequentially the maintenance of public buildings, monuments and sites became a function of the state as part of its elaborate public works activity.

In connection with the recent efforts by the state to preserve the cultural heritage, the *Protective Inventory of the Kathmandu Valley* has selected 888 individual monuments in 32 preservation districts, 46 monument zones and 29 natural preservation districts, which are of high artistic, historical or cultural value and are considered part of the national heritage. Sixteen of these monuments are located in Kirtipur. The Kathmandu Valley also has as many as ten thousand images and shrines, including the tiny ones. The amount of effort required in terms of manpower and materials to protect and conserve the man made environment calls for the obvious necessity for combined effort and mobilization of both the public and private sector.

These efforts should be viewed in terms of the conservation of a living organism, rather than the upkeep of a museum or archaeological site, since the cities and settlements of the Kathmandu Valley are alive with working populations carrying on a variety of occupations and trades. The preservation of individual monuments in isolation is not enough in a setting like the Kathmandu valley, which has such a large number of fragile artistic treasures. The overall environment, including the townships and settlements such as Kirtipur, needs to be planned comprehensively under a unifying and co-ordinating concept of physical planning and urban design. This calls for the integration of urban planning, transportation and infrastructure planning, as well as the preservation of the physical environment and cultural heritage within the general framework of national planning policies. The prohibitive, restrictive, and negative controls used so far have not led to a satisfactory solution. The success of preservation, conservation, and renewal depends on conscious interest and awareness, and real effort and participation by the citizen.

## PUBLIC AWARENESS, EDUCATION AND PUBLICITY IN THE COMMUNITY

While sufficient funding and appropriate legislation are vital for the success of conservation policies or projects, they are not adequate in themselves. The involvement of local people, sharing in leadership and participating in a real sense is essential for success. In places such as Kirtipur the conservation of a whole historical area as opposed to a particular feature is not an easy task. Attempts to maintain the architectural and visual order of the buildings and sites in a living urban setting can generate tremendous controversy. People are directly affected by the process and the resultant changes. Traders and other inhabitants may perceive the rehabilitation and conservation activities as a threat to their businesses. A conservative population may resent control and regulation in any form, seeing it as encroachment and bureaucratic intervention over their freedom of choice and style of life.

Lack of awareness about the benefits of heritage conservation among the community, as well as legislators, administrators, special interest groups, practitioners, and industrialists has been a great deterrent to the smooth execution of conservation projects. The first and most important step is to have the confidence of the people, and for them to be mobilized to build support for the project, and bring about the changes in the attitudes and behaviour of the entire community to develop a new ethic of living in harmony with the natural and cultural environment for the general betterment of the quality of life.

Educational campaigns and programmes should be directed at the various interest groups, with clear cut programme materials, and school students should be made aware of the necessity and advantage of the preservation of their cultural heritage. Media such as radio, television, newspapers, pamphlets, posters, and text books can all be helpful tools. Education on conservation should be given in a continuous sequence. Young people are a major group who will use the facilities offered by the restored and rehabilitated historic areas and it is important to engage their interest.

Neglect and decline over a long period in locations of cultural importance can lead people to ignore the possibility of interesting day to day activities in such places. In Kirtipur, for example, restored historic areas with their surroundings improved and integrated with recreational, commercial, working and cultural uses can well provide a lively living environment, and a natural location for parades and festivities. In this context conservation should include not only the restoration of old buildings and monuments, but also the creation or safeguarding of pedestrianized and traffic free zones, paving of lanes with stone and brick in the traditional manner, and keeping facades in scale and harmony in terms of style, texture, and materials. Care also needs to be taken over the design and installation of street furniture and lighting, as well as appropriate landscaping. The possibility of incorporating features to suit restored areas to the staging of entertainments can also be considered, as well as the promotion of local skills and crafts.

## PUBLIC PARTICIPATION IN PLANNING

Public participation in planning can result in more effective planning and control, as feedback from the local population is likely to lead to better and more realistic plans, as well as encouraging participation and contributions in terms of labour and funds from the community, willing co-operation, development of local talent, and political awareness. The following may be considered for an outline of the sequence of activities connected with public participation and mobilization which can be undertaken during a conservation project.

1 *Identification of potential personnel*: The main groups who can contribute to the realisation of the project should be identified, and their potential used in the best interests of the conservation programme. Private citizens, public officials and organizations, the local administration, *gūṭhīs*, businessman, ethnic groups, academics and media men can all play a useful role.

2 *Community involvement*: Once the key persons are identified and procedures discussed, the proposed plan of action can be transmitted to the whole community as a first step to wider participation.

3 *Meetings*: Meetings of special interest groups and the general community can be organized to review issues of a local nature or of political interest.

4 *Organization*: Existing resources in terms of manpower, materials and funds are to be assessed. The sources of funds are to be identified and located within the municipality, as well as from private organizations, individuals and central government. Project staff are to be selected for technical planning and field supervision. During this stage there should be regular consultation and contact with the media, administration, and citizens.

5 *Establishing goals*: An important step in planning is the setting up of clear goals. This also helps in the dissemination of correct information and in maintaining interest among the people. Publicity work can continue during this stage, as well as the selection of alternative solutions.

6 *Surveys and studies*: Feasibility studies and comprehensive surveys covering the various aspects of the environment, such as structural surveys for building conditions, land use, infrastructure, and preparation of maps can be undertaken. These should then be followed by more detailed surveys focussing on problems of a specific nature. Information available from within the local community should be gathered and scrutinized. In these surveys information from the citizens can be of considerable help, leading to economies in the cost of the project, as well as to increased public support. After these surveys have been analysed, workshops designed for community participation can be organized, and

publicized, making the public aware of the project's activities, and encouraging wider co-operation and support.

7 *Preparing objectives*: Following the surveys and studies, a schedule of objectives is prepared, which should reflect the local people's desires and ideas about the development of the area.

8 *Plans and implementation*: In conformity with the basic principal of conserving the heritage of the area, conflicting objectives need to be modified. Specialist planners, architects and urban designers can then prepare plans suitable for implementation, within the overall concept developed with local participation. Such plans are then approved and adopted for execution by the administration. Public hearings may also be organized.

9 *Monitoring and evaluation*: A continuous monitoring system should be developed to ensure effective management, cost control, and timely completion. On completion of the project, evaluation studies should be made, and the results used for the proper implementation of future projects. Promotional events to show the results of the project should also be organized to allow the local population and outsiders to share in the results of the project.

It cannot be over-stressed that the participation of the people is an essential element of conservation activity, as it helps increase the designers' and planners' awareness of what the people really want. Participation can take many forms such as exchanging ideas, taking an interest in community affairs, taking part in discussions, and responding to issues where public comment has been invited. The level of participation by the people will be determined by factors such as the personnel involved in the conservation planning of the area, the basis on which the plans are prepared, and how they are implemented and controlled. Conservation activities should be conceived as a continuing process, capable of absorbing new ideas, with plans and policies continually being reviewed.

# HISTORY

**MEHRDAD SHOKOOHY**

## ANCIENT ORIGINS

Kirtipur is one of the oldest settlements in the Kathmandu Valley, and its history goes back to ancient times. According to the *Padmagiri Chronicle*,[1] in the Brahmanical era Kirtipur was the home town of the earliest kings of the valley. The chronicle goes on to tell how the gods, after ruling the valley for many thousands of years, convened a general council in which it was decided that with the beginning of the Kālī era mortal men would be fit to rule. At this time Gopāla, a *brāhman* from Kirtipur who used to take his cow to the jungle of Slekhamavti, found a buried image of Paśupatināth under the ruins of a temple. Gopāla worshipped the image, and sometime later, when Ne Muni the sage came to the valley he bestowed the sovereignty of Nepal on Gopāla, who took the name Bhumangat. The Gopāla, or cow breeder dynasty ruled for five generations. The legend is particularly worthy of attention since it may be a reflection of a very ancient tradition of the existence of a settlement in Kirtipur even before the Buddhist period. It is not, of course, surprising that the earliest dynasty of the kingdom should be assigned to the cow breeders, as they were high in rank among the *brāhman*.

In Kirtipur there are still some places with names associated with the cowherd caste which perhaps reflect a link with the early settlement.[2] One of the areas of Kirtipur is known as Sāgāl Ṭol or Sā Gā Tvāḥ, meaning the area of the cow sheds. Until two centuries ago this part of the town was also known as Gopura, the Sanskrit word for the Newari *sā gā*.[3] To the west of Sāgāl Ṭol and near the site of one of the old city gates was once an old reservoir known as Gvā Pukhū or the pond of the *gopālas* or cowherds. The site of the pond is still known as Gvā or Giva. Until a decade ago on the festival day of Ghaṇṭākarṇa some of the rituals associated with the *gvā* cast, who trace their origins back to the *gopālas* or *gopakas*, were carried out at this pond. However, these rituals have now ceased as the *gvā* have recently lost their *guṭhi* land which was the source of revenue for their rituals.

The existence of Kirtipur is again reflected in the legends of the early Buddhist period. The mediaeval *vaṃśāvālīs* or chronicles of Nepal record that in the mid-3rd century BC the Emperor Aśoka made a journey to the valley and gave his daughter's hand to Prince Devapāli of Nepal. It is traditionally believed that on this journey the emperor himself founded the Chillaṅdeo or Chilaṅcho Stupa at Kirtipur, as well as the four stupas of Patan.[4] The stupa of Kirtipur (Plate 4) is still the holiest Buddhist shrine of the town, but its present appearance dates from later additions.

In the Nepalese *vaṃśāvālīs* there are several references to later reconstructions of Kirtipur. The *Padmagiri Chronicle*[5] records that the town was built by Raja Sadāśivadeva who 'gave it the appellation of Kirtipur'. Another chronicle[6] records the same event and gives its date as the 4015th year of the Kālī Era (c. 914 A.D.). Lévi,[7] without giving his source, suggests the 12th century for the date of the same event. However, historians have not yet been able to establish the exact dates of the early kings of Nepal.

## EARLY MEDIAEVAL PERIOD

Although the histories refer to the building of Kirtipur by Sadāśivadeva, the nature of his work in the town is not clear. References to the 'building' of existing towns are frequent in early records, but the extent of the works may vary between the renovation of an entire town, sometimes on a new layout, to the restoration of a few public buildings or the reinforcement of the fortification walls and gates. Kirtipur, however, appears to have a layout older than the other three towns of the valley, whose main feature is a central *darbār* or royal square developed in the late mediaeval period. Kirtipur does not have a *darbār* square, and the central square is not much larger than the other squares, each of which was

Plate 4 The Chilañcho complex, central stupa built over an ancient core which is said to date from the time of Aśoka.

Plate 5 Stone lintel carved with the image of a *makara*. The stone is now used as a step for a path, close to the site of one of the ancient gateways at the south of the town, in the Pore Ṭol.

traditionally at the heart of a neighbourhood known as a *ṭol*.

The early mediaeval appearance of the town can be envisaged from the description of the architecture of the valley given in a Chinese travel book of the time of the Tang Dynasty, probably based on the accounts of Wang Hiuen-t'se[8] who made a journey to Nepal in c. 657. It records that the houses were built of wood, and that the walls were carved and painted. Carved wood is still the most important feature in the roofs, as well as the door and window frames of the buildings, although since at least the 14th century red brick has replaced wood for the construction of the walls. The same account also speaks of pagoda style buildings in the valley, much earlier than the development of the style in China.

The archaeological evidence shows that, apart from wood, stone was one of the main building materials, usually finely carved on the exposed surfaces. As early as the Gupta period Kirtipur stone was known in the region for its durability.[9] The stone was quarried from the Kirtipur uplands and taken to workshops in Patan, where it was carved into religious images. In Kirtipur itself we found some carved architectural stones including a lintel which was probably from a mediaeval gateway (Plate 5). The lintel will be discussed in more detail in the chapter on the urban fabric.

## THE MALLA PERIOD

Kirtipur became a dependency of Patan probably as early as the 5th century when Rāja Viradeva developed Patan as the new capital of the valley. During the Malla Period (13th-18th century) the capital first remained in Patan, but was later moved to Kathmandu. In the late 15th century Kirtipur is recorded as being in the territory of the king of Kathmandu, Amaramalla, who established in Kirtipur the Nandurgā festival.[10] In the 16th century the Malla territory broke into three smaller kingdoms with their capitals in Kathmandu, Patan and Bhaktapur, and Kirtipur changed hands between Kathmandu and Patan.

In Kirtipur, as well as in other towns of the valley, there are a number of inscriptions dating from the Malla period, carved on votive objects, or on copper plates affixed to religious edifices. These inscriptions usually bear historical information. Dr. Dilli Raman Regmi[11] has already recorded some of these inscriptions, including a copper plate dated NS 707/1587 AD from the temple of Umā Maheśvara, referred to by him as Bhīmasena after the name of its deity, as well as two copper plates from the Bāgh Bhairav temple dated 852/1732 and 870/1750 respectively.

The last inscription is of particular interest as it records an order of Jaya Prakāśa Malla mentioning that no one in Kirtipur Fort was allowed to fell trees, and that there was a fine fixed for those who did not obey the order. This order apparently refers to the woodland which once covered much of the slopes of the Kirtipur hill, outside the town walls. The woodlands would not only have provided timber and fuel during peace time, but also could have formed a barrier against enemies at times of war. In the case of the order of Jaya Prakāśa Malla, it seems to be connected with the defence of Kirtipur from invasion by the Gurkhas. The northern slope of the Kirtipur hill is still wooded, although from aerial photographs taken from the 1950s on it appears that the original woodland had been gradually cut down, and the present woodland is not very old.

Apart from the few reported inscriptions in Kirtipur there are many other inscriptions of considerable age,[12] some of which probably came from old buildings of the town and were later brought to their present locations. Sucra Sagar Shrestha has carried out a survey of the more important inscriptions, and has made a preliminary study of their texts, given in Appendix A. While a thorough study of the epigraphical remains in Kirtipur is beyond the scope of the present work, his preliminary report shows that these inscriptions would no doubt throw new light on the history of the town, and indeed the history of the valley. Some inscriptions call the town Guṅ De and the *Gopālarāja Vaṃśāvālī*[13] mentions Guṅ de Kvātha (the forest town fortress) which was attacked by Kitapala of Patan in 362/1242. This is apparently a reference to the upper town of Kirtipur or perhaps its citadel. The name seems to have been commonly used to refer to the stronghold of Kirtipur in early mediaeval times, and in epigraphs of Kirtipur the deity of the Bāgh Bhairav temple is frequently referred to as the god associated with the upper town, mentioning his name as Guṅdesthanadhipāṭi. The Bāgh Bhairav complex, which is part of the upper town and most probably within the walls of the old fort is still known in Kirtipur as Guna.

In the Malla period, the people of Kirtipur were known for their skill in building. Kirtipur stone carvers and wood carvers were employed in constructing the monumental structures in the other towns of the valley. An incident of the early 18th century involving the builders of Kirtipur is worthy of attention.[14] At this time, towards the end of the Malla period, the towns were being increasingly embellished with grand architectural monuments and new buildings, and there was much rivalry between the rulers of the valley. The King of Bhaktapur, Ranjit Malla, planned to erect a monumental stone pillar, and requested Jaya Prakāśa, the Malla King of Kathmandu and Kirtipur, whose inscription has already been discussed, to send him skilled craftsmen from Kirtipur. Jaya Prakāśa, while complying with the request of Ranjit Malla, privately asked the masons to spoil the work. In Bhaktapur the pillar was prepared, but at the time of setting it up they let it fall. As a result the pillar broke into three pieces, which were put together and the patched up pillar then erected. Ranjit Malla was still obliged to give the masons robes of honour before sending them back to Kirtipur, where they received more robes of honour from Jaya Prakāśa.

## THE GURKHA CONQUEST

In the mid-18th century the hostility between the two Malla rulers brought their kingdom to an end, when the Gurkha King Pṛithvī Nārāyaṇ attacked the valley. The dramatic role of Kirtipur during the Gurkha invasion has been immortalized in the records of the Nepalese chronicles as well as in the accounts of the early Christian missionaries in the valley.[15] In c. 1743 Pṛithvī Nārāyaṇ made an attack on Kirtipur with the intention of taking over the valley. According to the *Vaṃśāvālī of Pṛithvīnārāyaṇa Shāh*,[16] an early 19th century Gurkha record, the Malla kings of the valley considered Kirtipur the gateway to Nepal, which, should the Gurkhas enter it, would allow them to occupy the three cities. Hence the Malla kings were determined to assist Kirtipur with all force. In the battle which took place near the reservoir at the south-west of the town the Gurkhas were defeated. Pṛithvī Nārāyaṇ himself had a narrow escape, but his famous army commander Kālū Pandey was killed, his head was cut off, and together with his sword and shield, as well as other Gurkha weapons was hung in the Bāgh Bhairav Temple at Kirtipur. While the head of the unfortunate commander was later removed, the Gurkha weapons still hang around the temple.

Sometime later Pṛithvī Nārāyaṇ, encouraged

Plate 6 Bāgh Bhairav temple, details of the tiered roof showing the Gurkha wepons captured in the 18th century and still hanging in front of the upper tier.

by an invitation from the king of Bhaktapur, returned to the valley and besieged Kirtipur. Once again the people of Kirtipur resisted, and finally with the help of Jaya Prakāśa, defeated the Gurkha king. However, Pṛithvī Nārāyaṇ eventually took over the valley, and in 1767 after another long siege, Kirtipur fell into the hands of the Gurkhas who devastated the town. The punishment of the inhabitants was also severe. The noses and, as some records suggest, the lips of all males were cut off. Only small children were spared.

In addition to the Gurkha destruction of the town, Kirtipur has also suffered from many earthquakes, frequent in the Himalayan region. Among those recorded in the last century are the 1808 and 1833 earthquakes.[17] The people of Kirtipur believe that the hill site of their town is one single solid rock and therefore earthquakes have little effect on their buildings. This claim is not entirely accurate, and while the good structure of some houses may have contributed towards their resistance, many buildings have been destroyed or damaged in earthquakes. Oldfield[18] who visited the town before 1880 mentions Kirtipur as a town with a population of less than 5,000, and records the dilapidated state of the buildings and even temples. His account is confirmed by Lévi[19] who saw Kirtipur early in this century. He records Kirtipur as a small town with a population of 4,000, and adds that the town once had over 6,000 households, and like Oldfield attributes its devastation to the pillage of the Gurkhas. The figure of 6,000 households for Kirtipur is, however, recorded by Kirkpatrick[20] to have included the area under the jurisdiction of Kirtipur. The town itself is unlikely to have been much larger than its present size, as only a few unbuilt areas are left on the hilltop, and there are no traces of any significant ruins around the town. Mediaeval Kirtipur appears to have been similar in size to the present town.

The last significant earthquake[21] was in 1934, during which many of the buildings of Kirtipur were destroyed or badly damaged. Some of these buildings are still uninhabited, and in a state of disrepair. Many others are replaced with new constructions which are not always in harmony with the architecture of the town. Amongst the buildings damaged in the 1934 earthquake were

Figure 5 The Bāgh Bhairav temple complex in the mid-19th century, from a drawing by Oldfield.

Figure 6 The ruins of the Darbār, with Umā Maheśvara in the background. Watercolour, 22.5 x 31.25 cm., c. 1855 by H. A. Oldfield.

some of the religious structures including the Umā Maheśvara temple and the Jagat Pāl Vihār. The former lost its top,[22] which was restored only a decade ago, but not in its original form, as is mentioned by Sudarshan Raj Tiwari in the chapter on the tiered temples. As for the Jagat Pāl Vihār, one of the best examples of Kirtipur architecture, it was only at the end of 1989 that basic repairs and re-roofing were carried out; until then it had been left in a ruinous state.

## NOTES

1 Bikrama Jit Hasrat, *History of Nepal as Told by its Own and Contemporary Chronicles*, Hoshiapur (India), 1970, 33-4; this account is confirmed in the *Parbatiyā*, see Daniel Wright, *History of Nepal translated from the Parbatiyā by Munshī Shew Shunker Singh and Pandit Shrī Gunānand*, Cambridge, 1877, 107-8 and 161; also see Sylvain Lévi, *Le Népal*, II, Paris, 1905, 72-3.

2 Dhana Bajra Bajarcharia, "*Mallakalka ek prakhyat Rājā Śiva Deva*", *Contributions to Nepalese Studies*, VIII, i, December 1980, 211.

3 Bābu Rām Ācharyā, *Pṛithvī Nārāyaṇ Shāhko jīvani*, Part III, 456. However, the normal meaning of *gopura* is a gate tower, and it is also possible that the name refers to a former gateway.

4 H. Ambrose Oldfield, *Sketches from Nipal, Historical and Descriptive*, II, 1880, 212-18; Perceval Landon, *Nepal*, London, 1928, I, 17-18, 256-7.

5 B. J. Hasrat, op. cit., 48.

6 Ibid.

7 S. Lévi, op. cit., I, 66. Lévi has apparently quoted the *Parbatiyā*, a copy of which is translated in Daniel Wright, *History of Nepal*, Cambridge, 1877, see p. 161-2. However, Wright's edition does not give any date for this event. On another occasion the *Parbatiyā* gives the date of the building of Paśupatināth by the same Rāja in the year 3851.

8 P. Landon, op. cit., II, 257; D. R. Regmi, *Ancient Nepal*, Calcutta, 1969, 290.

9 Ibid., 304.

10 *The Padmagiri Chronicle* in B. J. Hasrat, op. cit., 62.

11 D. R. Regmi, *Mediaeval Nepal*, IV, Patna, 1966, 35-6, 293-4, 300-1. Also see ibid., III, 100-3, 145.

12 Carl Pruscha, *A Protective Inventory*, I and II, Vienna, 1975, 261-5, gives some 16th to 18th-century dates for buildings in Kirtipur. The dates may have been taken from inscriptions, but the sources are not mentioned. During our survey we noticed many inscriptions, and made a photographic record of some of them for our archive.

13 D. R. Regmi, op. cit., III, 132-3.

14 P. Landon, op. cit., I, 58.

15 Most 19th and 20th century accounts of Nepal refer to the events of the Gurkha conquest in some detail, see Father Giuseppe, *Account of the Kingdom of Nepal*, Asiatick Researches, II, London, 1807, 316-19; William Kirkpatrick, *An account of the Kingdom of Nepaul*, London, 1811, 164 and 271; D. Wright, op. cit., 226 and 259; the *Padmagiri Chronicle* in B. J. Hasrat, op. cit., 92-3.
16 Ibid., 142-3.
17 Ibid., 95-7.
18 H. A. Oldfield, op. cit., I, 93-6.
19 S. Lévi, op. cit., I, 66.
20 William Kirkpatrick, op. cit., 165.
21 J. B. Auden and A. M. N. Ghosh, Preliminary account of the earthquake of the 15th January, 1934, in Bihar and Nepal, *Records of the Geological Survey of India*, LXVIII, ii, 1934, 177-239.
22 In 1934 Umā Maheśvara was already in ruins. Apart from frequent references to the ruinous state of this temple in the 19th century reports, a photograph in Landon, op. cit., I, 62, while not quite clear, shows that the top of the building was already in ruins in 1905, but perhaps not to the extent of the dilapidation after the 1934 earthquake.

# THE NEWARS, THE PEOPLE OF KIRTIPUR

MEHRDAD SHOKOOHY

Kirtipur is populated almost entirely by Newars, the indigenous, and oldest group of people of the Kathmandu Valley.[1] Like much of the ancient history of Nepal the origin of the Newars (*nevār*) is diffused in the mists of legend, and with the lack of extensive archaeological excavations historians have not yet been able to provide a commonly acceptable theory.

Dr. Regmi[2] holds the view that the Newars may have originally been a mixed group of different Asiatic tribes who migrated to the valley in pre-historic times. They gradually mingled, and, as it appears from the historical records, some time in the first or second century AD emerged as a single community with a common culture, and a social structure which incorporated a caste system. Regmi believes that if the rulers of the early kingdoms of the valley, the Lichhavis, and perhaps even the legendary Kirātaṣ were not themselves Newars, they certainly shared a similar culture with them.

A traditional belief is that the Newars came from the country of Nayera to the Kathmandu Valley in ancient times, under the guidance of their king, Nāya Deva. Some locate the land of Nayera somewhere in south India, but this belief may have developed at a much later date when the culture of the valley came under the influence of Hinduism. Other legends link the Newars with China and claim that the valley was once the site of a lake, and that the Bodhisattva Manjuśrī, who is believed to have come from Mount Sirsha in northern China, cut a gorge in the mountain and drained the valley,[3] making it habitable for the Newars.

The Newars differ linguistically from the main population of Nepal who speak Nepali, an Indo-Aryan language linked with Sanskrit. Nepali is the official language of the country, and is taught in schools and used for publications and broadcasts. It is also spoken widely in the three main towns of the valley. Newari (*nevārī*), however, is a Tibeto-Burmese language, and is spoken in Kirtipur, as well as among other Newar communities in towns and villages. It is generally believed that once the entire valley was populated by Newars, and although in the Malla period the Newar territories were reduced, it was Newari architecture which produced the townscapes of the Malla cities and villages, much admired today.

It is interesting that the Newars and their culture are limited to the Kathmandu Valley, and hardly penetrate outside the mountain range surrounding the valley, with the exception of the important community in the Tibetan capital, Lhasa,[4] where they are known historically for their skill in jewellery and metalwork. Today in the Kathmandu Valley there is still a wide distribution of Newars, but except in a few areas they are in a minority. The Newars also had their own script, but it has been replaced for several centuries by Devanāgarī, the Indian script used for Sanskṛit, modern Hindi, and also for Nepali. In mediaeval times Sanskrit was the literary language in the Nepalese courts, and many manuscripts and inscriptions are in this language. However, apart from many Nepali records there are also a number of old manuscripts and architectural manuals in Newari, and many of the inscriptions found on religious objects in Kirtipur are written in this language. Today Newari is becoming increasingly a spoken language only, and does not appear in printed form except rarely in scholarly reports.

## RELIGION

The position of religion and religious rites in Kirtipur is not very different from the rest of Nepal. The Newars were originally Buddhist, but during the middle ages the Hindu religion was introduced by the ruling classes. Unlike India, where the Hindu revival virtually eliminated Buddhism, in Nepal for many centuries the two religions have co-existed, and many of the rites and ceremonies of the two faiths have merged.

Plate 7 A shrine of the Hindu god Gaṇeś set at the south-east corner of the entrance to the Chilañcho stupa, the most important Buddhist site in Kirtipur. As with other shrines, both Buddhists and Hindus venerate this shrine.

However, in Newar communities, the proportions of people who practice Buddhism or Hinduism are not always the same. In Kirtipur the number of Hindus is larger than that of Buddhists, but each group regards the other's shrines with respect, and participates in the other's festivals.

## CASTE STRUCTURE

Although the principles of Buddhism do not advocate the Brahmanical caste system, under the influence of Hinduism a complicated caste structure has established itself amongst the Newars since at least early mediaeval times. According to the *Pārbatiya*,[5] at the turn of the 14th century Rāja Jayasthiti Malla reformed the caste structure of the Newars and divided them into 64 castes, based on religious status and occupation. The castes, in hierarchical order, were:

1 *Brāhman*: *dvija* and *bipra*
2 *Chhatrī*: (*kshatriya*) *bhūpa*, *rāja* and *narendra*
3 *Lekhaka*: writers
4 *Kāyasth*: scribes
5 *Mantrī*: governors and state officials, advisors
6 *Sachiva*: men of arms, companions, associates
7 *Āmātya* : ministers
8 *Pūjita*
9 *Devachinta*: priests
10 *Āchārya*: religious instructors, priests
11 *Grahachintaka*: astrologers
12 *Jyotisha*: (*joshī*) astronomers and astrologers
13 *Gaṇika*: mathematicians
14 *Daivagya*: lower ranking astrologers
15 *Ālama*
16 *Srichānte*
17 *Sajakāra*
18 *Sūpika*
19 *Chichhaka*
20 *Marīkāra*
21 *Śilpakāra*: craftsmen
22 *Bhārika*: porters
23 *Nāpika*: barbers, surgeons
24 *Lepika*: stucco carvers and plasterers
25 *Dārukāra*: wood carvers
26 *Takshaka*: carpenters, wood cutters
27 *Śriṅkharī*
28 *Kshetrakāra*: land measurers
29 *Kumbhakāra*: potters
30 *Tulādhara*: weighers
31 *Karṇikā*: weavers (?)
32 *Kānsyakāra*: white copper or brass workers, bell-makers
33 *Suvarnakāra*: goldsmiths
34 *Tāmrakāra*: coppersmiths
35 *Gopaka* or *gopāla*: cowherds
36 *Bhāyalāchanchu*
37 *Kāñjīkāra*: brewers, rice-vinegar makers (?)
38 *Tayoruta*
39 *Tankādhārī*
40 *Bimārī*
41 *Sūrppakāra*: cooks (?)[6]
42 *Natebaruda*
43 *Bāthahom*
44 *Gāyana*: (*gāyine*) musicians and singers
45 *Chitrākāra*: painters
46 *Surābīja*
47 *Naṭījīva*: actors and prostitutes
48 *Māndhura*[7]
49 *Byanjanakāra*: cooks (?)
50 *Mālī*: gardeners
51 *Mānsabikrī*: butchers
52 *Kirāta*: singers
53 *Badī*: musicians
54 *Dhānyamārī*: rice liquor makers (?)
55 *Tandukāra*: weavers (?)
56 *Nādīchhedi*: assistants for childbirth, midwives

Plate 8 Chilañcho stupa, an image of the Buddha visited daily by many Buddhists and Hindus.

57 *Kundakāra*: carvers of ivory and bones
58 *Lohakāra*: blacksmiths, coppersmiths
59 *Kshaṭṛikāra*: carvers and porters
60 *Dhobī*: launderers
61 *Rājaka*: dyers and sweepers
62 *Niyogī*
63 *Mātangī*: leather workers
64 *Charmakāra*: leather workers

The reforms of the Rāja appear to have been little more than an adaptation of the Indian caste system, and it is even more likely that he only confirmed an already existing caste structure, perhaps making some minor alterations. Many of these castes are unknown today, and there have been other adjustments to the castes by later kings of the valley. For example, after the battle of Kirtipur Pṛithvī Nārāyaṇ honoured those who carried his and his nobles' palanquins to Nāyākoṭ, and created a new caste, the *lamu* or royal palanquin bearers. Nevertheless, the hierarchy of the existing social groups has not altered greatly since Rāja Jayasthiti Malla's time, although the old names of some castes have been changed, and in some cases the occupations of members of a caste now differ from those with which it was traditionally associated.

While the caste system has now been legally abolished in Nepal, it is deep rooted and still affects most aspects of people's lives, particularly in the villages. In the towns, however, government policies with regard to equal opportunities, together with social and economic changes connected with modern urban life are causing the rigid social divisions between the various castes to loosen. In Kirtipur, still predominantly a farming town, the caste structure is still strong, and members of each caste tend to live together in the same area. Even the *gāyine*, a small non-Newar musician group settled in Kirtipur, have an area of their own outside the southern perimeter of the old town. Only in the newly developed areas such as Naya Bāzār has economic pressure, and to a lesser extent social awareness, resulted in a mixed caste community of people from outside Kirtipur. In the old part of Kirtipur many of the young and educated people, most of whom have employment in Kathmandu or Patan, are now increasingly challenging the old system of social divisions. Nevertheless, radical changes in the social structure of Kirtipur, and indeed the rest of Nepal, are likely to take many years to evolve.

In Kirtipur, as in other Newar settlements, not all castes are present and the ratio between the number of members of each caste is peculiar to the town, being the result of a long established socio-economic balance within the community of Kirtipur. In general, however, the social structure of the Kirtipur community is similar to that of other Newar farming towns. The caste system of the Newars, and its effect on all aspects of their lives has been the subject of many studies[8] and to analyse it further is outside the scope of the present work. However, a brief description of the Newar castes as found in Kirtipur is given below, as it is useful for an understanding of the social structure of the town. It should also be mentioned that the structure of Newar castes and their subdivisions into social groups is complex, and the local names of the castes and social groups vary from place to place. The reports of scholars, therefore, while agreeing in general, sometimes vary in details, as well as in the names and number of sub-castes delineated.

At the higher levels of the Newar hierarchy, the Hindu or *Śivamārga* castes differ from the Buddhist or *Buddhamārga* castes, but the lower castes of the two religions are mixed. The Buddhist castes are traditionally occupational, while the Hindu castes are religious, similar in structure to the four Brahmanical castes of India. The mixed castes are also occupational and are numerous, as every caste is associated with one or two specific types of work or trade. Being a farming town the main section of the Kirtipur population is of the farming caste: a mixed Hindu and Buddhist caste known as the *jyāpu* (*jiāpu*) or *maharjan*. The following is a summary of the present Newar castes and sub-castes of Kirtipur according to hierarchy.

## THE ŚIVAMĀRGA OR HINDU CASTES

### *The upadhyāyā*

The highest of the Hindu castes is the *upadhyāyā*, the members of which are *brāhmans*, and act as religious instructors (*guru*) and priests (*purohit*). Kirtipur has only a few *upadhyāyā* households, living near the Bāgh Bhairav temple. Other *brāhman* castes of slightly lower rank are the *lavarju* and the *bhāju*, whose duties are also linked with Hindu religious affairs and the temple.

### *The kshatriya*

In India this caste was originally associated with the ruling classes, nobles, and high ranking members of the army. In Nepal the *ṭhakur*, the main group of *kshatriya*, is considered to be associated with the Malla family who ruled in the valley before the Gurkhas. Other *kshatriya*

Figure 7 Map showing the distribution of castes.

groups, according to their rank, are the *nikhu*, originally the painters of religious objects, the *shiyashu* and *śreshṭha*, members of which were in the past responsible for the administration of the country and provided the officers of the army. Some *śreshṭhas* are also involved in trade. Although the number of *kṣatriyas* in Kirtipur must have been greatly reduced with the decline of the town in the 18th and 19th centuries, there are still some members of this caste living in Lāyaku, their traditional residential area near the site of the citadel. The members of the caste still enjoy some social advantages, in the administration of the town as well as having better opportunities for finding government employment outside Kirtipur. While caste is no longer the basis of employment in Nepal, wealth, better education, and local influence contribute towards the social advantages of the *kshatriya*.

### *The vaiśya*

This caste consists of two main groups, the *joshī* and the *āchār* or *āchārya*. The members of the first group in particular are present in Kirtipur and have their own *ṭol* north of Lāyaku, neighbouring the residential areas of the *kshatriya*. The social position of the *joshīs* appears to have been somewhat disputed in the 18th and 19th century. Buchanan writes of them as follows:[9]

> 'A kind of mixed breed of Newars are by the *Śivamārgas* acknowledged as very high rank... although their pretensions are disputed by the *Bangras*. They are called *Jauśī*, and are the only caste that ought to practice medicine; but at present all ranks profess that art. The *Jauśīs* are descended from the offspring of a Brahmin and a Newar woman; and if their mother has been a *Bangra* or an *Āchār*, they wear the thread, and act as instructors (*Gurus*) or priests (*Purohits*) for their brethren of mixed descent. These privileges are not allowed to such as are descended from low mothers. In imitation of their fathers the *Jauśīs* are mostly *Śivamārgas*, but in other matters they mostly follow the customs of the Newars.'

This is not an exceptionally complicated detail of the Newar caste network, but merely an example of the many ramifications to be found in most other Newar castes and social groups. There are also a number of other social groups of *vaiśya* caste, most of which are involved in trade.

### *The śūdra*

The *śūdra* form a small caste, consisting in order of rank of the *makhi*, the *lakhipar* and the *bagho shashu* groups. The members of all these groups were regarded as ritually clean by all Hindu and Buddhist castes and *śūdras* were therefore traditionally employed as cooks and domestic servants.

## THE BUDDHAMĀRGA CASTES

The highest rank of the Buddhist castes is the *Gubhājū* or *bajrāchārya*. The members of this caste act as *gurus* and priests in the Buddhist temples and *vihārs* (monasteries). Next in the hierarchy are the *śākyas* who are themselves divided into many social groups: the *baṛāju* (goldsmiths), the *nibharbari* (bronze workers and makers of holy images), and the *gamsabarhi* (woodworkers) to name a few. All these groups are regarded as Brāhman of Buddhist origin and are grouped as one larger caste known as the *bandya*. The members of all these groups can eat with each other and intermarry. In Kirtipur members of most of these groups are present and make a small community living together around the Chilañcho Stupa, as well as inside or near the *vihārs*.

Sharing the same area in the Buddhist quarter of Kirtipur are the members of the *uda* caste. The members of various groups of this caste were traditionally high ranking and usually prosperous metalworkers and traders, trading between the Kathmandu Valley and Tibet, and were responsible for the prosperity of the cities of the valley. The *uda* and *bandya* castes are closely linked, and are sometimes regarded as two branches of the same caste. The presence of members of these groups in Kirtipur is a reminder of the historical importance of the town, but in spite of their original association with trade and industry, in general they are no longer involved with their traditional occupations.

## THE MIXED CASTES

The most important group among the mixed castes is the *jyāpu* or *maharjan*: the farmers who constitute the largest social group of the valley, and two thirds of the population of Kirtipur. They occupy most areas of the town, and mix socially with the *śreshṭhas*. The *jyāpus* are subdivided into five classes including the *danghu*, land surveyors; the *kumbhakāra* (*kumhār*), potters; and the *karbujha*, the funerary musicians. Members of these groups also farm. The *jyāpus* are followed in the social hierarchy by the *chitrākārs*, painters; and the *bhāṭs* and *chipis*, both dyers. A very small number of members of these groups live in Kirtipur, and the *chipis* alone make one per cent of the population of the town.

Among other mixed caste groups present in

small numbers in Kīrtipur are the *nau* or *nāpika* who are barbers and traditional surgeons; the *kaua* or *nekarmi*: blacksmiths; the *garhtho* (*gāthu*): gardeners; and the *mānandhar*: oil pressers and farmers. The number of members in the last group is relatively larger than the others and they live together in a quarter at the north-west of the town. Similar to *mānandhars* in number in Kirtipur are the *khusals* or *tanḍukārs*: weavers. However, weaving in Kirtipur is not limited to this caste, as the *jyāpus* of Kirtipur have an active role in this craft. The *khusals* and *tanḍukārs* are now mostly farmers and live mainly in the same areas occupied by the *jyāpus*.

At the bottom of the social hierarchy are the "unclean" castes, the members of which live in separate areas. In Kirtipur their settlements have traditionally been outside the mediaeval town walls, though with the recent expansion of the town these areas are now surrounded by new housing belonging to people of different castes. There are altogether eight unclean castes in the Newar social system: *nay* or *kasāī*: butchers; *jogī* or *kusle*[10] or *kāpalī*: "tailors" and temple keepers; *dhom* or *badikar*, and *kulū*: musicians; *dhobī*: launderers; *poṛe*[11] or *dyola*, *chamakhallak* or *kūchikāra*, and *harahuru* or *saṅghar*: all sweepers and cleaners of houses and streets. In Kirtipur butchers still occupy a small settlement to the west of the town, and the cleaners, who are mainly of the *poṛe* caste, live in the south-west in a settlement which is very similar in its layout to a small Newar village.

A survey[12] of the distribution of the different castes in Kirtipur, including the newly developed area of Naya Bāzār, carried out by the Development Research and Communication Group in 1982 for HMG Nepal showed that the *jyāpu* alone constitute 70% of the population in the town. The Hindus of high caste including *śreshṭha*, *joshī*, *rājbandari*, *pradhān* and *āmātya* formed together 15% of the population. Other groups were the high ranking Buddhists including *bajrāchāryas*, *śākyas* and *urhays* accounting for 5%; while *mānandhars* made up 3%, *tandukāras* 2%, *kāpalīs* 1%, *poṛes* 1%, *gāthus* 1% and others 1%.

From these statistics it is clear that even with modern influences from outside, and the development of Naya Bāzār, Kirtipur has remained predominantly a farming town. The urban life of Kathmandu and Patan has not yet affected the basic balance of Kirtipur's social structure. The survey also reveals that the percentage of higher ranking Hindu castes is about three times that of their Buddhist counterparts. The reason for the difference may be found in the history of the town in the Malla period. At this time the administration of Kirtipur was in the hands of Hindus and a larger number of this group was needed than that of high ranking Buddhists, who remained mainly involved in the running of their own religious affairs. Our map of the distribution of castes in the town shows that there is only one Buddhist area, while there are two Hindu areas, one at and around Lāyaku, and another to the south-west of the town. Larger areas mainly occupied by a single caste are also shown. Those castes which constitute a very small percentage of the population are not shown in the map. They usually live in or near the areas occupied by castes close in rank. An interesting feature shown in our map is the area of modern development. These areas are occupied by members of all castes and show the beginning of a breaking down in the rigidity of the traditional caste structure in Kirtipur.

## NOTES

1 Most general studies of Nepal include chapters on the Newars, for some more recent studies see K. P. Chattopadhyay, An essay on the history of Newar culture, social organisation of the Newars, *Journal of the Asiatic Society of Bengal*, XIX, 1923, 465-560; C. von Führer-Haimendorf, Elements of Newar social structure, *Journal of the Royal Anthropological Institute of Great Britain and Northern Ireland*, LXXXV, ii. 1956, 15-38; G. S. Nepali, *The Newars, an Ethno-Sociological Study of a Himalayan Community*, Bombay, 1965; V. S. Doherty, Notes on the origins of the Newars of the Kathmandu Valley of Nepal, *Himalayan Anthropology, the Indo-Tibetan interface*, ed. J. F. Fisher, La Haye and Paris, 1978, 433-45; Gérard Toffin, *Société et religion chez les Néwar du Népal*, Paris, 1984.

2 D. R. Regmi, *Ancient Nepal*, 3rd ed. Calcutta, 1969, 29-33, 55.

3 H. Ambrose Oldfield, *Sketches from Nepal*, II, London, 1880, 185-7.

4 Perceval Landon, *Nepal*, II, London, 1928, 240; D. B. Jista, Nepalis in Tibet, *Himalayan Anthropology, the Indo-Tibetan Interface*, ed. J. B. Fisher, La Haye and Paris, 1978, 187-204.

5 Daniel Wright, *History of Nepal translated from the Parbatiyā by Munshī Shew Shunker Singh and Pandit Shrī Gunānand*, Cambridge, 1877, 185-7. Wright gives the date of the reign of the Rāja as NS 503-549/1383-1429.

6 *Sūrpa*, *sūpa*: a kind of basket, a ceiling punkah.

7 Probably *mānandhar*: oil pressers.

8 Francis Hamilton Buchanan, *An Account of the Kingdom of Nepal, and of the Territories Annexed to this Dominion by the House of Gorkha*, Edinburgh, 1819, 31-8; Sylvain Lévi, *Le Népal*, Paris, 1905, I, 237-44; K. P. Chattopadhyay, An essay on the history of Newar culture; social organisation of the Newars, *Journal of the Asiatic Society of Bengal*, XIX, 1923, 465-560; S. M. Greenwold, Newar castes again, *Archives Européennes de Sociologie*, XVIII, i, 1977, 194-7; E. P. Davies et al., *Kirtipur, A Newar Community in Nepal, Development in Debate*, Bristol, 1980, 46-51; Reinhard Herdick, *Kirtipur, Stadgestalt, Prinzipien der Ramordnung und gesellschaftliche Functionen einer Newar-Stadt*, Munich, Cologne, London, 1988, 110-137; G. Toffin, op.

cit., 221-32; also see A. Hofer, *The Caste Hierarchy and the State in Nepal, a Study of the Muluki Ain of 1854*, Innsbruck, 1979.
9 Francis Hamilton Buchanan, op. cit., 33.
10 Niels Gutschow and Bernhard Kölver, *Bhaktapur: ordered space concepts and functions in a town in Nepal*, Wiesbaden, 1975, 42.
11 Ibid., 30, mentions that the *poṛe* were originally fishermen.
12 Development Research and Communication Group, *Report on Evaluation Study of the Kirtipur Demonstration Project in Low-cost Sanitation*, prepared for the Department of Water Supply and Sewerage, Ministry of Water Resources, HMG. Kathmandu, 1982, 24.

# SOCIAL LIFE AND FESTIVALS

SUKRA SAGAR SHRESTHA

Social life in Kirtipur is organized into a tightly bound and regulated structure which has remained stable for many years, perhaps mainly as a result of the lack of change in the needs of the members of this farming community over the generations. Most people still live in extended families spanning three to four generations. Marriages tend to be arranged by the parents, the brides leaving their childhood home to become part of the husband's extended family. It is therefore common to find grand-parents, married sons and their families, and unmarried siblings together in one house. The male members of a family will include the father, possibly some of his brothers and their families, married sons with their own families, and unmarried sons. The female members comprise mothers, their unmarried daughters, and daughters-in-law.

The kitchen of a house has a particular role in defining family relationships. The definitive element is the hearth, considered sacred, and situated on the top floor, access to which is governed by caste rules and is allowed to few people apart from members of the family. The members of a family who eat food prepared at a particular hearth can be regarded as members of one kitchen, the smallest unit of Newari social organization. In an extended family there may be several hearths or 'kitchens', but they are tied together by cultural and religious practices, for example the distribution of *siu* (prescribed parts of a sacrificed animal) and preparations for the Divālī festival.

The head of the family is the *thakālī*, the eldest man. When he dies his wife may sometimes take his place, but usually it will be taken by the next male member. The role of the *thakālī* is that of leader and decision maker, and he is responsible for the well-being of the family. The male members of the family are responsible for earning money outside the house, and the female members also contribute to the family finances by weaving and other work carried on at home.

The women's role in the family is mainly confined to caring for the children, the day to day running of the house, and housework. For feasts and large gatherings, however, the food is prepared by the men, while the women are concerned with lighter work. In agriculture the heavy work, such as tilling the land, is done by men, and the jobs requiring less physical strength such as transplanting rice seedlings are undertaken by women. As well as the hearth, women are responsible for daily worship, alcohol distillation, and have their own role in festivals and rights of passage.

Marriages, particularly when arranged by the parents, are usually endogamous, but the localities from which the brides and grooms come vary from caste to caste. Most *śreshṭhas*, for example, have matrimonial relations with their counterparts in Patan, Chapagāoṅ, Thaiva, Pharping, Sāṅkhu, Panauti, and Bhaktapur, as well as Banepā, situated at the east of the valley. *Jyāpus*, on the other hand, prefer to marry people from Kirtipur itself, or Pāṅgā or Nagāoṅ, although they do also have matrimonial relations with Chobhār and Naikāp. With the recent improvements in communications a few marriages have also taken place between people of Kirtipur and Kathmandu.

In the case of a family splitting up, either as a result of mutual agreement or following a dispute, the inherited house will be divided vertically, and if there is not enough room one unit will go elsewhere. Most of the traditional dwellings of Kirtipur have gradually been divided in this manner into two or more units. The plots of land will also be subdivided. Even if a family is broken into a number of nuclear families, relations continue through participation in religious, cultural and customary practices. The collective term for members of an extended family is *phuki*, which includes up to three generations, and *bā-phuki* (half-*phuki*) for the fourth to the seventh generation. Membership is ritualized by ceremony, such as the custom of exchanging *siu*. Failure to give the appropriate

Plate 9 Procession of masked men in the De Pukhū Square during Gāi Jātrā. The stepped platform of the Nārāyaṇ temple in the background is used as amphitheatre by the spectators.

portion of the sacrificial animal to a person means a permanent break in the relationship, both religiously and socially. Another important duty for the *phuki* is that they must all mourn when a member dies.

The religious and social life of people is further regulated by the *gūṭhīs*, or organisations dedicated to the cult of a particular god or goddess, and supported by endowments of land and individual donations. The various *gūṭhīs* are concerned with social and religious matters such as the regulation of activities in temples and shrines, the maintenance of the buildings, and the cremation of the dead. The *gūṭhīs* now have income from funds deposited in local banks, and new *gūṭhīs* continue to be formed such as the Mṛityusamskara Gūṭhī, which is comprised of different castes.

The population of Kirtipur, with the exception of the *kusle* (temple keepers), cremate their dead at a place called Dathu Balkhu (middle Balkhu) near the river at the south of the Balkhu Gorge, where there is one main common crematorium for *śreshṭhas* and *jyāpus* with other cremation places for other castes to its west. An example of the role of the *gūṭhīs* is that of *de gūṭhī* (the town *gūṭhī*), which monitors the activities of the other *gūṭhīs*, and may, for example, punish them if they do not cremate the dead properly. For the last four decades the *bajrāchāryas* and *śākyas* of Kirtipur have been cremating their dead by the Bagmati River. There is no specific crematorium for them, and they may cremate their dead at any place where it is not opposed by the local people. In the past, however, they also used to carry out cremations at Balkhu Gorge, but they abandoned the site after a local dispute. The *kusle* bury their dead in the north-eastern part of the town, at the bottom of the northern slope.

## FESTIVALS

The Newars observe more festivals than any other population group in Nepal, to the extent that it is said that there is hardly a day in the year which does not have a festival being celebrated somewhere in the valley. These festivals may be observed nationally, or by particular communities, or in certain localities. A simple ritual for some Nepalese can be a major festival for the Newars, but within the Newar community there are also festivals which are only observed in specific villages or towns. The processions follow well defined paths, and details of the main festivals, or *jātrās* observed in Kirtipur every year are given below. They include Indrāyaṇī Jātrā, Bāgh Bhairav Jātrā, Buddha Jayanti, Gāi Jātrā and Kṛishṇa Janmāshṭamī.

### *Indrāyaṇī Jātrā*

Shrines of the mother goddess Indrāyaṇī are scattered all over the valley, and she is greatly honoured by Newars. There are temples specifically dedicated to her, as is one in Kirtipur, but, in addition, Shaivite and Vaishnavite temples are adorned with figures of the mother goddesses either in the decorative *toraṇas* over the doors, or in the struts of the roofs.

The Indrāyaṇī festival is celebrated with zeal in Kirtipur, as well as in the six neighbouring villages of Pāṅgā, Nagāoṅ, Naikāp, Satuṅgal, Lhonkhā and Machhegāoṅ. It is held in the month of Mārga (November-December) on the eighth day of the bright fortnight (*bakhumada ashṭami*). If there is any confusion about the exact date and time of the festival, it will be fixed by the *thakālī* of Kirtipur.

Plate 10 The main events of Gāi Jātrā take place at De Pukhū, the central square of the town.

Plate 11 Another view of the same event, masked men performing for the rest of the townspeople, especially those suffering from a recent bereavement.

Plate 12 A satirical street play during the Gāi Jātrā in Kirtipur. The audience are amused by a man in woman's dress who plays the role of a nagging wife critisizing her husband.

The festival in its present form was first celebrated in the 17th century, and the legend connected with it relates that an ogre living in the western part of the town used to kill many people. One day the townspeople made an agreement with the ogre to provide him each day with one man to eat, and every day a man from one of the families of the town was sent. When it came to the turn of the last surviving male member of one family, his affectionate old mother stopped him from going, offering herself in his place. On the way to the demon the helpless woman prayed to the goddess Indrāyaṇī, who, pleased by the prayers appeared in earthly form and killed the demon. The people celebrate the festival in gratitude for deliverance from the demon. One of the customs associated with the festival is for a man from a particular *gūṭhī* to be sent to the forest at the west end of the town. He is brought back the next day in a procession with music. The palanquin of the goddess is carried through the streets of the town and is worshipped by the people as it is brought in front of their houses. This is followed by two days of feasting, and a further procession in the upper part of the town.

### *Bāgh Bhairav Jātrā*

The Bāgh Bhairav festival is specific to Kirtipur, and is performed on the first of Bhādra (*siṅgha saṅkrānti*) which falls in the month of August. This is the only festival in Kirtipur which is observed according to the solar calendar. An image of Bāgh Bhairav is made specially, and is carried through the streets followed by *dāfās*, performers of ritual songs and music (*bhājans*) playing drums of different types (*dhime and nāyakhin*), together with girls offering lights, and the numerous devotees.

In the morning the procession follows the line of the ancient borders and fortifications of Kirtipur, and is known as the walk through the fort (*gā chā hyu wanegu*). In the evening hundreds of people circumambulate the temple as many times as they can, and throughout the night the whole Bāgh Bhairav complex is kept illuminated by *godāramata* and *mahādīp* (numerous or uncountable lamps).

### *Buddha Jayanti*

This festival is observed yearly on the full moon day of Baiśākh (April-May). It celebrates the birth of the Buddha in the *sāl* grove in Lumbini, about 400 kilometres south-west of the Kathmandu valley. This is a national festival observed throughout Nepal. In Kirtipur both Hindus and Buddhists go to Chilañcho Mahāvihār to pay homage to Lord Buddha on the morning of the festival, and a procession is taken out through the streets of the town. It used to be celebrated by numerous people following the procession with songs and music in the same manner as that of the Bāgh Bhairav festival, but since the time of the loss of the *gūṭhī* lands to the University, the *gūṭhī* has not had sufficient funds to put on the festival, and the procession is no longer taken out.

### *Gāi Jātrā*

The festival of Gāi Jātrā is widely observed by Newars all over Nepal, with the same central theme, but with local variations. During the festival families who have suffered a bereavement in the previous year send a cow, or a young boy decorated as a cow on a procession which goes around the streets of the town. The festival is to pay tribute to the dead and to assist their entry into heaven.

Plate 13 Procession with horn players passing a *chibhāḥ* at Lāyaku.

Plate 14 The *chibhāḥ* at Lāyaku, detail of the silver cladding fixed at the beginning of Gāi Jātrā, and removed after festivals.

During the festival processions take place both in the morning and in the afternoon, and in Kirtipur further carnival like processions take place in the evening in the De Pukhū square. The festival lasts for almost a week in July-August, until Kṛishṇa Ashṭami, but the main events take place in the two days after Gāi Jātrā. There is an interesting and curious story about the origin of the festival, according to which the festival was started in the 17th century by Rāja Pratap Malla (1641-74) after the death of his youngest son Chakra Vartendra Malla. The Queen was so much grieved by the sad demise of her beloved son that the Rāja ordered a festival to relieve her mental pain and to show her how many of his subjects had also lost a loved one during that year. Since then the festival has been observed every year.

In Kirtipur the festival is celebrated for three days. *Janaipurnimā* or *byān jā nakegu* (feeding the frogs) takes place on the first day, Gāi Jātrā or Sāpāru on the second, and Gaṇeś Jātrā on the third. Feeding the frogs is a unique tradition still prevalent in Newar farming communities. In the evening of the Gāi Jātrā carnival at De Pukhū there is a special event, the dropping of a buffalo head (*me chhyon kulkegu*).

### *Kṛishṇa Janmāshṭamī*

A week after Gāi Jātrā is Kṛishṇa Janmāshṭamī, in which the young girls and boys are the main participants. The festival is celebrated as the anniversary of Lord Kṛishṇa's birth. The palanquin of Kṛishṇa is taken out in a procession, which like in the other festivals is accompanied by various musical bands. Colourful traditional clothes are worn and lamps (*sukūdā*) are carried by the participants. Between eight hundred and twelve hundred girls and boys of the town join in the procession of *mata biyegu* (offering lamps).

### *Gāthu Pyākhāṅ*

One of the noteworthy minor festivals of Kirtipur is the Gāthu Pyākhāṅ or dance of the gardeners. It takes place once every twelve years, most recently in November-December 1992. The main theme of the dance is based on the acts of the Ashṭamātṛikās, and it is staged in Satako for several days. The festival lasts for almost six months, the drama being staged several times in different parts of the town. At the end of the festival the masks of the dancers are cremated at night in the same manner as human bodies, with a procession of mourners. The mourners are those who have participated in the dance for a year which includes six months of learning or teaching the dances before the festival. Thousands of other people, including those from the surrounding villages also take part in the funeral procession at mid-night, and observe it with zeal.

Other minor festivals peculiar to Kirtipur are Māghe Jātrā, Śrī Pañchamī, Ghanṭakarṇa, and Dvāre Jātrā. The Dvāre Jātrā is the only festival performed in honour of an administrator of Kirtipur: the *dvāre* or the village mayor. The ceremonies of the festival are similar to those of Gaṇeś Jātrā which takes place on the following day, but the Dvāre Jātrā is organized to honour the *dvāre*, and in its procession he is decorated and follows the palanquin of Gaṇeś. However, since 1984 this festival has not been observed. Among the other festivals observed by all Newars of the Valley are Dasaī, Tihār and Rām Navami.

# URBAN FABRIC

MEHRDAD SHOKOOHY

The Kirtipur hill is orientated north-west south-east, at an average of about 80m. above the level of the surrounding valley. The hill runs parallel to Mount Chandagiri, and is part of a range which connects Mount Indra Than at the west side of the valley to Mount Mahābharat to the south. Most of the peaks of this range of hills are occupied by small towns and villages: Naikāp, Gahirigāoṅ, and Badaregāoṅ are to the north-west of Kirtipur, and Chobhār is to the south-east. Kirkpatrick,[1] records that the Kirtipur hill was regarded by the Newars as a holy site, representing the body of Mahādeva (an epithet of Lord Śiva), whose head is denoted by the Chobhār hill. It is interesting that in spite of the association of the two sites with the Hindu deity, the Chilaṅcho Stupa in Kirtipur occupies the area which corresponds geographically with the site representing the heart of Mahādeva.

The northern flank of the Kirtipur Hill is steeper than the southern flank. On the top the hill has a saddle shaped formation with the middle being relatively flat, flanked by two small summits, one on the north-western side 30m. above the flat area, and another to the south 19m. above the flat area. The natural form of the hill seems to have been regarded as a suitable site for a fort since ancient times, but at present there is little evidence to help establish the location and size of the earliest settlement.

## MEDIAEVAL TOWN

From the historical sources it appears that at least from mediaeval times Kirtipur was a sizable fortified city. After the Gurkha pillage the fortifications of the town, together with most of the public and private buildings were left to disintegrate. Only in recent decades have some of the buildings been restored or reconstructed, while most of the late mediaeval fortifications have disappeared.

Oldfield's[2] eye witness account from the 1850's gives a vivid description of the town at the time of its decay. Besides describing the old layout of the town, and the state of its royal and religious buildings, the account is also valuable for its information on the traditional approaches to the town, which in turn may determine the positions of the gates.

> 'Since those days (the Gurkha conquest) the city has rapidly fallen into decay, no attempt having been ever made to restore its temples or repair any of its public buildings. The ancient walls and some of the gateways are still standing, but they are very much dilapidated. The city generally is in a melancholy state of ruin and decay. It is inhabited solely by Niwars, and it is doubtful whether it contains five thousand inhabitants. The air is very healthy, and the water is said to be so pure that cases of goitre very rarely are seen among those who dwell in Kirtipur.
>
> The principal approach to Kirtipur is by a winding road, which ascends the north-eastern face of the hill on which the city stands; but there are besides several foot-paths leading from the plain below to different parts of the town. The city is traversed through its entire length from east to west by a rather narrow, crooked, dirty street, which leads from its eastern entrance to the darbar, which is at the western end of the town.
>
> The ruins of the darbar and some adjacent temples are situated on and around a small conical hill, which rises out of the western extremity of the town, whence they overlook and command the whole of the city. In its best estate the darbar was never a large one, but it is now so utterly in ruins that even its form and extent cannot be traced. The body of a ruined temple (built of a peculiar purple or lake-coloured brick, which is not now manufactured) still survives, unroofed and overgrown with jungle, on the highest part of the hill, and some of its ornamental stone figures of elephants, lions, etc., are still in very fair preservation in front of its eastern entrance. It appears originally to have stood in the centre of a sort of square or quadrangle (probably part of the Basantpur), with which the level summit of the hill was crowned. This temple was built A.D. 1555. It was sacred to Parbati and Mahā Deo combined.
>
> The base of this little conical hill was strengthened and supported by terraces built of stone, and running up its sides, one above the other; and the

Plate 15 View from Kvācho looking towards Samal Ṭol in the northern part of the town. As Oldfield mentions: 'the base of this conical hill was strenghtened and supported by terraces built of stone'.

ascent was, and is still by a steep flight of steps, which in ancient days could easily have been defended against attack. Most of the temples in Kirtipur are more or less in ruin but there are some whose revenues have been partially spared by the Gurkha Government, and these are, therefore, still in good preservation.'

Oldfield's account raises a number of points which need to be considered to enable us to establish the layout and the fabric of old Kirtipur. The temple built with old fashioned purple bricks for the worship of Mahā Deo is the Umā Maheśvara temple, the second largest Hindu temple of Kirtipur. It may be assumed that his dating of the building to 1555 was taken from the date of an inscription in the compound, but such an inscription can no longer be found there, and even if there was an epigraph bearing a date corresponding with 1555, it may not have applied to the construction of the temple.

In the Kathmandu Valley, and indeed in all towns of Nepal and the Indian subcontinent, the distribution of urban spaces was determined by a rigid caste structure, with the quarters of the towns divided traditionally according to caste hierarchies. The caste orientated division of the urban areas is to a great extent still intact in Kirtipur, but in the past not all castes could live within the town walls.[3] The members of those castes which were regarded as unclean such as the *kasāī* (butchers), or untouchable such as the *poṛe* (sweepers) had to live outside the towns. Inside the town the members of the highest castes lived near the temples and the royal areas.

## TOWN WALLS AND GATES

The 16th and 17th century town walls and gates, dilapidated, but standing at the time of Oldfield, can still be traced, as at many points the lower parts of the town walls are preserved. The walls were constructed of brick, about 80cm. thick at base and encircling the present town almost in its entirety. It is said that there were 12 gates to the town. The gateway at the north, known as Deu Ḍhokā[4] still stands, and its lower parts are original, but the upper parts have been restored relatively recently. At the west of the town and at the south-west end of Pāliphal Ṭol the ruins of one of the piers of another gate, known as Pāliphal Ḍhokā, have also survived, and at most other points the stone thresholds of the gates can still be seen, but the gates themselves have disappeared. In the north-eastern side of the town parts of the wall stood on double stone ramparts, fragments of which are still traceable. Elsewhere

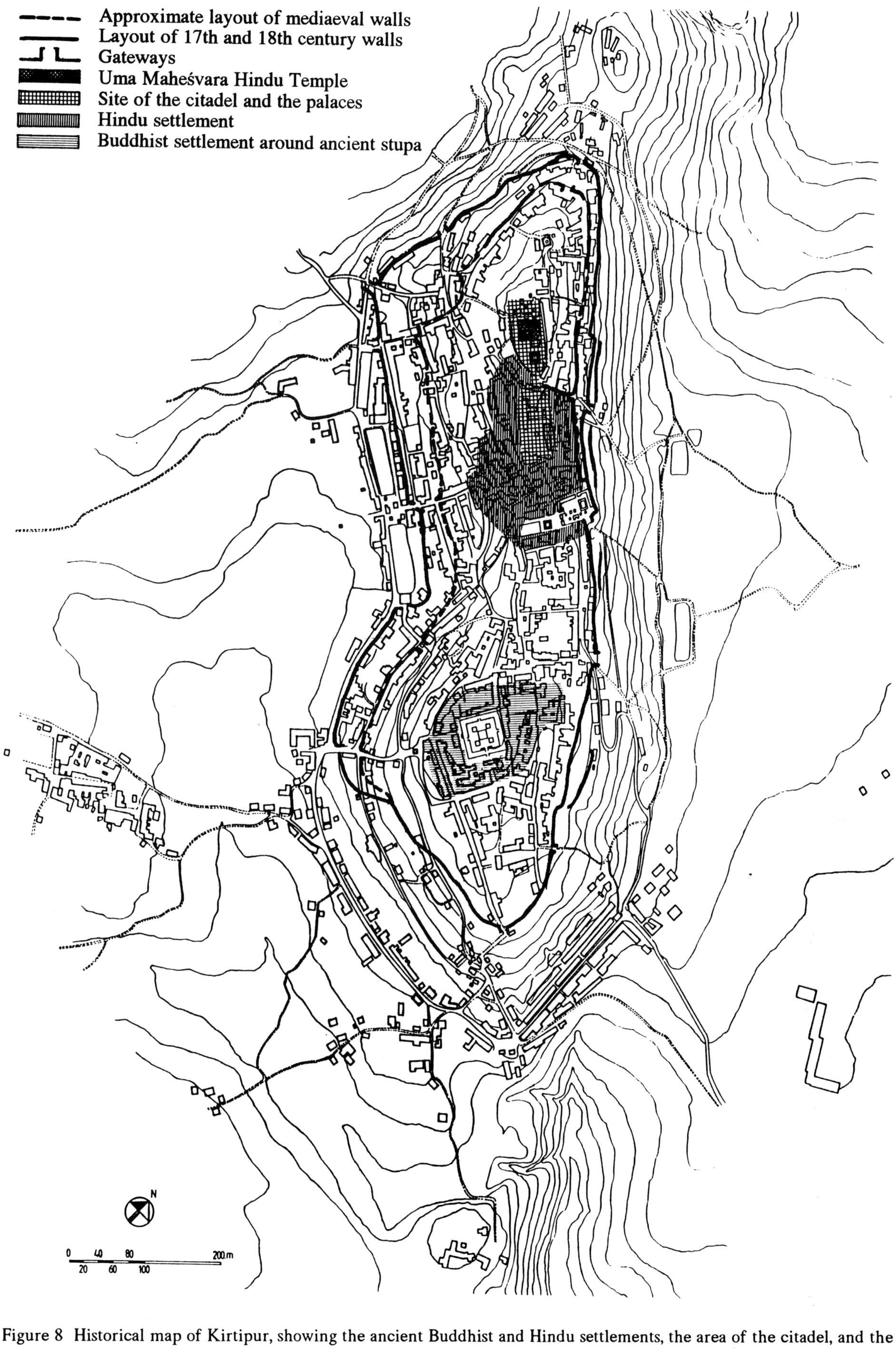


Figure 8 Historical map of Kirtipur, showing the ancient Buddhist and Hindu settlements, the area of the citadel, and the approximate outlines of the early and late mediaeval town walls and gates.

Plate 16 Poṛe settlement in an isolated area at the south-east of the town.

Plate 17 Ruins of the northern pier of the Pāliphal gate. A flat niche with a cusped arch has survived in the upper register.

Plate 18 Deu Ḍhokā, one of the main gates of the town at its north-eastern point. The steps descend to the Indrāyaṇī temple at Pīgāṅ.

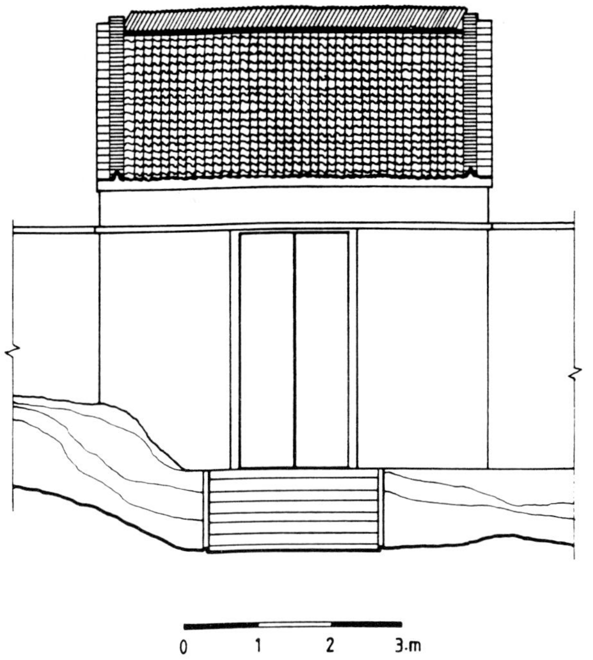


Figure 9 Deu Ḍhokā, north elevation showing the roof of the gate in its original tiled form.

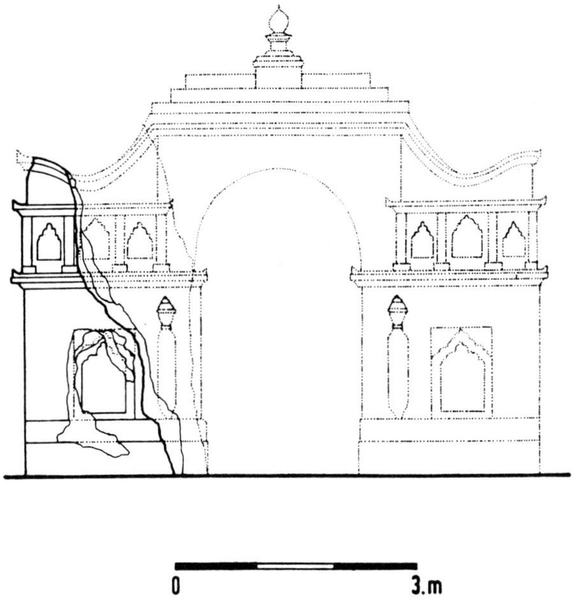


Figure 10 Pāliphal Ḍhokā, west elevation. The dotted lines are Herdick's suggestions, but it is more likely that the central arch was pointed in the "Indian" style.

Plate 19 Deu Ḍhokā, view from the town. The gate opens to a square which has a *chibhāḥ* (miniature stupa), a *maṇḍala* and a small pond. The gate has a single storeyed rest house (*pāṭi*) on the left and a double storeyed one (*sattal*) on the right. The vegetation around the pond can be seen in the foreground.

the wall had little re-enforcement and at the south-eastern side most traces of the walls have now been lost.

The size and the exact alignment of the town walls of early mediaeval Kirtipur are not, however, easy to establish. In our drawing (Figure 8) the line of the later walls is based mainly on the surviving evidence, but the perimeter of the early mediaeval town can only be suggested from the few existing features such as the remains of an old wall at Nagacho and Gachhen, and the contours of the Kirtipur hill. The sites of some of the early gates can also be conjectured where the main pathways entering the town meet the line of the wall. In our drawing we have suggested ten possible places for gates, most of which correspond with the site of a later gate.

In the late mediaeval period the city gates in the valley were usually constructed of stone or brick, with a rectangular portal framed by a lintel and timber jambs. An example of this type of gateway can be found in the palace at Thimi[5] where the gateway is flanked by colonnaded platforms on both faces, with the whole structure covered by a single pitched roof. The few existing examples of Nepalese city gates display a variety of designs and under the influence of Indo-Muslim architecture some later gates were constructed with pointed arches, like those to be seen in Patan. The Deu Ḍhokā of Kirtipur (Figure 9, Plates 18-19) has a simple rectangular wooden frame, covered by a modern pitched roof. However, the upper part of the gate is reconstructed and an original pitched roof cannot be ruled out. This gate does not appear to have had any flanking platforms, but within the town on either side of the square near the gate are two public buildings, one a roofed public platform or *pāṭi*, and the other a rest house of the type known as a *sattal* (Plate 19), both described with the public buildings of the town. Outside the town, a flight of stone steps descends to the valley.

The Pāliphal gate (Figure 10, Plate 17) seems to be later in date than the Deu Ḍhokā, and from the surviving pier, constructed of brick and decorated with arched flat niches, it appears that it was an arched gateway in the style of the later gates of the valley, with a pointed or semi circular arch. Herdick,[6] who has produced a conjectural reconstruction of this gate based on its surviving remains in the early 1970s, shows it with a semi-circular arch, but the pier has now deteriorated further making it difficult to form an accurate idea of its original profile.

From the city gates of the early mediaeval period very little is known. While nothing stands *in situ*, at the south side of Kirtipur we found stone fragments apparently of a sizable gate. These stones may be the remains of the southern gate of Kirtipur and are now incorporated into the steps on the path from the south going up to the *poṛe* quarter of the town. The stones consist of a number of large squared blocks, and a complete piece which appears to have been a lintel (Plate 5). The piece is finely decorated with carvings which appear to be part of a larger pattern probably representing a mythical beast. The rest of the pattern would have continued on the jambs. Among the stones incorporated into the steps a number of smaller fragments decorated with carvings could also be seen. While the tradition of stone carving is still strong in Nepal, for several centuries it has been employed exclusively for statues, commemorative pillars, water spouts for springs (Plate 116), *chaityas* and other religious objects. Architectural decoration has been limited to wood carving, and sometimes moulded terra-cotta. These stone elements may therefore date from a much earlier period, and are perhaps early mediaeval. An archaeological investigation of the site, and preservation of these pieces is of prime concern since as well as being rare examples of ~~architectural~~ carved stone in Nepal, they may also throw light on some of the architectural features of the valley in early times.

## THE CITADEL

In the three other towns of the Kathmandu Valley the traditional royal area is the palace complex, in all cases located on level ground in the core of the town. In front of the palace is the Darbār Square, a large ceremonial open space, occupied by a number of temples. In India, on the other hand, the royal area is fortified and is in the form of a citadel standing usually on higher ground than the town. From the account of Oldfield it is clear that the plan of Kirtipur was very different from the other cities of the valley, as its ruinous royal complex, incorporating the Umā Maheśvara temple, was on the highest point of the hill, and its surrounding walls were standing on stone ramparts. This arrangement is very similar to that of the citadels of Indian towns, but is unique in the Kathmandu Valley. In 1981 a 7th or 8th century image of Śiva (Plate 136) was accidentally found in the area behind the Umā Maheśvara temple at the time of the excavations connected with building the reservoir for the modern water supply of the town. This image, described elsewhere in this report, is the only archaeological

Plate 20 Lāyaku (the old palace area) looking north towards the Umā Maheśvara temple, which is set above the stone built rampart of the ancient citadel. The Gaṇeś image from Umā Maheśvara is housed in the rest house (*pāṭi*).

Plate 21 The site of the palace area between Lāyaku and Jochhe seen from the Umā Maheśvara temple looking south. A large part of the area is still vacant or used as vegetable gardens of houses built recently around the site. The rest of the town, including the mound of the Chilañcho stupa, can be seen in the background.

evidence indicating the old origin of the citadel, but in the absence of any systematic archaeological excavation it is difficult to establish the reasons for Kirtipur having an Indian type of town plan. However, we have seen that the chronicles of Nepal record an early mediaeval reconstruction of Kirtipur, and the layout of the town may be a result of this. The plan shows that the town was designed as a stronghold, perhaps in the days when the valley was coming increasingly under the influence of Indian elements, including the introduction of the Hindu religion.

At present the site of the citadel is still mainly vacant, and the only exceptions are the temple, a house occupied by the keeper of the temple, the modern water reservoir, and one or two other modern buildings. The ruins of the old palaces and most of the citadel walls have disappeared, but the stone faced ramparts upon which the platforms of the old palace complex stand are still partially intact (Plate 20). The citadel itself was on two levels, with an inner citadel, almost square in plan, standing on the higher level. The north-eastern and south-eastern sides of the outer citadel were aligned roughly on straight lines, but the other sides apparently followed the contours of the ground. The approach from the palaces to the citadel must have been at the south-eastern side, at the same place as the present entrance to the Umā Maheśvara temple, and the temple was probably in the outer court of the inner citadel. To the south-east of Umā Maheśvara there is another mound (Plate 21) that, according to Oldfield, was occupied by an extension of the palace complex, and some earlier temples. This area, still known as Lāyaku,[7] meaning palace, must have also been part of the late mediaeval citadel, and may have been added to the earlier citadel during a later expansion of the royal quarters towards the south. Excavation on this mound and the main part of the citadel may bring to light more information on the mediaeval history of the town.

## HISTORIC HINDU AND BUDDHIST AREAS

Kirtipur was, and to some extent still is divided into two main Buddhist and Hindu parts, designated according to the faiths of the two communities as *Buddhamārga* and *Śivamārga* areas respectively. At least from the time of the Malla dynasty Hinduism has always been the religion of the royal families as well as the ruling classes. In Kirtipur the north-western part of the town appears to have been occupied by Hindus, while the south-eastern part was dominated by Buddhists.

The nobles and high caste Hindus would have occupied the area between the Bāgh Bhairav temple in front of the central square (the De Pukhū square) and the citadel. This area is still occupied by high caste Hindus, and consists of some of the best houses of Kirtipur. The main thoroughfare of this area is also known as Lāyaku after the palace complex which once occupied its north-eastern flank.

In the centre of the southern part of Kirtipur and on the top of the southern summit stands the Chilańcho Stupa. The stupa occupies most of the area of a large square, almost four times larger than the De Pukhū square. The area surrounding the stupa has traditionally been occupied by Buddhists of the higher castes. Mediaeval Kirtipur was a farming town and the rest of the area within the old town wall must have been occupied mainly by the *jyāpus* or farmers. The distribution of population according to social hierarchy appears to have remained much the same, except that the high caste Buddhist community is probably reduced in size, leaving some of the area of Tananī Ṭol, to the west of the stupa to *jyāpus*, and some areas to the south of the stupa to high caste Hindus. On the northern side the Chīthuṅ Bahī, one of the old Buddhist monasteries of Kirtipur, located near the northern border of the town indicates the old limits of the Buddhist dwellings. This area is now occupied predominantly by *jyāpus*. The southern side of the town consists mainly of lately built or modern houses, indicating a relatively recent date for the establishment of a Hindu community in the area. The main temples in the area, the Lokeśvar and the Buddha Dharma Saṅgha, are both associated with the Buddhists.

Within the town wall there must also have been small communities of tradesmen living in their own groups, but among the main *jyāpu* population. With the alterations in the composition of the population of Kirtipur during the last two centuries it is not always easy to establish the former location of the trading communities. This is because their numbers would have been small, and although they were lower in the hierarchy than the *jyāpu*, the traders enjoyed a more flexible position than the very low castes. Today traders live together with *jyāpus*. In addition an area to the east of the northern part of the town is associated with the *mānandhars*, or oil pressers, whose traditional product is rapidly being replaced by commercially produced oil made by modern mechanical systems. Members of communities such as the *kasāī*, the *gāyine* and the *poṛe*, who all lived outside the walls, must have occupied the same areas as they do today.

The mediaeval division of the town into a Buddhist and a Hindu part may be a relic of the occupation of the site by much earlier settlements. We have already noted the local traditions claiming an ancient origin for the Chilańcho Stupa, connecting it with the Buddhist Emperor Aśoka. The tradition may reflect the possibility that the Buddhist settlement around the stupa has an earlier origin than the Hindu settlement. In early mediaeval times and with the introduction of Hinduism to Nepal, a Hindu settlement connected with the aristocracy and the army may have developed outside the Buddhist Kirtipur, on its northern border. The fortified core of this settlement would have been the citadel, occupied by the temples and the royal palaces. We have seen that the chronicles of Nepal record the construction of Kirtipur in the early mediaeval period by the Hindu king Sadāśivadeva. His construction of Kirtipur is very likely to be a reference to the building of the Hindu settlement and the citadel of the town.

## EXISTING DISTRIBUTION OF OPEN AND BUILT UP SPACES

The urban fabric of Kirtipur combines the elements of a multiple village with features common to the three cities of the valley. The general layout of villages in the valley, and indeed elsewhere in Nepal, consists of a wide open public square around which stand the houses, with their main elevation facing the square. The smaller villages do not have any lanes except a main path which connects their public central square to the network of roads and footpaths between the villages. The larger villages may consist of a combination of two or three squares. These squares are usually connected to each other by a very narrow lane, but long narrow streets are usually absent in their plan.

### *The ṭol*

In places where the community lives around more than one public square, the square and its surrounding neighbourhood is called a *ṭol*, and each *ṭol* usually consists of a number of households, sometimes over a hundred, comprising people of the same trade or rank according to the traditional social hierarchy. This arrangement for the neighbourhoods is found in Kirtipur as well as in the three cities, but in the cities the *ṭols* are not always adjacent, and are sometimes linked to each other by long narrow streets and bazaars.

Plate 22 De Pukhū square looking north. The pond is in the middle of the central square of the town connecting the old Hindu and Buddhist settlements, and is used for washing clothes and utensils, and by boys as a swimming pool.

Plate 23 Mvana Ṭol, one of the larger neighbourhoods built on three levels of terraces.

Plate 24 A grocery at Khasi Bāzār selling a limited selection of goods including cigarettes and fresh vegetables, and providing freshly brewed tea for passers by. A few other similar shops are scattered around the town, but the main shopping area has developed recently in Naya Bāzār.

The town plans of the cities were probably influenced by the north Indian and Bengali towns of the 16th and 17th century, at the time when, at the peak of Malla power the towns of the valley grew greatly in size. The main part of Kirtipur between the two hills, however, appears to have kept its more traditional arrangement, with the neighbouring *ṭols* being set very close to each other, a layout similar to that of the larger villages of Nepal. The open square of each *ṭol* has its own characteristics; it may be wide with a pond in the middle, or long and relatively narrow, and sometimes it is on several different levels. It is, however, generally well drained and paved with stone, brick, or more usually a combination of these materials.

The *ṭols* in Kirtipur are predominantly residential, but some contain one or two grocery shops. In the public area of each *ṭol* there are a number of *chaityas*, carved stone shrines mostly in the form of a small stupa.[8] The great number of these shrines, set up by individuals of the neighbourhood, is a reminder of the importance of religion in the everyday life of Kirtipur. In addition to the *chaityas* many of the *ṭols* have their own temple, varying in size and in design. The homogeneous quality of the buildings of the *ṭols*, and at the same time their diversity in scale and form, combines with the different settings of the temples and chaityas to produce a townscape full of variety.

All activities connected with the public life of a neighbourhood take place in the *ṭol*. In the traditional life of a Newar community the line between private and public life is not sharply drawn, and the *ṭol* should be regarded as an extension of the houses, where the families share their public interests — and activities — with the neighbours. In the *ṭol* the children play and grow up together, the mothers wash their utensils and laundry near the shared sources of water, marriages are arranged, and the fathers exchange views in daily afternoon meetings. The nature of life in the *ṭol* not only varies with the time of a day, but changes with the seasons of the year. For example, at harvest time early in the autumn

Plate 25 Stepped streets at Sāyami Ṭol, with a water tap in the foreground. The water supply is limited to a few hours per day. The taps, like the natural springs, not only provide drinking water for the locality but are also used for laundry and bathing.

the crops are brought to the *ṭol* to be dried before being stored. The pavements of the open squares are swept, and rice, grains and pulses are spread on mats for drying, while colourful garlands of chillies and corn cobs hang from the windows of the houses.

In a hierarchical society such as that of Kirtipur, it is not therefore surprising to find that the people of a *ṭol* identify themselves with their own neighbourhood rather than with the town as a whole. This is reinforced by the traditional caste structure of the society, and the fact that the people of a *ṭol* are of the same caste or at the same level in the social hierarchy, perhaps different from that of the people of the neighbouring *ṭol*. In the following pages we shall return to the subject of the *ṭols* of Kirtipur in more detail when we discuss the main areas of the town.

### *Streets*

Although the *ṭols* with open squares are the dominant feature of the fabric of Kirtipur, there are also streets, or rather, long and narrow lanes, in the town. These streets have mainly developed outside the central part of the old town and may be divided into two types: those which are stepped and link the network of country footpaths to the top of the hill, and those which are relatively flat, lying roughly along the contours of the ridge, and which were once parallel to the old town wall. Like the squares, all the streets were traditionally paved with flag stones or brick, or a combination of both, but in most areas the pavements have not been adequately maintained and need major repair.

The traditional streets of Kirtipur share some of the characteristics of the squares and their houses are again mainly occupied by people of the same caste. Some of these streets are known by the name of a *ṭol*, the wider part of the street playing the role of the public square, where most of the shrines and *chaityas* are set. It should also be mentioned that these streets may be the product of the enlargement of Kirtipur in the Malla period, when the other towns of the valley also grew in size, but unlike these towns, in Kirtipur the nature of the site determined the setting of the streets along the contour lines of the hill.

## MODERN DEVELOPMENTS

To the traditional streets those of the modern developments should also be added. Most of these streets follow the line of the old footpaths, originally outside the town, but now bordered by houses, shops and workshops. The main new streets are the two asphalted access roads, one at the eastern side starting from Naya Bāzār and winding up the hill to reach the De Pukhū square. The modern development alongside the roads has so far been limited to the lowest part near Naya Bāzār, and the top end where the road reaches the relatively flat area approaching the square. To the north of this road are the woodlands which have developed since the 1960s. The steep slope of the ground has to certain extent restricted building activities, but with uncontrolled development, the area is now being filled with new buildings.

The other asphalted road passes through Naya Bāzār, and encircles the flat ground on the southern and western flanks of the hill. It ends after passing the third traditional reservoir, Labhā Pukhū. The area at the southern part of this road is known as Bahirīgāoṅ, and the western section as Khasi Bāzār. The area alongside this road

Plate 26 Sāyami Ṭol, a neighbourhood alongside a long and narrow lane, without the usual *ṭol* square.

Plate 27 Naya Bāzār, the modern development at Kirtipur seen from the metalled road to the north-east.

is under rapid development. At Bahirīgāoṅ, when the road branches towards the village of Nagāoṅ a new built-up complex has developed with houses, shops and workshops, and the developing area will soon reach Nagāoṅ.

As already noted, Naya Bāzār itself is also growing rapidly, and at present consists of three parallel roads. The area is also developing eastwards, alongside an old stone paved pathway, and southward at the junction with the access tracks to the village of Saṅkhapur (or Pāṅgā), and the town of Chobhār. From the west Naya Bāzār has already joined Bahirīgāoṅ, and at many points side streets are now developing mainly towards the southern flat grounds.

At the eastern end of Naya Bāzār a new Tibetan monastry has been built, and another is situated in Pīgāṅ at the north-west of the town, outside the built up area and near a ropeway which transports materials from outside the Valley to Kathmandu. The Tibetan monasteries have no links with the Nepalese *bāhās* and *bahīs*, and belong to the Tibetan refugees who have been given the opportunity to settle in many locations in the Kathmandu Valley, and are now becoming gradually integrated into the life and economy of the Valley.

## NOTES

1 William Kirkpatrick, *An Account of the Kingdom of Nepaul*, London, 1811, 165.

2 H. Ambrose Oldfield, *Sketches from Nipal*, London, 1880, I, 127.

3 Ibid., I, 95; for the Hindu town planning rules see Parasanna Kumar Acharya, *Architecture of Mānasāra*, IV, New Delhi, 1980, 63-98; M. A. Ananthalwar, Alexander Rea and A. V. Thiagaraja Iyer, *Indian Architecture*, I, 1980, 1558-73.

4 Corrupt form of *de dhvākā*, defence gate.

5 Wolfgang Korn, *The Traditional Architecture of the Kathmandu Valley*, Kathmandu, 1979, 14-15.

6 Reinhard Herdick, *Kirtipur, Stadtgestalt, Prinzipien der Raumordnung und gesellschaftliche Functionen einer Newar-Stadt*, Munich, Cologne, London, 1988, 49, map 7.

7 H. Ambrose Oldfield, op. cit., I, 128; also see Francis Hamilton Buchanan, *An Account of the Kingdom of Nepal and of the Territories Annexed to this Domain by the House of Gorkha*, Edinburgh, 1819, 38.

8 The *chaitya* is a Buddhist shrine which in the past was set up at the end of a covered hall used somewhat like a church for everyday worship. A great number of these *chaitya* halls still survive in India. The form of a *chaitya* is similar to that of a stupa in every detail, the difference being that a stupa is generally regarded as the burial place of a relic of the Buddha or his associates, while the *chaitya* is purely symbolic, with no object buried in its core. The *chaityas* are described in more detail in the chapter on historic public buildings.

# THE NEWARI HOUSE

CHRIS MIERS

The traditional Newari house has evolved over hundreds of years into a uniform construction reflecting and integrating the demands of culture, religion and daily activities as well as the environmental considerations and availability of building materials. The dense urban settlement of Kirtipur is characterized by the terraced houses set up from the street on stone podia, their flat, red brick façades incorporating splendid carved timber doors and windows, and the large overhanging eaves of the roof projecting out on angled timber struts. Within the coherence of style and materials, building height, and elevational symmetry, there is a rich diversity of detail and decoration. Behind the houses lining the streets lie internal courtyards giving access to further houses, or open spaces providing vegetable gardens (*khebā*).

The complex social organization, centred around the extended family and ancestral worship has led to a cycle of expansion and regeneration of the inner town which has allowed Kirtipur to grow and adapt within its boundaries. When a family needs more space, they will either extend, if land is available, or demolish and reconstruct their house, rather than move to a different, larger house. The extensions are normally built on the *khebā*, the back garden, but the natural restrictions of the steep and rocky hillside prevent this open space being totally infilled and so maintain a balance of built form and planting and a limiting of density of population which is not found in the neighbouring Newari settlements of Pāṅgā and Nagāoṅ.

However, in recent years the newly constructed houses have tended to ignore traditional features and details. Instead within the traditional street the modern house sits incongruously higher than before, possibly with a different brick or even rendered façade, and typically a flat roof.

In conjunction with this internal regeneration, ribbon developments have sprung up in perimeter areas of the town where roads provide vehicular access. In Naya Bāzār tall modern houses differing in form, materials and details, and unsuited to the culture and climate, give an overall character quite foreign to the traditional town and an environment incompatible with the traditional life style. However, these new developments readily incorporate better services in the way of water supply and drainage, as well as meeting the aspirations of a younger generation of inhabitants who have recently moved to Kirtipur.

## THE FORM AND USE OF THE HOUSE

The traditional house has four storeys: three main storeys plus an attic. There are also some five storeyed houses, but they are unusual. Three storeyed houses belonging to members of the lower castes can also be found, mainly in the *poṛe ṭol*.

### *Podium*

The house is generally set on a raised podium (*phaṛ*) of between 300-1500mm. in height, which serves a number of functions. It raises the ground floor, hence reducing the dampness. It is generally made of stone rubble (occasionally brick) which, being largely non-porous, helps prevent the rising damp. The projecting eaves of the roof overhang fractionally further than the podium projects, helping to throw the monsoon water clear. However, any wind drives the rain onto the podium, saturating the lower parts of the wall.

The podium also acts as an intermediary zone, defining the transition between street and house, public and private, an attribute gained largely by the change in levels, but also often by a change in materials (stone and brick) or in the pattern of the stonework. Most of the daily activities for women, children and old men take place in the street, and the raised area becomes a semi-private space shared with neighbours, who sit and work on either side of the street, moving from one side

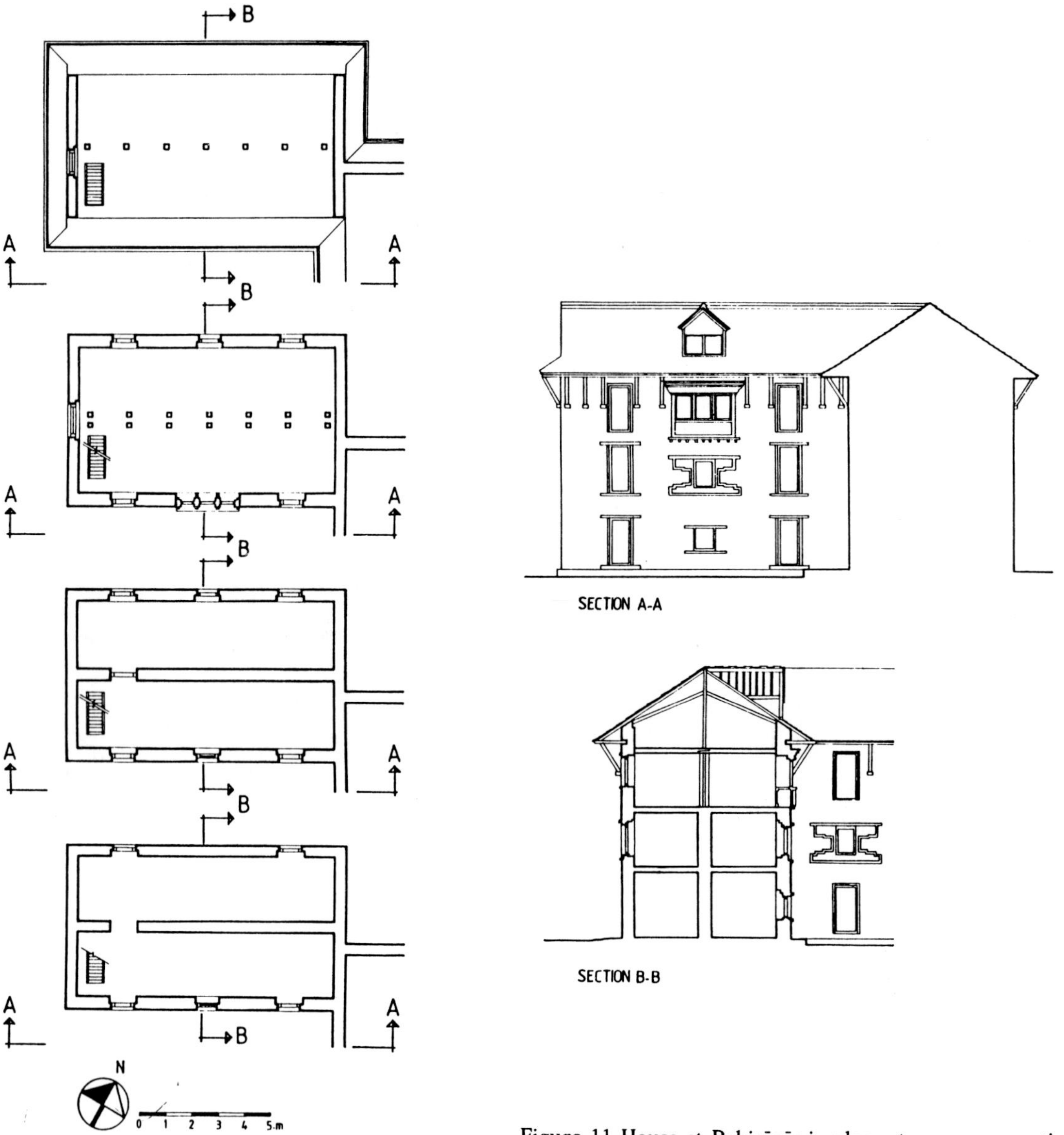


Figure 11 House at Bahirīgāoṅ, plans, transverse section and front elevation.

of the street to another to follow the sun.

Generally, in front of the entrance to a house are steps leading up. These are sometimes recessed into the podium, or sometimes protrude into the street, and they form an important street element, being used by children for games and by adults for sitting and conversing. In front of the steps is normally a circular *maṇḍala* inscribed in the street paving, representing Kumāra. This *maṇḍala* also indicates the start of the transitional zone of ownership. During *Tihār*, an annual festival, a stripe of red clay is painted from inside the house, over the raised threshold of the front door, across the podium and down the steps, terminating in a circle on the *maṇḍala* . Those who have no inscribed circle still create a circle of red clay. In the case of houses set well back from the street, the stripe is still brought right out to a circle in the street. Where one set of steps and one *maṇḍala* is shared by a number of houses, individual painted stripes leave each front door and descend independently until they are united in the *maṇḍala.*

## *Entrance*

The steps generally lead directly up to the front door, which may be set to one side of an otherwise symmetrical façade. The door surround is more ornate than any other element on the ground floor, often combining carvings with small paintings that are renewed for particular rites of passage, each carving or painting having a religious significance. Over the door is usually a

Plate 28 Traditional house with an L shaped extension at Bahirīgāoṅ. In the courtyard there is a a *chibhāḥ* and a *maṇḍala.*

Plate 29 Poṛe Ṭol seen from the south approach path with stone steps. The long monolithic step in the foreground is an old lintel, probably from an early gate in this vicinity. The traditional *poṛe* houses are in three storeys (two floors and the attic), but a newly constructed four storeyed house can also be seen.

Plate 30 Circular *maṇḍala* in the form of a six-pointed star within a lotus motif, set in front of the door of a house at Lāyaku.

paper image of a snake, intended to ward off reptiles.

*Ground Floor*

The ground floor is divided into a front and back space by means of a central spinal wall which runs along the whole of the structure and parallel to the front and back walls. This floor is dark, due to its small latticed windows giving security. It is damp, and considered to be uninhabitable, and is normally used for storage of agricultural implements, firewood, and for stabling animals. In Kirtipur a weaving loom is often kept at this level, which also functions as a workshop. In some houses part of the front wall at this level is replaced by carved wooden columns and beams, allowing the area to the front of the central spine wall to be an open space, with the rear area retained for storage. In these cases the front area may be used as a shop or workshop. Members of lower castes are usually allowed into the ground floor of a house, but often no further. From the ground floor a steep ladder-like stair rises to the first floor with a sliding or hinged trap door at first floor level to close it off.

*First floor*

The first floor is used for sleeping and partly for storage. The God Room is usually located on this floor. It is a locked and sacred room accessible only to "clean" members of the family and containing valuable and particularly significant religious objects as well as some foodstuffs. The first floor is characterized on the front elevation by the traditional square latticed windows, the *tiki jhyāḥ*, which maintain privacy whilst allowing in light. Shoes are normally left at this level before family or visitors proceed further.

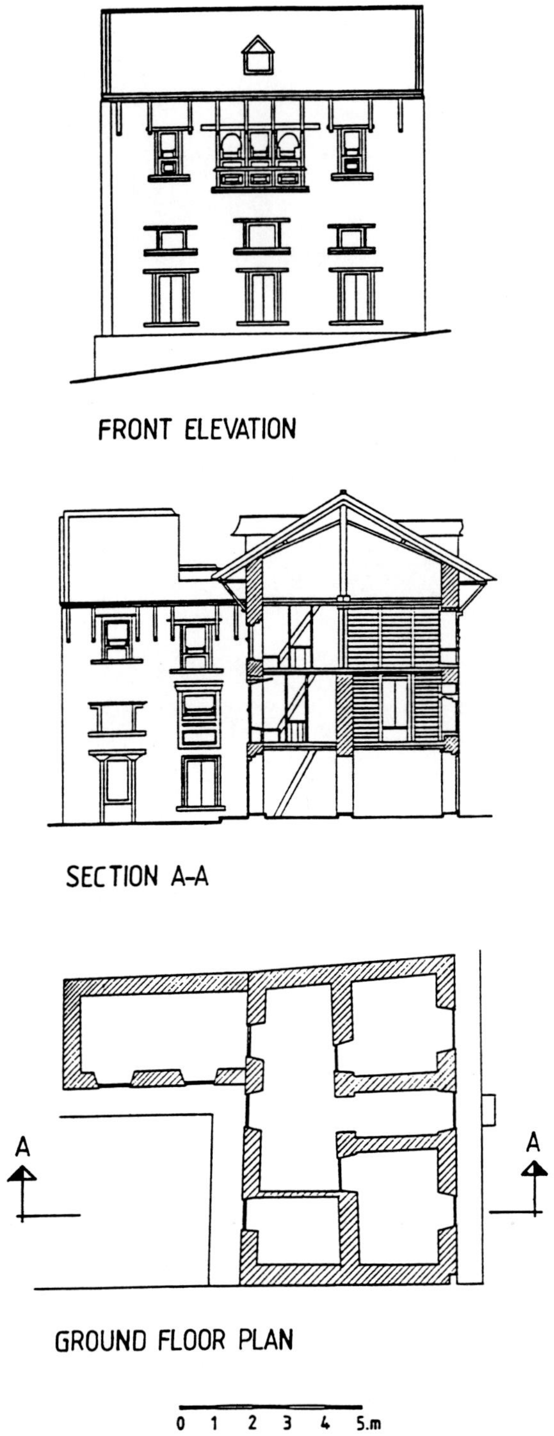


Figure 12 Traditional house with an extension situated at Pāliphal, ground plan, section and front elevation (survey by S. S. Shrestha).

Plate 31 House at Hva Kuncha, first floor divided by a timber partition wall and lightly furnished.

Plate 32 House at Sāgāl Ṭol divided vertically in two, with the façade of one side plastered over.

*Second floor*

Stairs up to the second floor run parallel over the lower ones. The stairs are generally open to the room, which at this level forms the primary internal living space, where visitors are received and family feasts and festivals take place. At this floor level the central spine wall is replaced with single or paired columns (*thāṅ*) supporting a beam (*nināḥ*) above, allowing the room to occupy the full depth of the house. In many houses this level is partially sub-divided with wooden partitions to create additional bedrooms.

The prominence of this space is traditionally marked on the front façade by the largest and most ornate window of the elevation, the *san jhyāḥ*. Centrally placed, this is usually a three bay window intricately carved with fine detail, projecting slightly from the plane of the brickwork. People sometimes sit at this window and call across to the neighbours opposite, or simply watch the goings on in the street. However, the room is usually deserted during the day because so much of the daily activity takes place in the street below. Only the more prestigious older houses in Kirtipur incorporate a *san jhyāḥ*, and more commonly an ornate single window is found in its place.

*Roof space*

The kitchen occupies the roof space. No member of a lower caste is allowed here, and its isolated position from the rest of the house removes it from any visitors. Cooking is carried out on an open hearth, with smoke escaping through a cowling tile in the roof. The underside of the roof is generally black with soot, and often infested with cockroaches. There is usually a small terrace leading off the kitchen, sometimes used for personal washing.

*Furnishings*

Traditional internal finishes and furnishings are simple throughout the house. Floors and walls are covered in a red clay slip that dries to a hard finish. This finish is renewed as part of regular purification rituals, such as before festivals, and the regular application often leads to characteristic rounded corners in an old house. Walls are generally painted blue or white. There is no furniture, only straw mats (*sukū*) woven from the rice straw reaped in the harvest, and occasionally flat cushions. The only seats of any sort are the bench seats usually built into the wall thickness inside the windows. In many houses there are also cotton mattresses which are rolled out of the way during the day.

In recent years, however, ready made furnishings such as simple beds, chairs, wardrobes and cupboards have become popular, and display the wealth of the families, as well as their desire to catch up with the modern life style promoted in the urban society of Kathmandu and Patan. The floors of the rooms in many houses are now covered by lino, which is easy to clean and unlike the traditional red clay does not need to be renewed regularly. Most households have radios, and television aerials are increasingly becoming a familiar feature on the roof-tops.

In the house religious icons and pictures are spread throughout the rooms, but in particular at second floor level. These images are worshipped daily as part of the *pūjā*, which protects the house and maintains a link with the family's ancestors and gods.

### *Services*

All houses have a supply of electricity, although internal wiring can be rudimentary. The supply is adequate in summer, but there can be frequent power cuts in winter. Electricity is mainly used for lighting, and sometimes for appliances such as radios, televisions and fans, as well as the running of power looms. Very few houses have private water taps. Water is generally collected in large brass pots from local public stand-pipes and then stored in the kitchen in earthenware pots. In the dry summer months the taps are only running for a few hours a day, and the collection of water for a family can be a time consuming business.

Until recently there was no sanitation within the house, and modern latrines are also located outside the house. Traditionally pits in the rear courtyard and underneath the stairs at ground floor level have in part filled this function combined with the use of communal outdoor latrine alleys. The new and properly constructed latrines are encouraging changing habits. No form of heating is provided. In the cold period in the winter small portable clay bowls (*makaḥ*) are filled with burning charcoal and carried around.

### *The front façade*

The façade of the typical traditional house is in principle symmetrical with the central elements being larger and more ornate. The central axis is marked by the three bay *san jhyāḥ* or an ornate single bay window at the second floor level, flanked by two smaller windows, and a large *tiki jhyāḥ* at first floor level, flanked by two smaller *tiki jhyāḥs*. The ground floor may have an ornate door set to one side, or may be entirely opened up to accommodate a shop.

The traditional windows and doors combined massive carved wooden lintels and sills projecting horizontally at either side of the window opening, giving a pronounced horizontal emphasis to the elevation. The date of the houses and their relation with the façade will be discussed in the next chapter, but in general it should be noted that on houses constructed between 100 to 200 years ago the projections of the windows were made shorter and the openings became somewhat more vertical. Windows from this century have dispensed with the projecting lintels and sills entirely and have taken on a vertical emphasis, being altogether taller, with steel railings over the lower section and most recently often having glass installed. The traditional, heavy, top-hung shutters have been replaced with light, side-hung shutters. *San jhyāḥs* are no longer incorporated, unless an old one can be installed in a new structure.

## CONSTRUCTION

### *Walls*

The traditional house is of load-bearing brickwork construction, with floor joists spanning between the front and back walls and the central spine wall. Typically the overall depth of the house is 6 to 6.50m. The walls are generally 450mm. thick, with an outer face of fired brick, but otherwise built of sun-dried mud bricks. It is more common now to use only fired bricks. Bricks may be either "Chinese" bricks: fired bricks made in large kilns in the Kathmandu Valley, or "Nepālī" bricks which are made locally. Around February when some fields are fallow, small kilns are constructed and bricks made in the neighbouring fields. Some of these bricks are fired, others merely sun-dried.

Foundations may go down to bed-rock, or may be formed from compacted broken brick and stone. No damp-proof course is incorporated. Mortar is usually made of a clay mud, but occasionally a cement-based mortar is used for the first few courses at ground level. Lintels over openings are of timber and often in three parts, stepping upwards towards the inside.

Plate 33 House at Hva Kuncha, ground floor lobby of the building at the south-west of the courtyard. The wooden stairs lead to the the upper floors.

Many houses suffer severely from brick erosion due to salt action. Salt carried by the rising dampness crystallizes on the brickwork about one metre up the wall causing the surface of the brickwork to break away and the mortar to be eroded. Modern houses are often built with thinner walls, using a better brick. They tend to be taller, taking advantage of better building technology, but still employ many of the traditional techniques and incorporate many faults.

*Floors and stairs*

The ground floor may be mud, tiled, or suspended timber if used as a shop. Other floors are of timber with the floor joists spanning front to back and usually projecting right through the external wall to show on the outer face, and internally lapping well over the central spine wall.

The joists (*dhalī*) are normally 75x100mm. laid flat at 225mm. centres. In general every third or fourth is pegged onto a wall plate which is on the inside edge of the wall. Floor to ceiling heights are very low, typically 1.75m. with exposed joists showing a timber or split bamboo lath supporting the broken brick and mud floor finish above.

Typically stairs run at approximately 55° pitch, with flights one above the other and with seven widely-spaced open treads. Nine and eleven treads are common with the higher floor-to-floor heights of the newly constructed houses.

*Roof*

The roof is double-pitched with the ridge on the line of the central spine wall, and a projecting overhang of 900mm. at front and back. The structure is of timber and comprises columns on the centre line supporting a ridge beam, intermediate purlins supported on primary rafters, a wall plate, an outer beam supported on angled struts, and then the rafters pegged together over the ridge beam and projecting out over the walls to the outer beam. Onto the rafters are laid timber or split bamboo laths, then a thick (150mm.) layer of sterile mud finished with small fired clay roof tiles (*jhingati*) embedded on it.

The larger "Indian" roof tile is also commonly used. In recent years corrugated steel sheeting is becoming more common. On the houses of the lower caste groups, the *poṛe* (sweepers), the *gāyine* (musicians) and the *kusle* (tailors), the roof may be covered in rice-straw thatch.

Flat roofs are not traditional except as small back terraces. These are built in the same way as floors, but finished with fired clay tiles. They frequently leak. Modern houses are often built with flat roofs of either in situ reinforced (or brick reinforced) concrete slabs, or corrugated steel. The former are expensive and built with little understanding of the materials. The latter, although quick to construct, are totally unsuited to the climate. As the modern houses are built taller, overshadowing the streets, so people are tending to use these flat roofs for activities that traditionally took place within the street areas.

### THE BUILDING OPERATION

Building work tends to take place in February and March when labour is not required in the fields. Traditionally it is accompanied by a number of ceremonies, and the extent to which these are adhered to depends on the wealth of the family. Auspicious dates must be established by the local astrologer for the selection of the site and the laying of the foundation stone. Further ceremonies follow with the completion of each floor, the roof, and finally, when the house is ready for occupation. This last ceremony may well be accompanied by the sacrifice of a goat or buffalo.

Generally the actual construction is carried out by local men, but the carrying of materials is often done by women, as is the treading of the mud mortar until it reaches the right consistency. Bamboo scaffolding is erected where necessary. No plans are prepared, or drawings referred to.

In the built up areas it is common that an old house is first pulled down and the new house then built up on the same site. The traditional inheritance laws leave old houses sub-divided between the next generation, and on occasion a house is literally cut in half, even down to the sawing in half of a window, in order to allow one family to rebuild its own half in a new, "modern" style. Where possible the materials from the old house are incorporated into the construction of the new one. Timber can be re-used. Old bricks can also be re-used mainly for internal work, and broken bricks can be utilized in foundations and floor construction. Old mud bricks may be ground up for mortar.

The style of the new building is indicative of the prestige of a modern house. The low floor to ceiling heights of the traditional dwelling are changed to give greater height and a more spacious feeling. This generally results in an increased height of façade to street. Modern vertically proportioned windows are incorporated, and in most cases they include glass. The new roof often dispenses with the overhanging eaves and double pitch, and corrugated steel is laid flat, allowing a quickly constructed low-maintenance roof on a minimal timber structure.

If examples of carefully designed and constructed modern houses could be created, demonstrating the feasibility of incorporating new technology and current aspirations into the sophistication of the traditional house, to meet cultural, social and environmental demands, then a positive lead could be offered to encourage better building. Until this happens it is unlikely that building methods will improve.

A considerable amount of work has been carried out in restoring palaces and temples within the Kathmandu Valley, and in the course of this work many techniques have been developed to improve the performance of traditional materials and techniques and thus to improve the life expectancy of the buildings. However, none of this experience appears to have trickled down into new house building technology. It is to be hoped that a restoration and conservation programme in Kirtipur would also have an educative role for the local Newar craftsmen. Since they are some of the most skilled builders in the valley, any lessons learnt could have considerable beneficial impact.

# TRADITIONAL HOUSES OF KIRTIPUR, THEIR TYPES AND THEIR BUILDING MATERIALS

RAMENDRA RAJ SHARMA

Kirtipur is known for the skill of its inhabitants in masonry and carpentry. These traditional skills are no longer in such high demand in the modern market, where modern methods of construction and material are the norm. The townspeople also had to depend on seasonal, seldom bumper, incomes from agriculture, and their lives have not been as affluent as those of the people of Kathmandu, Patan and Bhaktapur. In spite of this they have been able to create in Kirtipur temples and private dwellings enriched with ornaments and carvings, even if they are more modest in scale than the grand monuments of the other towns.

The houses of the Newars of Kirtipur, both Hindus and Buddhists, cluster along the streets. The houses have a rectangular layout, with the longer side of the rectangle set alongside the street. The ceilings, including those of the ground floor, are barely two metres high. The floors are smoothed with mud plaster and covered with straw mats. There are fewer courtyards (*chauk*) in Kirtipur than in the other towns of the valley, and houses sharing a common courtyard, or *nanī*, are fairly rare. Good examples of houses around a *nanī* are the two groups of dwellings at Hva Kuncha to the south of Bāgh Bhairav Temple, but other examples can also be found elsewhere in the town, such as those in Tananī Ṭol, Mvana Ṭol and Joshīnanī. Unlike in Kathmandu and Patan, the neighbourhoods are not usually known after a monastery or *bāhā*, but as is discussed elsewhere in this report there are a number of monasteries in Kirtipur, some of which are surrounded by private dwellings.

Most of the domestic buildings of Kirtipur date from the 19th century, and, as a result of earthquakes some of the older buildings have been hurriedly reconstructed sacrificing architectural embellishment. Yet there are a number of buildings which have withstood great tremors and retain signs of their earlier grandeur. The Iṭāchhen of Sinaduvā is an example of the old style of domestic architecture of Kirtipur (Figure 13). Other buildings, for example a row on the north-western side of De Pukhū, also retain their traditional façades.

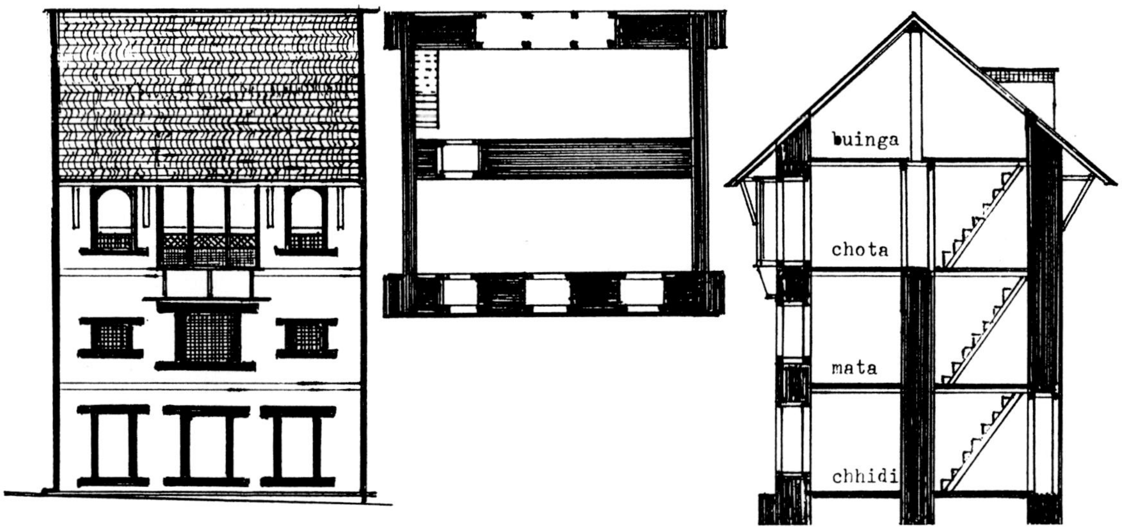


Figure 13 The Iṭāchhen in Sinaduvā, elevation, plan and section (drawing by R. R. Sharma).

Plate 34 Jochhe from the north-west, showing a row of dwellings and infill of various periods.

BUILDING MATERIALS AND METHODS

As in the other Newar towns in the valley, the houses of Kirtipur are built out of red baked brick. The region has a very good type of clay which when fired at a high temperature produces fine quality red brick and tile, and the traditional brick moulds produce bricks similar in form and size to modern bricks. Other types of mould have also been used for cornices and mouldings. The best type of brick, used for front elevations, is known as *chikā apā*, and is smoothed and polished with oil before firing, giving it a shiny surface. The mortar of old houses is mainly clay, as in the past lime was not widely available in the valley. The walls are usually as thick as 70 cm. However, in most houses fired brick is used only for the surface of the walls while the core of the walls is constructed of un-baked brick. Stone is rarely used, except for the retaining walls of the podium. The core of the podium is usually dry laid stone, and sometimes debris from earlier buildings.

Figure 14 Typical elevations of houses showing the changes in design of doors and windows from the 17th to 20th century.

Plate 35 Courtyard of a house in Hva Kuncha, with the ground floor entrance colonnade walled up.

The houses are roofed with small roof tiles, known as *jhingati*, also made of smooth surfaced terra-cotta, and the roof-line of the houses tends to be uniform, giving an appearance of continuity to a block of houses. Roof and floor structures, as well as doors and windows are made out of timber, usually brought from outside the valley. The outer walls overlooking the street have doors to the ground floor, the frames of which are carved and bear symbols pertinent to the occupation of the householder. As timber, like all other commodities, had to be carried through the mountains by porters, the size and weight of the wood to be used was limited. The rooms are therefore narrow and low, and the columns squat.

The houses are usually rectangular in plan, with the longer side set alongside the street. The depth of the dwellings rarely exceeds six metres, while the length varies, and may be as much as ten metres or more. The depth is, however, divided into units called *nāla* by a structural spine wall or by a series of twin posts carved with simple patterns. In some houses the ground floor (*chhiḍi* or *chheli*) has a colonnade, but in most

Plate 36 De Pukhū, well preserved houses on the north-west side of the square, with fine examples of carved windows.

Plate 37 Weaving loom in the ground floor of a house in Hva Kuncha.

cases this area is walled and is used traditionally as a barn or shed for animals. In Kirtipur this area is now normally the weaving workshop of the household. In some cases a colonnade is provided when access is needed to the area beyond, such as to a central courtyard shared by a group of dwellings. In the above mentioned examples of groups of houses at Hva Kuncha the ground floor of the sides facing the street originally had colonnades, but parts of the colonnades have been walled up subsequently to provide extra accommodation.

## BUILDING TYPES

The ancient street layout of the old town of Kirtipur has not changed greatly, but the oldest houses in the town seem not to be earlier than the 17th century, while a number of the houses may be datable to the late 18th and early 19th century, when the town was reconstructed to a certain extent after the destruction of 1767. The bulk of the houses, however, as already noted, date from the 19th and early 20th century, when the town started to flourish again, and most of the ruinous buildings were rebuilt. There is no tradition in Kirtipur of recording the date of construction of private dwellings, but an approximate dating of the buildings can be established by studying

Plate 38 *San jhyāḥ* in Sāyami Ṭol, in the style of the 18th and early 19th century, with "Mughal" style cusped arches.

the woodwork, and the form of the front elevation. In this respect consideration should also be given to the house plan and building materials, such as the type of brick. However, in the past the traditional plan remained more or less the same, and in many of the reconstructed buildings of Kirtipur it appears that the old bricks and carved wooden elements have been reused.

In general the front elevation of the traditional houses in Kirtipur may be categorized into three types (Figure 14). The oldest, dating from the 17th century or earlier, have a central entrance on the ground floor. In some cases there are no windows at this level, but more usually there are one or two small latticed windows, which cannot be opened, and which admit limited light to the front chamber at this level. The three windows of the first floor, including the central window, have wooden lattices (*tiki jhyāḥ*). In most houses these windows are nearly square, but the central one is larger in size and has more elaborate carving. In a few of the more elegant examples of these windows found in the town the outer frame is rectangular, and divided into three or more latticed openings. In the earlier buildings the inner frames of the central windows are square, but from the 17th century on, while the square frame continued, the inner frames were made in the form of an arch, or a lobed arch. The form must have been introduced to the region through the influence of the Mughal architecture of North India.

In early houses the most elaborate window is the *san jhyāḥ*, the large opening of the second floor, which takes most of the middle part of this floor, and extends to beneath the roof. These windows are composed of a bench projecting outside the wall in the form of a balcony with lattice work in front sloping outwards from the bench to meet the edge of the roof. In the examples dating from the 17th and early 18th century arched and lobed arched forms can also be found in the inner frame of these bays.

The second type of front elevation can be found in the buildings constructed, or heavily restored, after 1767 and up to the middle of the 19th century. The fenestration of these houses differs from that of the earlier type mainly on the ground and second floor. The fenestration of the first floor, is, however, comparable to that of the earlier houses, although the carving of the window frames is sometimes less elaborate.

Since the 19th century weaving has increasingly become an important economic factor in the life of people of Kirtipur, and most farming households have adapted the ground floors of their houses for use as workshops. We have already noted that this area was originally dark and used as store or animal shed, but the change of use required better lighting and ventilation as well as better access. As a result the traditional blank wall, or small windows of the ground floor were replaced with doors, similar to the main entrance of the house, and in this type of house three doors, usually of the same size, can be seen on the front elevation of the ground floor. In some houses similar doors are also provided on the rear elevation, improving the ventilation and light, as well as increasing the access to the back garden (*khebā*).

The form of the *san jhyāḥ* in the second type of house is perhaps the best indication of the date of a building. In general the *san jhyāḥ* is still in the form of a large latticed window enclosing a balcony projecting from the wall. The walls of the bay, however, are vertical, rather than having the sloping form of the earlier type. The arched form has been once again used on the inner frame of many of these *san jhyāḥs*. In some late 19th century houses the *san jhyāḥ* no longer projects out from the wall, and in many houses extra windows have been added to one or both sides of the *san jhyāḥ*. These additions occur in particular when a house has been divided vertically to accommodate an extra household.

The third type of front elevation can be found in the houses built during the 20th century, and particularly in the last fifty years. In these houses, three doors to the ground floor are more or less the norm. The traditional *tiki jhyāḥ* and *san jhyāḥ* are replaced by ordinary upright rectangular windows, three to each floor. Decorative carvings are absent or are minimized to narrow borders on the frames. The elegance of the decorative woodwork of the earlier houses is not to be seen in the relatively modern houses, nevertheless, the size and proportion of the house fronts have remained comparable to those of earlier dates, making the newer houses blend relatively well with the earlier buildings. Only very recent buildings fail to harmonize with the traditional townscape. These buildings are often four, five and even six storeys high, and are sometimes constructed with a concrete frame and brick walls. In many cases the walls are faced with cement, and sometimes older buildings are given a coat of cement plaster in an attempt to modernize their appearance.

So far the whole-scale development of new buildings has been confined to the Naya Bāzār area, and the southern ring road. However, in recent years much of the infill in the old town consists of modern buildings, and many of the older houses are plastered with cement. These modern buildings are plain and monotonous both on the exterior and the interior. The ground floors of modern houses, with wider windows and some with damp proof treatment, are less damp and dim and can therefore be profitably used for commercial purposes. The function of the middle floors of modern houses, unlike the traditional ones, is often identical, and all areas are used as bedrooms. The kitchen, and the private shrine, if any, are located on the forth or fifth floor.

The modern houses of Kirtipur reflect the gradual changes in the social structure, and the habits of the townspeople. However, there is no reason why the older houses cannot be adapted to the requirements of modern life. The introduction of latrines to the houses in Kirtipur may be regarded as one of the first steps towards this adaptation, but in many other ways the buildings can be improved. A damp proof course can make living and working in the ground floor more comfortable. Larger windows towards the *khebā* also provide extra light. Providing realistic and simple guide-lines, and enforcing the existing ones, can also help keep the further development of infill in harmony with the rest of the town. We have already seen that in Kirtipur extensions to the houses are usually towards the *khebā*. Encouraging such extensions with controlled planning may help to reduce the pressure of further vertical divisions of the houses to accommodate the growing number of households.

# THE RESIDENTIAL UNIT - SYMBOLIC ORGANIZATION

**MARC BARANI**

Newar society, though based on agriculture, has an essentially urban quality, and in Kirtipur the role of the religious monuments in structuring the town is immediately apparent. The temples, shrines and other places of worship are placed in the urban network to reflect an ideal image of the universe, and the whole city can thus be seen in terms of a sacred diagram. The city walls with their 12 gates separate the organized and sacred city from the rough and non-structured outside. Although within the walls the city has predominantly Hindu and Buddhist areas, the divisions of territory in the city should be seen as complimentary rather than divisive. The routes of processions during the festivals take in the shrines of both faiths, demonstrating the fundamental unity of the city.[1]

Newar social organization, which is principally defined by the system of caste, lineage, and the *gūṭhīs*, is deeply rooted in a system of complex interrelations with the territory of the city. The distribution of castes, the grouping of the family around the ancestral house, and the role of the *gūṭhī* with regard to precise spatial unities demonstrate the coherence of the way territory is organized, and the importance of urban space for the sense of community. Kirtipur is divided spatially and socially into six districts each subdivided into two. These 12 areas each face one of the city gates, and each has a Gaṇeś shrine and a Kāji Gūṭhī house (*ākhā chhe*). The three principle north-south streets, and the same number of main east-west streets link the 12 gates. All these features indicate that Kirtipur may at some time in its history have been planned according to the principles of the Hindu urban models, integrated with the characteristics of the hill.

Within the town, the residential units too manifest the spiritual beliefs and hierarchical organization of their inhabitants. When analysing the nature of the houses, it is important to be aware of what may be called the area of influence of the dwelling, in other words, not only the ownership of the plot of land, but the well defined rights to use the semi-public and public areas of the *ṭol* or group of houses of which it forms part. It should also be born in mind that at all times the Newar family space is being protected according to the rules of pure and impure.

The Newar residential unit can, like the town, be seen as a complex symbolic system. This system is based on the house (*chhe*) taking its roots in the underground world, rising above the earth where people live, and pointing towards the celestial regions. It is for an astrologer to determine the suitability of the land for building, and the date and time when construction should start. Sacred tests regulate the different stages of the erection of the building, and the necessary rituals to be performed. A text on architectural science (Figure 15) belonging to Buddha Ratna Bajracharya, shown to the author by Suresh Sakya, is an example of an invocation to the deities, and gives details of the beliefs regarding various types of site:[2]

" I salute the God Viśvakarman. I salute the God Bighnaraj, (the god invoked not to destroy the habitat) and with the permission of the King Bhojdeva, I start to construct the house. For the benefit of all the world, O God of Architecture Viśvakarman, I pay homage to you. The science of architecture is described herewith by salutation to that god who is free from all false notions, and adorned with all the best qualities.
A man will achieve prosperity if he makes his house on a rectangular site.
A man will benefit or earn money if he builds his house on a square site.
A man will get much satisfaction if he builds his house on a high plain.
A man will be very poor if he makes his house on a circular site.
A man will experience sorrow if he makes the house on a site that is not well shaped.
A man will face trouble from rulers if he makes his house on a circular site.
A man will loose money if he makes his house on a hexagonal site.
A man will loose domestic animals if he makes the house on a stick shaped site.

Figure 15 Newar text on architectural science, 1849, mentioning the beliefs associated with different shapes of site.

A man will loose his life and wealth if he makes his house on a trapezoid shaped site.
A man will face trouble if he makes his house on a tortoise shaped site.
A man will loose rice if he makes his house on a site that has the shape of a serpent.
I salute you (God Viśvakarman) who gives these fruits (benefits or troubles) to him who starts to build his house...
[In the year] 969 NS (1849 AD) in the month of Śrāvaṇ (July-August) on the eighth day of the dark moon on Saturday. This manuscript has been copied, and on this day it was completely copied. Śrī Kulajoti of Saka Bāhā copied it and presented it to Śrī Bhājunanda of Chhve Bāhā."

The rectangular or square outline of the building sites, noted in the manuscript, are the beneficent forms according to the Hindu and Buddhist urban models.[3] The residential unit is the sacred territory of the family, with the different levels of the cosmos represented by the different levels of the building. As an individual goes up to the attic of a house he is also making a metaphorical ascent to the sky. The sacred territory of a house is therefore a place of communication with the cosmos, and the benevolent and evil divinities. The balance of forces in the unit is protected with vigour, and the actions of people, which are believed to have repercussions on the cosmos and vice versa are regulated accordingly. Daily offerings performed at the key points of the house — the door sill, the god room and the attic — as well as major rituals, contribute to preserve the purity, harmony and unity of the domestic territory, and its role as a place of communication with the cosmos.

As well as the qualities of the site and the interior spaces, each part or "organ" of the house has a precise symbolic value (Figures 16 and 17). For example, the foundations represent the king of snakes, Śiśu Nāg; the windows are the eyes of the house; the bricks ninety million stars; the clay the sky; the posts of the second floor Mahādeva; their capitals Pārvatī, the main beams the Ashṭabhairavas; and the joists of the floor the Ashṭamātṛikās.

In the same way domestic objects have their religious meaning. The loom represents Chandramāha Roshanī; the broom Brahmā; the small stone mortar for grinding spices Kumārī; its pestle Vishṇu; and the winnowing basket for cleaning rice Maheśvarī. The assembling of the various

Plate 39 Joshīnanī, house with vertical and horizontal extensions seen from its back garden.

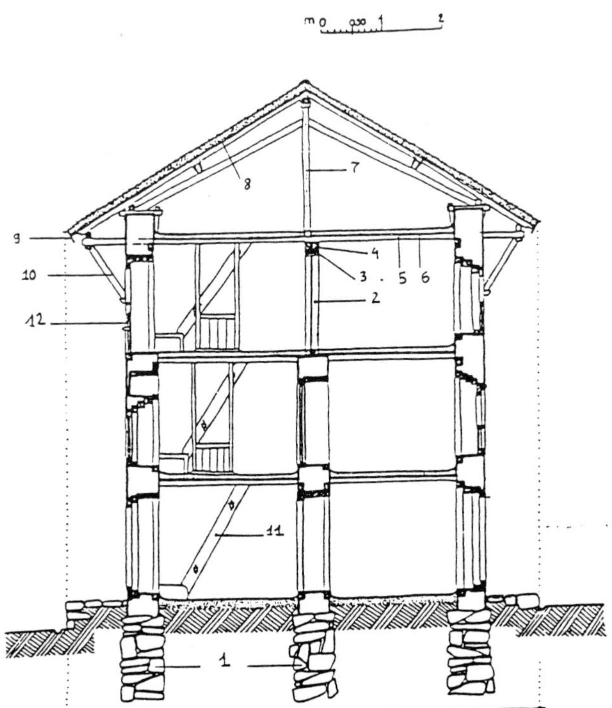


Figure 16 Section of a Newar house showing the symbolic meaning of its components (M. Barani).

Key: 1 *jag* = Śiśu Nāg; 2 *thā* = Mahādeva; 3 *metha* = Pārvatī; 4 *nidalā* = Ashṭabhairava; 5 *dhalī* = Ashṭamātrika; 6 *chisī* = Moddha; 7 *thā* = Pañchā Tathagata; 8 *musī* = 64 Yoginī; 9 *mhutaḥ* = Ashṭa Nāgā Rāj; 10 *tunāḥ* = Garuḍa; 11 *svāne* = Sapta Ṛishi (seven hermits); 12 *san jhyāḥ* = Buddha Dharma Saṅgha. *pau* (roof) = *chhatra*, the umbrella which protects the gods; *apā* (bricks) = 90 million stars; *chā* (clay)= the sky; *kuthi* (rooms) = secret; *dhukū* (treasure room) = Lakshmī.

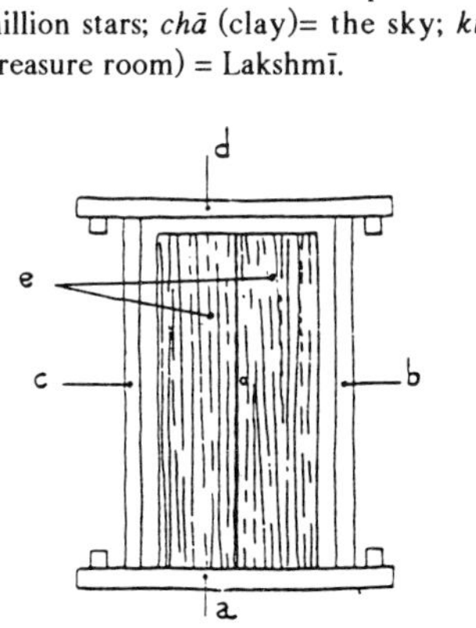

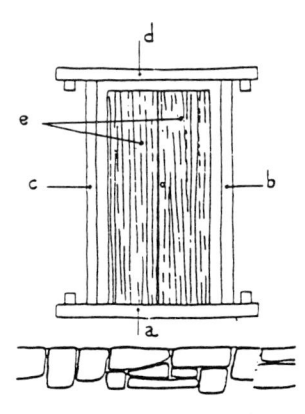


Figure 17 Entrance door of a Newar house showing the symbolic meaning of its components (M. Barani).

Key: a. *khalu* = Betāla; b. *java vaha* = lioness; c. *khagu vaha* = tigress; d. *taṅgāya* = rays of the moon; e. *khāpā* = Śiva Śakti.

Plate 40 Carved doorway to a complex of dwellings on the corner of Kuṭujhol.

Plate 41 Hva Kuncha, courtyard of a house with the colonnade partially walled up.

elements of the house, the arrangement of the rooms, as well as the objects in them, the family hierarchy and their activities, are all organized in space and time according to a symbolic outline in keeping with "the order of things".

## USE OF SPACE

The way these beliefs, and spiritual values in general, influence the use of the dwelling can be seen when the residential unit is analysed (Figure 18). The plinth in front of the house is a semi-private area sometimes delimited by a different floor covering, and is known as the *pikhā lākhi* area after the god of the doorway, or sometimes simply front. The formal boundary of the house is the line where the rain runs down from the over-hanging eaves, and it is believed that if someone is attacked by supernatural forces he should take refuge behind this boundary, which is also the place where a symbolic last meal is prepared for someone who has died, before the body is taken for cremation. The plinth area is an extension to the house, and is vital for a multitude of daily activities which can be done in view of the neighbours, and which may involve mixing with other castes. Women's daily chores, and jobs such as weaving and spinning are carried out here according to the season, and the plinth, and particular spaces on the street in front of the house are used for drying grain. For special occasions such as weddings or the return from a pilgrimage, the front is used, sometimes with an awning, to accommodate guests. It is the responsibility of the householder to keep the plinth in front of his house clean, and maintain the surface, and a house is judged by its surroundings. All these factors reinforce the sense of territory, but as the limits are well understood, disputes are rare.

The back of the house may have a courtyard, sometimes shared between several units. This is often dirty, with a manure pit also incorporating liquid waste from the kitchen, and a gutter to drain away rainwater. The point where this gutter crosses the boundary of the plot of land, or goes underground, is considered to be the dwelling of a snake who is responsible for the inhabitants'

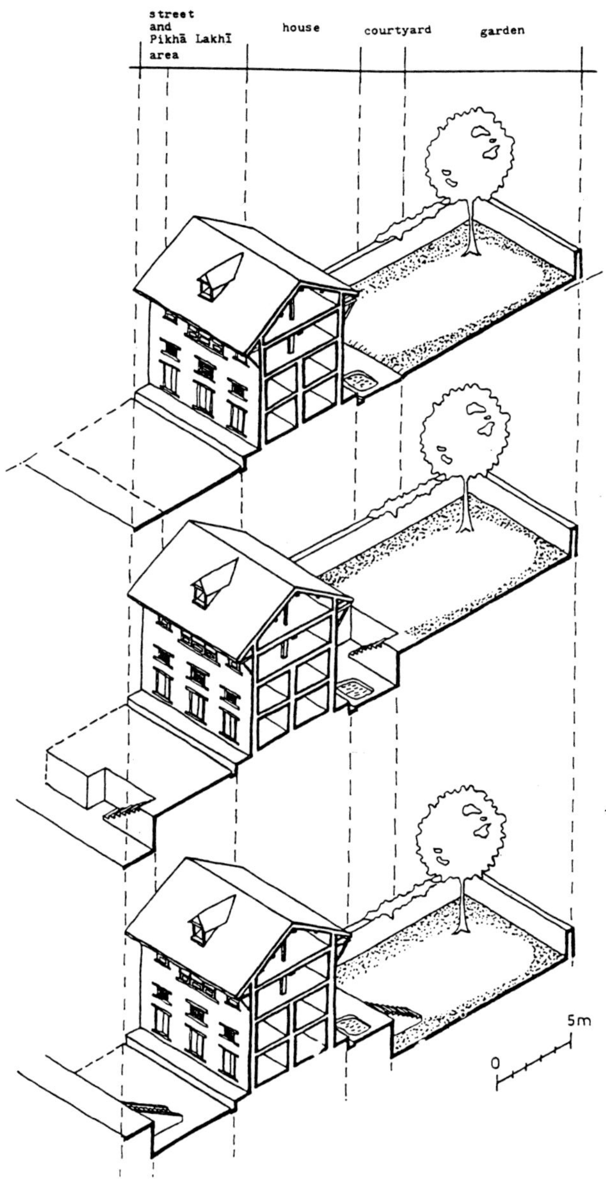


Figure 18 Residential units, showing how the layout of the dwellings is adapted to fit different sites while retaining the hierarchy of public and private, or impure and pure, space (M. Barani).

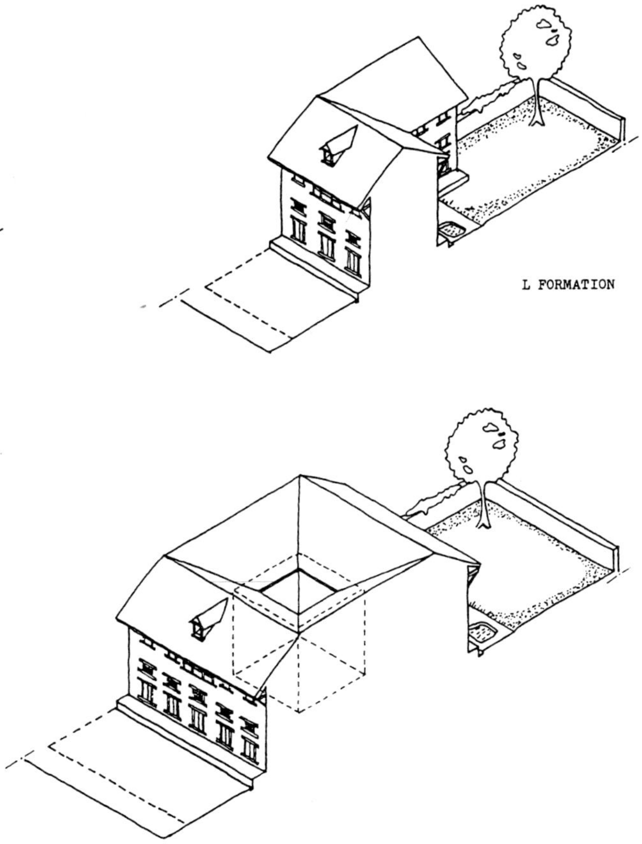


Figure 19 Densification of dwellings, showing typical extensions (M. Barani).

bad health, and offerings are made there when someone falls ill. If the courtyard is sufficiently large and exposed to the sun it may however be well kept, and tiled or lined with slabs of stone. In the case of higher caste households, who prefer a greater degree of privacy for their daily activities, the courtyard provides an open space out of view of the rest of the *ṭol*.

The courtyard leads to a vegetable garden (*khebā*) surrounded by low walls and thorn hedges. These gardens are very important in Kirtipur, and occupy about half of the area of the town. Trees and fruit trees are planted, and vegetables are grown there for the daily needs of the family. Particular beliefs also govern the way the garden is planted, for example, banana trees and bamboo should not be close to the house, and care is taken where ginger and soya are grown, as it is believed that these plants can make one ill.

Bearing in mind the symbolic function of the house and considering how this regulates its use, we see that the ground floor is a zone of transition where impure castes can enter. It can therefore be a place for carrying on business, as well as a circulation area and storage space. The first floor (*mātā*), entered by a trap door, is where the family space starts being subjected to the concepts of pure and impure. The front or back bay, according to the position of the staircase, is a place for the reception of pure castes, and is a

Plate 42 Hva Kuncha, complex of dwellings around a courtyard, with the centre house retaining its old *san jhyāḥ*, and the house on the right rebuilt.

transitional space between the ground and first floor. The rest of the first floor is divided into bedrooms and rooms for storing valuable items, food, and for housing the domestic deities. The windows of the front elevation of this floor have lattices, which increase the feeling of privacy and security. Legends relate that evil spirits passing through the streets of a city might try and snatch children, and the lattices would prevent them. The second floor (*chvatā*), spacious, light, and airy is the main living and reception room for the family, friends and relations. It is the most frequented floor and tends not to be divided up, though a small room where some of the family sleep may be made in an angle of the back bay.

The most exclusive area is, however, the attic (*baigaḥ*). This is the place for the kitchen, and is, together with the room for the household gods, the purest area of the dwelling. It is essentially reserved for the women of the family, the men only going there to eat. The attic may also have a terrace where the dishes are washed and plants are grown for offerings. The importance of the role of women in a Newar house can be surmised from their responsibilities with regard to the protected and hidden parts of the dwelling. The position of the kitchen, and the hearth, with its ritual importance, at the top of the house conforms to a vertical hierarchy in the specialization of the rooms. The higher one goes, the more specialized is the use of each floor, and the less likely it is that the area will be divided up.

Each caste has its own rules about who may or may not enter the upper floors, for example, a *jogī* may go up to the second floor of a *jyāpu* house, but in the case of a house of a *śreshṭha*, *joshī* or *pradhān*, a *jogī* may only go as far as the corner of the first floor. In the houses of the higher castes only relations may approach the hearth on the top floor, whereas among *jyāpu* members of that caste may also do so.

## DENSITY

A fundamental factor in the pattern of densification of the urban network in Kirtipur is the desire to live in the house of the ancestors (*mūl chhe*). Thus, as the family expands, extensions (*yaḥnaḥchhe*) are built along the length of the plot and around the courtyard, resulting in an L shaped or U shaped formation. The consequent grouping of dwellings around a courtyard or

Plate 43 Tananī, the central square with grain spread to dry, and household chores being done near the water tank. The houses on the left are marked nos. 42 and 43 in the plan, and nos. 2-13 form a row on the south-western side.

Plate 44 The pond at the south-western end of Tananī Ṭol.

*chauk* allows the branches of the family to share resources while retaining a separate dwelling for each family unit (Figure 19). This can be seen as an ideal model, with the lineage gathered round its leader, the *thakālī*, the head of the family. If the plot of land is big enough, the extensions can be built incorporating the same succession of elements found in the original house. When the head of the family dies, his property is equally divided among his male children. This may lead to vertical divisions of the dwelling, including the courtyard and the garden, where a low wall may mark the dividing line. The new units created in this way may be very narrow, but all the residential unit space is still defined according to the considerations discussed above. In the case of high densification the extensions may continue into the area of the garden, until little space is left for cultivation.

The availability of modern building materials in recent years has meant that some recent extensions to the traditional houses retain only some of the symbolic aspects of a Newar house. The hierarchical arrangement of the floors is retained, but when large windows are provided at all levels and the roof is flat forming a terrace, the daily activities tend to be concentrated more in the house and less in the street. This can be seen as a gradual tendency towards the isolation of family units, and perhaps as a forerunner to radical changes in the use of Newar domestic space.

The traditional residential unit, in its material and symbolic organization, appears as a system which consolidates and symbolizes the unity of the family according to principals similar to those which define the layout of the town. In order to understand the relationship between the typology of the residential unit and the urban morphology, we should also consider the role of the street in the organization of social practices and the symbolic structuring of the urban network. For this purpose two representative examples of groups of houses will be considered in some detail, Tananī, a square occupied principally by farmers, and Sinaduvā, a street inhabited by a mixed population, not directly linked with agriculture.

*Tananī*

Tananī or Taninī, meaning the big square, is located to the east of the town in the district of the same name. It takes the form of a splayed rectangle, with steps to accommodate the changes in level of the ground. It is surrounded by houses, and is accessible from the lanes at each ends of the square. It is one of the stopping places for religious processions, and the square contains a *pāṭi*, a concrete water tank, and the Tananī Stupa, connected with Chilañcho and discussed together with the public buildings, as is the *pāṭi*. Out of the houses studied, 44 were of *jyāpu* families (farmers), one *pamā* (traders, a *śreshṭha* subcaste), and one *nau* (barber).

When observing the plan of the whole area (Figures 20 and 21), the structuring role of the built on plots is immediately apparent. The division and development of the houses is within the plot, following the system of extending the houses in an L or U shaped formation until the back yard becomes an enclosed courtyard. The plots are arranged in an orderly pattern and the ideal model of a group of houses around the house of the *thakālī* thus appears as a structuring and regulating element in the urban space. This is the case even when successive divisions have to some extent altered the coherence of the original layout, and where the courtyards have lost their communal function and have been reduced to dilapidated dumping grounds.

The *pikhā lākhi* area in front of the house is of particular importance in Tananī. Almost all the inhabitants have fields, and the large quantities of grain harvested determine a strict organization of the areas for threshing and drying. Each house has the plinth in front, and a designated area of the street for these purposes. Sheaves of wheat are carefully arranged before being threshed, in a precise way which avoids the grain mixing with that of the neighbour. When large quantities of grain (rice, wheat, maize, soya) or pepper or wood are being dried every inch of the surface is used.

In a house where the family has expanded, and the residential unit has been divided, the area in front that was designated for the house before the divisions is used in turn by the inhabitants, according to who lived there first. It may happen, in particular after the rice crop, that there is not enough room, and some people are obliged to dry their grain outside the town. In addition, the building of the concrete water tank has deprived houses numbers 19-23 of their drying area, and they either have to go outside the town, or ask permission of their neighbours to use their spaces when they have finished with them. On the whole everyone knows the exact limits of their area, although when the quantities are smaller the limits are naturally conformed to with less rigour.

However, disputes do occasionally arise. For example on one occasion a woman wanted to dry

Figure 20 Tananī Ṭol, plan, showing the private vegetable garden and the area of the communal square associated with each group of dwellings (M. Barani).

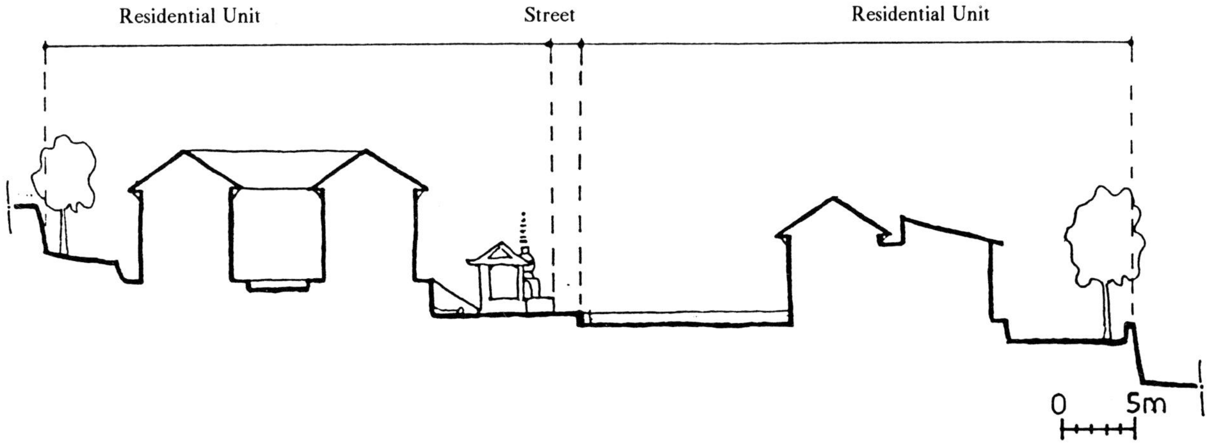


Figure 21 Tananī, section A-A through residential units, showing extensions built on the vegetable gardens (M. Barani).

Plate 45 Courtyard of a house in Tananī.

rice and found that a neighbour had appropriated her place and refused to go. The matter was referred to the local *pañchāyat* committee, and the Pradhān Pañcha ordered the neighbour to stop encroaching, showing that the dispute was considered important enough to be dealt with at *pañchāyat* level. The ruling of the *pañchāyat* also reinforced the traditional rights with regard to that space. Farming activities in urban areas, particularly in Newar towns can only be carried out if flexibility in the use of public space is maintained.

### *Sinaduvā*

The households of Sinaduvā are in many cases high caste Buddhists closely connected with the nearby Chilañcho complex, and there is a far smaller proportion of farmers than in Tananī, so the priorities as far as the way public space is used are different. The houses are arranged on either side of a street (Figures 22 and 23), relatively wide, but without the large space for threshing and drying grain found in Tananī. The religious structures are more numerous than at Tananī, and include the Śākyamuni Buddha Mandir, a *śikhara* temple discussed together with the public buildings, as well as the ruins of the platform of a temple dedicated to Lokeśvar. There is also the *lukama-dyo*, the *pikhā lākhi* of the Chilañcho Stupa, below the steps leading to the stupa, and a Gaṇeś altar, as well as three old monasteries, Chhve, Ikhā and Kve Bāhā. Of the 23 houses ten belong to *jyāpu* families, eight to *gubhājū* (Buddhist priests), three to *pamā*, and two were unoccupied at the time of survey. Like Tananī, Sinaduvā is also a stopping place for religious processions.

In Sinaduvā the built on plots are smaller than those of Tananī, and very few houses have a private garden. The limits of the plots are also less obviously apparent because of the accumulation of buildings, but the structuring and regulating of the space in the buildings is still determined by the same factors as the other houses in Kirtipur. The *bāhā* or monastery buildings have their own typological characteristics, described in detail in the section on Buddhist monasteries. The *bāhās* are situated in courtyards containing miniature stupas (*chibhāḥ*) visited by the faithful, but with the decline in importance of the *bāhās* as places of pilgrimage the *bāhā* buildings, with the exception of the main shrines built to house the icons, are now used as dwellings, and their courtyards are used by the surrounding houses for daily activities. The families living in Sinaduvā have far less land than those of Tananī, some *gubhājū* having no land at all. The organization of the areas in front of the houses is therefore far less strict. Houses 6-9 and 11-12, for example, use the yards of the *bāhā*, and houses 17-21 use the street in front of their houses. However, when the monsoon rains flood the yards of the *bāhās*, the householders do have their own areas in the street for drying crops.

We therefore see when we compare Tananī and Sinaduvā, that the occupation of the inhabitants has had a marked effect on the planning of their areas. Like many other *jyāpu* areas in Kirtipur, Tananī is built round a large open space, but in Sinaduvā, although a considerable area was once provided for the use of pilgrims, an extensive space for drying crops was not a priority.

In conclusion we see that while the occupation of the inhabitants has an effect on the way their housing is arranged, it must be born in mind that for the Newars there is little distinction between sacred and profane. Spiritual and symbolic considerations therefore play an important role, and are seen at every stage, from the grouping of

Plate 46 Sinaduvā, block of houses south-west of the Śākyamuni Buddha Mandir, marked in plan as numbers 17-20.

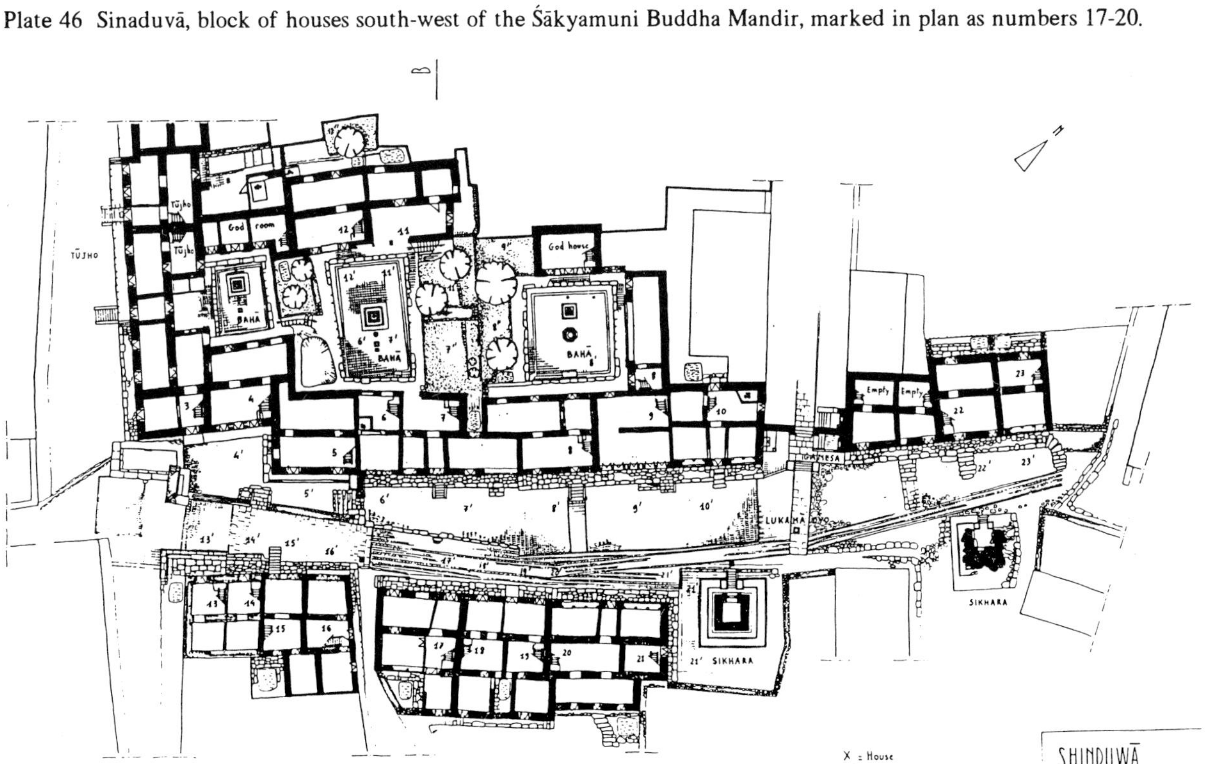

Figure 22 Sinaduvā, plan of an area incorporating a number of monasteries (M. Barani).

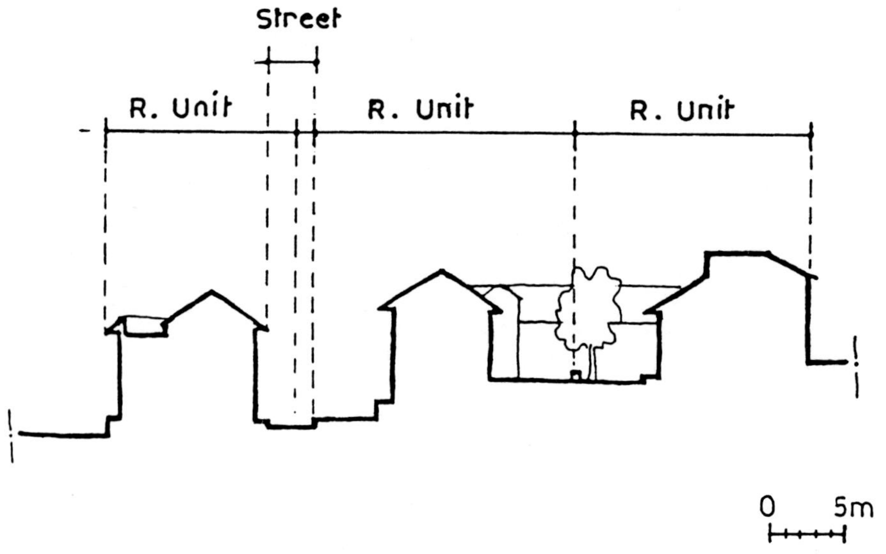


Figure 23 Sinaduvā, section B-B. Compared with Tananī, the households have less space for vegetable growing and farming activities (M. Barani).

castes together, the beliefs with regard to the choice of site and the components of the actual structure, to the organization of each part of the interior and exterior space. The hierarchies governing the use of domestic territory allow for an analysis in terms of duality. The relationships between open and hidden, high and low, pure and impure, masculine and feminine, youth and age, are central to a system of belief which ties in the spiritual dimension of the life of the townspeople with every detail of their daily life.[4] The residential unit is therefore not merely a "machine for living" but a receptacle for spiritual forces, and all aspects of its organization reflect this.

## NOTES

1 Reinhard Herdick, *Kirtipur Stadtgestalt, Prinzipien der Raumordnung und gesellschaftliche Funktionen einer Newar-Stadt*, Munich, Cologne, London, 1988, 160-178.

2 The translation of the text was kindly made by Sukra Sagar Shrestha.

3 The rules may be compared with those given in the *Kamikāgama*, see M. A. Ananthalwar and Alexander Rea (eds.), A. V. Thiagaraja Iyer (compiler), *Indian Architecture*, I, Delhi, 1980, 61.

4 For further discussion on the spacial and symbolic organization of Newar urban space see: Gerhard Auer and Niels Gutschow, *Domestic Architecture of Nepal*, *AARP*, XII, December 1977, 64-9; Niels Gutschow, The Pujahari Math: a survey of Newar building techniques and restoration methods in the valley of Kathmandu, *East and West*, XXVI, 1976, 191-204, figs 7-30; Niels Gutschow and T. Sieverts (eds.), Urban space and ritual, proceedings of an international symposium on urban history of South and East Asia, 2-4 June 1977, 2nd ed. *AARP*, 1978; Niels Gutschow, Functions of squares in Bhaktapur, *AARP*, XVII, March 1980, 57-64; Niels Gutschow, Bernhard Kölver and Ishwaranand Shresthacarya, *Newar Towns and Buildings: an Illustrated Dictionary, Newari-English*, Sankt Augustin, 1987.

# HISTORIC PUBLIC BUILDINGS

SUKRA SAGAR SHRESTHA

Religious edifices are the main traditional public buildings in Kirtipur. These include temples and shrines of both the Hindu and the Buddhist faiths, as well as Buddhist stupas, *chaityas* and the buildings associated with all these structures. In addition to these there are a number of rest houses provided in the town for both religious and secular purposes. As discussed by Gauri Nath Rimal earlier in this report, the responsibility for the upkeep of religious structures rests with the *gūṭhīs* or traditional associations of townspeople. The *gūṭhī's* funds come from land endowments and donations. In recent years the central government has also provided funds for the restoration of historic buildings in the country, either directly or through the *gūṭhīs*.

The *Protective Inventory*[1] recommends preservation of a number of buildings in Kirtipur. They are the Hindu temples of Bāgh Bhairav, Nārāyaṇ, Umā Maheśvara and Indrāyaṇī, the Buddhist Chilañcho Stupa complex and the Buddhist temples Loṅ Degaḥ (Buddha Dharma Saṅgha Śikhara), Śākyamuni Buddha Mandir and Lokeśvar Mandir. Among the Buddhist monasteries Chilañcho Mahāvihār (Jagat Pāl Vihār), Chithuṅ Bahī, Chhve Bāhā, and Kve Bāhā were also noted. All these buildings are described below, and the Buddhist monasteries are also discussed in a separate chapter.

### TEMPLES

The Buddhist and Hindu temples of Kirtipur and the rest of the Kathmandu Valley share common architectural forms, but house images connected predominantly with one faith or the other. Two different styles of temple are to be found in Kirtipur, the most usual being the tiered type, typical of traditional Nepalese architecture, and built on a square or rectangular plan with a multiple pitched roof.

The other style is an adaptation of the north Indian type of Hindu temple, and was built in Nepal from the late Malla period onwards. In this style the temple is normally based on a square plan in the form of the sanctum of a North Indian temple, and has a spire known in Indian architecture as the *śikhara*.[2] The plan follows the outline of a *yantra* or sacred diagram, as do the horizontal sections of the tower. The *śikhara* is crowned with a circular lobed moulding known as the *āmalaka*, and is topped with a *kalaśā* representing the container of the nectar of immortality. In India the *kalaśā* is in the shape of a vase, but in Nepal it is bell shaped, and also appears above stupas. In Kirtipur the two *śikhara* temples are both Buddhist.

## HINDU TEMPLES

### BĀGH BHAIRAV TEMPLE

The Bāgh Bhairav temple complex is situated at the heart of the town and is the only temple dedicated to the fierce form of Bhairav as a tiger. As the town's main guardian deity, Bāgh Bhairav is paid the highest respect by the populace, and the complex is the main religious and social centre of Kirtipur. The complex (Figure 24, Plate 47) consists of the main temple set in a rectangular walled enclosure, measuring about 30 x 50m. The main gateway is on the south-western side and is flanked by *pāṭis* (rest houses) on the outside. There is also access to the complex via an entrance in the north-west, and another in the south-east side. A number of subsidiary buildings are around the courtyard, which also has several small temples and shrines. The complex contains numerous images, some as early as the 4th century AD. The oldest inscription so far discovered in Kirtipur, dating from Nepali Saṃvat 623/1503 AD is to be found in one of the subsidiary temples, known as Māna Binayak. The most recent addition to the complex, an image of Dhartī Mātā installed in 1980, exemplifies the continuing tradition of devotion by the people of Kirtipur.

The main temple (Plate 48) is rectangular in

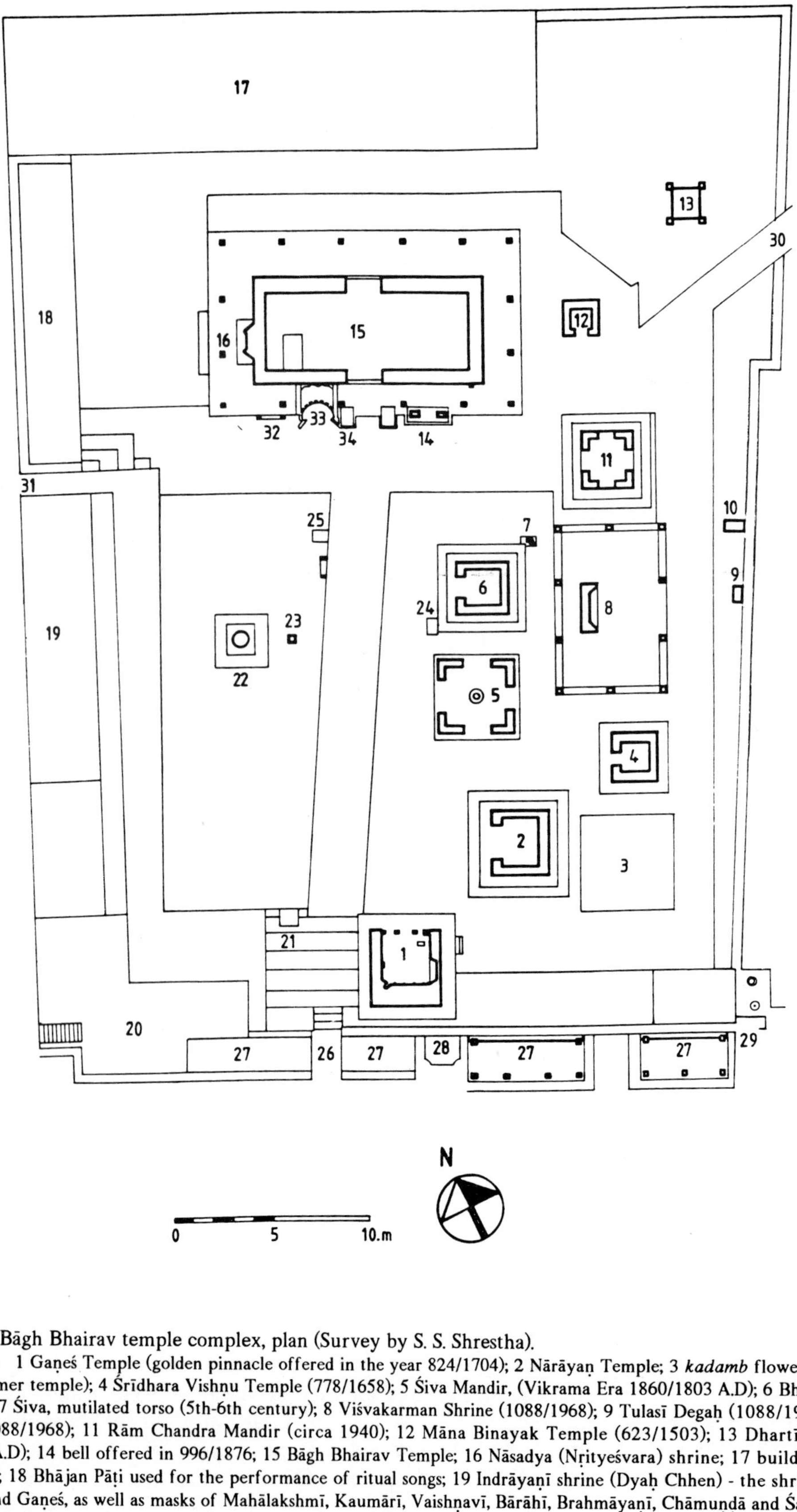


Figure 24 Bāgh Bhairav temple complex, plan (Survey by S. S. Shrestha).

Key to plan: 1 Gaṇeś Temple (golden pinnacle offered in the year 824/1704); 2 Nārāyaṇ Temple; 3 *kadamb* flower tree (planted on the site of a former temple); 4 Śrīdhara Vishṇu Temple (778/1658); 5 Śiva Mandir, (Vikrama Era 1860/1803 A.D); 6 Bhavānī Śaṅkar Temple (838/1718); 7 Śiva, mutilated torso (5th-6th century); 8 Viśvakarman Shrine (1088/1968); 9 Tulasī Degaḥ (1088/1968); 10 Gaṇeś image (marble) (1088/1968); 11 Rām Chandra Mandir (circa 1940); 12 Māna Binayak Temple (623/1503); 13 Dhartī Mātā (Vikrama Era 2036/1979 A.D); 14 bell offered in 996/1876; 15 Bāgh Bhairav Temple; 16 Nāsadya (Nṛityeśvara) shrine; 17 building used by Kirtipur High School; 18 Bhājan Pāṭi used for the performance of ritual songs; 19 Indrāyaṇī shrine (Dyaḥ Chhen) - the shrine housed images of Indrāyaṇī and Gaṇeś, as well as masks of Mahālakshmī, Kaumārī, Vaishṇavī, Bārāhī, Brahmāyaṇī, Chāmuṇḍā and Śaivi, all were stolen in the 1970s; 20 living quarters of *jogis* (temple keepers); 21 Hanumān *stambha* (17th-18th century); 22 Tulasī Degaḥ (796/1676); 23 *dharma stambha* (Vikrama Era 2010/1953 A.D.); 24 Bāsuki Nāg (17th-18th century); 25 Nandī (5th-6th century); 26 main (south-west) entrance to complex; 27 *dāphā phalechā*; 28 *jarū hiti*; 29 Gaṇeś image (17th-18th century); 30 entrance from south-east; 31 entrance from north-west; 32 *ghaṇṭa stambha* (bell frame) 811/1691; 33 *hi pha dyaḥ* (sacrificial altar); 34 gold plated lions of main entrance to temple.

Plate 47 Bāgh Bhairav Temple complex from the south-west with the Śiva Mandir in the foreground.

plan and is built of rough brick faced with the type of brick known as *chikā apā*, which is smoothed and polished with oil before firing. The structure is in three tiers with projecting pitched roofs. The ground level has a main entrance on the south-western side (Plate 49) with two large guardian lions in front (no. 34), gold-plated in 1041/1924; a copper plated *toraṇa* dated 815/1695; as well as golden flags of 1044/1921. There is also a subsidiary door in the northern side (Plate 50) which is used as an exit during festivals. The image of the deity is housed in the ground floor and faces eastwards. It is lit at dawn by the sun shining through a small window known as *dyo pvāḥ*. Although the building is in three tiers there are only two more floor levels above the shrine, with access by a ladder from inside, at the south-east corner. The exterior walls are plastered and preserve unique examples of wall painting, discussed in the section on antiquities. The main *hi pha dyaḥ* (sacrificial altar) is on the south-western exterior, and includes a wooden *toraṇa* with Ashṭabhairavas and Ashṭamātṛikās of 782/1662 (Plate 147); another wooden *toraṇa* of the 15th-16th century; a stone *toraṇa* of the 16th-17th century; an iron *khaḍga* of the 17th-18th century; as well as two figures of Hanumān, 837/1717. On the north-western exterior is, in addition, a shrine of Nāsadya (Nṛityeśvara) (Plate 51), where animals are also sacrificed. This shrine appears, from the style of the carved figures, to be of the 13th or 14th century, or possibly earlier.

A row of wooden pillars supports the projecting roof of the first tier, making a colonnade around the ground level. A horizontal beam rests on the pillars and is tied into the temple wall by means of timbers projecting at right angles from the walls of the rectangular core. This beam supports the rafters, which fan out from the central core at an angle of less than 45°, and project beyond the beam. The overhang is supported by a series of struts fixed to the pillars at an angle of about 45°.

The rectangular core becomes smaller at each successive level of the structure. The second tier has windows with carved wooden frames (Plate 52). Cornices set into the walls serve to buttress wooden struts supporting the projecting balconies and roofs of each tier. The balconies are enclosed by wooden screens which follow the angle of the struts. The fourth level of the temple is open on all sides and the roof is clad with gilt copper, as is the roof of the third tier. The other roofs have small clay tiles, known as *jhingati* or *āmypā*, set on boards plastered with mud. The first roof has a single pinnacle in the middle of the south-

Plate 48 Bāgh Bhairav Temple from the south-west. Gurkha weapons are hung around the third tier.

Plate 49 Main entrance to Bāgh Bhairav, with copper plated *toraṇa* of 815/1695.

Plate 50 North-east entrance of Bāgh Bhairav, with another wooden *toraṇa* above.

western side, the second roof has six, the third ten, and the top roof is crowned by a single one.

The temple preserves some fine examples of carved woodwork, including the struts of the balcony of the second level, carved with the figures of gods and goddesses (Plate 52). The following list, with the struts numbered anti-clockwise starting from the west, is given as an aid to identification.

| | | | | | | | |
|---|---|---|---|---|---|---|---|
| W | 32 | 31 | 30 | 29 | 28 | 27 | N |
| 1 | | | | NW | | | 26 |
| 2 | | | | | | | 25 |
| 3 | | | | | | | 24 |
| 4 | | | | | | | 23 |
| 5 | | | | | | | 22 |
| Entrance | S-W | | | | N-E | | rear door |
| 6 | | | | | | | 21 |
| 7 | | | | | | | 20 |
| 8 | | | | | | | 19 |
| 9 | | | | | | | 18 |
| 10 | | | | SE | | | 17 |
| S | 11 | 12 | 13 | 14 | 15 | 16 | E |

SOUTH-WESTERN SIDE: 1 Brahmāyaṇī, 2 Gaṇeś, 3 Pañchamukha Brahmā, 4 Rudrāyaṇī, 5 Indrāyaṇī, 6 Bāmana, 7 not visible, 8 dated 974/1854, 9 not visible, 10 Brahmā (?);
SOUTH-EASTERN SIDE: 11 Tribhuvan (?), 12 Śrī ... Deva, 13 Agni Deva, 14 obscured by other carvings, 15 obscured by other carvings, 16 obscured by other carvings;
NORTH-EASTERN SIDE: 17 not visible, 18 Nārāyaṇa, 19 not visible, 20 not visible, 21 Bhairav, 22 Vishṇu Deva, 23 obscured by other carvings, 24 Mahālakshmī, 25 Chāmuṇḍā, 26 not visible;
NORTH-WESTERN SIDE: 27 Kāprankā Devi (?), 28 Brahmāyaṇī, 29 Kumāra, 30 Kaumārī, 31 Bhairav, 32 Maheśvara.

Bāgh Bhairav, the guardian deity of the town and the most venerated, is known locally as Ājudyaḥ, or "Grandfather God", and an inscription of 796/1676 (Apx. A, no. 17) from the complex refers to him as Ājaju Byaghreśvara or "Great great grandfather Byaghreśvara". Other terms of address are Bhīmsen Bhaṭṭāraka, given in an inscription of 707/1587 and Bhīmeśvara, in an inscription of 838/1718 (Apx. A, no. 23). However,

Plate 51 Nāsadya (Nṛityeśvara) shrine on the north-west side of Bāgh Bhairav, from the north east. The wall paintings are now covered with white wash.

the most commonly used name is Bāgh Bhairav, and this deity is worshipped by Hindus and Buddhists alike. He is also honoured at the time of rituals or renovations at other shrines, as is seen from an inscription referring to the establishment of Umā Maheśvara (Apx. A, no. 7), and also one referring to the renovation of the Chilañcho Stupa.[3]

The main icon of Bāgh Bhairav is of clay, and is partly covered by a silver mask offered by a local citizen during the reign of Chandra Shumsher (1901-1929). When the icon becomes damaged by rats and the weather it is repaired or replaced by the Buddhist *bajrāchārya* priest in accordance with esoteric requirements. These involve the collection of clay from seven places around the shrine of Mhaipi, a shrine situated between Pakanājol and Bālāju. The icon is replaced every fifteen to twenty years.

The origin of the god Bāgh Bhairav in Kirtipur has an interesting legend. According to local belief some shepherd girls, grazing their sheep in the jungle (*gā*) on the northern slope of Kirtipur, were amusing themselves by moulding the figure of a tiger out of clay. When the figure was finished the girls went in search of a suitable leaf to use for the tiger's tongue, but to their great surprise, when they returned with the leaf the sheep were missing. They wept and wailed and asked the people in the vicinity if they had seen the sheep but no one could locate them. They decided that the sheep must have been eaten by the clay tiger, so they questioned him. In reply he opened his mouth wide and the girls saw that it was full of blood. Angry with the tiger, the girls punished him by not fixing the tongue in his mouth, and therefore the image of Bāgh Bhairav has no tongue, and the mouth is wide open. It is said that he is asking someone to provide a tongue for him. In connection with this story the image of a standing Śiva now housed in the Gaṇeś temple of the Bāgh Bhairav complex is regarded locally as a shepherd, and those of the Mātṛikās in the same temple as sheep.

It is not known exactly when the god Bāgh Bhairav was established. A local chronicle[4] mentions Bāgh Bhairav being established a year after the founding of the city. The antiquity of the complex is indicated by the images, particularly those housed in the Gaṇeś temple (Plate 57), and discussed in the section on antiquities. As well as a Gaṇeś which may be as early as the 4th century AD, there are images of Śiva, the Mātṛikās, and Umā Maheśvara. It is possible that Śiva Deva (r. circa 1099-1126) established the shrine of Bāgh Bhairav in an existing complex dedicated to other deities, whose importance declined gradually as that of Bāgh Bhairav increased.

The first historical record connected with the temple itself is the inscription of 635/1515 of Jagat Pāl Varmā[5] a famous Mahāpātra of Piṇḍa Bāhā in Patan, recording the renovation of the temple which included the addition of three *chulikā* (pinnacles) and the performance of the ritual fire sacrifice. The legible part of the inscription mentions "*Śrī Byāghreśvarasya Bhaṭṭārakasya nivās jirnodhāra yāngā*" meaning "the temple of Bāgh Bhairav is renovated". The temple must, of course, have been in existence for some time before this restoration.

Further inscriptions recording offerings include one of 707/1587 mentioning the offering of a golden *kalaśā*.[6] In 782/1662 the installation of a wooden *toraṇa* above the *hi pha dyaḥ* (sacrificial altar) is commemorated.[7] A bell on the side of Nāsadya (Newari name of Naṭarāj) and a golden window and a flag were offered in 814/1695.

Plate 52 Details of the carvings of the upper tier windows of Bāgh Bhairav.

Plate 53 The upper tiers of Bāgh Bhairav, showing the wood carvings.

Two images of Hanumān[9] on either side of the sacrificial altar were erected in 837/ 1717. According to an inscription[10] of 882/ 1762 a door and a garland of *mohara* (coins) was donated. Apart from inscriptions recording gifts, there is also an inscription[11] of 870/1750 on the entrance which, as is mentioned elsewhere in this report, prohibits the felling of trees in the forest on the northern slope of the town, with a penalty of 12 rupees for offenders.

Further renovations are recorded to have been carried out by Jaifal, son of Hastikā, the wetnurse of Rānā Bahādur Shāh.[12] The renovations were carried out in NS 923/1803 AD (Saka Era 1725). One of the struts of the roof of the second level is, however, dated 974/1854. In 996/1876 a bell was installed by a *mānandhar*, which according to its inscription weighs 31 *dhārni*, and was moulded by Byāpāri Bidyādhana of Naudvan Bāhā of Patan.[13] The most recent record[14] concerns the offering of the golden flag at the entrance in 1022/1902.

Apart from the inscriptions, evidence of changes to the temple can also be seen from Ambrose Oldfield's sketch (Figure 5) which shows that at the time of his visit in 1855 the upper floor of the temple had an open verandah, which was later to be enclosed by latticed windows. The objects displayed on the outside of the temple include armour and weapons captured at the time of the Gurkha conflict, such as the helmet of Kālū Pandey, the army commander of the Gurkhas.

The most recent renovation to the main temple was carried out in 1087/1967 by the Gūṭhī Saṃsthān of the Government of Nepal. On this occasion the metal plates on the floor of the temple were replaced by marble. In addition, in January 1986 a team from Italy[15] carried out some experimental cleaning and fixing of a portion of the paintings of the temple.

## SUBSIDIARY TEMPLES IN THE BĀGH BHAIRAV COMPLEX

The Bāgh Bhairav complex includes a number of subsidiary temples and shrines built within the enclosure, mainly on the south-eastern side of the courtyard. They are in various styles, and house a number of important images. They date from the

Plate 54 Eastern side of the Bāgh Bhairav complex, with the main temple to the right, and from right to left the subsidiary temples of Māna Binayak (no. 12), Bhavānī Śaṅkar (no. 6), Śiva (no. 5), Śrīdhara Vishṇu (no. 4), Nārāyaṇ (no. 2) and Gaṇeś (no. 1).

early 17th century to the present day and the following temples and shrines are described below in approximate chronological order: Māna Binayak Temple, Śrīdhara Vishṇu Temple, Tulasī Degaḥ, Gaṇeś Temple, Bhavānī Śaṅkar Temple, Śiva Temple, Nārāyaṇ Temple, Rām Chandra Temple, Viśvakarmā Shrine, and Dhartī Mātā.

*Māna Binayak Temple*

The earliest of the small temples in the complex is that of Māna Binayak (no. 12, Plate 54), standing on the south-eastern side of the main temple. It is a small square brick building with a single doorway to the south-west and a pyramidal roof with a finial. An inscription (Apx. A, no. 4) on a stone slab above the entrance gives the date of the building as 750/1630, but the image of Gaṇeś housed inside is even earlier, its inscription, (Apx. A, no. 1) the earliest dated epigraph in the town, giving the year of the installation of the image as 623/1503. Gaṇeś is shown with the seven headed serpent forming a canopy. This is one of the few Gaṇeś images in the Kathmandu Valley where no animal sacrifice is offered.

*Śrīdhara Temple*

On the south-eastern side of the complex, to the east of the Nārāyaṇ Temple is the stone temple of Śrīdhara Vishṇu (no. 4, Plate 54). It is square in plan with a pyramidal roof in three tiers, and a single north-western entrance. The roof imitates the form of a wooden roof, and includes details such as cornices with the ends of the rafters depicted in stone. It is topped by a finial. Instead of windows at each side of the three upper levels there is a face of the deity flanked by his consorts under an arch.

The inscription (Apx. A, no. 8) attached to the temple gives the date 778/1658. The image of Śrīdhara Vishṇu housed in the temple is considered by Lain Simha Bangdel[16] to be of the 10th century. Although the inscription is now partly

Plate 55 The Tulasī Degaḥ (no. 22) south-west of the main temple in the Bāgh Bhairav Complex.

defaced, there is a clear and readable ink rubbing of the epigraph in the National Archive at Kathmandu, the text of which gives details of the renovation of the temple, as well as the establishment of a Vaṃsa Gopāla icon.

*Tulasī Degaḥ*

In front of the main temple on the western side of the courtyard is the Tulasī Degaḥ (No. 22, Plate 47, 55), a miniature stone *śikhara* standing on a podium 1.5m. square and 1.5m. high. A blind niche with a semi-circular arch is provided on each face of the shrine, and the roof tower with its slightly bowed profile is topped by a finial. According to the inscription (Apx. A, no. 17) the *degaḥ* was established in 796/1676, and the text of the inscription praises the *tulasī* (basil) plant, and the following deities: Garuḍ Nārāyaṇa, Bhavānī Śaṅkar, Vaṃśa Gopāla, and Mādhaveśvara. The images now housed in the niches are, however, Nārāyaṇa, Sarasvatī, Rādhā Kṛishṇa, Umā Maheśvara and Garuḍ Nārāyaṇa. There is a place for a basil plant on the podium.

*Gaṇeś Temple*

The Gaṇeś temple (Figure 24, no. 1, Figure 25, Plate 56) stands on a low stone platform close to the western wall just inside the main gate of the complex. The building is rectangular in plan, measuring 3.89 x 2.95m., and is built of brick faced with polished brick. It has a two tiered tiled roof, with the projecting eaves resting on slanting struts. As the back of the building is very close to the enclosure wall, there is less overhang on the roofs of this side. The carved woodwork of the temple includes windows on the upper levels, cornices, and a colonnade of two columns and two pilasters on the north-eastern side at ground level. The colonnade leads to the shrine on the ground floor. There is also an upper floor, which is not accessible except by the windows. The wooden pillars and windows are well carved, but until its repair in 1989 the building itself was in a neglected state. The upper tier of the roof had collapsed on one side. The lower roof was also dilapidated, and the brickwork of the walls had developed cracks. Panelling had been added between the lower part of the columns flanking the entrance.

The temple has an inscription (Apx. A, no. 21) mentioning the erection of the temple together with the performance of the *sahaprānhuti yagya* sacrifice. In this ceremony both male and female animals are sacrificed together. The inscription also records the offering of a golden pinnacle in 824/1704, but the pinnacle is no longer in situ. The temple houses eight ancient images which are arranged around the walls of the lower chamber (Plate 57), with a standing Śiva in the eastern corner, a Gaṇeś against the north-western wall, Umā Maheśvara (Śiva Pārvatī) against the south-eastern wall, and a row of Mātṛikās (the Divine Mothers) — Vaishṇavī, Brahmāyaṇī, Kaumārī, Śaivi and Bārāhī along the south-western wall. The images are the most ancient to be found in the complex; that of Gaṇeś may be datable to as early as the 4th century. The images are discussed in more detail in the section on antiquities.

*Bhavānī Śaṅkar Temple*

To the south-west of the main temple is a stone temple of Bhavānī Śaṅkar (no. 6, Plate 54), established in 838/1718 (Apx. A, no. 23). The temple is built on a double podium and is square in

Plate 56 The Gaṇeś temple in the Bāgh Bhairav complex, from the north.

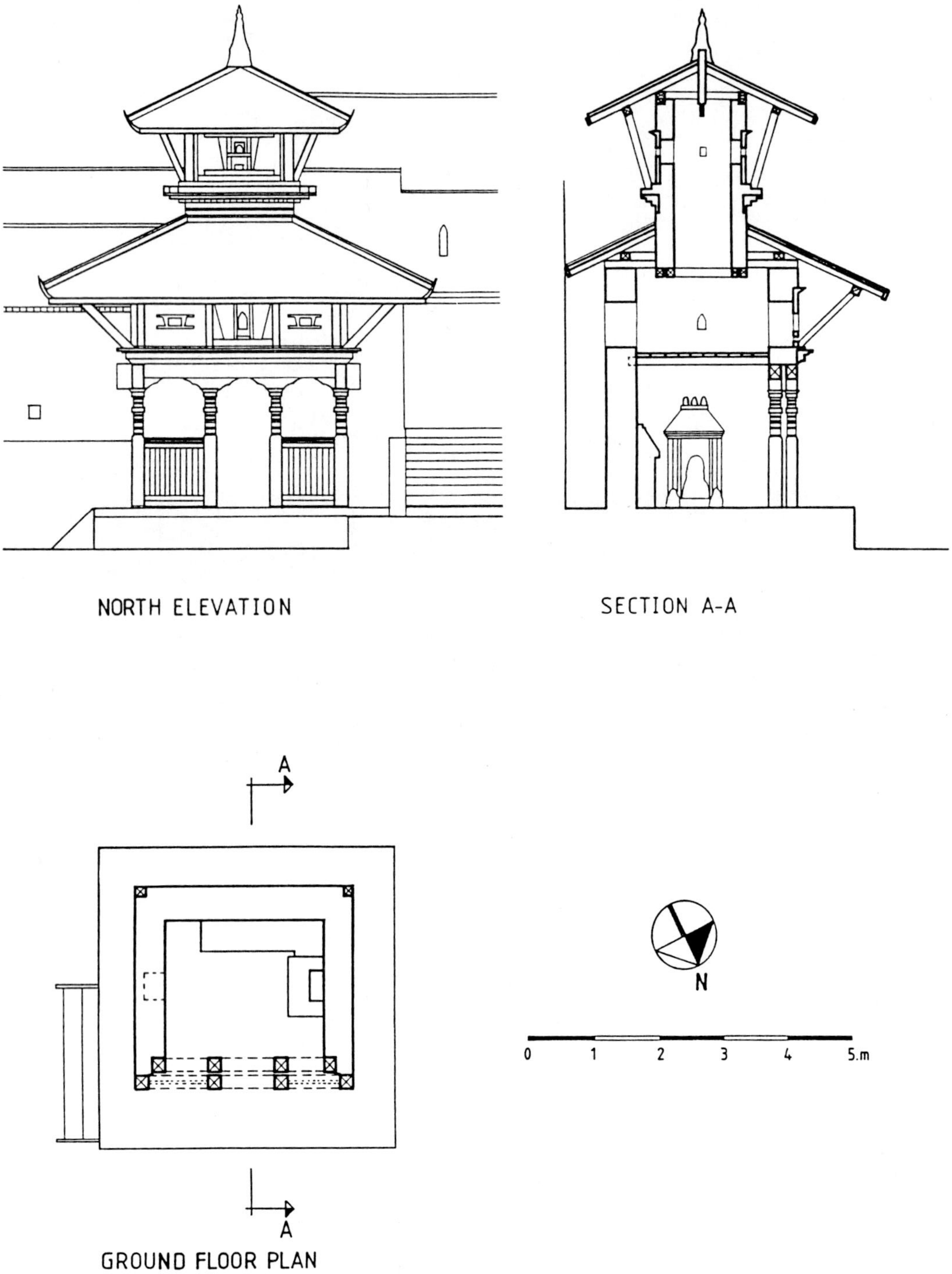


Figure 25 Gaṇeś temple in Bāgh Bhairav complex, plan, section A-A, and north elevation. Key: a. standing Śiva (Jhavā Dya) (4th cent.); b. Śiva Pārvatī; c. Mātṛikās (Vaishṇavī, Brahmāyaṇī, Kaumārī, Śaivi, and Bārāhī); d. Gaṇeś (4th cent.).

plan with a pyramidal roof. It has a doorway on the north-west side, with a semi-circular arch decorated with carved stone. As in the Śrīdhara Temple, the other façades have blind arches. The building is in a fair state of preservation, but the image of Bhavānī Śaṅkar, housed in its chamber, was stolen in 1984 and has not been recovered.

*Śiva Temple*

On the south-west side of the Bhavānī Śaṅkar Temple is a temple of Śiva (no. 5, Plates 47 and

Plate 57 The interior of the Gaṇeś temple with the images of the Ashṭamātṛikas.

54). It stands on a low stone platform and is square in plan and built of brick faced with polished brick. It has openings in all four sides, as is the case with many other Śiva temples of the valley, and it contains a Śiva *liṅga*. All four façades of the ground floor are in a good state of preservation, and have exquisitely carved wooden doors with stone sills, and a wooden cornice running round the building (Plate 58). The original date of the temple is uncertain, but it was renovated by Jaifal in 923/1803.

The building was, however, in a roofless and dilapidated condition by the time Oldfield visited the town in 1855. His sketch (Figure 5) shows that the temple had a *toraṇa* over the north-west entrance, and the traditional type of windows. Now the upper part of the building has been completely rebuilt, with un-ornamented windows and a dome. The dome is covered with cement and stands on a zone of transition which is square on the outside. The window on the south-west side of the ground level, shown in Oldfield's drawing, has been filled in. From the features shown in the drawing we can assume that the original building would have been in at least two tiers, with projecting roofs, and possibly a colonnade at ground level.

*Nārāyaṇ Temple*

The Nārāyaṇ Temple (no. 2, Plate 54), to the south of the Śiva Temple, was built in the 19th century by Hastikā the mother of Jaifal. It is square in plan, on a platform in two tiers, and is built of brick. The single entrance is in the traditional Nepalese style, with an elaborate carved wood frame with the usual extended lintel and side wings (Plates 59 and 60). The entrance is provided with a massive stone sill.

The building is now roofed by a dome, crowned by a bell shaped cap and pinnacle, both covered with gilt copper. There is a vase shaped finial in each corner of the parapet around the dome. In Vikrama Era 2009/1952 the exterior of the building was coated with lime plaster, and the building was given its present shape, while a *gūṭhī* was established for the religious observances and the upkeep of the temple. The temple houses the images of Nārāyaṇ followed by his two consorts Sarasvatī and Lakshmī, of which the

Plate 58 Śiva temple (no. 5) in the Bāgh Bhairav complex. The lower part retains the original carved entrance, but the upper part of the building is reconstructed.

Plate 59 Carved entrance of the Nārāyaṇ Temple (no. 2) in the Bāgh Bhairav Complex.

Plate 60 Detail of the wood carvings of the Nārāyaṇ Temple (no. 2).

Sarasvatī image was stolen on the night of 28th January 1984.

*Rām Chandra Temple*

The complex includes a number of modern additions including a small temple of Rām Chandra (no. 11) built in the 1940s and situated to the south of the main temple. It houses images of Rāma, Lakshmaṇ, Sītā and Hanumān, and is usually kept locked up.

*Viśvakarman Shrine*

Another modern addition to the complex is the Viśvakarmā (locally known as Biśvakarmā) shrine (no. 8), built of cement in 1088/1968 to the south-east of the Bhavānī Śaṅkar Temple. On its eastern side is a marble image of Gaṇeś made in the same year, and an object of veneration for local masons, labourers and carpenters. Before 1960 there was a small garden on the present site of the shrine. The deity Viśvakarman is greatly venerated by all masons, labourers, carpenters and workers in other technical trades in the Newar community.

*Dhartī Mātā*

The most recent addition to the complex is the shrine of Dhartī Mātā (no. 13), established in Vikrama Era 2036/1979 AD, to the east of the main temple. It is open to the sky and contains a carved image of Dhartī Mātā giving birth (Plate 145). The image is discussed with the art objects elsewhere in the report.

## UMĀ MAHEŚVARA TEMPLE

The Umā Maheśvara Temple (Figure 26, Plate 61), also known locally as Kvācho Degaḥ, occupies the most commanding position in the town, at the highest point of the northern ridge, and is a prominent landmark in the Valley (Plate 1). The temple is reached via a flight of steps on the south-eastern side and the present structure is

Plate 61 Umā Maheśvara Temple from the north-west.

Plate 62 Umā Maheśvara Temple, interior from the south-east with the Umā Maheśvara icon in the centre.

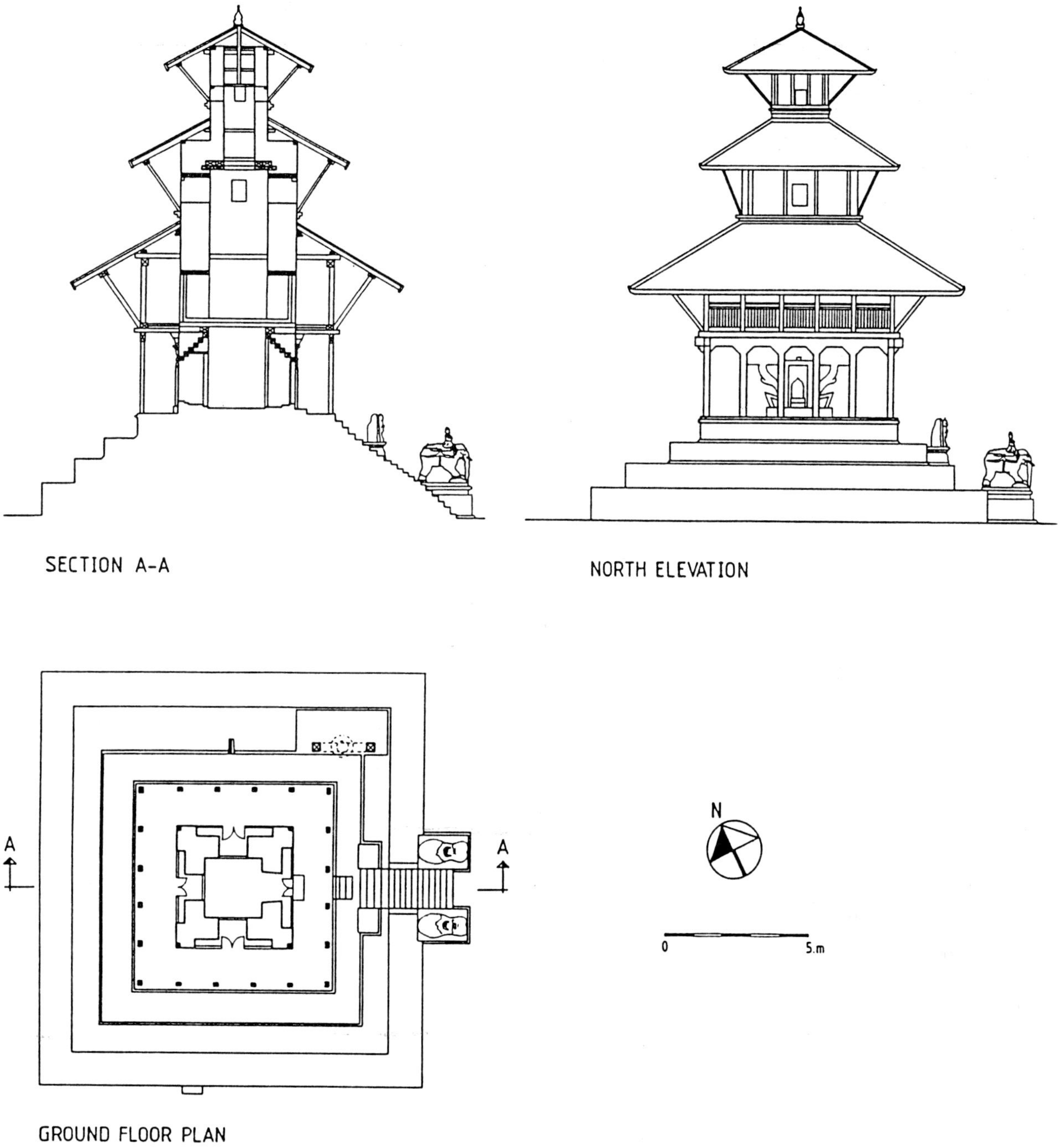


Figure 26 Umā Maheśvara temple, plan, section A-A, and north elevation.

in three tiers standing on a platform.

There are conflicting views on the date of the building. Hari Ram Joshi[17] writes that the temple was constructed by the *pradhāns* of Dathu Tajhya Ṭol, Mangal Bāzār in Patan giving the copper plate inscription attached to the temple as his source. However, the copper plate inscription (Apx. A, no. 7) attached to the wall behind the main image (Plate 62) does not mention a builder, but rather a certain Rāṭhaura Bishva Nāth Bābu who established the image, and made endowments to the temple in 775/1655. We can therefore assume that the temple already existed at this time. Bernier[18] gives the date of the temple as 1673, and also states that the temple was originally in four storeys, without giving his sources. It is very unlikely that the temple would have been built eighteen years after the instalment of the image. As the site of Umā Maheśvara is at the highest and most prominent position in Kirtipur, a temple must always have existed there during the life of the town. The present building must have been founded earlier than its image, perhaps sometime at the end of

Plate 63 Stone elephants installed in 782/1662 flanking the steps of the plinth of Umā Maheśvara.

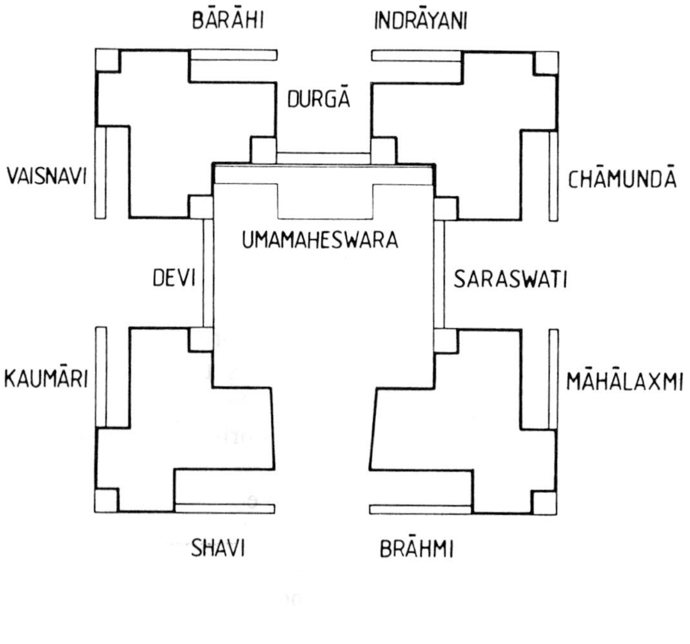


Figure 27 Umā Maheśvara temple, plan showing the location of the images (Sketch by S. S. Shrestha).

Plate 64 The entrance to the principal shrine of Umā Maheśvara.

Plate 65 Umā Maheśvara, trident of Śiva on the south.

Plate 66 Umā Maheśvara, Sarasvatī image at north-east.

the 16th century or more probably early in the 17th century, but further evidence is needed before a more definite date can be established for the building.

The original form of the temple is also a matter for debate. The structure has suffered considerable damage during its history. Oldfield's drawing of the Lāyaku area in about 1855 (Figure 6) shows that the temple, which had been damaged in the 1833 earthquake was still in a dilapidated state, with the upper part missing. The building remained in the same state for nearly a century, but after the 1934 earthquake it was renovated using corrugated iron sheeting for the roof. However, a storm in 1947 caused the upper portion and the pinnacle to fall to the ground.[19] It remained in need of repair until 1982 when the temple was brought to its present condition by the local authority,[20] the Lāyaku Village Pañchāyat, in collaboration with the Local Development and Pañchāyat Ministry of the Government of Nepal. From close study and measurement of the upper walls of the building, together with comparison with Oldfield's sketch, it appears that the building may have always been in three storeys, and Bernier's suggestion of four storeys needs further investigation.

The temple stands on a stepped plinth in four levels over a platform. A gateway dated 835/1715 (Apx. A no. 11 c) on the south-eastern side opens onto a flight of steps leading to the temple. The plinth is paved with stone and polished brick. The core of the building is square in plan and built of brick. There are entrances on all four sides, but only that on the south-east now gives access to the interior (Plate 64), the other three being boarded up to provide niches for images. The temple in its present form has three floors inside, and on the outside there is a colonnade around the lower level supporting a balcony and the struts of the first roof, which has been reconstructed together with the two upper roofs.

On either side of the steps at the lowest level of the plinth are two stone elephants installed in 782/1662 (Apx. A, no. 11 a, b) (Plate 63). Above the elephants, on the third level of the plinth, are images of Kubara and Bhīmsen. It appears from other examples that it was customary to install these images in Śiva temples. A stone slab of 651/1531 in the Bhaktapur Art Gallery has a Śiva *liṅga* flanked by Bhīmsen and Kubara, and the 1627 Bisheśvara temple of Patan has these two figures on the plinth. On the southern side of the

Plate 67 Detail of the carvings of the jamb of the entrance to the principal shrine of Umā Maheśvara.

Plate 68 Details of the carvings of the south-west side of Umā Maheśvara.

plinth of Umā Maheśvara at the level of the platform is a shrine consisting of a colossal stone *triśūla* (Plate 65), with six carved niches on either side. The stepped plinth itself was renovated in 839/1719 (Apx. A, no. 11 a).

The south-eastern door leads to the principal shrine (Figure 27), with a stone image of the main deity of the temple, Umā Maheśvara (Plates 62 and 139), a fine example of the Malla period. The copper plate inscription (Apx. A, no. 7) mentioned above describes the generous contributions made by the people for the installation of the icon of Bhavānī Śaṅkar, a synonym of Umā Maheśvara. Two images of Śiva Pārvatī and two images of Vishṇu Nārāyaṇa are also housed in the sanctum. Behind the door on the north-eastern façade is an image of Sarasvatī (Plate 66), and behind that of the north-western side Durgā (Plate 140). The Gaṇeś originally behind the door of the southern façade is now housed in the Gaṇeś Phalechā in Lāyaku (Plate 20), and an image of a Devī takes its place in Umā Maheśvara.

The temple preserves excellent examples of architectural decoration in its wooden elements, although much of the woodwork has been replaced at the time of renovations. The present pillars and struts supporting the verandah are replaced, and are un-carved, but two carved struts from the temple have been reused in the Gaṇeś Temple in Dabujho Ṭol and indicate that these elements would originally have been elaborately carved. None of the old pillars replaced in the first half of this century can now be found. The wooden door frames and lintels of the façade at ground level are in a good state of preservation, and are shaped to extend well into the brickwork in the traditional manner (Plate 64). These elements are intricately carved with images of deities such as Indra, Śiva, Sūrya, Chandra, Vishṇu, and Brahmā, in attitudes displaying readiness to combat demons. The Ashṭamaṅgala or the eight auspicious symbols are also depicted, as well as scenes of carnivorous beasts hunting in the jungle. The brackets of the lower level are profusely carved with the figures of gods and goddesses. On either side of the door frames are carved wing-shaped wooden panels which bear fine examples of images of the Ashṭamātṛikās, the eight divine mothers, in the upper portion (Plate 68), with (starting from the east, going clockwise) Brahmāyaṇī, Rudrāyaṇī, Kaumārī, Vaishṇavī, Bārāhī, Indrāyaṇī (now lost), Chāmuṇḍā and Mahālakshmī. The lower portion of these panels have carvings of the Ashṭa-

Plate 69 Umā Maheśvara, corner showing lions' heads carved on the ends of the joists of the first tier.

Plate 70 Gaṇeś shrine at Tuṅjho, south of Chilaṅcho.

Plate 71 Nārāyaṇ Temple to the north-west of De Pukhū, from the west.

bhairavas. The carvings of this part of the temple are as far as it is known original, and represent the finest examples of wooden sculpture to be found in the town.

The bell hung in the temple was originally a quarter striking bell from the Ghanṭaghar clock tower in Kathmandu. When the clock tower was destroyed in the 1934 earthquake the then prime Minister Juddha Shumsher offered the bell at the request of the Kirtipur *dvāre* Jagat Bahādur Pradhān (also known as Sipāhī Bājyā). The bell was cast by Gillet and Johnston Founders of Croydon, England in 1895. The original bell of the temple is said locally to have been taken away by one of the kings of Bhaktapur in the first half of the 18th century, and it seems from Oldfield's 1855 watercolour (Figure 6) that it was missing at the time of his visit. Sipāhī Bājyā died in 1982, but in 1981 told the author his version of the story. According to him the King of Bhaktapur sent men to steal the bell because of its fine tone and intense echo. They took it away, passing across the territory of Patan, but as the night was ending and they did not want to be caught with the stolen bell in daylight they hid it in a field and fled. Seeing this, the King of Patan took the bell and had it hung in the Taleju Temple. It was said that the bell was hung below a deity and that if the bell were taken out the deity would fall, therefore no one dared to take it back. Sipāhī Bājyā went to Taleju Temple to see the bell, but because it could not be removed a request was made for the present bell, which was finally granted. The present author tried to acquire more information on the position of the original bell, but was unable to gain access to the interior of this royal temple.

## GAṆEŚ TEMPLE IN DABUJHO

There are a number of small Gaṇeś temples and shrines in Kirtipur, some of architectural interest, for example that at Tunjho (Plate 70), south of Chilañcho. Another one, the Gaṇeś temple of Dabujho is particularly significant as it preserves two of the original struts of the Umā Maheśvara temple. The Gaṇeś temple lies on the south-west of the steps leading up to the Umā Maheśvara temple complex, and houses the images of Gaṇeś and Sūrya (the sun god) both dating from the 16-17th century. There are also two miniature temples inside the building although the Gaṇeś temple itself is built in the form of a *pāṭi* or rest-house against the wall of a house.

The two struts are all that is left of the pile of struts from Umā Maheśvara, which were put aside after its reconstruction. The struts lay for half a century in a *pāṭi* near the Gaṇeś temple, and all the other struts have now apparently decayed and no longer exist. In front of the Gaṇeś temple there is also a *chaitya* of recent origin.

## NĀRĀYAṆ TEMPLE

The Nārāyaṇ Temple to the north of the De Pukhū and south of the Bāgh Bhairav complex is a brick temple rebuilt early this century in the style of that time, incorporating a dome and western details (Figure 28, Plate 71). It seems that the original temple must have been destroyed in the earthquake of 1833. Oldfield[21] mentions "two or three ruined temples" on the north side of De Pukhū. The old people of the town still recall the site as a big heap of bricks and earth, but it is not remembered precisely when the temple was re-erected. However, according to Lakshmaṇ Pradhān of Kirtipur who was born about 1921, his father, Kaziman Pradhān was responsible for the reconstruction of the building, giving it the present appearance some time in 1920-21. Lakshmaṇ Pradhān was told by his father that the temple had been a heap of earth and brick for many decades, and that the original building was, according to his ancestors, constructed twelve

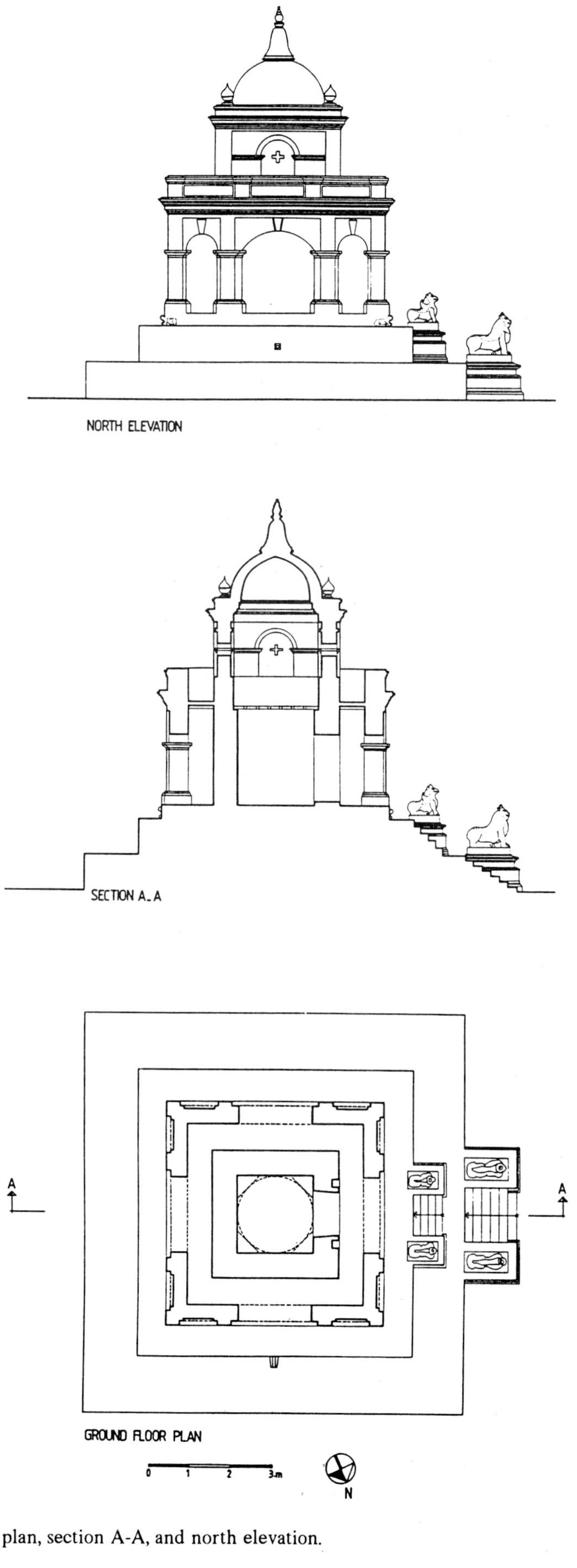


Figure 28 Nārāyaṇ Temple, plan, section A-A, and north elevation.

Plate 72 Lions flanking the steps of the plinth on the west side of the Nārāyaṇ Temple.

generations before him. In its latest form, before its destruction the building was in the "pagoda style" with three storeys and had a large pinnacle with four smaller pinnacles around set on the cardinal points, like those of the Paśupatināth Temple at Kathmandu. Lakshmaṇ Pradhan's father also told him that the present two pairs of lions (Plate 72) were carved from stone brought from Dukuchhap, behind the Dakshiṇkālī shrine. The reconstruction work was supervised by Bahādur Bajrāchārya, who was also responsible for the re-erection of the Sat Tale Darbār in Nuvakoṭ after it fell in the 1934 earthquake.

The present building stands on a two tiered platform made of a combination of brick and stone, with a flight of steps on the north-western side flanked by monolithic lions and griffins set on carved stone plinths. It appears that the platform and these sculptures survived the earthquake, and it was the structure above that was rebuilt. Although the appearance of the temple is not in the traditional style, its layout follows Nepalese traditions. The walls of the inner shrine rise above the level of the surrounding corridor, giving a two tiered elevation. The corridor has an opening with a semi-circular arch with a keystone on each of the four sides, but the sanctum chamber has only one entrance, on the north-west. The upper tier of the sanctum has blind arches on the exterior. It is possible that the original temple may have had a circumambulatory passage, in the style of that of the Tvā Dvāra (the Jagannāth Temple) in the Kathmandu Darbār Square.

The main image in the sanctum is of Nārāyaṇa, but the date of installation is not known. There are also images of Sūrya and of Śiva Pārvatī, dated 772/1652 on either side of the entrance. According to an inscription of 797/1677 a restoration of the platform was carried out by Kvātha Nāyaka Lakshmīnārāyaṇ Bharo, and an inscription of 834/1714 gives details of further restoration carried out by Kvātha Nāyaka Dristi Rāj, and the installation of an Umā Maheśvara image.

To the north of the temple is a platform which was used for the performance of the ritual dances known as *sikhāli pyākhan* and *khapyākhaṅ*. The custom has now died out, but a manuscript[22] describes the *khapyākhaṅ* staged in 1020/1900 and in 1059/1939 in this location. In spite of being built comparatively recently, the temple is

Plate 73 Indrāyaṇī Temple at the north of the town, stone lion.

Plate 74 Lioness offered with the lion to the Indrāyaṇī Temple in 1661, with inscriptions.

now neglected, and in poor condition, with vegetation growing in the brickwork. It is, however, still visited by devotees in the mornings.

## INDRĀYAṆĪ SHRINE

The Indrāyaṇī shrine lies in Pīgāṅ, at the north-western end of the town, and is considered by the townspeople to be equal in importance to Bāgh Bhairav and the Chilaṅcho Stupa. This is in spite of the fact that the old building has been completely destroyed by a sacred pipal tree (*ficus religiosa*).

The shrine preserves a pair of stone lions (Plates 73 and 74) offered to the goddess Indrāyaṇī in 781/1661, as well as a stone tympanum carved with the figures of the Ashṭamātṛikās and dated 790/1670. The date of the lions indicates that there would have been a temple prior to the installation of the tympanum. The shrine is probably the site of one of the oldest temples of the town, and archaeological excavation of the site may well produce valuable information. There is now a new brick canopy over the deity at the base of the tree, and a modern wall has been built around it. Old carved stones associated with the temple, including an inscribed slab at the foot of the lioness, are also kept in the shrine.

## SARASVATĪ TEMPLE COMPLEX

The Sarasvatī Temple complex is situated in the north-west of the town, about half way between Umā Maheśvara and the Indrāyaṇī Shrine. The main temple (Plate 75) is dedicated to Sarasvatī, the goddess of learning, locally known as Nagacho. An inscription (Apx. A, no. 24) on the south-western wall (Plate 77) records the renovation of the stone temple and the establishment of the image of Sarasvatī in 841/1721 by Kvātha Nāyaka Lakshmī Singh Bharo. The temple stands on a platform in three tiers, and is approached by a flight of steps on the south-eastern side. The temple is built of stone and is square in plan with a pyramidal roof on an octagonal base. Each side has an opening with a

Plate 75 Sarasvatī Temple from the east.

Plate 76 Interior of the Sarasvatī Temple, with the image of Sarasvatī and other icons.

Plate 77 Sarasvatī Temple, inscribed slab on the south-west exterior recording the renovation of the temple, and the establishment of the image in 1721.

semi-circular arch of carved stone, but the north-west and south-west openings are closed with inscribed slabs of stone. The interior consists of a single chamber containing an image of Sarasvatī and other icons (Plate 76) set into the stone work, as well as a further inscribed slab of stone. In 1984 the temple was again restored by the Lāyaku Panchāyat in collaboration with the Department of Archaeology, and trees growing between its stones, making the structure unstable, were removed.

On the north side of the temple are other shrines, notably a shrine of Manjuśrī dated 911/1791 and another of Gorakh Nath. Below the Manjuśrī shrine a small stone temple has an inscribed stone slab of the year 804/1684 which describes the temple as Ishtachoni Mahākāra. The image is now lost and the meaning of this name is no longer known. People from the surrounding area make an offering here of the first milk given by their domestic animals after the birth of a calf or a kid. It is believed that the goddess Sarasvatī lives in Tibet from the first day of Baiśākh until the day before Śrī Pañchamī. The place is crowded with devotees on Śrī Pañchamī day, and she is worshipped until Baiśākh.

## BUDDHIST STUPAS AND CHAITYAS

### CHILAÑCHO STUPA

The Chilañcho Stupa dominates the eastern part of the town, and is perhaps the oldest monument in Kirtipur. The complex (Figure 29, Plate 78) consists of the great stupa in the centre of a platform built around a natural mound, with the *mahāvihār* (principal monastery also referred to as *mubāhā*) (Figure 29 no. 42, Figure 40, Plates 97-8) on the south-western side of the complex. The Jagat Pāl Mahāvihār is discussed elsewhere in this work, together with the other monasteries of Kirtipur. A number of secondary stupas and shrines have also been added to the complex, which is surrounded by a wall and houses. The stupa is generally known as Chilañcho Chaitya, but in inscriptions found in the complex it is also referred to as *chaitya ranga bhaṭṭāraka*, *chitra ranga bhaṭṭāraka*, and *dharmadhātu vagiśvara* (Apx. A, nos. 12, 16).

The main entrance to the complex is via a gateway (no. 1) on the south-eastern side. An image of Tārā (no. 6) offered in 636/1516 is to be found inside the main entrance on the north-east wall. The gateway leads to flights of steps (Plate 79) up to the three levels of the platform on which the main stupa stands. The lowest level of the platform has two rest houses (no. 7) flanking the steps, and four miniature *chaityas* (*chibhāḥs*) of differing styles. In front of the north-eastern rest house a small tank or *jarū hiti* (no. 12) is provided for the use of devotees. It has a damaged image of Padmapāṇi Lokeśvar of about the 17th or 18th century. The tank used to be kept filled by the *gūṭhī*, but with the loss of the *gūṭhī* lands and the installation of a piped water system to the town the tank is now dry and out of use.

More steps lead up to the second level, which has a small *chaitya* (no. 14) on the eastern side and watchman's quarters (no. 38) on the southern side. Another flight of steps leads to the topmost level, a platform 32m. square, on which stands the great stupa and the principal monuments and images of the complex. The top of the steps is flanked by two rest houses (no. 15) where ritual songs (*dāphā*) are performed. The northern rest house contains an image of Sukhāvati Lokeśvara of the 17th or 18th century. In front of the steps is the *dharma stambha* (no. 16, Plate 80) of 793/1673 with images of devotees, and an

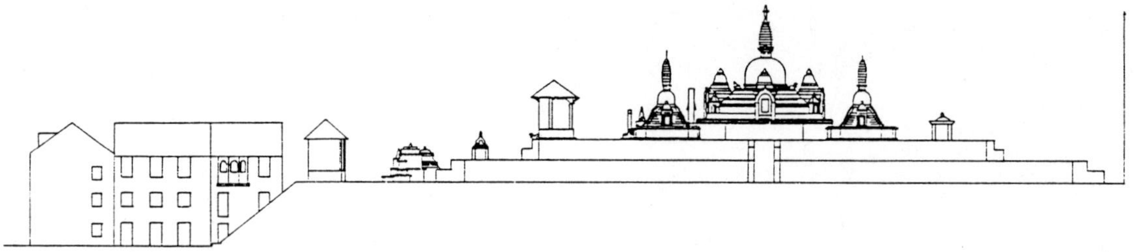

NORTH ELEVATION

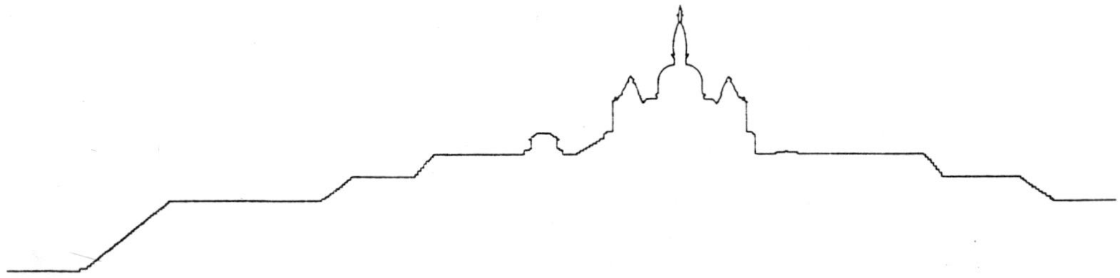

SECTION A–A

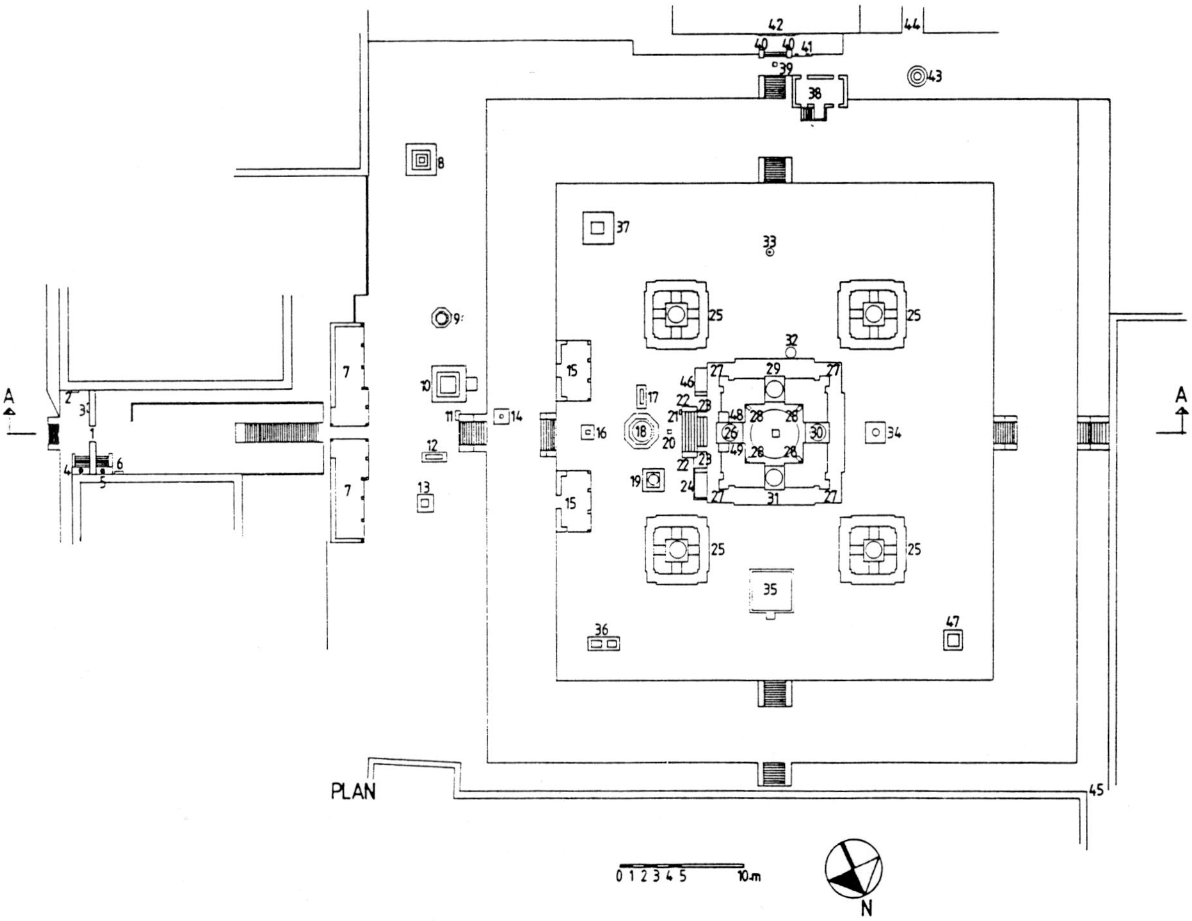


PLAN

Figure 29 Chilañcho Stupa complex, plan, section A-A, and north elevation (Survey by S. S. Shrestha).

Key to plan: 1 Main entrance to complex; 2 image of Hanumān; 3 image of Rām Chandra; 4 image of Gaṇeś (16th-17th century), *dvārapāla* of the *vihār*; 5 image of Mahākāla (16th-17th century), *dvārapāla* of the *vihār*; 6 place of a stone image of Tārā dated 636/1516, once set on a house wall, and now lost; 7 *phalechās* (*pāṭis*); 8 *chibhāḥ* (2 m. high); 9 octagonal *chibhāḥ* (2 m. high); 10 *chibhāḥ* 898/1778 (3 m. high); 11 Gaṇeś; 12 *jarū hiti* with Padmapāṇi of the 17th-18th century; 13 *chibhāḥ* (2.1 m. high); 14 *chibhāḥ;* 15 *phalechās* (*pāṭis*), the northern one has a Sukhāvati Lokeśvar of the 17th-18th century; 16 *dharma stambha* 793/1673 (the images of individual devotees are of the same date, the inscription of the installation of the Tri-ratna is now attached to the *stambha*); 17 frame for bell (788/1688); 18 *dharmadhātu maṇḍala* 789/1669; 19 *chibhāḥ* (1040/1920); 20 *agniśālā* (791/1671); 21 inscription referring to renovations of 635/1515; 22 two elephants (789/1669); 23 two images of Krodharāj (788/1668); 24 bell (876/1756); 25 four subsidiary stupas; 26 Achhyobhya; 27 four Tārā Devīs (793/1673); 28 four *jarumanuchhyas* (790/1670); 29 Ratna Sambhava (Bodhisattva and Tārā added in 797/1677); 30 Amitābha (Padmapāṇis installed in 797/1677); 31 Amoghasiddhi (Tārās installed in 797/1677); 32 *satungāchā* (stone tub for mixing lime for painting the stupa) 935/1815. The inscription mentions that 12 *man* of lime are required. 33 *dvādaśa tirtha* (twelve points), small holes representing the twelve sacred Buddhist pilgrimage points in the Kathmandu Valley; 34 small *chibhāḥ* (*pañcha mandi*); 35 Vasigā; 36 images of individual devotees and *kalāśa maṇḍala, dharmadhātu maṇḍala* (788/1660); 37 Sadāchhyari Lokeśvar (1099/1979); 38 sleeping quarters for the *bāhā* keepers; 39 *agniśālā* of the main *āgam* (shrine); 40 lions of *āgam chhen*, Phālguna to south, Karttik to north, (835/1715); 41 bell; 42 main *bāhā* building, Jagat Pāl Vihār; 43 *chibhāḥ* (2.5 m. high) (832/1712); 44 approach from south-west; 45 approach from north-west; 46 Tri-ratna shrine (793/1673); 47 small square stupa plastered with lime (Vikrama Era 2003/1946); 48 Bairochana with Pūjāevi (791/1671); 49 Padmapāṇi Lokeśvar.

Plate 78 The *phalechās* and *dharma stambha* on the platform of Chilañcho Stupa, from the north.

Plate 79 Chilaṅcho Stupa from the west with a small *chibhāḥ* (*paṅcha mandi*) in front.

Plate 80 The main approach to the Chilaṅcho Stupa from the south-east, flanked by two *phalechās* where ritual songs are performed.

Plate 81 The south-eastern side of Chilancho with two guardian images of Krodharāj Raj dating from 1688.

inscription of the installation of a Tri-ratna shrine. Close by is a small *dharmadhātu maṇḍala* and *kalaśā*, added in 788/1688, and to the south is a frame (17), dated the same year, for hanging a bell (no longer *in situ*). The main *maṇḍala* (18) is dated 789/1669, and there is a miniature stupa (19) of 1040/1920 to the north of it. The *agniśala* (20) between the *maṇḍala* and the main stupa was dug in 791/1671.

The principal stupa appears to have been constructed over the top of the natural mound of rock and is of brick, standing on a brick platform reached by stone steps on the south-eastern side. Steps flanked by a pair of elephants (no. 22) dated 789/1669 and images of Krodharāj (no. 23, Plate 140) dated 788/1668 (Apx. A, no. 13) lead up to the platform on which the stupa stands (Plate 81). The south-eastern side of the platform has a Tri-ratna shrine (no. 46, Plate 82) the inscription of which is now attached to the *dharma stambha* (no. 16) and gives the date of installation as 793/1673 (Apx. A, no. 16). To the east of the steps is a bell (no. 24) offered in 876/1756.

The central stupa takes the form of a stepped pyramid surmounted by a solid dome topped by the *harmikā*, a solid tower. The base of the tower is square in plan with the eyes of the Buddha painted on each face. Thirteen concentric circles stand above the base on a moulded slab with triangular pediments on each side. These thirteen circles represent the Buddhist paradise, and are known as the *trayodaś bhūmi*. They are named Pramudita, Bimala, Prabhākari, Archismati, Sudurjaya, Abhaimukhī, Durāngamā, Achchhāla, Sādhumati, Dharmameghā, Samantaprabhā, Nirupaṃa, and Gyānavāṭī.[23] The thirteen circles are topped by a pinnacle, and over the pinnacle is a square *toraṇa* supported independently by four iron poles set around the base of the dome. The height of the pinnacle from the base of the pyramid is slightly over 10.5m.

The lower levels of the stupa are faced with intricately carved terra-cotta, and the dome is plastered, while the thirteen circles and the pinnacle are clad with metal and gold plated. The south-eastern façade of the pyramid is more elaborately decorated than the others, and has additional chambers on the façade with Achhyobhya (no. 26) in the central niche flanked by Bairochana (no. 48) with Pūjāevi, both installed in 791/1671 on its southern side, and Padmapāṇi Lokeśvar (no. 49) on the north. The central chambers on the other sides have the following images, all installed in 797/1677: Amoghasiddhi (no. 31) with Tārās above in the north-eastern niche; Amitābh (no. 30) with Padmapāṇis to

Plate 82 Chilancho Stupa, Tri-ratna shrine (no. 46 on plan) dating from 1673.

the north-west, and a Ratna Sambhava (no. 29) with the Bodhisattva and Tārā on the south-west. The four corners each have miniature shrines (no. 27) housing the four Tārās (Pāṇḍurā, Māmaki, Lochani and Tārā) facing the cardinal points. The images were carved by Rāghava Bharo of Patan in 793/1673. At the base of the dome, at the cardinal points of the top of the pyramid, are four *jarumanuchhyas* (no. 28, Plate 141), anthropomorphic images of aquatic creatures, dated 790/1670 (Apx. A, no. 15).

At each corner of the main stupa is a subsidiary stupa (no. 25) built on a plinth about a metre high. These house the images of Dhyānī Buddhas. There is also a small modern flat-roofed shrine (no. 37) in the southern corner, with an image of Sadachhyari Lokeśvar added in 1099/1979 by Chandra Bahādur Bajrāchārya of Kirtipur and Badri Ratna Bajrāchārya of Kathmandu. This is one of the most recent additions to the complex.

In the section on the history of Kirtipur it has already been noted that Landon mentions the foundation of the stupa as being the work of the Emperor Aśoka during his pilgrimage to Kathmandu. The chronicles which mention this visit are of a later date, but the local *bajrāchāryas* are of the same opinion as Landon. Alterations to the stupa over the years have, however, changed its appearance drastically, and excavation of the complex may help to establish the origin of Chilancho. In addition, the monastery preserves many documents and records which might contain important historical evidence. These documents, not easily accessible, also await future study.

As well as records of offerings, renovations and restorations to the stupa complex have also been documented. One of these renovations was in 635/1533 on the initiative of Jagat Pāl Varma, one of the Sapta Kuṭumbas from Piṇḍa Bāhā in Patan.[24] He also added the chambers of the five Dhyānī Buddhas in the four directions, which caused many other alterations to the complex to be made. The inscription (no. 21) on the north-eastern side of the steps of the main stupa gives the following information:

> "In the month of Phālguna in NS 635/1515 *pādasthāpanā* was done and on the same month in Daśamī Tithi the door was erected (*dvārasthāpanā*). In Baiśākh Sūcṛa Dvitiyā the god Trasisāngha Bibakhādeva was established. In Jestha the *agnisthāpanā* was performed. All these constructions were done when Ratna Malla, Rānā Malla,

Plate 83 Padmapāṇi Lokeśvara (no. 49 on plan) on the south-east side of Chilaṅcho.

Plate 84 Majā Degaḥ.

and Rām Malla were ruling Nepal together. After all these necessary rites an image of Chakra Sambhara was inaugurated in the monastery. After the reconstruction a series of donations and offerings were made."

The stupa complex has a large number of inscriptions giving detailed information on the numerous offerings of new structures and repairs as well as images. As can be seen from the dates mentioned above, a century and a half after the renovation of the stupa many decorative elements were added in the five years between 788 and 793/1668-73. The succeeding generations, following the example of their predecessors, added a number of other shrines. In the year 832/1712 a miniature stupa (no. 43) (*chibhāḥ*) was installed near the monastery. In the same year a stone tub for mixing lime (*satungāchā*) (no. 32) was made below the main stupa on the southern side. There are then no records of offerings until the beginning of this century, when a copper plated *toraṇa* was offered for the *āgam chhen* of the monastery in 1031/1911. The site has been encircled by a brick wall in 1099/ 1979, when the *gūṭhī* of Godaramata was reactivated, involving the lighting of 133 lamps on the full-moon night of Kārttik and of Baiśākh (Apx. A, no. 28). Beside the offerings mentioned there have been many other structures, images, miniature stupas, and shrines added for which there are no inscriptions or records giving details of their date or donor.

## MAJĀ DEGAḤ

Majā or Mazā Degaḥ, meaning "the never to be completed stupa" (Plate 84) stands to the southwest of Chilaṅcho. Below Majā Degaḥ was a small cistern (*kuti*) with a water spout (*hiti*) the water of which is used for the daily worship at Chilaṅcho. The stupa has four of the five Dhyānī Buddhas depicted facing in the four directions in the prescribed fashion, as well as 24 miniature images connected with the Buddhist faith. The stupa and its images are in the style of the 18th or 19th century, but there are no inscriptions to

Plate 85 Tananī Stupa and *pāṭi* from the north.

give us a precise date.

The stupa stands on a four tiered platform of brick and stone, the upper tier faced with dressed stone decorated with mouldings. The platform is much larger than the stupa itself, and appears to be considerably older than the stupa.

TANANĪ STUPA

Outside the Chilañcho complex, in the Buddhist quarter of the town there are a number of minor stupas which include the elements found in the main stupas, but on a smaller scale. These include

Plate 86 Adi Buddha Stupa, the *chaitya* at Gutapau.

Plate 87 Aśoka Chaitya of the 11th-12th century, Gūṭhī Saṃsthān Collection, Kathmandu (photograph by S. S. Shrestha).

the stupa in Tananī (Figure 20, Plates 43 and 85), a large square to the north-east of Chilaṅcho. The stupa stands on a plinth of polished brick and is greatly venerated by the townspeople.

An inscription of 750/1630 mentions an offering of jewellery and a golden cover for the Buddha image, and we can assume that the stupa itself dates from well before the time of the offering. Further offerings include a stone *toraṇa* on the north side in 798/1678, followed by a golden pinnacle and a garland of gold. The *dharmadhātu maṇḍala* on the south-eastern side is a recent addition. An indication that the stupa was erected earlier than these offerings is another inscription, now illegible, but which appears to be of considerable age.

## GUTAPAU CHAITYA

In the square called Gutapau to the north-west of Chilaṅcho is a large white stupa (Plates 86 and 123), located in a corner of the square. It is believed locally that there was once a nine storeyed temple in this area. The stupa has an inscription which shows the structure to have been built in the 17th-18th century.

The stupa stands on a brick and stone platform 85cm. high, with steps on the south-eastern side, similar in form to the platforms of the other stupas in the town. However, the stupa itself has an unusual form. The lower part, 90cm. high, is solid but is in the form of a temple on a Bhairav *yantra* plan, commonly seen in North Indian temples. This part is divided into two registers by a moulding, and at the top has the form of eaves. The mound above is a truncated cone with bands of decoration, and the stupa is in the shape of a concave cylinder instead of the usual hemisphere. It is topped by a square platform supporting the thirteen tiered tower. The lower part has niches with images of four of the Dhyānī Buddhas, and the south-eastern niche has a miniature stupa over the niche, as well as a *toraṇa* over the arch. Two finely executed stone elephants stand on either side of the arch.

## CHAITYA OF CHĪTHUṄ

In front of the Chīthuṅ Bahī complex to the north-east of Chilaṅcho is a stupa with an inscription of 786/1666. The stupa has, as usual, the four Dhyānī Buddhas, but it is at present considered to be of lower status than the other stupas, and is in a dilapidated condition.

## MINIATURE STUPAS - CHIBHĀḤ

As well as the important stupas mentioned above, Kirtipur has a number of miniature stupas or *chibhāḥs* dotted around the town. The earliest example is the Aśoka Chaitya (Plate 87), now in the Gūṭhī Saṃsthān collection at Kathmandu. This cast metal *chibhāḥ* consists of a hemispherical dome, flattened at the top, and having a band of moulding round the base. It stands on a square plinth with a moulded collar between it and the dome. There is an arch in the centre of each side of the plinth, framing instead of Pañcha Dhyānī Buddhas, a book, a box and a lotus flower on a stalk with leaves.

The tower above the hemisphere has seven concentric circles, instead of thirteen, as is usual in later stupas, and the finial is square in plan and in two registers, and is crowned by a tiny replica of a stupa, again not the usual arrangement. On stylistic grounds this *chibhāḥ* can be dated to the 11th or 12th century, and is not only a very early example of its type, but also provides us with an indication of the form and proportions of the ancient stupas in Nepal.

The *chibhāḥs* are often carved of black

Plate 88 Loṅ Degaḥ (Buddha Dharma Saṅgha Śikhara) built in 1664, south-west façade.

marble, and are usually in the form of a square podium with a lotus in full bloom with Chaturmahārājas beneath it, and resting on the lotus a solid square chamber with niches on the four sides for the four Dhyānī Buddhas. Above the Buddhas is a small stupa. There may also be a separate *dharmadhātu maṇḍala*, but not in every case. Macdonald and Stahl[25] record eight different types of stupa, but the examples in Kirtipur fall into five categories, the earlier ones, apparently dating from the 16th century, being simpler in both structure and decoration, while the later ones are more elaborately ornamented.

There are as many as 25 *chibhāḥs* in Kirtipur, most of them established in the 19th and 20th century. Dated examples include the one in front

Plate 89 North-west entrance to Loṇ Degaḥ flanked by guardian lions and Mahākāla.

Plate 90 The interior of Loṅ Degaḥ showing the place of the missing images.

of the Chilaṅcho Stupa, of 1040/1920 (Figure 29 no. 19, Plate 4), and the one in Lāyaku installed in 1082/1962. The Lāyaku *chibhāḥ* is of white Godavārī marble, and as far as we know is the only one of its kind in the valley.

## BUDDHIST ŚIKHARA TEMPLES

The *śikhara* temples in Kirtipur are in the *devagala* part of the town, and are built of blocks of stone assembled without mortar, and have wooden doors. Unlike in many other places, the *śikhara* temples of Kirtipur are associated with the Buddhists, and house images of Śākyamuni Buddha.

### LOṄ DEGAḤ (BUDDHA DHARMA SAṄGHA)

The larger of the *śikhara* temples in Kirtipur is dedicated to the Tri-ratna (Buddha, Dharma and Saṅgha) and is known as Loṅ Degaḥ, meaning the stone temple (Figure 30, Plate 88). It stands at the intersection of three roads coming from Baku Nanī, from the north-east and from the Chilaṅcho Stupa. The temple is set on a plinth in three levels, and has a pair of guardian lions and two guardian deities (*mahākāla*) flanking the steps which lead to the entrance on the north-eastern side (Plate 89). On the eastern side of the entrance on the lowest level of the platform is an inscription[26] which gives the following information:

> "Loṅ Degaḥ was built in 784/1664 by a Bajrāchārya. It took one year to complete the temple which was started in Kārttik 784 and completed in the same month of the following year. The temple was built in *granthakuta* style, and the final ritual was held in Paush 785, two months after the completion of the temple. The ceremony was attended by the King of Patan, Śrinivās Malla. There was a solar eclipse on that day."

Another inscription (Apx. A, no. 30) on the entablature of the façade, has Sanskrit *slokas* in praise of Śākyamuni Buddha, his consort, and his mother.

The temple is square in plan, and consists of a

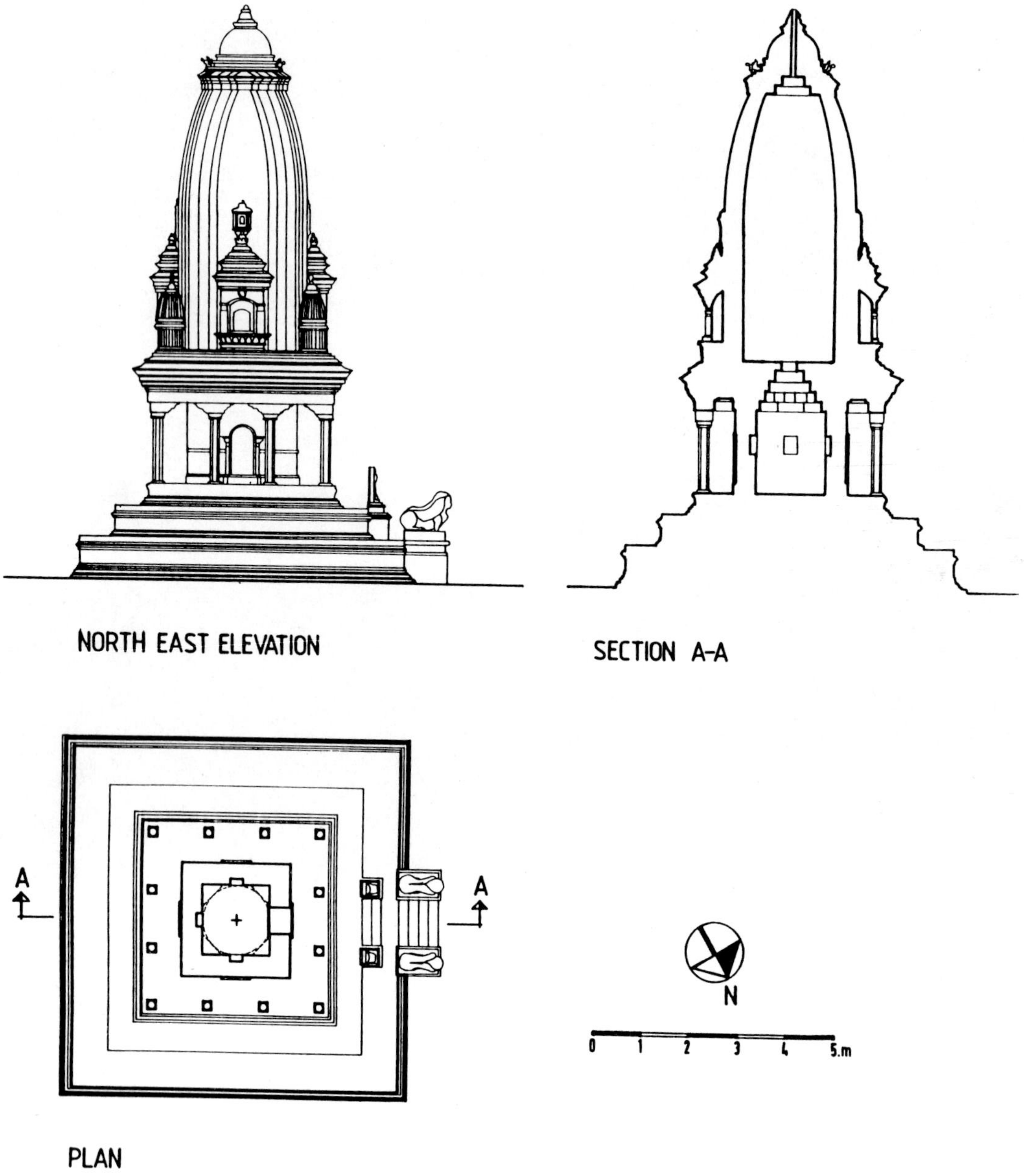


Figure 30 Loṅ Degaḥ (Buddha Dharma Saṅgha), plan, section and north-east elevation.

central chamber with an entrance to the north-east. The entrance has an upper and a lower niche on either side. There are blind arches on the other three sides, again flanked by niches. The chamber is surrounded by a colonnade of 12 columns, which supports an entablature, and in turn the tower, crowned by a gilt pinnacle. The capitals of the columns and the entablature have small carved niches with images of deities. Around the base of the tower, which has the characteristic slightly bowed profile, are shrines on each face in the form of projecting windows, with smaller niches above, and on each corner is a miniature *śikhara*. The ceiling of the chamber is corbelled, leaving only a small gap in the centre. There are no steps on the interior (Plate 90) to give access to the inside of the tower, but there is a small opening in the centre of the ceiling of the shrine. The top of the tower also has a narrow shaft, open to the sky.

The temple formerly housed images of Śākyamuni Buddha, Pragya Devī, and Padmapāṇi Avalokiteśvara. In the years between 1979 and 1982 all the images were stolen and were never recovered, leaving the temple empty. The temple, however, incorporates some fine carving (Plate 91), including the *toraṇa* or arch over the main entrance, which is embellished with figures of the Pañchā Dhyānī Buddhas. The *dharma chakra mudrā* of Bairochana is shown in an unusual form

Plate 91 Loṅ Degaḥ, guardian deity on the exterior.

Plate 92 Tree shrine in Sinaduvā Ṭol housing an image of Lokeśvar.

with the forefingers crossed and the palms facing inwards. The niches of this façade of the chamber have a Gaṇeś and a Mahākāla in the lower niches, and Dhyānī Buddhas above. The other façades of the chamber have Mahākālas in the lower niches, and Dhyānī Buddhas in the upper ones, arranged according to iconographic requirements. The projecting shrines above the entablature have Bairochana and Dhyānī Buddhas, and the small *śikharas* on the corners each have a figure in the *yogapaṭṭāsana* posture.

The present condition of the temple up to the level of the entablature is fairly good, but above the entablature a heavy growth of weeds and lichens is damaging the stonework. The maintenance of the temple is the responsibility of the Gūṭhī Saṃsthān.

## ŚĀKYAMUNI BUDDHA MANDIR

The Śākyamuni Buddha Mandir (Figure 31, Plate 93), the smaller stone *śikhara* temple of Kirtipur, is situated in Sinaduvā Ṭol to the south-east of the Chilaṅcho Stupa. It houses an icon of Śākyamuni Buddha (Plate 143), discussed in this report together with the antiquities. An inscription (Apx. A, no. 6) beside the icon informs us that the construction was completed in 769/1649 in the month of Māgha Dvādasi and the image of Śākyamuni was installed with the performance of the twelve fire sacrifices to achieve that which was destined (*lachhyāhuti dvadasa agni kriya*). In addition there were five different musical sounds (*paṅchāśvara bādyadhārā*), and the different dances performed. The kings of Patan, Siddhi Narasiṃha Malla and Śrīnivās Malla were present during the ceremony. The inscription further mentions that all these ceremonies were performed when these two kings were ruling Patan together, and that the temple was donated by Dānapati Śākyavamsa Hākuju, who also established the nearby Harshakīrti Mahāvihār (Chhve Bāhā).

The temple is built of stone, but the tower is brick clad with blocks of stone, rather than solid stone. The building stands on a platform in two

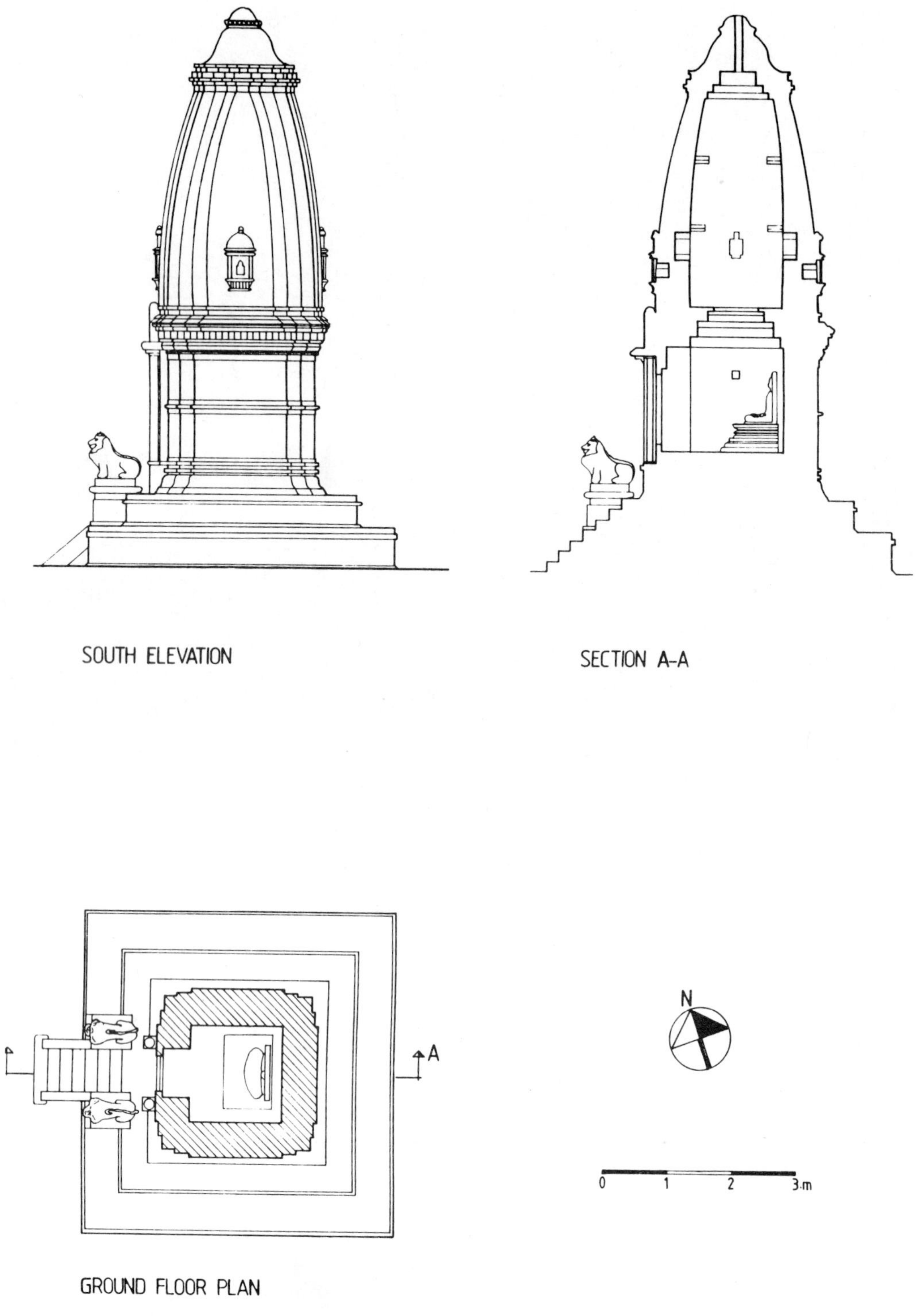


Figure 31 Śākyamuni Buddha Mandir, plan, section A-A, and south elevation.

tiers, and has a single entrance with octagonal monolithic columns reached by a flight of steps on the north-west side, flanked by a pair of stone lions. The façade of the lower part of the temple is divided into two registers by a moulding and carved borders, but is relatively plain. The tower is four sided with a slightly bowed profile, and is topped by a bell shaped cap, with a rounded finial. There is a decorative niche in the form of a window on each side of the tower. The interior (Plate 94) of the temple consists of a single square chamber with a corbelled ceiling; the

Plate 93 Śakyamuni Buddha Mandir, completed in 1649, from the north.

Plate 94 Interior of the Śakyamuni Buddha Mandir showing the structure of the tower.

brickwork of the tower can be seen through an opening in the centre. Unlike Loṅ Degaḥ the temple has no circumambulatory path on the platform, and people circumambulate on the pavement. The temple is fairly well preserved, but as with Loṅ Degaḥ, weeds and bushes have taken root in the structure of the upper level.

### LOKEŚVAR TEMPLE

A large sacred pipal tree in Sinaduvā Ṭol has a platform around it with steps leading to a shrine inside the trunk of the tree (Plate 92). The shrine houses an image of Lokeśvar, and a stone inscription informing us that the temple was built by Gunajyoti Śākya in 1683, and consecrated in the name of Hākuju and his wife, who became *satī*, immolated on her husband's funeral pyre. The donors were the sons of the deceased. Hākuju was also responsible for the erection of the Śākyamuni Buddha Mandir and the Chhve Bāhā. The steps of the Lokeśvara shrine are guarded by a pair of stone lions, and it appears that the shrine was once a building, now destroyed by the tree.

## PUBLIC REST HOUSES

A feature of Kirtipur, in common with other Newar towns, is its numerous public rest houses built in the squares and streets. They are mainly of two different types. The more common type is known as a *pāṭi* or *phalechā* which is a single storeyed roofed platform. The other type, known as *sattal* always has more than one storey, usually two. Both types are present in Kirtipur, although of the second type there is only one probable example preserved.

### PĀṬIS

A *pāṭi* takes the form of a rectangular brick platform floored with planks and roofed by a pitched roof supported by a row of wooden columns open to the streets and courtyards. The rear wall is provided with a niche for images. As well as providing shelter for travellers, they are used by the neighbourhood as a meeting place, and place for everything from the singing of ritual songs to card playing. Straw is stored in the *pāṭis* during the wheat harvest, women use them to do their laundry when it rains, elderly people sit and chat in them and children play, while the space underneath serves as a home for street dogs. A *pāṭi* may be constructed for the public by a group of householders of a particular *ṭol*, a *gūṭhī* or an individual person.

There are dozens of *pāṭis* in Kirtipur, as well as in the fields, near roads, cross roads, wells, ponds, and in the vicinity of temples and shrines

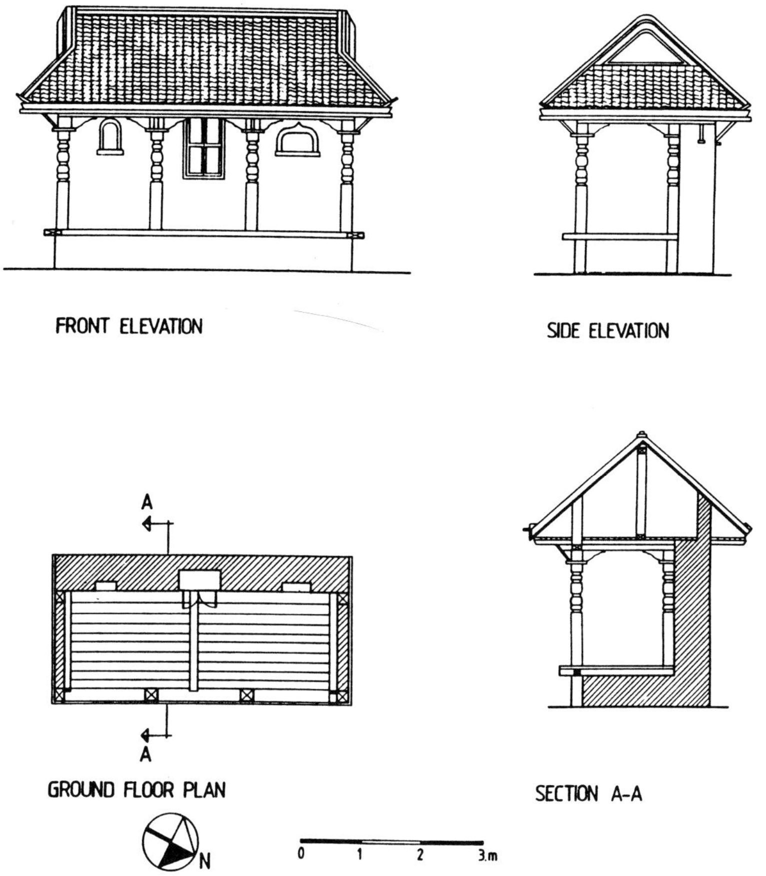


Figure 32 Pāṭi in Tanani, plan, section A-A, and front and side elevations (Survey by M. Barani and S. S. Shrestha).

all over the Kathmandu Valley. The lay out of the *pāṭis* in Kirtipur varies according to the space available, and the needs of the neighbourhood. They can be free standing or attached to buildings, and different Newari names are used for the various types. *Yāka phale* is the commonly found free standing form seen in Tanani Pāṭi, shown on our drawing (Figure 32, Plate 85). *Pāṭis* set in the corner of a square, such as the one in Dabujho Ṭol are known as *kuṅ phale*, the large *pāṭis* set against the enclosure walls of Bāgh Bhairav would be described as *tāhā phale*, while those set against a house, such as the *pāṭi* housing the Gaṇeś image in Pāliphal Ṭol, are known as *lidhan phale*. There is also a type known in Newari as *dhamā phale*, but no examples of this type have survived and their past existence is only known from manuscript records. No one, however, has been able to give us information on the layout and function of a *dhamā phale*.

At each end of Kirtipur there is also a type of *pāṭi* called *manda phalechā*, one in Sāgāl Ṭol, and one in Amalshi, now Naya Bāzār. This type has sixteen pillars, is open on all sides, and has a drinking water tank (*jarū hiti*) with a tap for travellers to quench their thirst. The tanks were traditionally kept full by the *gūṭhīs*. The author was informed by an elderly man of the town, Satya Lal Bhansāli, that these *pāṭis* were used as a halting place for porters, and as the place for the collection of customs duties levied on goods passing through Kirtipur, which was on the trade route connecting the towns of the valley with India and Tibet. The informant is a member of the *bhansāli* cast (custom collectors) and a descendant of the local revenue collector.

The practice of building new *pāṭis* seems to have ceased, and the ones that still exist have in some cases lost their multiple public functions and have been appropriated for use as police offices, primary schools, health clinics, guardians quarters, and even for housing high tension electricity transformers. In addition some have been taken over for use as club houses by groups of young people who have carried out renovations. The *pāṭis* are also in many cases taken over by private house holders. There were once more than a hundred *pāṭis* in the town, and many of the free standing examples are still in use. However, those attached to dwellings have in many cases been appropriated by the owners of the houses, who have gradually encroached on the *pāṭi* by building an upper floor with a door through to the dwelling, and after 20 or 30 years claiming ownership of the whole structure.

## SATTALS

The usual type of two storeyed *sattal* consists of a timber colonnade on a brick platform with one or more chambers above. The function of the colonnaded platform below is similar to that of a *pāṭi*, but the upper floor traditionally provided shelter for travellers and those in need of temporary housing, such as *gurus* and *sādhus*. *Sattals* are usually located near the gates or main temples and squares of a town but they never existed in great numbers. With the changes in the traditional lifestyle *sattals* have lost their original function and many have been taken over by townspeople.

In Kirtipur there is a *sattal* now occupied by the *jogīs* and its building is no longer in its original form. However its original function is still clear and is reflected in its present name, Satako which is a derivation of the word *sattal*. Another probable example in Kirtipur is located at the east side of the Deu Ḍhokā gate. The elderly people of Kirtipur do not refer to this structure as a *sattal* and consider it as a *loṅ phalechā* (stone *pāṭi*). They mention that there were two *pāṭis* at either side of Deu Ḍhokā gate. One was this *loṅ phalechā*, and the other a *sī phalechā* (wooden *pāṭi*) opposite (Plate 19). This wooden *pāṭi* still survives in its original form.

The building known as the *loṅ phalechā* is in two storeys, and the upper chamber appears to have been reconstructed and is now attached to an extension of a neighbouring house. In spite of the name, the building has a timber structure and from the exposed timber above the lower colonnade it appears that the chamber may have been in the form of a wooden structure with fretwork screens, but nothing of the original structure of the upper level has survived and the present roof of the upper chamber is also in need of repair. The colonnade below has, however, retained its function, and is the main gathering place of the people of the neighbourhood, as the *sī phalechā* opposite is now used as a dispensary.

We have already noted that some of the old *pāṭis* have been taken over by the townspeople, and upper floors added to them. It is, therefore possible to assume that this building was also a *pāṭi*, but as its levels do not correspond with the adjoining house it is more probable that the building was originally a *sattal*. Its location near one of the gates of the town is also another indication that it is a *sattal*, as the site is an appropriate one for such a building.

## NOTES

1 Carl Pruscha, *A Protective Inventory*, Vienna, 1975, 66, 118-9, 262-5.
2 Alice Boner and Sadāśiva Rath Śarmā, *Śilpa Prakāśa: Medieval Orissan Sanskrit Text on Temple Architecture*, Leiden, 1966, introduction p. 38.
3 D. R. Regmi, *Mediaeval Nepal*, III, Calcutta, 1966, 102-103.
4 Hari Ram Joshi, "*Kirtipurko stapana*", *Madhuparka*, VIII, no. x, 1976, 7.
5 D. R. Regmi, op. cit., III, 100-102.
6 Ibid., IV, 35.
7 Sukra Sagar Shrestha, *Three mediaeval inscriptions from Kathmandu*, Nepalese Culture, IV, no. 4, 1984, 57.
8 The inscription is attached to the side of the tynpanum, and has not been published.
9 The inscription is on the pedestal and has not been published.
10 The inscription is on the entrance and has not been published.
11 D. R. Regmi, op. cit., IV, 300.
12 Bajracharya Dhana Bajra, *Shahkalin Abhilekh*, Kirtipur, VE 2037 (1980), 360.
13 The inscription is unpublished and the information is given from a reading carried out on site.
14 The inscription on the flag is unpublished and the information is given from a reading made on site.
15 Eugenio Galdieri, Nepal: Campaign held between September 1985 and January 1986, Report of Centro di Studi Storici e per la Conservazione dei Monumenti, *East and West*, XXXV, vi, 1985, 500-503.
16 Lain Simha Bangdel, *Early Sculpture of Nepal*, New Delhi, 1982, 66.
17 Hari Ram Joshi, "*Kirtipur Umā Maheśvara mandirstit Sarasvatī ek adhyayana*", *Prachin Nepal*, no. 21 (Kārttik VE 2029) 1972, 56.
18 Ronald M. Bernier, *The Temples of Nepal*, Kathmandu, 1970 revised New Delhi, 1978, 144-5.
19 Information given to the author in 1984 by Birananda Joshi of Kirtipur, who had been the *dvāre* (keeper) at the time of the damage on Jestha 4 of that year.
20 E. P. Davies et al., *Kirtipur, a Newar Community in Nepal, Development in Debate*, Kirtipur Programme, Bristol, 1979-80, 11, shows a photograph of Umā Maheśvara before restoration.
21 H. Ambrose Oldfield, *Sketches of Nepal*, London, 1880, reprinted New Delhi, 1981, 129.
22 Manuscript in the possession of Tuyu Bahadur Maharjan of Salichhen Ṭol.
23 Hem Naj Śākya, *Nepal sanakritiya mulukha*, Lalitpur, 1089/1969, 117.
24 Ibid., 4; D. R. Regmi, op. cit., III, 102-3.
25 Alexander W. Macdonald and Anne Vergati Stahl, *Newar Art: Nepalese Art during the Malla Period*, New Delhi, 1979, 144.
26 Reading by the author from a rubbing of the inscription made by CNAS in 1979-80 for the Bristol University Kirtipur Programme team.

# TIERED TEMPLES OF KIRTIPUR, A STUDY OF THEIR FORM AND PROPORTION

SUDARSHAN RAJ TIWARI

Although the township of Kirtipur was settled by king Śivadeva II, its history as a fortified temple site is probably much older. The layout of the town shows a strong connection with religious planning ideas, and it is possibly the only town planned in the Malla period where a segregation of the Buddhist and Hindu sectors was attempted (Figure 8). However, if we consider the street layout, it is clear that the two sectors are fully integrated into a plan reminiscent of a city laid out on Vedic rules: three parallel streets in both the north-south and the east-west directions, crossing each other within the area bounded by the roads around the edge of the settlement.

The major religious determinants of the town as a whole also follow Hindu principles, for example the locations of Śiva, Vishṇu, Gaṇeś and Śaktī Pīṭhs are symmetrically distributed in both the *Śivagala* (Hindu) and *Devagala* (Buddhist) sectors.[1] Here we are concerned only with the cosmological aspects of the tiered temples of Umā Maheśvara and Bāgh Bhairav, and the system used for achieving the proportions of the structures. However, there was formerly at least one other tiered temple in Kirtipur, the Nārāyaṇ temple, now roofed with a dome (Plate 71) from the time of the renovations by Bhīm Shumsher Rānā (1928-32). In the Gutapau area the local people also believe a nine storeyed temple existed in the distant past, a tradition which is worthy of closer investigation, as remains of wide foundations are commonplace in this area.

## UMĀ MAHEŚVARA TEMPLE

The Umā Maheśvara Temple (Plate 20) is sited just below the highest point of the town, the highest spot being reserved for Taleju Chhe, the abode of the clan goddess of the Malla kings. The temple has suffered earthquake and storm damage over the years, and it is said that long after the damage in 1833 it was rebuilt in four tiers by Bhim Shumsher Rānā. After the 1934 earthquake it was again repaired, this time with a three tiered corrugated iron roof, and the renovations of 1982 incorporating tiled roofs retain this form. Only the core wall of the sanctum level, its carved doors and the images inside are true to original, the upper levels having all been rebuilt. The paved courtyard, the multi-staged plinth, the gate to the complex, and the guardian elephants (Plate 63), as well as the images of Kubara and Bhairav also appear to be in the original form. The earliest dated icon was established in 1655, and it can be assumed that the temple was built some time before that date. Based on the parts that we can be reasonably sure are in the same proportions as the original building, and records such as Oldfield's drawing (Figure 6) we can consider what the original form would have been.

The temple is square in plan with a colonnaded circumambulatory at the level of the sanctum, with five bays on each side. The original outer wall above the colonnade has been replaced by a balconied floor with a plain railing, the original railings having been lost or reused elsewhere, as we have seen earlier in this report with regard to the struts reused in the Gaṇeś Temple in Dabujho Ṭol (p. 96). The three carved windows shown in Oldfield's sketch have been replaced by a central door, an element not used in the upper part of any other temple of this style. The inner sanctum wall, which continued upwards to take the second roof, also had three carved windows, now replaced by one plain window frame for the first floor. The width of this wall seems to be true to original, but the finial of the third roof is too small in proportion to the rest of the building to be so.

The building adheres to the principals of a *maṇḍala* plan, as can be seen from the sides of the three temple plinths being in the ratio 34:28:23. The sanctum colonnade is accordingly 18. The core wall exhibits a ratio of 3:5 to the sanctum colonnade, and the *cella* exhibits the ratio of 1:2 to the inner core wall. On the basis of

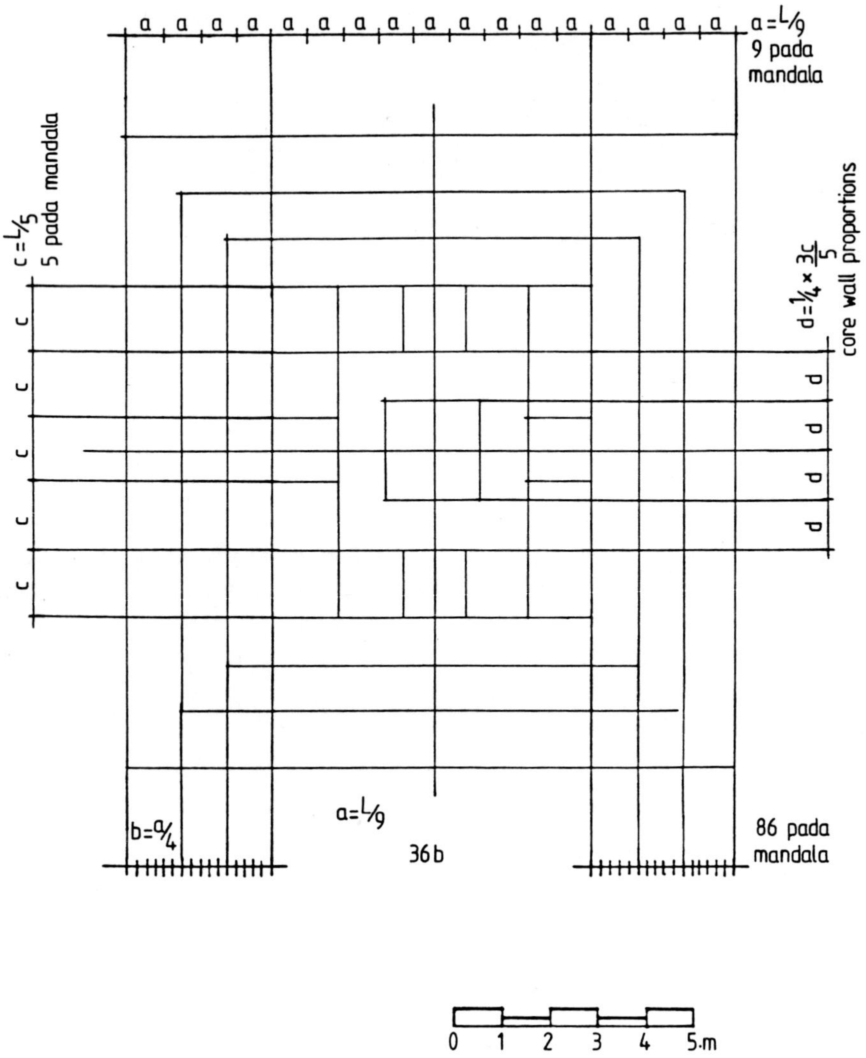


Figure 33 Umā Maheśvara, *maṇḍala* plan and *sūtras* (S. R. Tiwari)

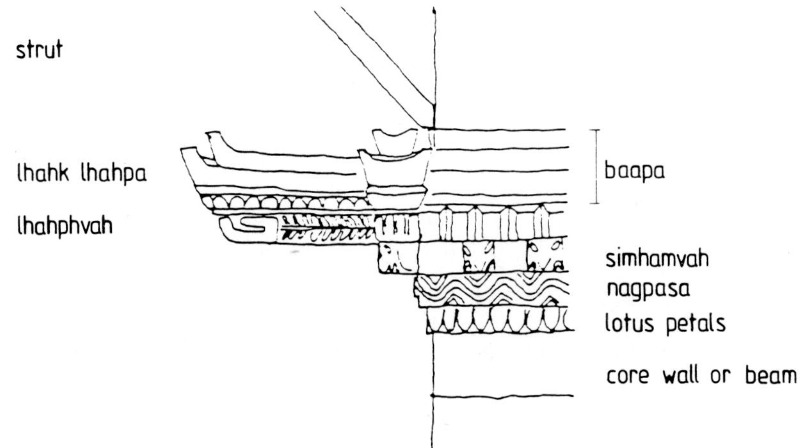


Figure 34 Detail of missing strut from Umā Maheśvara (S. R. Tiwari)

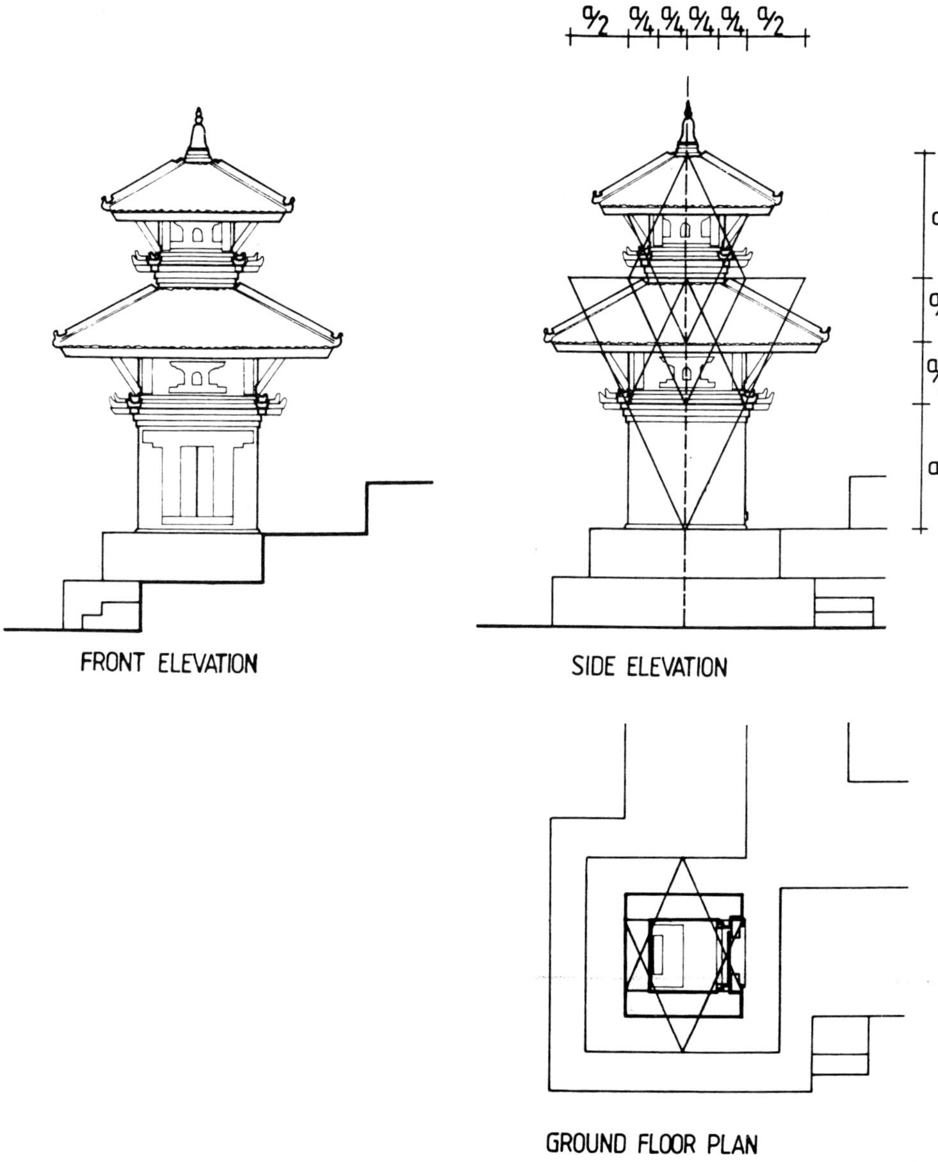


Figure 35 Nārāyaṇ Degaḥ (after W. Korn), showing proportioning triangles.

this a plan *maṇḍala* can be drawn (Figure 33). The ratio of the three plinths suggest that the *maṇḍala* used in this context is a 36 *pāda* (square) *maṇḍala* (representing Śiva and Śaktī, or 3 x 2 or $2^2$ by $3^2$) as only on this basis can the proportioning lines (*vīṇāyasūtras*) for the plinths be established.

That the upper part of the current structure is not original can be seen from a number of missing or misrepresented elements. From a study of other temples of the time, as well as earlier examples built in the tiered style, such missing elements can be listed.

(a) None of the levels have the usual course of moulded brick (*bāapā* type *mvaḥapā* and *khālapā*) immediately below the take off point of the struts. These courses usually have dog-eared bricks (*lhāḥkā lhāḥpā*) supported by the fisted hand element (*lhāḥphvaḥ*) at the four corners of the building. Immediately below such a course of bricks there would typically be a projecting course with a band of lion faces (*sīṃhamvaḥ*), and below it the *nāgapāsa* band and lotus petal bands, but all these elements have been omitted. This greatly affects the proportions of the temple. If we examine the length (1.93 m.) of the two struts reused in the Gaṇeś temple we see that such a band would be needed, and the angle between the strut and the wall would be more than the present angle (Figure 34).

(b) At the sanctum level, instead of the outer core wall, which would normally be built above these decorated courses and finish under the first roof, there is an open verandah, and no sign of the three windows on each façade shown in Oldfield's sketch.

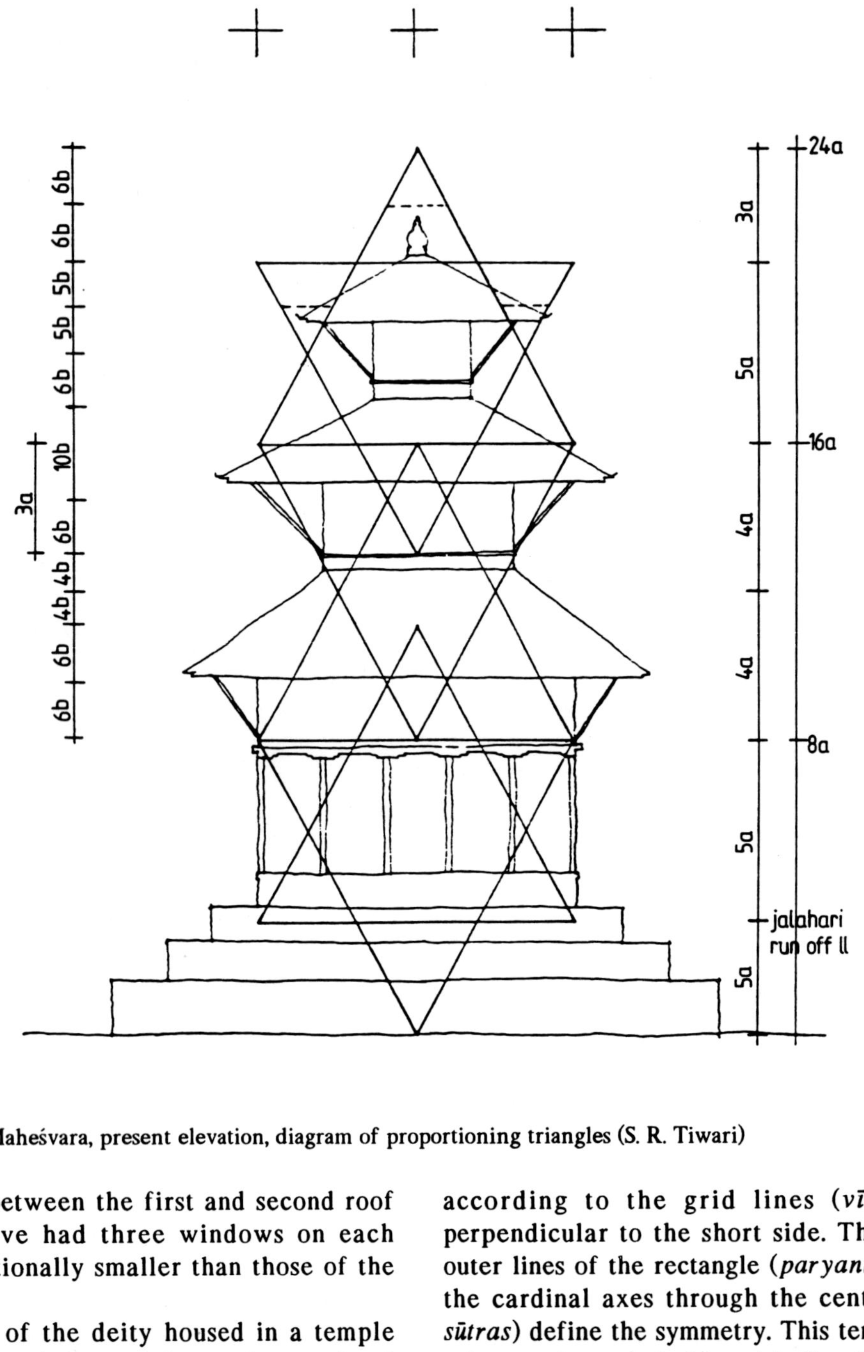


Figure 36 Umā Maheśvara, present elevation, diagram of proportioning triangles (S. R. Tiwari)

(c) The wall between the first and second roof would also have had three windows on each façade, proportionally smaller than those of the lower level.

The nature of the deity housed in a temple and the number of tiers of the roof are related factors, and other temples dedicated to Umā Maheśvara elsewhere in the valley, the Bhagavatī Temple at Nālā[2] (Plate 95) to the east of Bhaktapur, and the Harisiddhi Bhavānī Temple[3] (Plate 96) at the village of Harisiddhi five kilometres south of Patan, indicate that four tiers would have been needed for the Kirtipur temple.[4] There is, however, a one-tiered temple dedicated to Umā Maheśvara in Khauma Ṭol, Bhaktapur. The Nālā Bhagavatī Temple is rectangular in plan, and the lower two roofs are proportioned on the basis of the grid lines perpendicular to long side, and the upper two roofs are proportioned according to the grid lines (*vīṇāyasūtras*) perpendicular to the short side. The containing outer lines of the rectangle (*paryantasūtras*) and the cardinal axes through the centre (*pramān-sūtras*) define the symmetry. This temple also has a long colonnaded side with five bays, and the inner core wall parallel to the long side exhibits a ratio of 3:5 to the outer colonnade.

The other four tiered temple, the Harisiddhi temple, has all the Bhavānīs as well as Śaṅkar dedicated to it and housed inside. The temple is square in plan and the sanctum is on the first floor. Some of the elderly inhabitants of Kirtipur think of the multiple plinth of Umā Maheśvara as a lower floor below the sanctum level. The design of Harisiddhi[5] appears to be based on a 32 *pāda maṇḍala* in which 32 is $2^5$, and further study of this temple would be likely to shed more light on the original form of Umā Maheśvara.

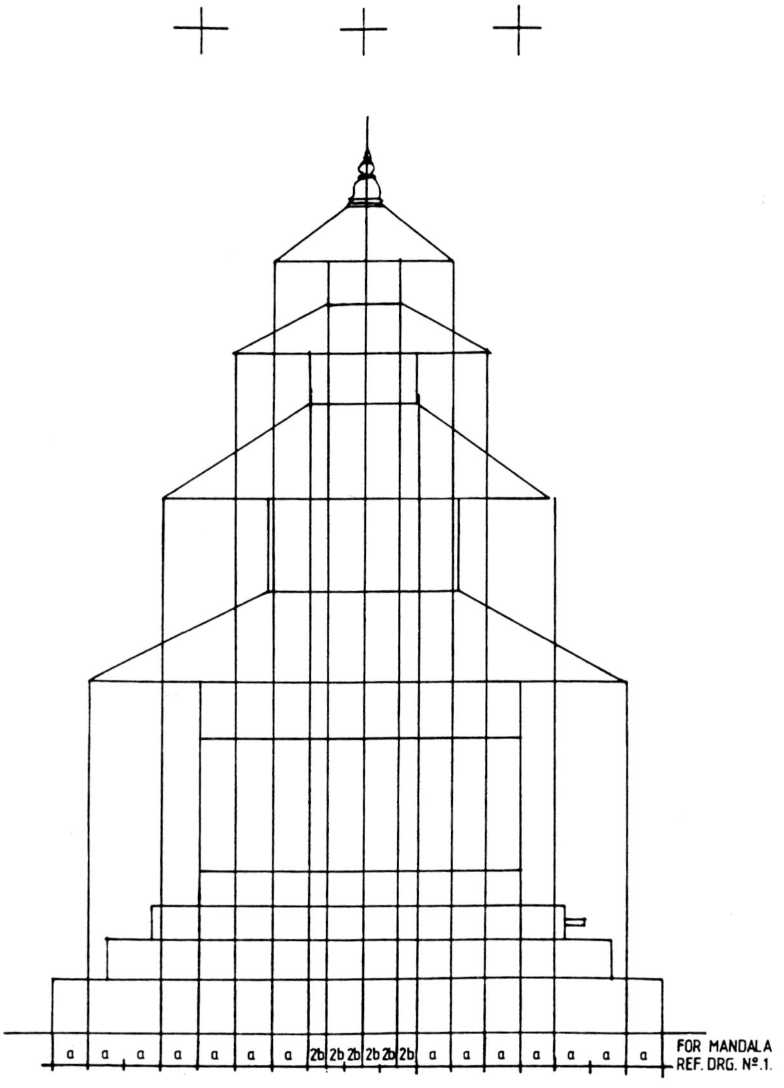


Figure 37 Umā Maheśvara, diagram of vertical proportions of the original form of the temple (S. R. Tiwari)

The Hindu precepts relating to the proportion of plan and elevation in temples can be found in many ancient scriptures. The temples type I and III described in the *Matsyapurāṇa* are significant for the study of Nepalese temples, as it is known that the height of most tiered temples in Nepal is 3$y$ where $y$ is a variant of the width of the outer wall or colonnade of the sanctum floor ($x$). The exact relation of $y$ to $x$ is controlled by the nature of the division of the *maṇḍala*.

An anonymous manuscript,[6] outlining the steps to be taken for the repair and maintenance of a temple, clearly shows the use of three proportioning triangles to arrive at the correct proportions for the elevation. The accuracy of the system given in the manuscript can be seen when it is applied to existing temples such as Nārāyaṇ Degaḥ (Figure 35) at Tripureśvar, Kathmandu[7] which completely follows the dictates of the *Matsyapurāṇa*. Even the *cella* (*prāsāda*) is an exact cube, and the height of the first tier of the roof structure is twice the width of the *cella*. The height of this proportioning triangle is not, however, universally equal to $x$.

Study of other extant temples indicates that the ratio of the height of the triangle to the length of the *paryantasūtra* can vary from 9:9 to 8:9, 7:9, 6:7 or 4:5, depending on the divisions of the plan *maṇḍala*. However, the lower inverted triangle always reaches up to the level of the *lhāḥphvaḥ*. The simple principal (*sāmānya paddhatī*) for the wall thickness of the sanctum floor, which according to the *Matsyapurāṇa* is a quarter of the *prāsāda* width, is also followed, making the wall thickness one fourth of the length of the *paryantasūtra*, and the sanctum room a square whose side is one half of the length of the *paryantasūtra*.

The proportioning principal of the Umā Maheśvara Temple can be arrived at by imposing

Plate 95 Bhagavatī Temple at Nālā (S. R. Tiwari).

Plate 96 The four tiered Harisiddhi Bhavānī Temple at Harisiddhi (S. R. Tiwari).

such triangles over a drawing of the elevation of the temple (Figure 36). The lower portion only is considered, as the authenticity of the proportions of the upper structure is not certain. Because the *sīṃhamvaḥ* and *lhāphvaḥ* bands have been left out in the renovations, the height of the proportioning triangles has to be assumed. For this reason the height of the triangle was calculated on the basis of various possible ratios of height to width: 9:9, 8:9, 7:9, 6:7 and 4:5, so that the most likely one could be chosen.

As the usual height of the element from the top of the column capital (*metha*) to the top of *sīṃhamvaḥ* is between 381 to 535 mm., the only possible ratios would be 9:9 and 8:9 (which give a height of 6.86 m. and 6.10 m.) as the other ratios give heights (5.33 m., 5.49 m., and 5.87 m. respectively) which allow less than 230 mm. for the *sīṃhamvaḥ* band. From the details of the door it can be concluded that the position of the *metha* is correct, and cannot be lower than at present. A ratio of 9:9 gives a space of 1.22 m. for the *sīṃhamvaḥ* band, and 8:9 gives 460 mm., which is nearer to what would be expected, and indicates that 6.10 m. would be the height of the proportioning triangle of the temple. If this is indeed the case, the height of the temple to the base of the finial (*gajū*) would be 2.44 m. higher than the present structure. This would correspond to a correctly proportioned four tiered temple with four bands of *sīṃhamvaḥ* and other decoration. Based on this triangle the possible elevation is illustrated (Figure 37), the width of the roofs being based on the plan *maṇḍala*, and the levels of the elements being decided on the basis of the points where the triangles intersect.

## BĀGH BHAIRAV TEMPLE

Bāgh Bhairav, the other extant tiered temple of Kirtipur, may be one of the oldest sites on the hillock. Although it now occupies a central place, in earlier times it could have been at the north-east corner of the settlement, the location most suited to Śiva according to the ancient scriptures. References to Bāgh Bhairav as Guṅ De Jhavā Dya indicate its pre-Lichhavi importance, but the current name is found almost as early as the establishment of Kirtipur, although it is not clear what sort of a structure the temple had. As

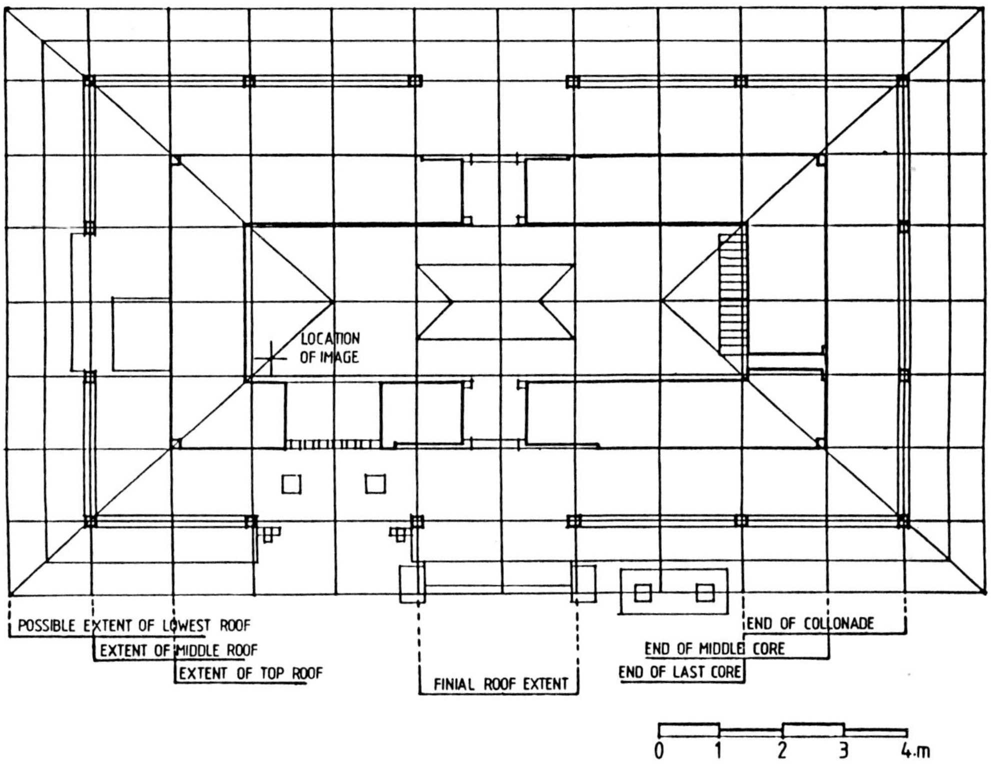


Figure 38 Bāgh Bhairav Temple, plan and *maṇḍala* (S. R. Tiwari)

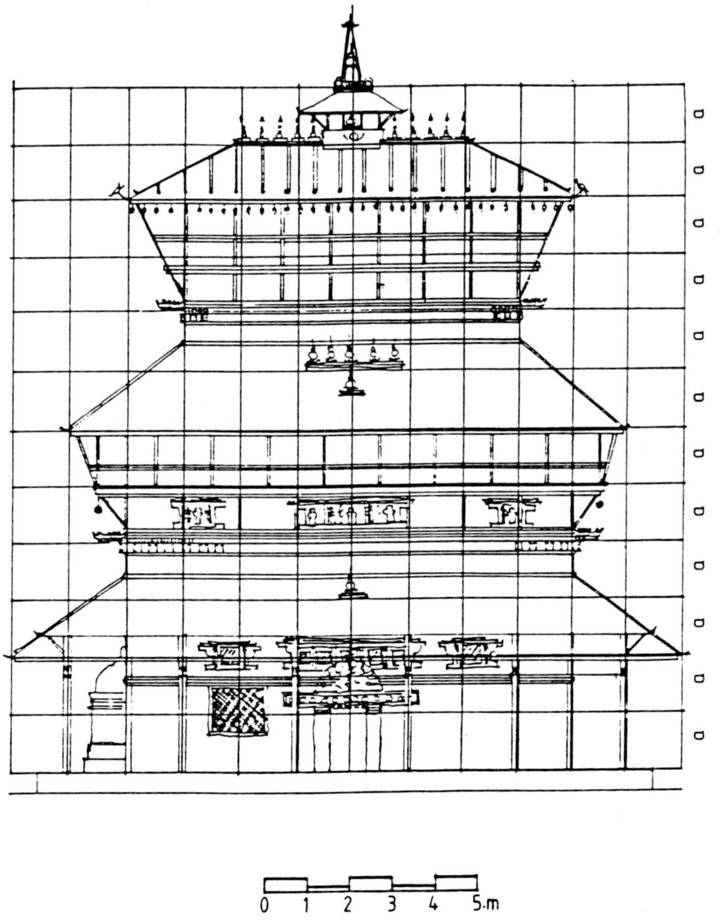


Figure 39 Bāgh Bhairav, sketch diagram of vertical proportions (S. R. Tiwari)

mentioned previously in this report the temple was restored in 1515, and we can assume that the original structure dates from well before this time.

The temple is rectangular in plan (Figure 38), which is typical in the Kathmandu Valley for Bhairava, Bhīmsen, and some Devī temples.[8] The current structure (Plate 48) has certainly remained unchanged since 1855, and is probably true to its form in 1515. Although the temple has a three tiered roof, the interior has four intermediate floors. A rectangular form for a temple is not seen in the ancient scriptures, and does not conform to the theoretical basis of the *vāstu purusha maṇḍala*. A rare example of a major temple in India with a rectangular sanctum is Vaitāl Deul of Bhubaneśvar (circa 800) which may possibly be a Bhairava temple. In the Kathmandu Valley the form is used for the Bhairava temples, with the exception of Tika Bhairav in Patan, and for the temples of Bhīmsen, with the exception of Hadigāoṅ Bhīmsensthan, Kathmandu. The same form is also used for Devī temples such as those known as Bhubaneśvari and Jayabhageśvari at Deupatan, and Nālā Bhagavatī and Bagkumārī of Patan.

It is possible that temples with a congregational pattern of worship such as those of Bhairava, or those housing gods with more human qualities such as Bhīmsen, or those dedicated to gods previously resident in royal palaces (*Bālakumārīs*) were all built on the pattern of human residences. Many of these temples also have other peculiarities such as a large number of finials (*gajū*) on each roof — Bāgh Bhairav has 18, the main sanctum being located on the first floor, as seen in Bhīmsensthan, Kathmandu and Patan, and Bhairavsthan, Bhaktapur, and walls dividing the ground floor as seen in Bhīmsensthan, Kathmandu, and Bhairavsthan, Bhaktapur.

The relationship between the sides of the rectangle is not uniform. The Indian example is 3:4, but this ratio is not evident in the examples in Kathmandu. In Bāgh Bhairav the colonnade is 5:9, the core wall is 4:9, and the cella of the sanctum is 3:9. According to the *Śilpa Prakāśa*[9] the Bhairav *yantra* has a proportion of 6:9 and this does correlate with Bāgh Bhairav. Some striking geometrical relations are worth noting here. The proportions of the three roofs are in a ratio of 4:5:6, the top, middle and colonnade of the core wall are in a ratio of 3:4:5. From these ratios it is possible to deduce the *maṇḍala* for Bāgh Bhairav. As the relationship of the side to the front of the temple appears to be based on 9 divisions, and that of the roofs to the core walls on 10 divisions, the minimum working measure for Bāgh Bhairav, taken by dividing the long side by 90, could be 140 mm. (one *kuret*).

It appears that the heights of the internal floors, which were not all accessible for measurement, are $3a$, $5a$, $7a$ and $9a$ in height from ground level ($a$ being one tenth of the long side of the building). The eaves of the first, second and third roofs are at heights of $2.5a$, $6a$ and $10a$, and the levels of the first *sīṃhamvaḥ*, the second *sīṃhamvaḥ*, and the top of the building are $4a$, $8a$ and $12a$ respectively. One may therefore conclude that the lowest roof has been reduced in size during renovations, to its current height of $2.5a$. The original height of the eaves from the design plane could well have been $2a$ (Figure 39). It is possible that the proportioning triangle used for this temple had a base width equal to three fifths of the length, and that the height of the triangle was two fifths of the length.

Of the three tiered temples of importance in Kirtipur, Bāgh Bhairav is probably nearest to its original form. Umā Maheśvara has been reduced in size and stripped of many decorative elements. The Nārāyaṇ Temple, originally a three storied tiered temple, was reconstructed inappropriately as a domical building. Fortunately the true proportions can still to a large extent be deduced based on the elements which remain.

## NOTES

1 Reinhard Herdick, *Kirtipur: Stadtgestalt, Prinzipien der Raumordnung und gesellschaftliche Funktionen einer Newarstadt*, Munich-Cologne-London, 1988, 96-102.

2 Ronald M. Bernier, *The Temples of Nepal, an introductory Survey*, New Delhi, 1970, rev. 1978, 144-8; S. R. Tiwari, The tiered temples, a cosmological overview, *Tribhuvan University Journal*, XI, i, 1980, 18-19.

3 *Physical Development Plan for the Kathmandu Valley*, HMG Nepal, Kathmandu, 1969, 150-51.

4 Idem.

5 Tiwari, op. cit., 16-18.

6 A photocopy of the manuscript is in the possession of the author and a microfilm of the manuscript is kept in the Archives of the Department of Archaeology, Kathmandu.

7 Wolfgang Korn, *The Traditional Architecture of the Kathmandu Valley*, Kathmandu, 1979, 72-3.

8 S. R. Tiwari, The non-conformist temples, *The Rising Nepal*, 30th November 1973.

9 Madhu Khanna, *Yantra, the Tantric Symbol of Cosmic Unity*, London, 1979.

# BUDDHIST MONASTERIES

NATALIE H. SHOKOOHY

In Kirtipur there are eight traditional Newar monasteries, the hereditary organization of which is associated with the monasteries of Patan. According to the *Pārbatiya*[1] in the early 17th century at the time of the Malla King Narasiṃha, the monasteries in the Kathmandu Valley were re-organized, and, as Kirtipur was at that time under the jurisdiction of Patan, the monasteries were also amalgamated with those of Patan. Buddhist monasteries are known in Nepal[2] as *bāhā* or *bahī*, both words derived from the Sanskrit *vihāra*. The word in its original form also appears in the Sanskrit texts of Nepal. The word *vihār* or *bihār*[3] is still used in more literary contexts and in Kirtipur it is usually given to the main monastery of the town, the Jagat Pāl Vihār. The terms *bāhā* and *bahī* referred in the past to two distinct types of institution, but their function is now very close, although people still distinguish them by name and there are usually some differences in the plans of the buildings. The Newars pay equal respect to the two types of monastery, but the administrators of the *bahīs* are regarded as being of a slightly inferior caste to those of the *bāhās*. On the grounds of a passage in the *Pārbatiya* concerning the description of the *vihāras* John Locke[4] suggests that the *bahīs* may be of more ancient origin than the *bāhās*, but while relics of some early rites and traditions still survive in the *bahīs*, the differences between the two types of institution are rapidly diminishing. In Kirtipur only one of the monasteries is a *bahī*.

Although the establishment of Buddhist monasteries goes back to the early days of Buddhism in India and Afghanistan, and the religious principles of monastic life are observed, with regional variations, in Buddhist countries from Tibet to South-East Asia and China, in Newar society the nature of the administration and the function of the monasteries has its own peculiarities. Each monastery is run by a *saṅgha*, a community of monks or sometimes a single monk, who unlike monks elsewhere in the Buddhist world is not celibate and who, together with his family observes the rites and daily rituals of his institution. The family also live in the monastery, and part of the monastery functions as a dwelling, not very different in its interior arrangement from any other house in the town. The *saṅgha* and his family constitute a *gūṭhī*, or kinship organization which traditionally retained agricultural land, the revenue of which was spent on the maintenance of the monastery and on holding the ceremonies and festivals.

During the last two centuries in the Kathmandu Valley in general, and in Kirtipur in particular, the revenue of the monasteries has diminished drastically. The decline of these institutions in Kirtipur is said to have been exacerbated by the Gurkha conquest of the town, as the new rulers had little inclination to support the institutions of the section of the population who were perceived to be out of sympathy with them. In the last decades social changes as well as the loss of the monasteries' lands to Tribhuvan University have further reduced the ability of the *saṅghas* to maintain the buildings, which are among the best examples of the traditional structures of the town. As a result the buildings are gradually decaying. In the case of the most important monastery, the Jagat Pāl Bāhā, the building was damaged in the earthquake of 1934, and was closed for many years. During the background study of the present report, between 1986 and 1988, a large part of the upper storey of the building collapsed.

Apart from the Jagat Pāl Vihār, the other monasteries of Kirtipur are the Kve Bāhā, the Chhve Bāhā, the Ikhā Bāhā, the Kusi Bāhā, the Yāka Bāhā, the Padmochcha Bāhā and the Chīthuṅ Bahī.[5] The architecture of these buildings is analogous but the extensive detailed wood carving varies according to the wealth and importance of the monastery in the past. The ground plans of the buildings follow the general layout of monasteries in the Valley, which in turn derive from the plans of ancient Buddhist monasteries. The foundations of such monasteries

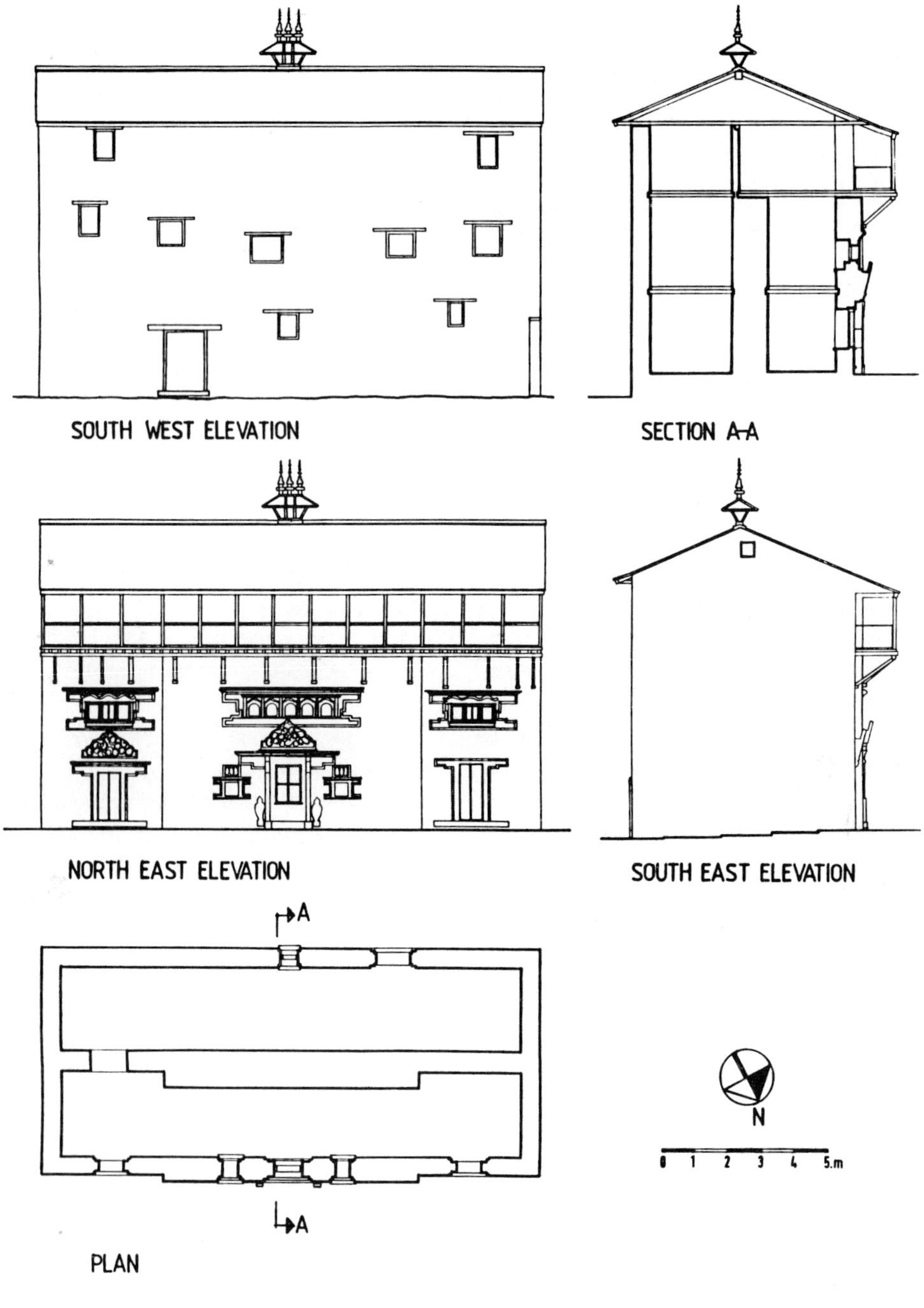


Figure 40 Jagat Pāl Vihār, plan, section and elevations.

have been excavated in many sites in Afghanistan such as Gul Darra[6] and Hadda,[7] and in the Indian sub-continent in places such as Nalanda,[8] Sarnath,[9] and Sāñchī.[10] These monasteries all share a common layout, consisting of a courtyard surrounded by a series of small cells in which the monks are thought to have resided. In addition there is usually a chamber opposite the main entrance, in the middle of one side of the courtyard, housing the main image of Lord Buddha. This chamber is regarded as the focal point of the monastery. The ancient monasteries are usually built near a sizable stupa, and in many cases have a large assembly hall with a *chaitya* built inside. Rock hewn versions of these halls are to be found associated with the *vihāras* in the caves at Aurangabad, Kanheri, Ajanta, Ellora, Karle and other sites in India.[11] These examples represent in stone the exquisite detailing of the timber and masonry supper-structure of ancient Buddhist buildings, of which only foundations have been found by archaeologists.

The monasteries of Kirtipur, although far less grandiose in scale than the monuments of the ancient world, still incorporate many features of the old tradition. Five of the monasteries are constructed in the area immediately surrounding the Chilañcho Stupa, while the other three are

Plate 97 Jagat Pāl Vihār, north-east façade in 1986 before repairs.

also near the stupa, and in the area of the old Buddhist town. Each monastery also has at least one *chaitya* set in the courtyard. The tradition of building a *chaitya* hall, has, however, been abandoned in Nepal since mediaeval times. The layout of the Nepalese monasteries still follows the ancient traditions in its arrangement around a courtyard, with the grander examples in the other old capitals of the valley.[12] In Kirtipur the courtyard can be found in all monasteries, and in at least four of them it was originally centrally located. The sanctum is referred to by the people of Kirtipur as the "god room", and is present in all monasteries except in Ikhā and Padmochcha, which, as we shall see, are said to have lost this chamber some time ago. The main non-Tantric deity is enshrined here, and is known as *kvāpā dya* (the guardian), in one of the forms of the Buddha, enthroned on a lotus and sometimes flanked by other deities. The courtyard and the sanctum are for public worship, and the door of the sanctum is mainly left open during the day. The public leave their offerings inside the sanctum through the door, but do not enter it. This right is preserved for the *saṅgha*, and sometimes a close member of his family only. The other rooms in the complex are used by the *saṅgha* and the members of his household, and are not accessible to the public. In the first floor is the *āgam chhen*, the private shrine for the Tantric deities of the *saṅgha*, with the *āgam*, a specific room for the images, and the *digi* or meeting room.

## JAGAT PĀL VIHĀR

The Jagat Pāl Vihār or Bāhā is also sometimes referred to as the Chilaṅcho Bāhā (Plate 97). The monastery is located to the south-west of the Chilaṅcho Stupa and its entrance is aligned with one of the axis of the main stupa. The people of Kirtipur regard it as the oldest Buddhist institution of the Valley, and claim that it originates from ancient times.[13] At the time of the reorganization of the *vihāras* of the Valley by Narasiṃha the Jagat Pāl Vihār was made one of the fifteen

Plate 98 Jagat Pāl Vihār, detail of the *toraṇa* over the northern entrance, and the window of the upper chamber.

Plate 99 The lower level of the south-east side of the platform of the Chilaṅcho Stupa, looking towards the rear of the three storeyed Ikhā (Sinaduvā) and Kve Bāhās. The *chaitya* dated 898/1778 (no. 10 in Figure 29) is on the left.

main monasteries of Patan, and today in Patan the Jagat Pāl Vihār is still referred to as Kyapu Bāhā, after the old name of Kirtipur. The formal Sanskrit name of the monastery is *Jagatpālavarma Saṃskārita Padmakāshṭha Giri Mahāvihāra*. The term *māhāvihār* (great monastery) is only given to the principal institution at the head of a number of branches, or to a single institution, much larger than usual. In the case of Kirtipur the *saṅghas* of all the other *bāhās* of the town are associated with that of Jagat Pāl. The existing monastic building is only the focal point, or the sanctum of *kvāpā dya*, with some associated chambers. The institution of the monastery, however, consists of a *saṅgha* of 128 *bajrāchāryas*, who are also responsible for the upkeep of the Chilaṅcho Stupa, and the performance of all the rituals associated with it. Only one person carries out the daily rituals, but a council of 10 members is responsible for governing the monastery.

The present building is a rectangular structure (Figure 40) in three storeys, in the form of a Newar house, with three doors at the ground level opening towards the stupa. The interior is divided into two long and narrow halls by means of a spinal wall, as is usual in Newar buildings. The first floor has a similar layout and has windows with fine carvings corresponding with the doors below. In the upper storey, instead of the spinal wall the ridge of the roof is supported by a series of columns, and there is a balcony, 1.20 m. wide running along of the whole of the front façade. Different parts of the building, however, appear to have been constructed at different times. The oldest part of the structure is the central front bay, which seems to have consisted originally of a small two storeyed building, with a single chamber at each floor. The probable back wall of this building, which is now the central part of the spine wall of the whole structure, is 1.20 m. thick, about twice the thickness of the other walls. Behind the building is now open ground or *khebā*, which may have been the courtyard of a much larger institution with many other buildings. The present building appears to have had a central door opening into the yard but it has been blocked, and beside it another door has been opened at a later date.

The Jagat Pāl Vihār is among the oldest and most important buildings of Kirtipur, and has preserved some very fine wood carvings. Two of the entrances to the building on the main façade have a *toraṇa* or decorative arch form set above the lintels, and decorated with coils of *makaras* (sea monsters) and figures of other deities. The *toraṇa* of the central entrance was made in 1031/1911 of copper plate, backed by wood, but that above the eastern door (Plate 98) is sculptured in wood and appears to be much older. The central entrance is reached by means of three steps flanked by two lions, one dated 837/1717, and the other 839/1719. The building itself, however, is at least a century earlier, some of the struts being dated 749/1629, among the earliest dates appearing on the monuments of the town. A major restoration to the building seems to have been carried out in around 800/1680, a date which appears on some of the other struts. Inside the building were preserved some of the important early bronze images to be found in Nepal. These sculptural pieces, dating from the 6th and 7th century AD, have now been taken to the National Museum of Nepal, and are noted in the chapter on the art and antiquities of the town, and in Appendices B and C.

The Jagat Pāl Vihār, damaged in the 1934 earthquake, was later restored. The lattice work of the upper storey and the present balcony seem to date from this time. However, the restoration was superficial, and major cracks in the building were left unrepaired, resulting in the gradual dilapidation of the structure which, as noted, is now unsafe and is left unused. The roof has lost all its tiles, which have been replaced by sheets of corrugated iron, and parts of the roof structure and timber floors have collapsed. Although the building had some basic repairs and was given a new roof of corrugated iron in 1989 it is perhaps a matter of urgency to carry out a scientific and appropriate restoration work on this important architectural monument, and the shrine of one of the oldest Buddhist establishments in Nepal.

### KVE BĀHĀ

In a complex of buildings situated to the south of the Chilaṅcho Stupa are situated three adjoining *bāhās* called Kve, Ikhā and Chhve Bāhā (Figures 41-2). The southern most monastery is the Kve Bāhā (meaning lower), the formal name of which is recorded in an inscription as Karṇātaka Mahāvihāra. The monastery (Plate 100) is constructed on three sides of a square courtyard, open at the north-east side to a small *khebā* leading into the courtyard of the Ikhā Bāhā. The *khebā*, however, is the site of an earlier building the foundations of which remain, and which once enclosed the courtyard of the Kve Bāhā. The entrance to the Bāhā is through a colonnade at the south-west (Plate 101), and the sanctum of *kvāpā dya* is on the north-western side of the courtyard.

Until recently the main income of this Bāhā was from the agricultural fields to the east of the

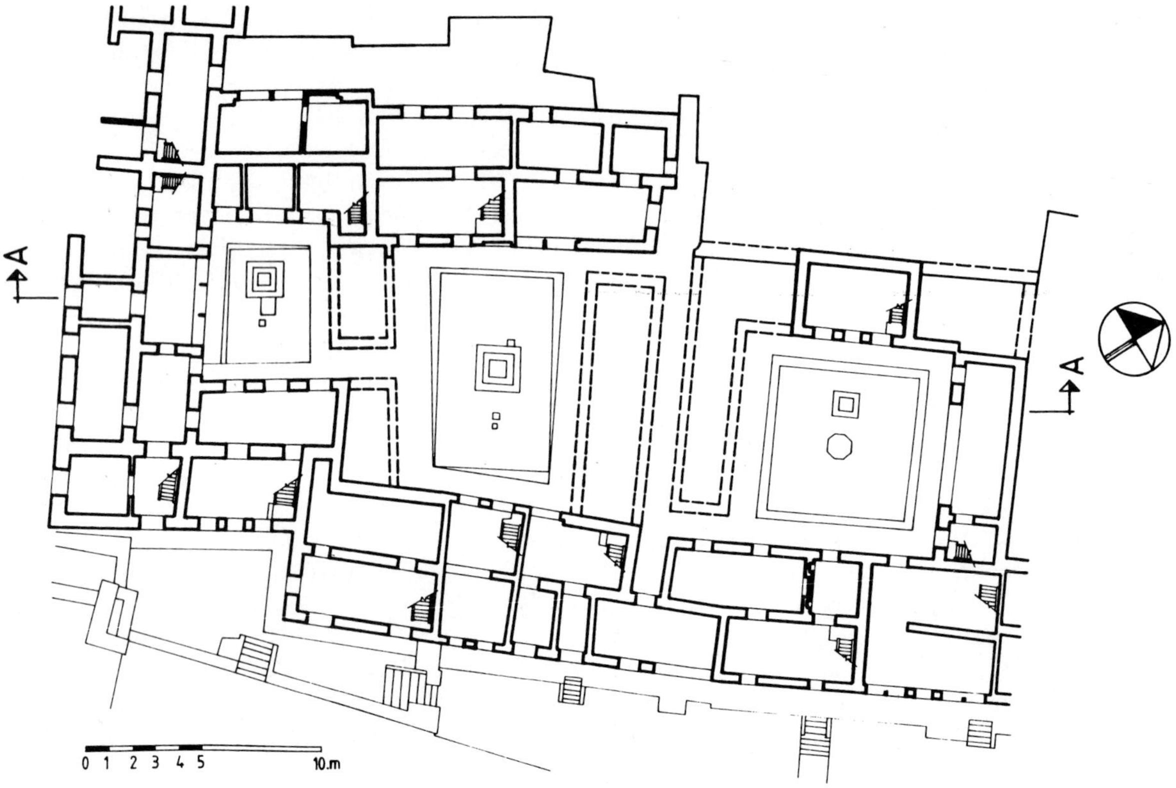


Figure 41 Kve Bāhā, Ikhā Bāhā and Chhve Bāhā, plan.

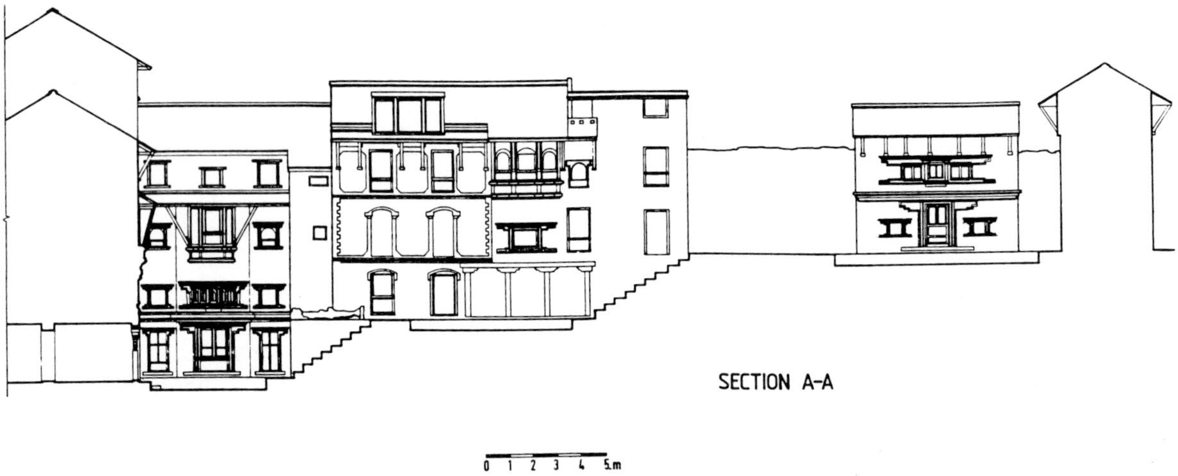


Figure 42 Kve Bāhā, Ikhā Bāhā and Chhve Bāhā, section A - A showing the façades of the buildings facing the north-west of the courtyards

town, taken over by Tribhuvan University. In compensation the Bāhā has some income from the Gūṭhī Saṃsthān for the maintenance of the building, performance of the annual festival and daily rituals. The *saṅgha* of Kve Bāhā consists of four households associated with the Jagat Pāl Bāhā, who also perform their initiation there. In the Kve Bāhā the daily rituals are performed by the members of only one of the four households.

The original buildings of the Bāhā were in three storeys, built at different periods, but to house the growing family of the *saṅgha* during

Plate 100 Kve Bāhā and its *chaitya*, from the courtyard, showing the state of dilapidation of the upper levels.

Plate 101 Kve Bāhā from the east, showing modern additional storeys.

this century a fourth storey was added to the structures and recently a fifth floor to the building at the south-west of the courtyard. The extra load on the old building of the sanctum is particularly noticeable as the structure is now unsafe and the wall of the façade is in danger of collapsing. This building is perhaps the oldest part of the monastery, and judging from the form of its windows may be datable to the 17th or early 18th century. The door frame of the sanctum is finely carved and has an image of Akshobhya on the centre of its lintel. Above the entrance, the window of the first floor, the *chhapa jhyāḥ* with its five openings, is also decorated with carvings.

In the centre of the courtyard is a single *chaitya* with a relatively tall pedestal standing on a platform, all carved in stone. The *chaitya* bears an inscription recording its installation in 753/1633, probably close to the date of the construction of the building of the sanctum. The building at the south-west side of the courtyard with its entrance colonnade is of a later date and from the lobed arched openings of its windows may be datable to the 18th or early 19th century. The other building, opposite the sanctum, is relatively modern.

## IKHĀ (SINADUVĀ) BĀHĀ

At the north-west of the Kve Bāhā is the Ikhā (Ukhe) or Sinaduvā Bāhā which has been heavily reconstructed and at present does not have its own ground floor shrine or an *āgam chhen*. It uses those of Chhve Bāhā, and all three *bāhās*, now interconnected, are sometimes referred to as Ikhā.[14] From the layout of the site, however, it appears that the monastery once consisted of a courtyard surrounded in all sides by buildings. At present the north-east and part of the south-west of the courtyard are open sites, with the remains of older foundations to be seen in some places. To the south-east of the courtyard are three buildings, the central one is a narrow four storeyed building constructed recently, flanked by two other buildings which date probably from the 19th century. All these buildings are two rooms deep and have their entrances at the street side, opening to the Sinaduvā Tol. The south-east building is in two storeys, and the one to the north-east in three storeys and at ground floor has a corridor with carved wooden columns leading to the courtyard of the *bāhā*.

To the north-west of the courtyard are two three storied buildings (Plate 102); one, adjoining the Kve Bāhā, is again a modern structure, but the other is perhaps the oldest building of the *bāhā* and probably dates from the 18th century. This building has been recently renovated, and its brick façade plastered with cement. However, it has preserved its original timber elements, including the columns and lintels of the ground floor, and the carved windows of the upper storeys. The *tiki jhyāh* or upper window has the three lobed arched openings usual for buildings of the period.

The Ikhā Bāhā must have been one the larger monasteries of Kirtipur. The courtyard is rectangular and twice as large as that of the Kve Bāhā. Although it no longer has a sanctum it is still regarded as a *bāhā*, and we were told that it has a *saṅgha* associated with the Jagat Pāl Vihār. In the centre of the courtyard is the stone *chaitya* with the usual niches at the four sides and the images of the standing Buddha.

## CHHVE BĀHĀ

The Chhve Bāhā (Figures 41-2) opens on the south-east to Sinaduvā, and adjoins the Ikhā Bāhā

Plate 102 Ikhā Bāhā from the south-east. The sanctum has been replaced by a later building, and the foundations of other old buildings can be seen on either side of the courtyard.

on its north-east side. While at present the name Ikhā Bāhā is used locally for all the monasteries at this site, the *bāhā* is generally known as Chhve (meaning upper) Bāhā,[15] as it stands on higher ground than the other two *bāhās*. At the other sides of the monastery are the open ground in front of the Chilañcho stupa and its stepped street leading to Sinaduvā. As with the other *bāhās* the Chhve Bāhā has lost some of its original structures, but as a whole it is one of the better preserved monasteries of Kirtipur, with a relatively large square courtyard set in the usual manner with its corners alined roughly with the cardinal points, and once surrounded by buildings at all sides. The buildings at the south-western side once adjoining the Ikha Bāhā have disappeared and those facing the Sinaduvā Ṭol are modern. The sanctum (Plate 104), however, dates from the mid-17th century, and the building at the north-east of the courtyard is also of old origin. The layout of the Chhve Bāhā closely conforms with the standard central courtyard plan of the monasteries of the Kathmandu Valley. The sanctum is a free standing two storeyed building with a finely carved door in the middle of the ground floor chamber, and a window at either side. The upper chamber has a *chhapa jhyāḥ* window with five openings, the central one bearing extensive decoration. At either side of the window is a wooden panel set into the wall and carved with images. The brickwork was once covered with white plaster and probably had paintings, but only small fragments of the plaster have survived. The tiled roof is supported by wooden struts with modest carvings.

The other old building of the Chhve Bāhā is a three storeyed structure (Plate 103) only one room deep, and has two doors at either side opening to the courtyard and between the doors three windows faced with lattice screens. The middle floor has five windows, all finely carved, but the upper storey seems to have been reconstructed and the window with three openings replacing the traditional *tiki jhyāḥ* is modern, while the tiled roof has also been reconstructed in recent decades. In the monastery some of the old wooden elements are preserved, including a carved window and column shafts. These elements come from the older buildings of the *bāhā*, now replaced by modern structures.

Plate 103 Chhve Bāhā from the south, showing the later windows and screening of the colonnade, and an old carved window removed and kept in the courtyard.

Plate 104 Chhve Bāhā from the south-east showing the sanctum.

Plate 105 Kusi Bāhā, showing the sanctum with the painted stucco medallions on the façade.

Plate 106 Kusi Bāhā looking towards the side colonnade, with the entrance colonnade on the right side of the courtyard.

The stone *chaitya* of the monastery is in the middle of the north-western side of the courtyard, and in the centre of the courtyard is an octagonal pedestal with a lotus form platform, on the flat surface of which is a copper *maṇḍala*, the geometric representation of earth and the heavens. All monasteries in the valley have a stone or copper *maṇḍala*, but only in some of them is the *maṇḍala* presented on a lotus set on a pedestal. In an inscription on the *maṇḍala* of the Chhve Bāhā the formal Sanskrit name of the monastery is recorded as Harshakīrti Vihāra, and the date of its foundation is mentioned as 761/1641. The *maṇḍala* itself is noted to have been erected in 936/1816. The monastery is said to have been badly damaged in the 1934 earthquake, and in the following decades some of the buildings were replaced by modern structures and the remaining buildings were restored. The main income of the monastery was from farm land at the east of the town which was compulsorily purchased for Tribhuvan University; the Gūṭhi Saṃsthān provides some compensatory income used for the maintenance of the *bāhā* and daily rituals, but the yearly festival is no longer performed. The *saṅgha* of the monastery at present consists of one household, who perform their initiations at the Jagat Pāl Bāhā.

### KUSI BĀHĀ

Kusi Bāhā, a small but well preserved monastery in Kirtipur, is situated in the Kusicha Ṭol on the steep slope west of the Chilañcho Stupa. The Kusicha is a very small neighbourhood and consists of only the Kusi Bāhā and eight other houses, of which three are occupied by *bajrāchāryas*, one by a *pradhān* family and three by *jyāpus*. The monastery itself is occupied by a household of *bajrāchāryas* of Jagat Pāl Vihār. This household constitutes the *saṅgha* of the Kusi Bāhā and observes the daily rituals and the yearly festival, although at present the monastery does not have any direct income. Kusi Bāhā is also one of the two monasteries in Kirtipur where the members of the *śākya* families perform their initiations. These families moved to Kirtipur some generations ago, and the *bajrāchāryas* of the Jagat Pāl gave them permission to use the Kusi Bāhā and the Yāka Bāhā for their initiations.

The existing buildings of the Kusi Bāhā (Plates 105-6) are constructed around a square courtyard with its corners aligned approximately with the cardinal points, and there are remains of another building at the south-west of the courtyard indicating that this monastery also had a central courtyard plan. The entrance to the Bāhā is in the Kusicha Ṭol leading via a number of steps down to a colonnade at the north-east of the courtyard. The building at this side is in three storeys, but the windows are set in a haphazard manner, and from the type of the bricks it appears that the structure was in two storeys originally, but the upper storey was partly reconstructed and a third storey added to it.

The window above the entrance colonnade is particularly interesting for its finely carved images and serpentine motifs of the jambs, an uncommon specimen in Kirtipur. The entrance colonnade itself stands on a high plinth with a flight of steps at each side leading down to the courtyard. Opposite the entrance is the sanctum of *kvāpā dya* which has a relatively plain entrance but above it is a very fine wooden cornice running along the façade of the building, and the chamber above the sanctum has a *chhapa jhyāḥ*, with five openings enriched with deeply carved figurative and floral patterns. The jambs of the windows are carved to imitate pilasters with mouldings and pot and foliage patterns derived from the decoration of the column shafts of ancient and mediaeval India. The bases of the jambs are decorated with lotus motifs, and those at either side of the window rest on crouching elephants. A number of images of guardian deities are also represented.

Part of the façade, below the cornice and at either side of the door jambs, is plastered with white stucco decorated with paintings. Their date is uncertain but they seem to be a later addition to the building. The stucco panels at either side of the door jambs have floral paintings, and the paintings below the cornice consist of a row of roundels each with a central figure and a lotus border. The colours have faded but blue, red, yellow and brown are still recognizable. The paintings of the Kusi Bāhā are neither as refined nor have the complexity of design seen in the stucco paintings of the Bāgh Bhairav temple, nevertheless they are rare examples of their kind in Kirtipur.

The north-western building is a simple two storied structure with a three bayed colonnade below and a chamber with a central window above. There is also a smaller window at the left side of the central window but both windows are relatively plain. The destroyed structure opposite this building may have been in a similar form, with a colonnade at the ground level. Such a layout, with colonnades at three sides of the courtyard, is common in the monasteries of the Kathmandu Valley. In the Kusi Bāhā there is a

Plate 107 Yāka Bāhā founded in 769/1649, view from the south-east.

single *chaitya* carved in stone set in the courtyard in front of the sanctum entrance.

## YĀKA BĀHĀ

The Yāka Bāhā (Plate 107) is situated at the corner of Mvana Ṭol, and south-west of Loṇ Degaḥ. The *saṅgha* of the monastery consists of a household who take turns in performing the daily rituals. They also observe the annual festival of the *bāhā*, although their monastery no longer has any direct income. As we have noted, the Yāka Bāhā is also used by the *śākya* of Kirtipur for their initiations.

The Yāka Bāhā (Figure 43) is constructed around a central courtyard with the sanctum at its north-west and the main entrance at the opposite side opening to the street between Loṇ Degaḥ and Mvana Ṭol. To the south-west of the entrance and at the corner of Mvana Ṭol is an old *pāṭi*. In the monastery, apart from the building of the sanctum which dates from the mid-17th century, all other structures have been reconstructed at later dates, and two of them are modern. Nevertheless, in some of the buildings parts of the older structures are preserved, and in the three storied building which incorporates the main entrance some of the old windows have been reused.

The sanctum is on the ground floor of a two storeyed structure, and has a door with carved jambs and lintels opening to the courtyard. At either side of the door is a small window, and above the door an elaborately carved cornice runs along the façade. The entrance is guarded by a pair of stone lions resting on the backs of crouching elephants and dated 830/1710. The room above the sanctum has a large carved window with five openings filling most of the upper register of the façade. The central window is rectangular, flanked by pilasters carved with elaborate capitals, and a pair of three lobed arched openings on either side. The jambs, which are decorated with guardian deities, are in turn flanked by small blind windows (*gaḥjhyāḥ*) with carved wooden frames and an arched niche in the centre. An inscription dated 802/1682 in the monastery gives the formal Sanskrit name of the

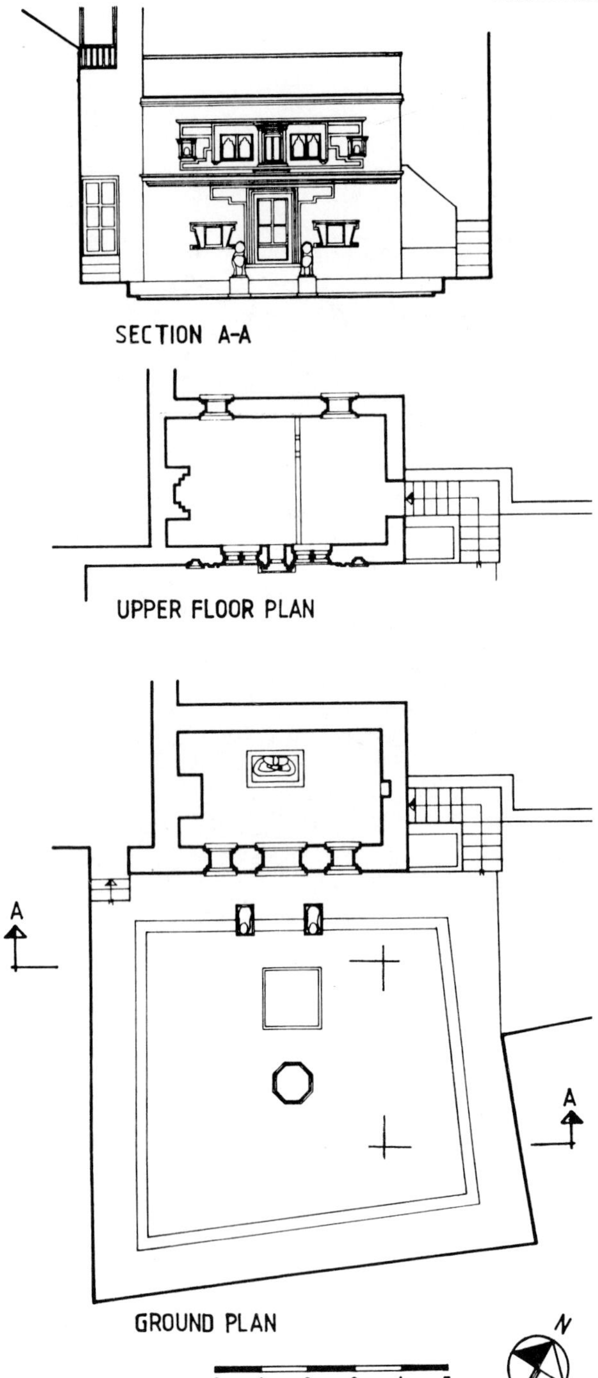


Figure 43 Yāka Bāhā, plans and section A - A.

monastery as Jīvadharma Vihāra and notes that it was founded in 769/1649 and was consecrated in the presence of the king of Patan, Siddhi Narasiṃha Malla. The inscription also lists donations given to the monastery in 783/1663 and 802/1682 including images of deities and some land, the income from which was to be been spent on the yearly festival and the monthly and daily rites and rituals.

In the courtyard and in front of the door of the sanctum is a stone *chaitya*, and at the centre of the courtyard is a *maṇḍala* with a lotus on an

Plate 108 The site of the Padmochcha Bāhā, with its *chaitya* dated 868/1748.

octagonal stone pedestal comparable to that of the Chhve Bāhā. There are also two other stone images in the courtyard.

## PADMOCHCHA BĀHĀ

The Padmochcha Bāhā, also known as Tuṅjalaychvaṅgu Bāhā, is situated off a modern paper making workshop in the Tunjho Ṭol, south of the Chilaṅcho Stupa. Little remains from the original monastery except a courtyard with one of the auxiliary buildings of the *bāhā* (Plate 108). In past decades the building has been heavily reconstructed in three storeys, with a fourth storey added sometime later. However, the ground floor has kept its three bayed colonnade which, until recent years, was open into the courtyard, but is now bricked up and made into rooms. Next to this building a modern house has been constructed, occupying a large part of the old site of the monastery. At present there is no sanctum for the *kvāpā dya* in the site, but it is still regarded as a

Plate 109 Chīthuṅ Bahī, the courtyard with the *maṇḍala* and *chaityas* in front of the old building of the sanctum, and reconstructed buildings of the complex on the left side.

Plate 110 Chīthuṅ Bahī, the entrance to the courtyard with what may be the remains of a colonnade.

*bāhā* and it was said that there was such a sanctum in the past, which disappeared many years ago, apparently before the 1934 earthquake.

The main remaining part of the *bāhā* is its stone *chaitya* which stands in the middle of the courtyard and bears the date 868/1748. The date may be close to the time of the foundation of the monastery. In the absence of the *kvāpā dya* image the daily rites are performed at the *chaitya* by the *saṅgha* which consists of one household, and is initiated at the Jagat Pāl Bāhā.

## CHĪTHUṄ BAHĪ

The only *bahī* of Kirtipur is the Chīthuṅ or Chīthu Bahī (Plate 109) situated in Chīthuṅ Ṭol north of the Chilaṅcho Stupa. The official Sanskrit name of the Bahī is Padmakīrtigīri Mahāvihār, and as appears from its name the monastery is a large institution independent of other monasteries of Kirtipur and Patan. The *saṅgha* of the Chīthuṅ Bahī consists of forty-five *śākyas*, with five elders who are the descendants of the first *śākya* families who came from Patan and were originally members of the Nhāykaṅ Bahī, a large and well preserved monastery there.[16] Chīthuṅ Bahī has lost almost all of its revenue, and the yearly festival of the monastery has been abandoned, but the buildings in the compound are maintained, and the daily rites are carried out in turn by the members of the *saṅgha.*

The monastery consists of a rectangular courtyard with the sanctum of the *kvāpā dya* at the south-west and the entrance on the opposite side. At the west and north-west of the courtyard there are a number of buildings, but they are all modern, and the only old structure is the two storeyed building with the sanctum at its ground floor. This building has also been restored and while the old carved door to the sanctum is preserved, the original upper floor window has been lost. In later dates a two storied timber porch has been added to the front elevation of the building. However, it appears that in the past the Chīthuṅ Bahī was a large monastery, probably with a colonnade at three sides of its spacious courtyard, a structural form which is peculiar to the larger *bahīs*, and distinguishes them architecturally from *bāhās*. In the Chīthuṅ Bahī parts of an old colonnade have survived at either side of the entrance (Plate 110) and have been made into two *pāṭis*. From the form of the finely carved columns of these *pāṭis* a 17th century date may be suggested for the monastery. This date may be confirmed by a votive inscription on a copper plate on the sanctum recording offerings by one Brahmācharya Bhikshu Śrī Deva Ratna[17] in 779/1659. Other inscriptions in the *bahī* record that the courtyard was paved in 827/1707; the sanctum was renovated in 831/1711; and a wooden *toraṇa* and a stone *maṇḍala* were installed in 832/1712. The *toraṇa* is apparently lost, but the *maṇḍala* is still in the courtyard.

Apart from the *maṇḍala,* with its lotus base on the usual octagonal pediment, in the courtyard there are two stone *chaityas* which differ in form from one another, although many examples of both forms can be found in Kirtipur and elsewhere. The *chaitya* in the middle of the courtyard consists of a small hemispherical top, resting on four images of sitting Buddhas facing the four directions. The images are on a lotus set on a square base above a larger stone pedestal. The other *chaitya,* set in front of the entrance of the sanctum, has a larger miniature stupa on the top and a pedestal which at each face has a niche with an image of the standing Buddha. Other stone carvings in the shrine include two lions guarding the doors of the sanctum.

## NOTES

1 Daniel Wright, *History of Nepal translated from the Pārbatiya,* Cambridge, 1877.

2 For a detailed study of the Nepalese monasteries see John K. Locke, S. J., *Buddhist Monasteries of Nepal, A Survey of the Bāhās and Bahīs of the Kathmandu Valley,* Kathmandu, 1985.

3 The pronunciation of *vihāra* as *bihār* and *bahār* in the regions of the Hindu Kush and the Himalayas goes back to at least early mediaeval times, and even appears in Persian in reference to the ancient monasteries of Afghanistan. See Yāqūt Hamawī, *Geographisches Worterbuch (Mu'jam al-buldān),* ed. Ferdinand Wustenfeld, Leipzig, 1869, IV, 817-21.

4 John K. Locke, op. cit., 185-7.

5 Ibid., 178-84; the monasteries are also listed in Carl Pruscha, *A Protective Inventory,* Anton Schroll & Co. for HMG Nepal, Vienna, 1975, II, 118; E. P. Davies et al., *Kirtipur, a Newar Community in Nepal, Development in Debate,* Bristol, 1979-80, 13.

6 Warwick Ball, *Archaeological Gazetteer of Afghanistan,* Paris, 1982, I, 113 site no. 389; II, 442. This source also gives a bibliography of all other Buddhist sites in Afghanistan.

7 Ibid., 116, site no. 404; II, 443.

8 A. Ghosh, *Nalanda,* Archaeological Survey of India, New Delhi, 1939, 6th ed., 1986, site plan, also see p. 57 for a selected bibliography of the site.

9 V. S. Agrawala, *Sarnath,* Archaeological Survey of India, New Delhi, 1956, 4th ed. 1984, pl. 11, site plan, bibliography p. 29.

10 *Archaeological Survey of India Annual Reports, 1912-13,* Calcutta 1915, part i, 17-24, pls. 6-9: *1913-14,* Calcutta, 1915, part i, 20-23, pls. 19-21, part ii, 1-39, pls. 1-24; *1936-7,* 84-7; John Marshall and Alfred Foucher, *The Monuments of Sāñchī,* 3 vols., Delhi, c. 1944, see in particular II, pl. 2, monasteries nos. 36-8 and 44-5; III, pl. 123.

11 J. Fergusson and J. Burgess, The Cave Temples of India, 1880 (repr. Delhi, 1969), 232-40, 289-, 350-3, 377-9, pls. XI, XXVIII, LIII, LXII.

12 Wolfgang Korn, *The Traditional Architecture of the Kathmandu Valley,* Kathmandu, 1979, 26-37.

13 In Patan the Kvā Bāhā of this town is regarded as the most ancient institution, and the Jagat Pāl of Kirtipur as the second most ancient *vihāra* see John K. Locke, op. cit., 31-40, 180.

14 Ikhā or Ukhe Bāhā is not mentioned by Locke, nor is recorded by Pruscha, but is noted as Sinaduvā Bāhā by Reinhard Herdick, *Kirtipur: Stadtgestalt, Prinzipien der Raumordnung und gesellschaftliche Funktionen einer Newar-stadt,* Munich-Cologne-London, 1988, 45.

15 John K. Locke, op. cit., 182-4; Carl Pruscha, op. cit., 265.

16 John K. Locke, op. cit., 217.

17 Ibid., 221.

# KATHMANDU VALLEY LAND USE PLAN AND KIRTIPUR

PADAM B. CHHETRI

The *Kathmandu Valley Land Use Plan* was officially adopted in 1976 by HMG Nepal. This plan, concerned with a general policy for the land use of the whole valley was the outcome of an earlier work, the *Physical Development Plan for the Kathmandu Valley*, carried out by the Department of Housing and Physical Planning with technical assistance from the United Nations, the report of which was published in 1969. The Land Use Plan does not consider the conditions of each individual site in detail, but consists of broader land use classifications and their area delineation, with the major emphasis given to the urban areas of the Kathmandu, Lalitpur (Patan) and Bhaktapur Town Pañchāyats.

The areas outside the boundaries of these towns are either designated as Rural Settlements or Agricultural Areas. The historical localities with monuments (the Monument Zones) within the Rural Settlement areas have been identified, but the actual areas are not clearly defined. Kirtipur is regarded as a Rural Settlement area lying next to the Educational Institution Zone (Tribhuvan University).

## BUILDING REGULATIONS

In the context of Land Use Plan enforcement, the Kathmandu Valley Town Development Board has prepared a set of land use and building regulations, which were officially adopted in 1976. Their aim is to deal specifically with the various types of land use within the urban areas, but they also provide general regulations applicable to all Rural Settlements within the valley. The regulations dealing with building construction in the Rural Settlements and applicable to Kirtipur are as follows:

1 Buildings to be constructed within the Rural Settlement areas should retain the look and character of the adjacent houses, but can make provision for such physical facilities both within or outside the building which are essential for living.

2 Ground coverage ratio of the buildings shall not be more than 50% of the plot, and the height of the building shall not be more than four storeys.

3 New buildings should be set back at a distance of five metres from the edge of motorable roads in the rural areas.

4 Plastering or pointing of the walls on the outside shall be allowed where necessary.

5 If a building is to be constructed within or adjacent to a designated Monument Zone it is to be constructed according to guide-lines and directions of the concerned Town Plan Implementation Committee (TPIC).

6 As far as possible new building construction on good agricultural land will be discouraged in the rural areas.

7 Small scale cottage and agriculture based industries only shall be permitted in the rural areas. The permission of the concerned TPIC is necessary for starting such an industry in rural areas.

8 Building permits shall be issued by the concerned village authorities according to land use and building regulations prescribed by the TPIC.

These regulations, while providing guide-lines, show that land use planning for the historic settlements outside the administrative limits of the three main towns of the valley was virtually ignored. When the Land Use Plan was adopted in 1976 the urban growth pressure was limited to areas adjacent to the main towns, and other settlements were more or less continuing to function as traditional agricultural communities. However, the construction of the Ring Road during the late 1970s greatly increased people's access to new areas, and the old traditional settlements did not remain un-affected by this development.

In the last decades Kirtipur in particular,

Plate 111 Aerial view of the area south-east of Kirtipur in January 1985, showing the new area of Naya Bāzār at the south-east of the town, and the Tribhuvan University campus.

Plate 112 Naya Bāzār, the main street seen from the south end looking north. Many of the buildings which were in three storeys originally now have additional floors, some up to six storeys.

along with other settlements, has been subjected to strong pressure for urbanisation and has undergone an irreversible change in its traditional way of life and socio-economic characteristics. The absence of effective and comprehensive land use and building regulations for a town of the size of Kirtipur has already resulted in uncontrolled urban growth there, particularly in the south-east of the town, which if it is to continue will create serious problems, especially in the old core of the town, affecting its historic character and the conservation of its monuments.

### INSTITUTIONAL ARRANGEMENTS FOR ENFORCEMENT OF REGULATIONS

For administration and enforcement of the Land Use Plan HMG has established the Kathmandu Valley Town Development Board (KVTDB) at the valley level, and three TPICs at district levels. In order to provide logistic and other technical support the Department of Housing and Physical Planning has set up a specific team, the Kathmandu Valley Town Planning Team. The KVTDB is mainly concerned with broad policy issues and provides guide-lines and directions in the planning and implementation process. The TPICs are the main institutions entrusted with the responsibilities of implementing the provisions of the Land Use Plan effectively, and the role of the Kathmandu Valley Town Planning Team is to carry out detailed planning work to create a firm and well worked out planning frame-work for effective implementation of the Land Use Plan. However, so far the detailed planning exercises have not, unfortunately, been carried out, and therefore the problems of Land Use Plan implementation and enforcement have now assumed much larger and more complex dimensions.

For new constructions in the three towns, building permits have so far been issued by the Town Pañchāyats, which were obliged to follow certain prescribed norms by law in the issuance of such permits. The village authorities (formerly the Village Pañchāyats) have been rather freer, and therefore in the areas under Village Pañchāyats, such as Kirtipur, building permits have not been absolutely necessary, and usually there has been no insistence on implementing the set rules, such as the submission of drawings and other usual processes. Thus it is clear that Kirtipur, and indeed many other old settlements of the valley, which have strong historical character and are of cultural importance, have not received the necessary attention in the Land Use Plan, and deserve immediate attention if the conservation of their heritage is to be included within their future development.

# LAND USE AND POPULATION SURVEY

SHANKER M. PRADHAN

Centuries of habitation in Kirtipur show the importance of man's role in the creation of the existing physical environment. The prominent settlement of Kirtipur as it appears today dates back to the beginning of the 13th century, and has remained in the compact form that was established then. The closely spaced brick houses with their kitchen gardens are built in blocks with narrow streets and small courtyards, and are located mainly on the high ground, leaving the slopes for grazing and woodland and the more level ground for cultivation.

The morphology of Kirtipur is not radically different from other compact settlements in the Kathmandu Valley, irrespective of whether they are called towns or villages, in spite of variations in their size, geographical situation, and the economic activities of their inhabitants. These settlements are far from being merely smaller or larger groups of housing units designed to provide shelter. Each settlement is an institutional and social base which provides a common environment to retain and reinforce the kinship patterns and relationships of particular groups of people through their daily life and the performance of their traditional rituals.

Aside from the necessity of proximity to cultivated fields, a compact form of vertically orientated dwellings is motivated by a strong concern for preserving the rich agricultural land and avoiding its inefficient use. As an outgrowth of, as well as a motivating factor for this compact settlement pattern of Kirtipur, the social cohesion and organization of its inhabitants shows marked differences from the situation found in the more dispersed type of traditional agricultural settlements, both in and outside the Kathmandu Valley. The settlement of Kirtipur also represents a strong socio-economic framework for maintaining compact groups large enough to broaden associations beyond tight extended family circles, and includes a number of castes which have evolved on the basis of their occupations.

The physical townscape of settlements in Nepal is based on the unifying factor of a direct association with particular gods and temples. The central land of the towns is marked by an open space on which streets and lanes converge. In Kirtipur one of the main open spaces is the site of the temple to the town god, Bāgh Bhairav, and forms a nucleus around which this part of the settlement has grown. The association of a settlement with a physical structure dedicated to the gods is very important to its organization. The temple is located within the core of the settlement, set in an extensive open space which also accommodates its subsidiary structures. As discussed in the chapter on the symbolic organization of the residential unit, the layout of the dwellings is in turn orientated to the temples and shrines, and geared to vertical rather than horizontal expansion, with the plan details adapted to the geographic characteristics of the site.

Kirtipur is one of the oldest settlements in the valley. With its unique geography it had good natural defences as well as being situated at a strategic point on one of the traditional southern trade routes from the valley to India. With recent changes in land use, Kirtipur now has a relatively low percentage of families engaged primarily in agriculture. Cottage industries and crafts have always been important to Kirtipur, and the town is known for its artisans, particularly masons and carpenters. However, in recent years the pattern of people's earning has gradually changed and most of those employed on a wage basis now work outside Kirtipur, going each day as far as Kathmandu and Patan. Kirtipur has relatively few commercial activities, and serves only to a small degree as a market centre for its region. For most of its goods Kirtipur depends on sources in Kathmandu. In turn, the majority of the textiles produced in Kirtipur are sold in Kathmandu.

Kirtipur, with a population of 16,000 according to the local Pañchāyat records of 1988, has many claims to special attention. It has historic importance as a very old settlement, and commands a magnificent site with an impressive

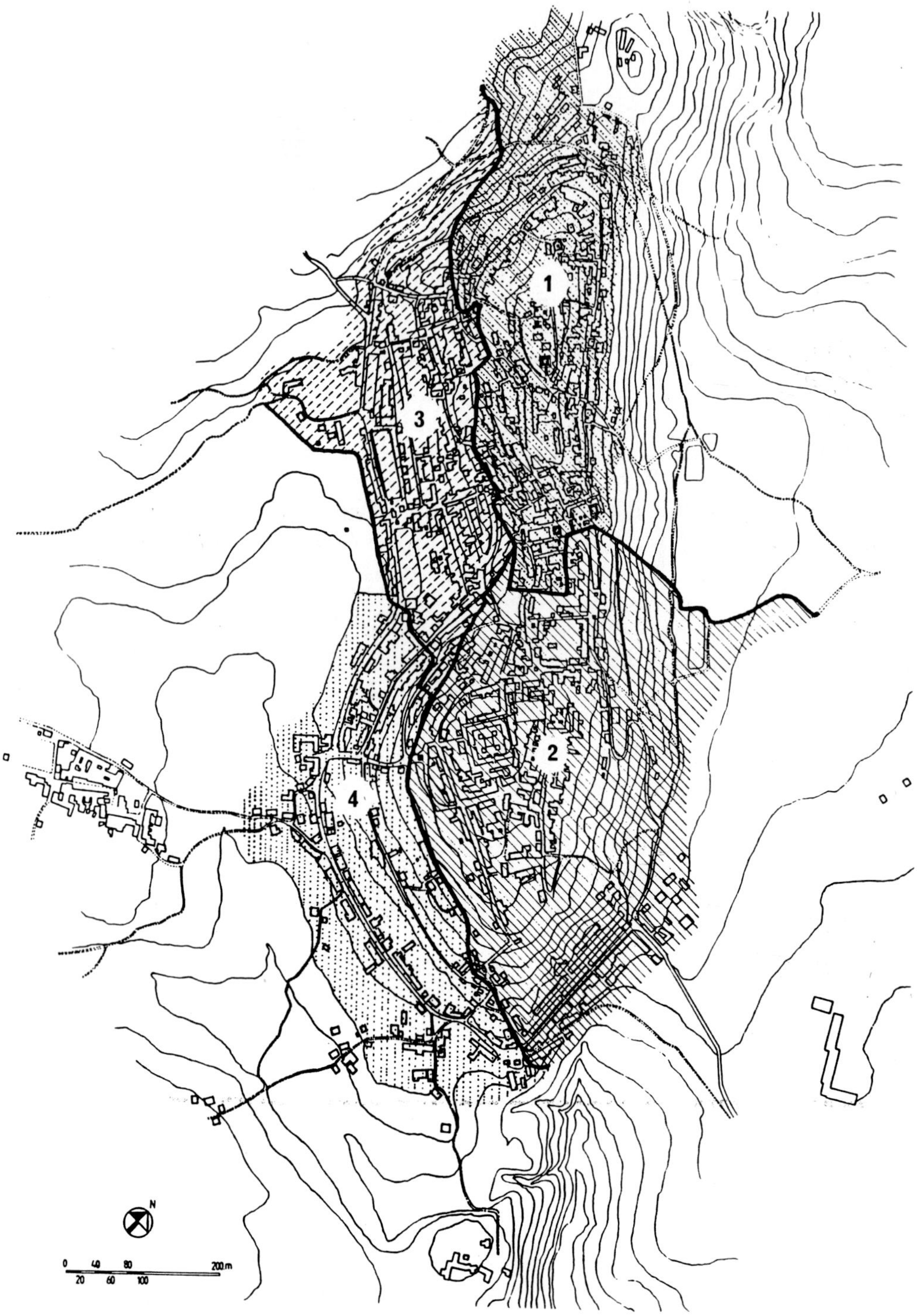


Figure 44 Map of Kirtipur showing the administrative divisions under four Pañchāyats, which were replaced by Village Development Committees covering the same areas in 1990.
Key: 1 Lāyaku; 2 Chīthuṅ Bihār; 3 Pāliphal; 4 Bahirīgāoṅ.

urban landscape. It has a tradition of activity in the crafts, and houses a significant number of important monuments of architecture and sculpture. Finally, in spite of its relative proximity to Kathmandu, which makes it an ideal goal for tourists, the old town has not been greatly spoiled, even after incongruous recent additions and a good deal of new construction in Naya Bāzār, at the foot of the hill.

In the built up area of Kirtipur almost all houses have an electricity supply. There is one high school and five primary schools. The town

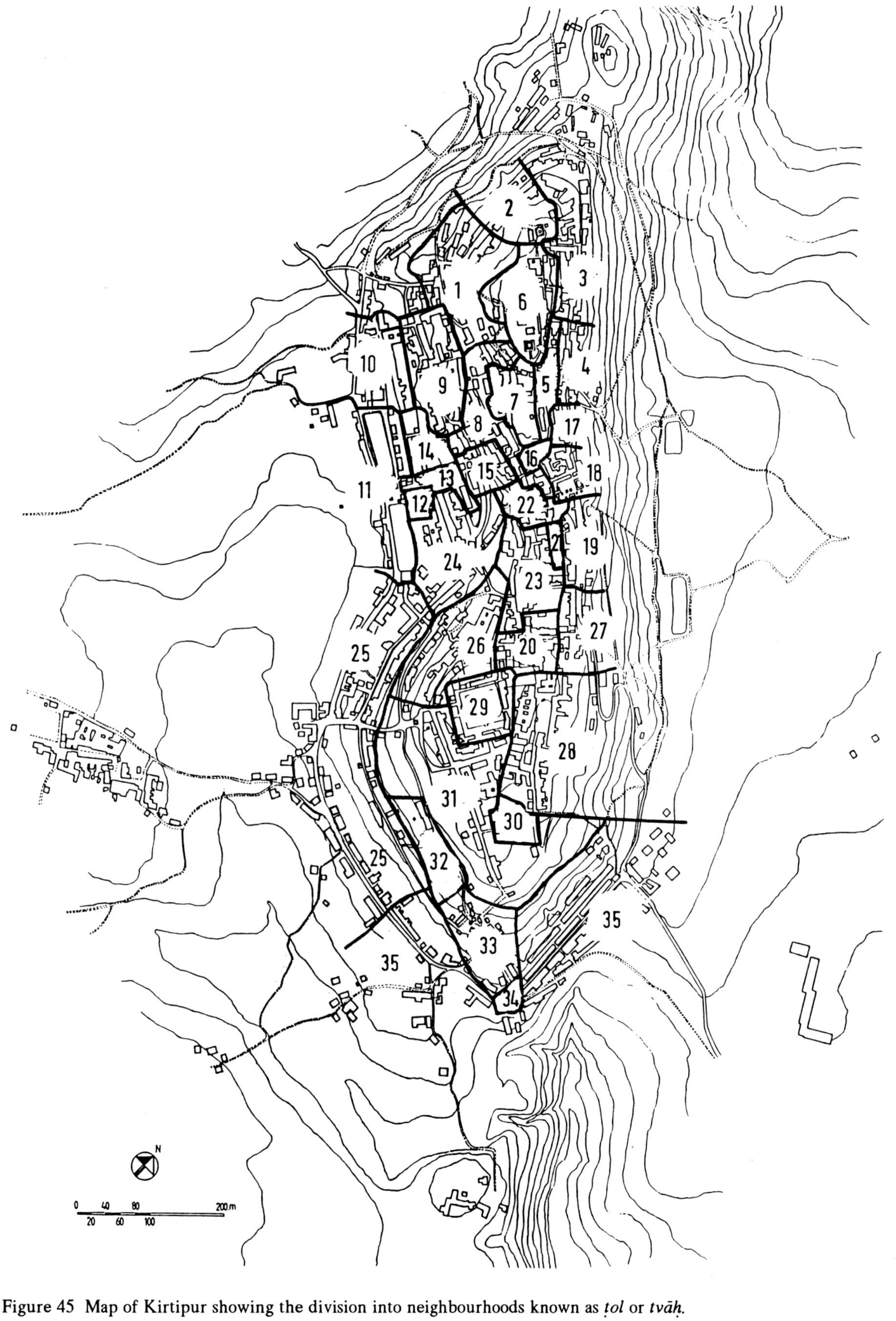


Figure 45 Map of Kirtipur showing the division into neighbourhoods known as *ṭol* or *tvāḥ*.

Key: 1 Samal; 2 Nagacho; 3 Deu Ḍhokā; 4 Gachhen; 5 Jochhe; 6 Kvācho; 7 Lāyaku; 8 Kochhen; 9 Sāyami; 10 Sāgāl; 11 Khasi Bāzār; 12 Hitigaḥ; 13 Pāliphal; 14 Dopacha; 15 Chaphal; 16 Satako; 17 Salichhen; 18 Bāgh Bhairav; 19 Iṭāchhen; 20 Loṅ Degaḥ; 21 Hva Kuncha; 22 De Pukhū; 23 Gutapau; 24 Kuṭujhol; 25 Bahirīgāoṅ; 26 Mvana; 27 Chīthuṅ; 28 Tananī; 29 Chilaṅcho; 30 Mārakhyo; 31 Tuṅjho; 32 Gāyine; 33 Poṛe; 34 Amalshi; 35 Naya Bāzār.

has a police station and a post office, as well as a health centre. There are offices of the electricity corporation and cooperatives, and branches of the Banijya Bank and the Agricultural Bank, and in 1988 there were five rice mills, one oil mill, one wheat mill and three *chūrā* (bruised grain) mills in the town. The public and private land and the buildings in public and private use in Kirtipur are marked in our drawings. According to the statistics prepared by the Development Research and Communication Group[1] in 1982 from a sample of 167 households out of a total of 1362, the major source of income for about 19% was agriculture, and for 42% was from waged labour including construction work. Nearly 8% had their income from business, and 27% from employment in services. Although cottage industry and particularly weaving plays an important role in providing supplementary income to most households, less than 2% of the population relied on income from cottage industries alone, and nearly 2% on other sources, including remittances. In 1988 it was estimated that 79% of the population of the town were employed in construction work, 5% in carpet weaving, 4% in business, 3% in weaving, 2% in service, and the rest in agriculture. It is interesting to note that carpet weaving is a new craft in Kirtipur, and has developed with the demand for Tibetan style carpets in Kathmandu, mainly connected with the foreign tourist trade, and exports. The proportion of people working inside and away from the town is discussed below in the article on transport and communications.

The access roads to the town follow the lines of the old footpaths, originally outside the town, but now bordered by houses, shops and workshops. The main new roads are the asphalted access roads leading from Naya Bāzār, up the eastern side of the hill to reach De Pukhū, and to the west through Bahirīgāoṅ. Naya Bāzār is now growing rapidly, and at present consists of three parallel roads.

## COMPOSITION OF USAGE

Looking at the composition of the town, we can see characteristics associated with the process of urbanization and industrialization. The more recent the built up area is the more we find mixed residential and commercial use. The area at the southern part of the town is known as Bahirīgāoṅ, and the western section as Khasi Bāzār. At Bahirīgāoṅ, where the road branches towards the village of Nagāoṅ, a new built up complex has developed with houses, shops and workshops.

In a town like Kirtipur, planning of old town renewal, as well as the reconstruction of individual features, needs to be the responsibility of a body concerned principally with conservation and renewal questions. General urban development planning is not only a local community task, and the responsible body needs to reconcile various views to ensure the preservation of the historic monuments and the fabric of the town.

The major source of income for households in 1982 and the general land use of Kirtipur as calculated in 1988 are shown in the following tables.

MAJOR SOURCE OF HOUSEHOLD INCOME IN 1982

From a sample of 167 households out of a total of 1362

| | | | |
|---|---|---|---|
| Agriculture | 18.88% | Livestock | 0.38% |
| Cottage Industries | 1.90% | Business | 7.70% |
| Wages | 42.17% | Services | 27.16% |
| Remittances | 0.38% | Other | 1.43% |

LAND USE TABLE, 1988

| | |
|---|---|
| Residential | 50,000 sq.m. |
| Commercial | 5,000 |
| Public ponds | 7,000 |
| Public open spaces | 4,000 |
| Temple squares (preservation areas) | 8,000 |
| **Institutions:** | |
| Schools | 2,000 |
| Post Office | 50 |
| Offices | 1,500 |
| Paṅchāyat offices | 950 |
| Old town gates (12) | 72 |
| Reservoir | 140 |
| Public clinic | 90 |
| Public land | 25,000 |
| Private land | 40,000 |
| Woodland | 32,000 |

NOTES

1 Development Research and Communication Group, *Report on Evaluation Study of the Kirtipur Demonstration Project in Low-cost Sanitation*, prepared for the Department of Water Supply and Sewerage, Ministry of Water Resources HMG Nepal, Kathmandu 1982, 53, 57, Table 5 (our figures and table take all the sample together).

# LAND USE CHANGES IN KIRTIPUR

UTTAM SAGAR SHRESTHA

The distribution of the built up areas and farmlands of Kirtipur appears to have remained stable until recent decades. In the chapter on the urban fabric of the town the extent of the mediaeval town is discussed in detail, and it can be seen that the boundaries of the town have remained largely unaltered.

Since the 1950s there have, however, been marked changes in land use, and much of the agricultural area has now been taken over for other purposes. Here we examine the changes between 1954 and 1989 using information from aerial survey photographs provided by the Topographical Survey Branch of the Forestry Department, and the Central Department of Geography at Tribhuvan University. There has been no previous systematic study of land use in the town, but valuable information was given by the *pañchāyats* and townspeople about particular transactions.

## CHANGES IN THE URBAN AREAS

The main factors responsible for the recent changes in land use have been the proximity of the town to the capital, the availability of low priced land, the development of modern roads, the growth in population and the need for accommodation for large families. The most significant area of land taken out of agricultural use is that acquired in 1957 for Tribhuvan University and the Horticulture Research Station. The largest increase in built up land has occurred as a result of the distribution by Chīthuṅ Bihār and Lāyaku Pañchāyats of grazing land to homeless and landless local people, and others, for building houses. The area of land used for brick kilns is also increasing, as is that of fallow land. In spite of the government's aim of introducing a Basic Need Programme by the year 2000 and encouraging farmers to produce more food for the growing population, farmers are tending to pay less attention to their land and more to activities not directly associated with farming.

The changes in the built up area and in agricultural land are given in the tables below. The urban area comprises areas of settlement including open spaces, circulation areas and ponds, as well as kitchen gardens, grazing land, quarries and bad land, but not cultivated fields. Between 1954 and 1964 there was no change in the composition of the urban area. All the blocks of houses were concentrated within the latest phase of the defensive walls, known locally as De Paḥkhāḥ, with the exception of one linear settlement of 23 houses at Khasi Bāzār. The settlement area constituted only 245.67 *ropanis* (18.31%), and the kitchen gardens covered 270.11 *ropanis* (20.10%). The largest proportion of land was set aside for grazing, part of this land in the northern side being covered with vegetation and woodland. In 1957 the Department of Cottage Industries (Gharelau Udhyog) erected one building at the side of Mabhī Pukhū, and in 1962 the road from Tribhuvan University to Kirtipur was widened, but these activities did not account for a significant change in the built up area.

### 1964-1972

In 1969 there was a change in composition of the urban area following the decision of two of the *pañchāyats* to re-allocate certain public lands for the development of private dwellings. The aim of the redistribution and the change of use of the land was to provide accommodation for landless people (*sukumbāsi*) and also make rentable accommodation available for university students. The Chīthuṅ Bihār Pañchāyat divided the grazing into 20′x28′ building plots and sold them at the nominal price of Rs.100 to landless people. In the same way the Lāyaku Pañchāyat distributed the grazing land in the south-west of the town to local people. As a result the built up area increased by 49 *ropanis*. Many of the plots changed hands before they were actually built. In addition during this period the area of kitchen gardens in Amalshi Bāzār also increased by about

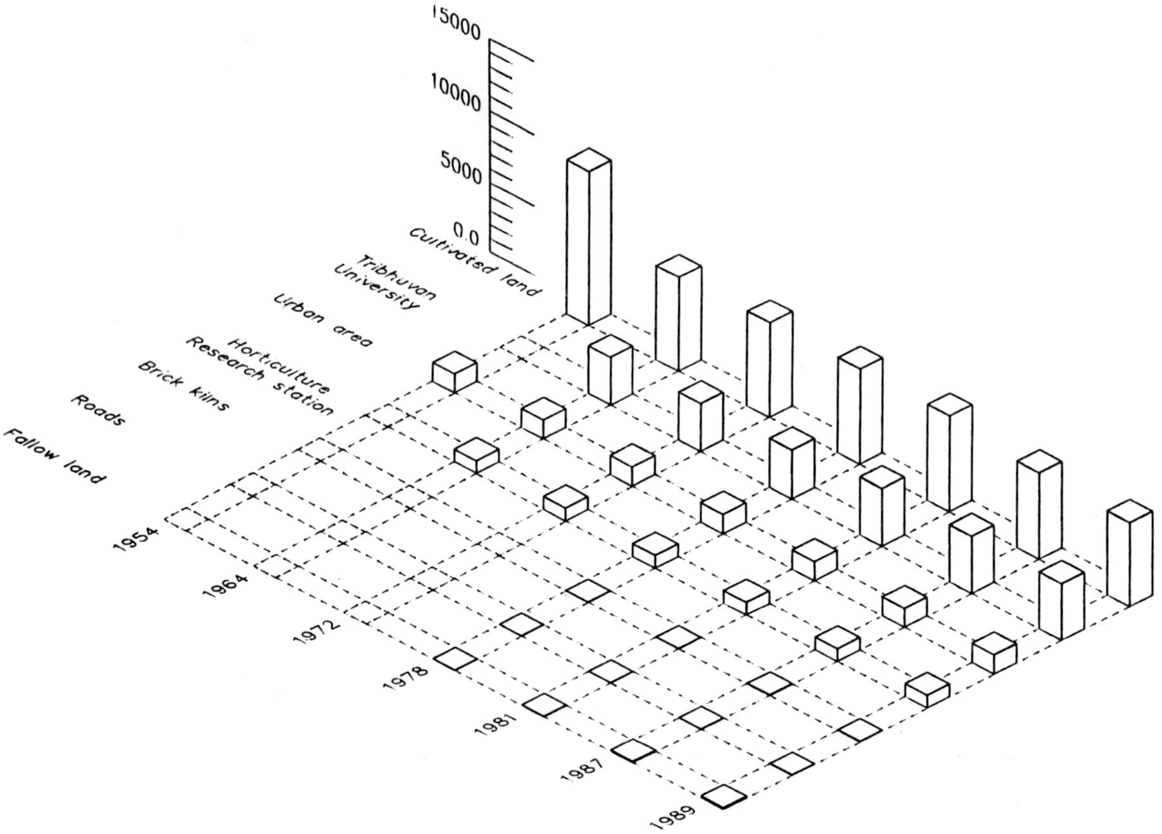


Figure 46 Graph of changes in agricultural land use between 1954 and 1989. The most significant decrease in cultivated land is due to farmland being taken over by the University and the Horticultural Research Station, and the increase in land used for roads and brick kilns, or left fallow, is another recent trend.

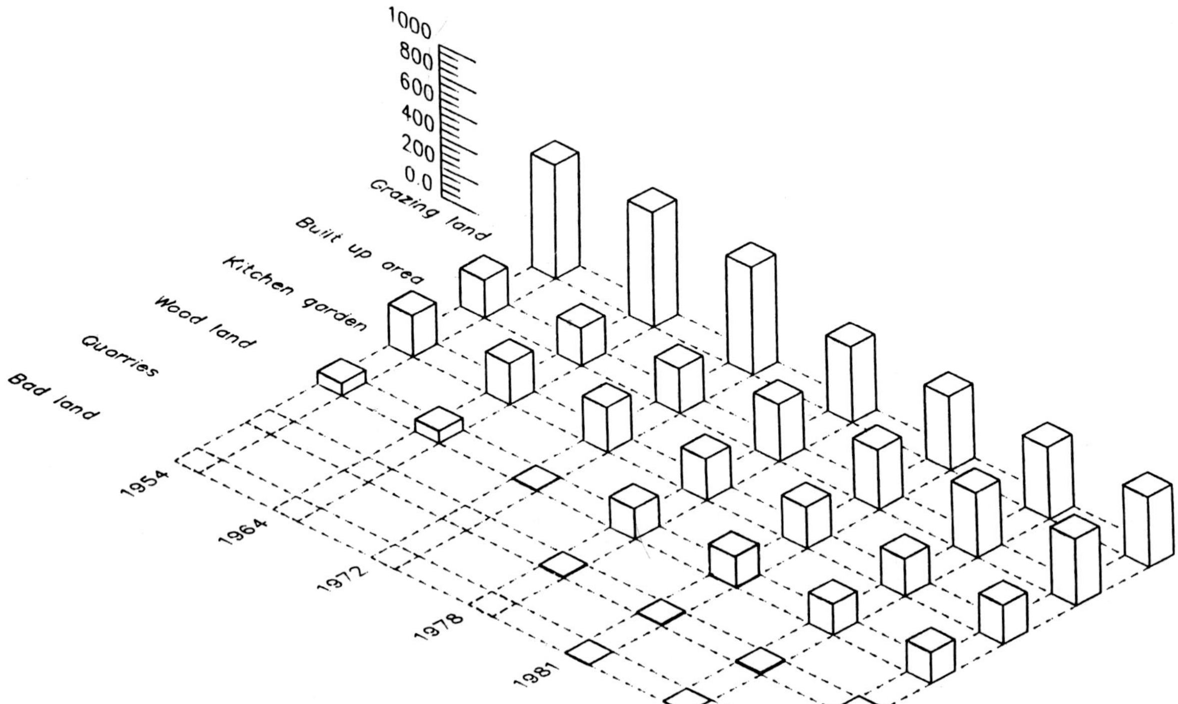


Figure 47 Graph of changes in the urban area between 1954 and 1989, showing the decrease in grazing and kitchen gardens, and the increase in the built up area.

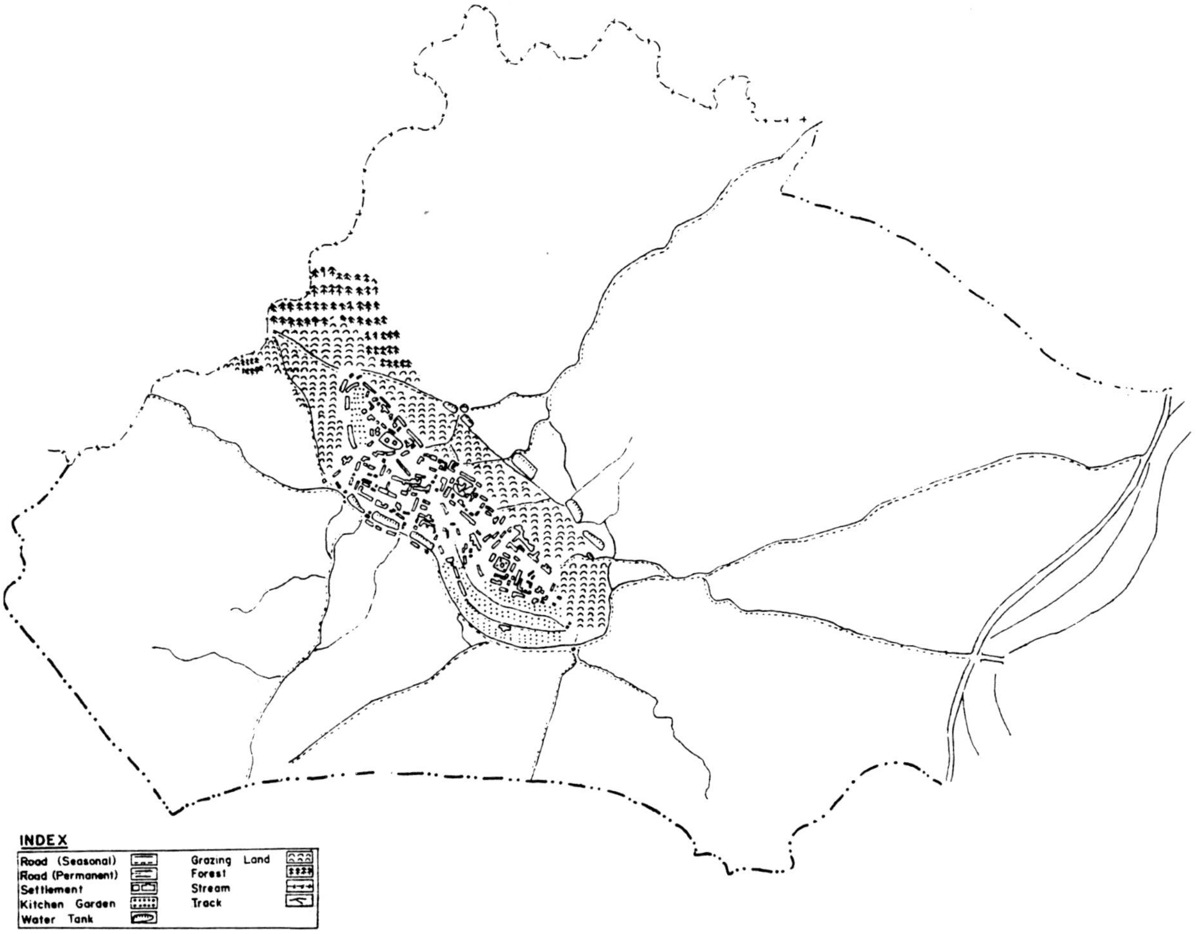


Figure 48 Land use map of Kirtipur 1954 (U. S. Shrestha). The compactness of the historic settlement can be seen on the high ground, with the old defensive woodland to the north, the vegetable gardens between the former inner and outer fortifications, and the grazing land on the slopes around the town.

24 *ropanis*, as householders enlarged their gardens by encroaching into the grazing land, and later bought the land from the Kirtipur and Bāgh Bhairav Pañchāyats.

With the construction of a great number of new houses, local people began quarrying stone in various places around the town to provide materials for erecting the new dwellings. One of the larger quarries was in Amalshi Bāzār, but this quarry has now been exhausted and is out of use. In Pīgāṅ the surface stone (*pucha loṅ*) has also been quarried both by local people and by people from the nearby village of Tīn Thana situated west of Kirtipur and at the opposite side of the Balkhu River. The houses were built sporadically in two lines, in the area which was later to become known as Naya Bāzār. From the aerial photographs it is also apparent that the woodland at the north-western side of the town decreased at this time by some 75 *ropanis*. This destruction was unplanned, and took place after a strip of vegetation was cleared by a team of labourers when the ropeway for transporting goods from the west of the valley to Kathmandu was erected passing the north end of Kirtipur. The local people understood that they were permitted by the government to clear the woodland, and with the help of people from Dhupa (part of the Tīn Thana Village Pañchāyat) the wood was cleared. Another increase in the built up area took place in the area of the old fortified wall in Khasi Bāzār when the wall was demolished by civil servants and local people to widen the road from the University as a response to the "Go to Village Campaign" (*gāoṅ phark rastriya abhiyan*).

1972-1978

With the improved road access from Tribhuvan University to Amalshi the built up area in this part of the town began to increase. Land which had been previously distributed to the landless

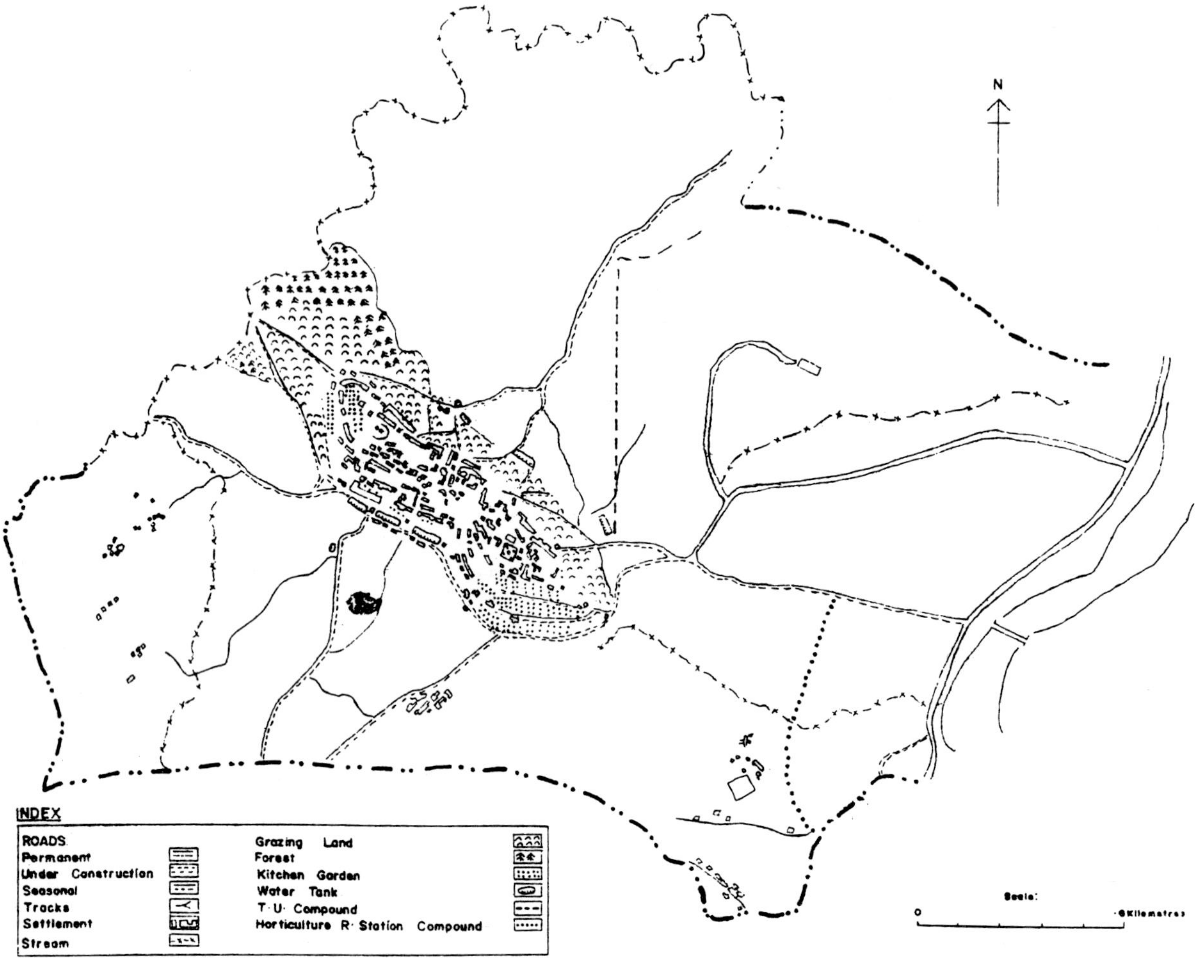


Figure 49 Land us map 1964 (U. S. Shrestha), showing the farmland acquired from Kirtipur for Tribhuvan University and the Horticultural Research Station in 1957, including the new road. The urban area, woodland and grazing of Kirtipur remain with little change.

was purchased by wealthy businessmen who built houses, and people from the old core of Kirtipur began to move to this area. Many well-off people in Chīthuṅ Bihār Paṅchāyat now own property in Amalshi Bāzār. With improved road access the number of houses in Bahirīgāoṅ also increased, and the new building of the Kirtipur Madhyamik Vidyalaya (Kirtipur High School) was built. The settled part of the urban areas increased at this time by 70 *ropanis*, and the grazing decreased by 206 *ropanis*.

In the north-western part of Lāyaku Paṅchāyat area at this time an afforestation programme was undertaken which involved the widening of the road from Amalshi to Pīgāṅ, and the planting of *pinus ruscebergi*, *pinus specie*, eucalyptus (*schima wallichi*), and mixed vegetation in 1974, 1975 and 1976. According to the Pradhān Paṅcha this raised the wooded area by 192 *ropanis*, and constituted the most significant increase in woodland since the destruction during the previous decade.

## 1978-1981

The period between 1978-81 saw a number of the ponds of the town sold by the local *paṅchāyats* to private people and converted to built up areas. These include the site of the present Red Cross building, the pond west of Labhā Pukhū in Sāgāl Ṭol, and the site of the Vishow Rastriya Primary School in Dhalpāḥ, south of Sāgāl Ṭol. The built up area was thus increased by 12 *ropanis*.

## 1981-1987

Within this period the development of the built up area on both sides of the road between Amalshi and Khasi Bāzār took place. The gravelled road from Tribhuvan University to Kirtipur was metalled in 1983, and with the facilities of piped

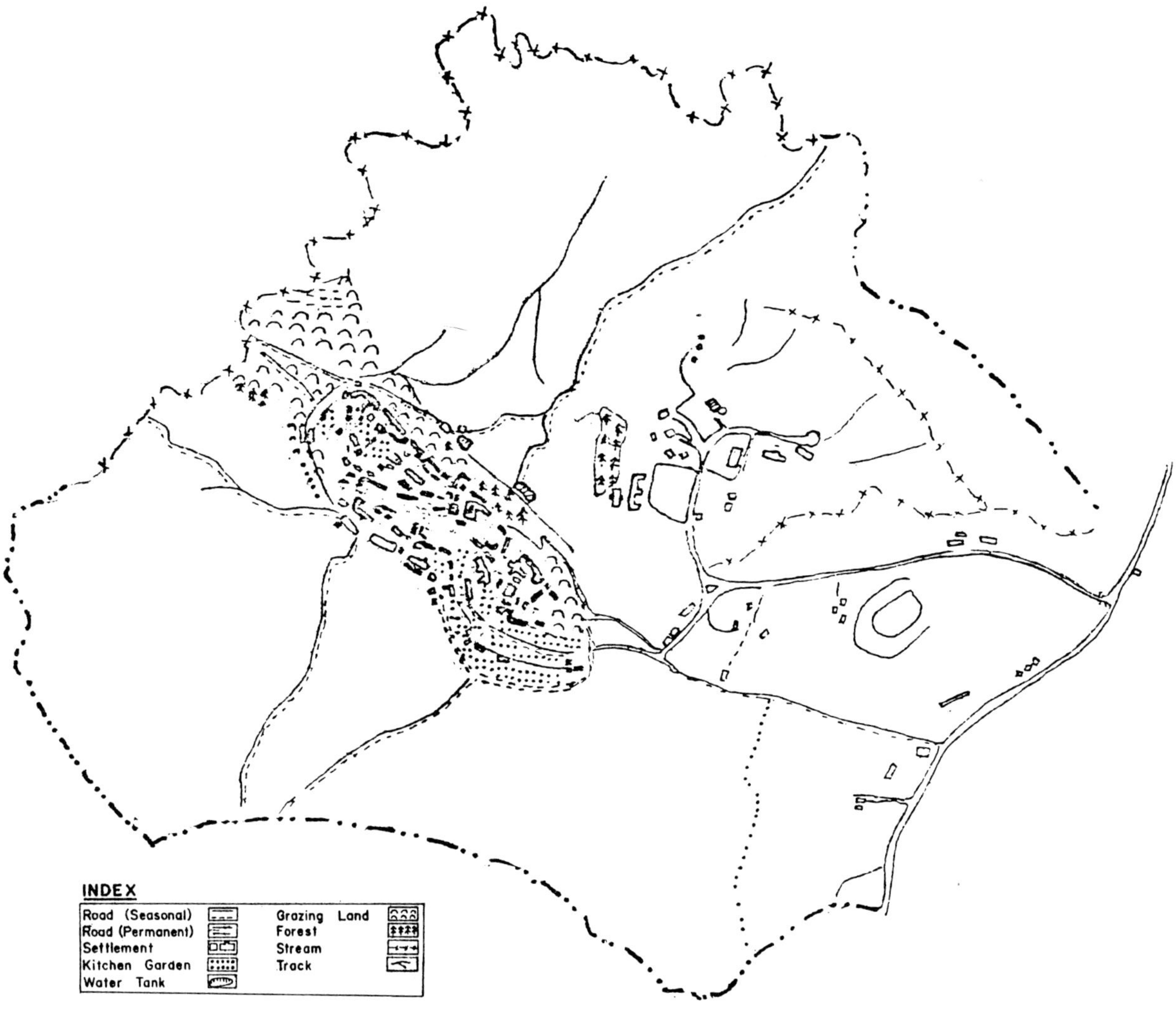


Figure 50 Land us map 1972 (U. S. Shrestha). The old woodland to the north was cleared at the time of the construction of a cable transport system.

drinking water, electricity, the clinic and the bank, people of the core area of the town were encouraged to build in this area, accounting for an increase of 47 *ropanis*. The kitchen gardens and grazing land decreased by 25 and 18 *ropanis* respectively. The effects of the clearance of undergrowth and forest in the west of the town between 1964 and 1972, already causing erosion by 1981 had become more marked by 1987, as is seen by the increase in bad land on the steep slope known locally as Ta Dhang Ga near Balkhu Khola.

1987-1989

The settled area in Amalshi Bāzār and Khasi Bāzār has become denser day by day. For example, where the fortified wall was destroyed ten houses were erected, and other private houses and the Gurkha Nath School have further increased the density. The grazing land on the western side has decreased by ten *ropanis*, mainly by the setting up in one night in 1988 of 23 squatter houses with their own kitchen gardens. In the central area of the town some grazing land has also been turned into kitchen gardens by the old building of the Kirtipur Madhyamik Vidyalaya. More quarrying is being carried out on the route to Ta Dhang Ga in the west. The District Forest Controllers Office has been responsible for the afforestation of 28 *ropanis* of land in this period, but because of factors such as erosion the area of forested land has in fact only increased by two *ropanis* between 1978 and 1989.

CHANGES IN USE OF CULTIVATED LAND 1954-1964

In 1954 the cultivated land was 11,110 *ropanis*, accounting for 89.21% of the total area of Kirtipur, while the urban area of 1,343 *ropanis* made up the remainder. Cultivated land lying three or more kilometres from Kirtipur was

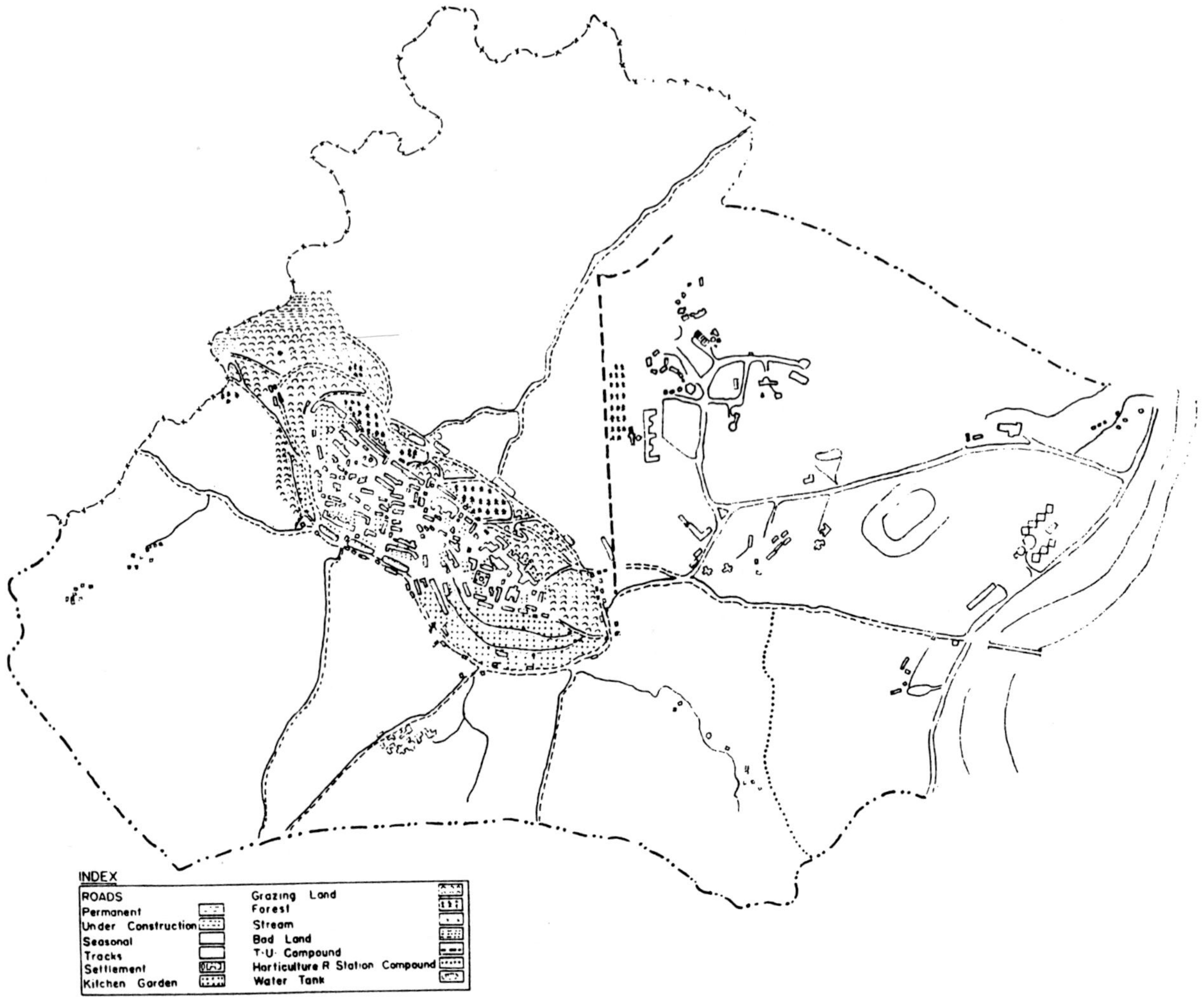


Figure 51 Land us map 1978 (U. S. Shrestha), showing the new woodland planted to the north-east of the town, and the development of the University Campus.

rented to farmers of other areas for cultivation. The greatest changes in land use in Kirtipur occurred with the setting up in 1957 by the government of Tribhuvan University and the Horticulture Research Station. This involved the acquisition of 3,408 *ropanis* (27.37%) of land for the University, and 900 *ropanis* (7.25%) for the Horticultural Research Station, with a result that the town lost a third of its cultivated land.

The land acquired for the University was initially left uncultivated because of the possibility of buildings being erected, but later the University decided to lease land not being built on for cultivation at a rent of Rs.200 per *ropani*, or 45 kilogrammes of paddy per *ropani*. According to the tenants of the University land, they do not have the right to claim one third of the cultivated land because it is owned by an institution, a right which exists where the land is owned by an individual. Rice paddy and other crops are therefore cultivated right up to the University buildings. The University administration also has the right to cultivate. Graziers may not graze in the area, and the University administration has to check all the grazing within the compound, but there is some flexibility about this. Outside the compound and in the fields people graze where they like.

### 1964-1972

Between 1964 and 1972 no significant change was seen in the area of cultivated land.

### 1972-1978

The completion of the ring road around Kathmandu brought about a marked increase in land prices in Kirtipur. Land formerly valued at Rs.25,000 per *ropani* began to be sold at

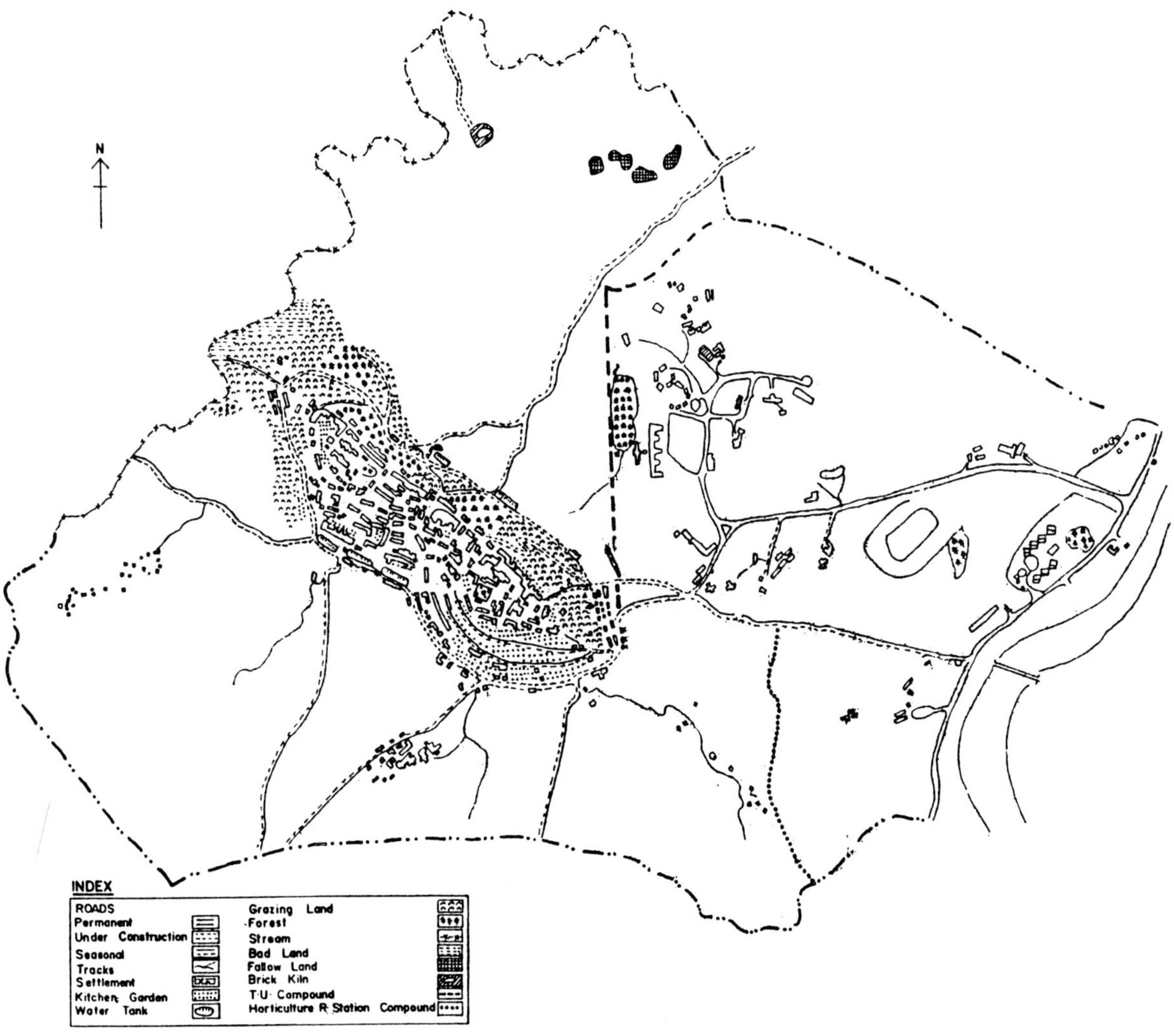


Figure 52 Land us map 1981 (U. S. Shrestha). A brick kiln and its connecting road can be seen at the north of the town, and the new development at Naya Bāzār on the south-east edge of the town is shown.

Rs.80,000 per *ropani,* in some cases to people from outside the Kathmandu Valley. In Kirtipur 15 *ropanis* of former agricultural land became brick kilns, and some eight *ropanis* of land were left fallow in Naravocha to the north of the town. As the law stands, if the land is rented to a tenant the cultivator has a right to claim one third of it, which discourages owners of land bought as a speculation from letting it to farmers.

1978-1981

Between 1978 and 1981 there were more changes in land use. The University acquired a further 600 *ropanis* of land by compulsory purchase, 18 *ropanis* of land were taken for roads to give access to the brick kilns, and the area of fallow land in Naravocha increased to 47 *ropanis.* In 1978 only one of the brick kilns was in operation, covering an area of approximately 60 *ropanis.* The figures given in the tables represent the area used for the kilns throughout the year, and in the Land Use Maps the diagonal hatching represents the area of clay used for brick making. This may also be used for winter cropping, and in Summer for paddy cultivation, apart from the area of the actual chimney. All these activities reduced the cultivated land to 6,716 *ropanis* or 50.27% of the Kirtipur area.

1981-1987

Between 1981 and 1987 the trend of land being left fallow continued for a number of reasons. Rumours that land in Khoyanala was likely to be acquired by the government for the establishment of a main bus terminal for Kathmandu caused a number of owners to sell land quickly at the market price rather than run the risk of having it taken over by the government for a nominal

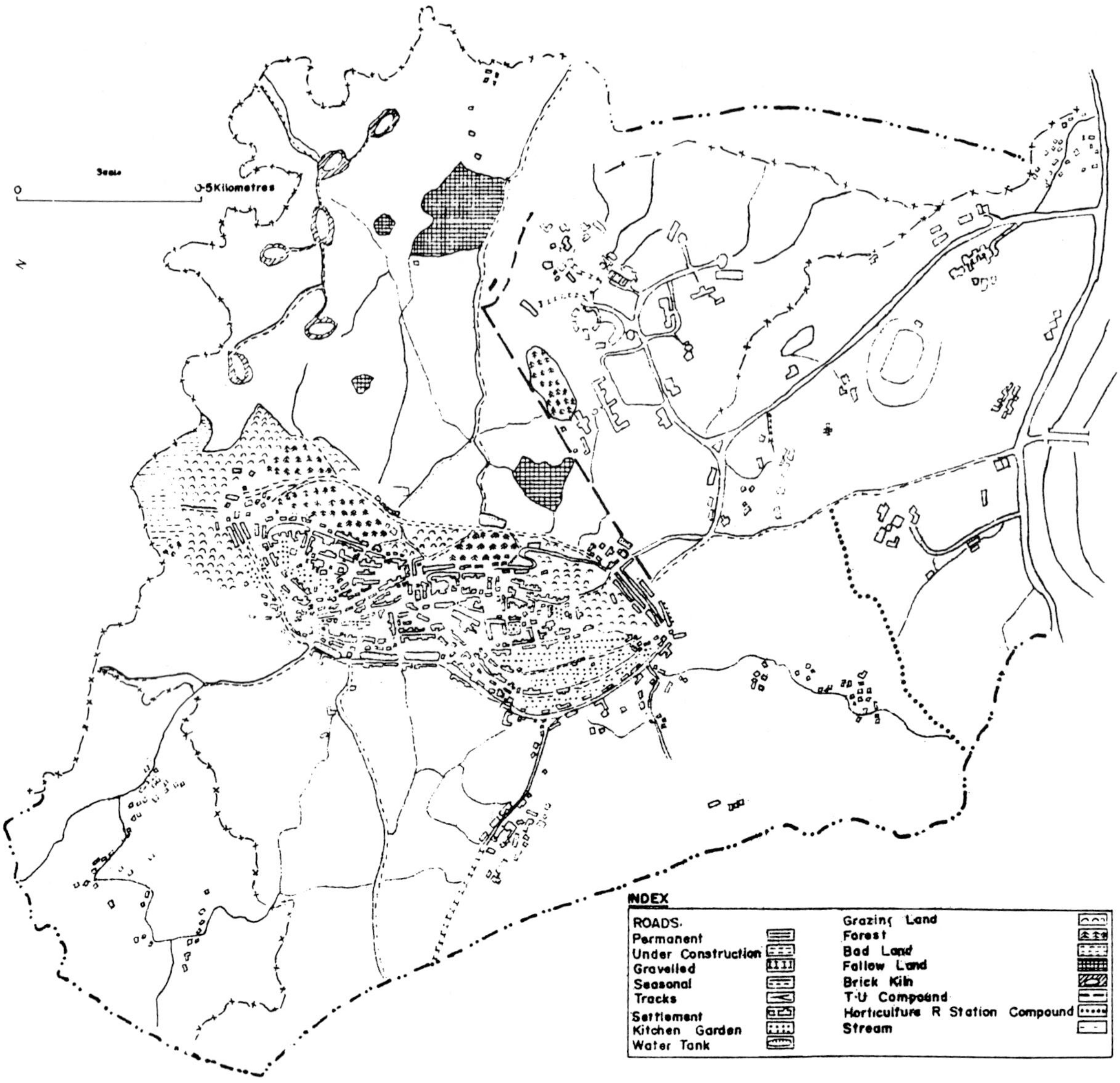


Figure 53 Land us map 1987 (U. S. Shrestha). There is a increase in land left uncultivated, and some land to the north-west has been eroded following previous deforestation. Naya Bāzār has become a significant development, served by a metalled road.

payment. By 1987 a total of 105 *ropanis* at Naravocha and Tyangla which had been bought for investment were lying fallow.

In 1986 the construction of the gravelled road from Kirtipur to Salyanthān village, two kilometres south of the town, increased the value of the land nearby from Rs.45,000 to Rs.70,000 per *ropani*. The proximity to the road, as well as facilities such as water and electricity also led to encroachment on cultivated land for house building in the south-eastern part of the town, particularly in Salayanch near the road junction to Pāṅgā and Bhājangal. Only one house was built on cultivated land to the north of the town at this time. A number of brick kilns were also built on another 30 *ropanis* of former farm-land to the north-east, bringing brick making up to the foot of the Kirtipur hill. The decrease in the total area of cultivated land during these six years was from 6,716 to 6,015 *ropanis*.

## 1987-1989

Between 1987 and 1989 more agricultural land on the northern side, and some on the southern side was sold following reports that the government was to launch an Urban Development Plan in the northern part of the town, and rumours that there was a possibility of a military barrack being constructed to the south. Fallow land on the northern side increased by 17 *ropanis*. The construction of a gravelled road from Kirtipur to Naravocha by the Lāyaku Village Pañchāyat brought a change in land value from Rs.60,000

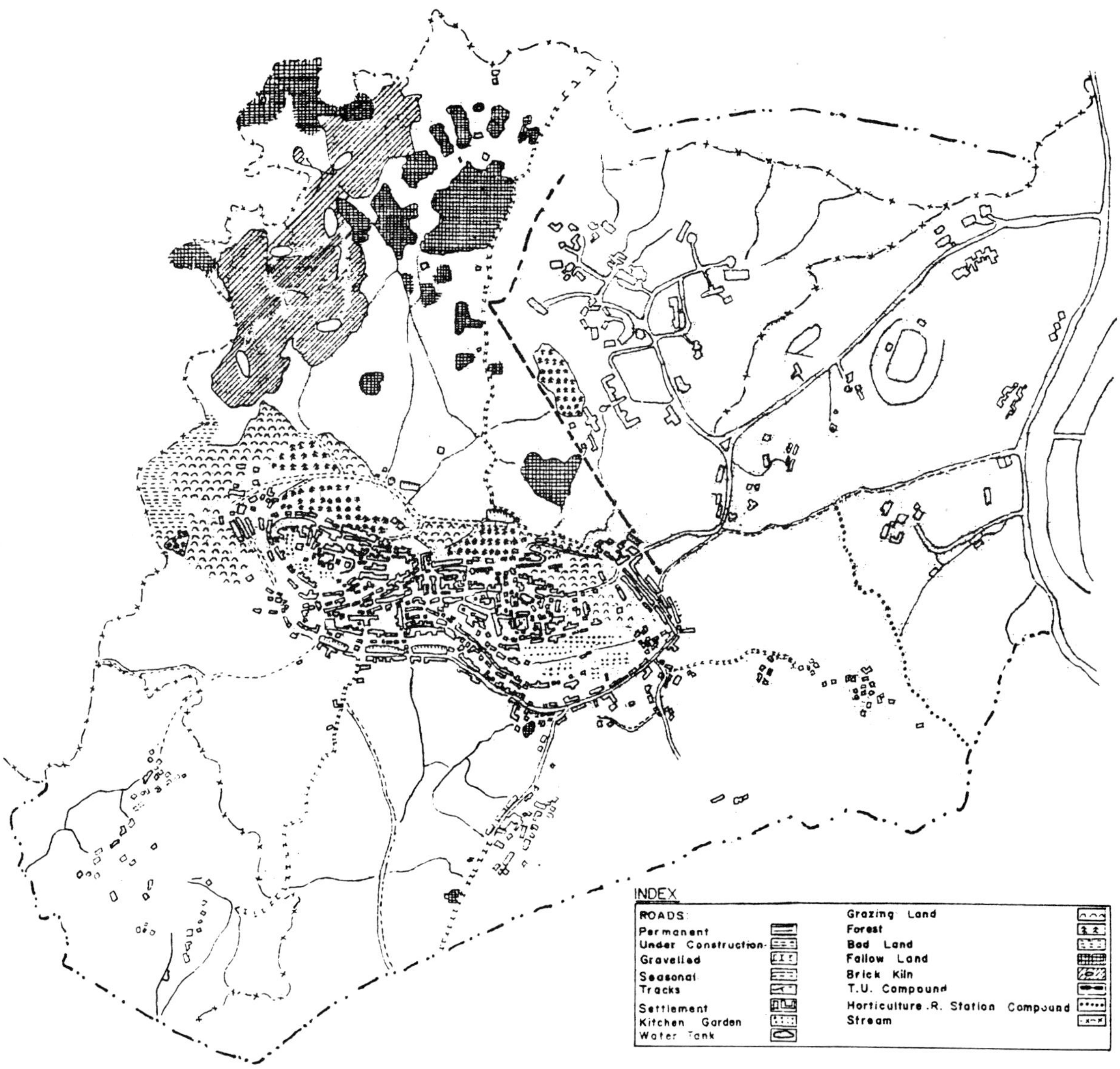


Figure 54 Land us map 1989 (U. S. Shrestha). There has been a considerable increase in land used for brick production or left fallow. In the built up area there is a continued increase in the density of housing.

per *ropani* to Rs.100,000 per *ropani* or more, and people began to build on the cultivated land on the northern side. According to the estimate of the Pañchāyat Secretariats of Chīthuṅ and Lāya-ku, 30% to 35% of landholders sold their land in Naravocha and Ikhā Bāhā. Four houses were erected by local people by selling half of their land.

People from outside the Kathmandu Valley were also attracted to Kirtipur because of the prospect of future urban development. This is the case with most of the irrigated fields at Khoya-nala north-west of the town. The land there has been bought by kiln owners and industrialists from outside Kirtipur. According to an interview with a kiln owner, the area used for brick production has increased from 45 to 408 *ropanis* between 1978 and 1989. The exhaustion of the land results in the land becoming unproductive as the subsoil is brought to the surface. The traditional irrigation channels are also disrupted by the extraction of clay. Where the level of the land has been reduced, it prevents the flow of water to the paddy fields, while, on the other hand, the level of some plots has been raised by spoil, preventing water retention, and making it impossible to grow paddy in some areas. On the whole the land level is dropping, and the topsoil is thinner than previously. There is also a possibility of cutting into the bed of the River Balkhu, which could in the near future cause it to change course, exposing boulders and increasing the area unsuitable for cultivation.

The land in Naravocha has also been bought

Plate 113 Mabhī Pukhū, photograph taken in 1986 before the pond was filled in to provide a recreation ground at Khasi Bāzār. It is situated near the metalled road, where there has been a spate of new building activity.

for both industrial and residential purposes. On a number of occasions the original owners of the land were manipulated by land brokers who propagated various rumours of the possibility of the land being acquired by the government, for the University, or for the Horticulture Research Station, which caused people to sell their land as fast as possible.

Proximity to the motorable roads has been responsible for most changes in land use. Arable land near the ring road and the University is gradually changing to residential areas. The local people tend to be reluctant to encroach on cultivated land as they do not have the resources themselves to develop it as residential plots. However, with the possibility of a decrease in the value in the future because of acquisition by the government, the owners have in some cases taken the option of selling, and investing the money in secondary activities. In the case of western countries on the point of industrial development a similar situation has been described, where in the earlier stages wealth and effort were still put into preparing the land for agricultural use, whereas in the later stages, with the growth of population and transport facilities, time and wealth were put to the task of taking the land out of agricultural use.

In the case of Kirtipur, the last three decades have brought about substantial changes in land use both in the urban and cultivated areas. The causes have been a combination of the growth of population through natural increase, immigration from other parts of Nepal to the Kathmandu Valley, the government programmes of road building and the establishment of various institutions, and the policies of the local *panchāyats* with regard to municipally owned land. The changes have been mainly in the north and south because of the location of the University campus to the east and the natural barrier of the Balkhu River gorge and the steep slope to the west. The result between 1954 and 1989 has been an overall decrease in cultivated land of 5,233 *ropanis*, and an increase in the urban area of 21 *ropanis*. Tribhuvan University and the Horticultural Research Station account for 4,912 *ropanis* of the former farm-lands of the town, and brick kilns and roads for 45 and 33 *ropanis* respectively. 122 *ropanis* of the cultivable land have been bought for investment and are left fallow to prevent a cultivator acquiring rights over the land.

A detailed break down of the changes in the urban area itself shows that the housing has become denser, with 200 *ropanis* more land used for buildings by 1989. The total area of kitchen gardens has decreased by 15 *ropanis*, which considering the increase in population and density of housing means that individual families now have far smaller gardens than previously. The areas used for communal grazing have also decreased, by 288 *ropanis*, but the woodland and vegetation have increased by 119 *ropanis*. Quarrying now accounts for 12 *ropanis* of land, and erosion has rendered 2 *ropanis* of land unusable.

The changes in land use are a result of the gradual modernization and development of the Kathmandu Valley, and reflect an improvement in the facilities available to the citizens. There have, however, been some unplanned and unforeseen consequences of the changes, and these should be born in mind when considering future recommendations for the development of the town. The removal of a third of the farm land has made the economy of the town depend less on agriculture and more on other sources of income. The increase in land prices has led to short term financial gain for some individuals, but not necessarily to improvements in the quality of life in the town.

## TABLE 1

### CHANGES IN URBAN AREA

Figures in *ropanis*, with percentages below
1 *ropani* = 72 x 72 ft. or 21.96 x 21.96 m.
8.4 *ropani* = approx 1 acre, 20.73 *ropani* = approx 1 hectare

| | 1954 | 1964 | 1972 | 1978 | 1981 | 1987 | 1989 |
|---|---|---|---|---|---|---|---|
| **Built up area** | **246** | **246** | **295** | **365** | **380** | **422** | **436** |
| % | 18.31 | 18.31 | 21.96 | 27.17 | 28.18 | 31.28 | 31.98 |
| **Kitchen garden** | **270** | **270** | **294** | **271** | **270** | **245** | **255** |
| % | 20.10 | 20.10 | 21.89 | 20.17 | 20.02 | 18.16 | 18.70 |
| **Grazing land** | **745** | **745** | **747** | **497** | **485** | **467** | **457** |
| % | 55.47 | 55.47 | 55.62 | 37.00 | 35.97 | 34.61 | 33.52 |
| **Woodland** | **82** | **82** | **7** | **199** | **200** | **201** | **201** |
| % | 6.10 | 6.10 | 0.52 | 14.82 | 14.83 | 14.89 | 14.74 |
| **Quarries** | | | | **11** | **11** | **12** | **12** |
| % | | | | 0.81 | 0.81 | 0.88 | 0.88 |
| **Bad Land** | | | | | **2** | **2** | **2** |
| % | | | | | 0.14 | 0.14 | 0.14 |
| **Total** | **1343** | **1343** | **1343** | **1343** | **1343** | **1343** | **1343** |
| % | 100. | 100 | 100 | 100 | 100 | 100 | 100 |

## TABLE 2

### CHANGE IN AGRICULTURAL LANDUSE

Areas in *ropani*, with percentages below.

| | 1954 | 1964 | 1972 | 1978 | 1981 | 1987 | 1989 |
|---|---|---|---|---|---|---|---|
| **Cultivated land** | **11110** | **6802** | **6802** | **6761** | **6113** | **6020** | **5978** |
| % | 89.21 | 54.62 | 54.62 | 54.29 | 49.08 | 48.34 | 48.00 |
| **Urban area** | **1343** | **1343** | **1343** | **1343** | **1348** | **1349** | **1363** |
| % | 10.78 | 10.78 | 10.78 | 10.78 | 10.82 | 10.83 | 10.95 |
| **Tribhuvan University** | | **3408** | **3408** | **3408** | **4012** | **4012** | **4012** |
| % | | 27.37 | 27.37 | 27.37 | 32.22 | 32.22 | 32.22 |
| **Horticulture Research Stn.** | | **900** | **900** | **900** | **900** | **900** | **900** |
| % | | 7.23 | 7.23 | 7.23 | 7.23 | 7.23 | 7.23 |
| **Brick kilns** | | | | **15** | **15** | **45** | **45** |
| % | | | | 0.12 | 0.12 | 0.36 | 0.36 |
| **Roads** | | | | **18** | **18** | **22** | **33** |
| % | | | | 0.14 | 0.14 | 0.17 | 0.26 |
| **Fallow land** | | | | **8** | **47** | **105** | **122** |
| % | | | | 0.6 | 0.38 | 0.84 | 0.98 |
| **Total** | 12453 | 12453 | 12453 | 12453 | 12453 | 12453 | 12453 |
| % | 100 | 100 | 100 | 100 | 100 | 100 | 100 |

# ROAD TRANSPORT AND COMMUNICATIONS

UTTAM SAGAR SHRESTHA

The roads and tracks in Kirtipur follow their mediaeval layout and have kept their ritual and practical functions from early times. The majority of the streets in the town are paved in the traditional way with stone slabs or brick, or a combination of the two. There are interesting parallels between the streets of Kirtipur and those of the Indus civilization which flourished in Asia between 3250 and 2750 BC. Excavations at Mohenjo Daro[1] and Harappa[2] show that some of the streets of these cities may have been paved with burnt brick, and in most streets drainage was provided. Archaeological and historical evidence shows that there were many types of carts and chariots in use in India in ancient times, and by 75 AD various methods of road construction were known there. As well as brick pavement, stone slab pavement and a kind of concrete used as a foundation course or as the actual road surface has been found, and the principle of grouting with gypsum lime mortar was known.[3]

In Nepal, in the relatively flat terai region bordering India there is some evidence of cart tracks at Kapilvastu[4] and Lumbini, the birthplace of Lord Buddha, 425 kilometres from Kathmandu. The tracks may be datable to the 3rd century BC, the time of the Emperor Aśoka's visit to Nepal, and roads dating between the 7th century BC to the 2nd century AD have been discovered near the gateway within the city of Kapilvastu. A road of the 2nd century BC is of particular interest. It was built with an eight inch layer of iron slag and a surface of brick with stone edges, and has traces of ancient wheel tracks four feet apart, the same spacing as the wheels of bullock carts still used in the locality. In the Kathmandu Valley itself there are inscriptions of the 5th to 7th century AD[5] mentioning three categories of tracks: elephant tracks (*hastimarg*), horse tracks (*asvamarg*), and general tracks, presumably footpaths (*marg*), but because of the mountainous terrain carts were not practical for long distance transport in Nepal.

The Chinese traveller Wang Hiuen-t'se crossed through Kathmandu in about 657 AD on his way to Patna and Benares, giving one of the earliest descriptions of the route in his account. In the 17th, 18th and 19th centuries numerous Capuchin friars crossed the Kuti pass, now called Kodari, in the Himalayas on their route between Peking via Lhasa and Kathmandu, to Benares and the ports of western India. Kirkpatrick[6] also gives extensive details of routes and methods of travel to and within Nepal from his journey in 1793, accompanied by a map.

## HISTORIC STREETS AND PROCESSIONAL ROUTES IN KIRTIPUR

Kirtipur's importance as a fortified town was increased by its position on the trade routes from the south and south-west of the country to Kathmandu. As Kirtipur was under the jurisdiction of Patan, customs duty was levied on goods passing through Kirtipur. The route from India coming via Chitlang and Pānīghāṭ to Kathmandu reaches the western end of Kirtipur at Sāgāl Ṭol and passes Sāyami Ṭol and Bāgh Bhairav to reach the track to Kathmandu. The main route from the west of the country to Patan also entered Kirtipur at Sāgāl Ṭol, and passed via Khasi Bāzār and Bahirīgāoṅ to Amalshi, crossing the river at Sundarighāṭ, where there is now a bridge. The trade route from India to Patan forked at Chisapani, and came via Pharping.

The network of streets in Kirtipur (Figure 55) consists of broad streets known as *taphā lan*, connected with subsidiary streets (*lan*). The street called Dathu Lan (middle street) running south from Bāgh Bhairav to Khasi Bāzār, and the broad street leading from the Poṛe Ṭol to Lāyaku can be considered the principal streets of Kirtipur, with the subsidiary streets leading off in a swastika pattern to the twelve town gates. When the gates were closed the city was safe from invaders in mediaeval times. Because of the lack of wheeled transport steps are often provided where there is a change of level, and many of the

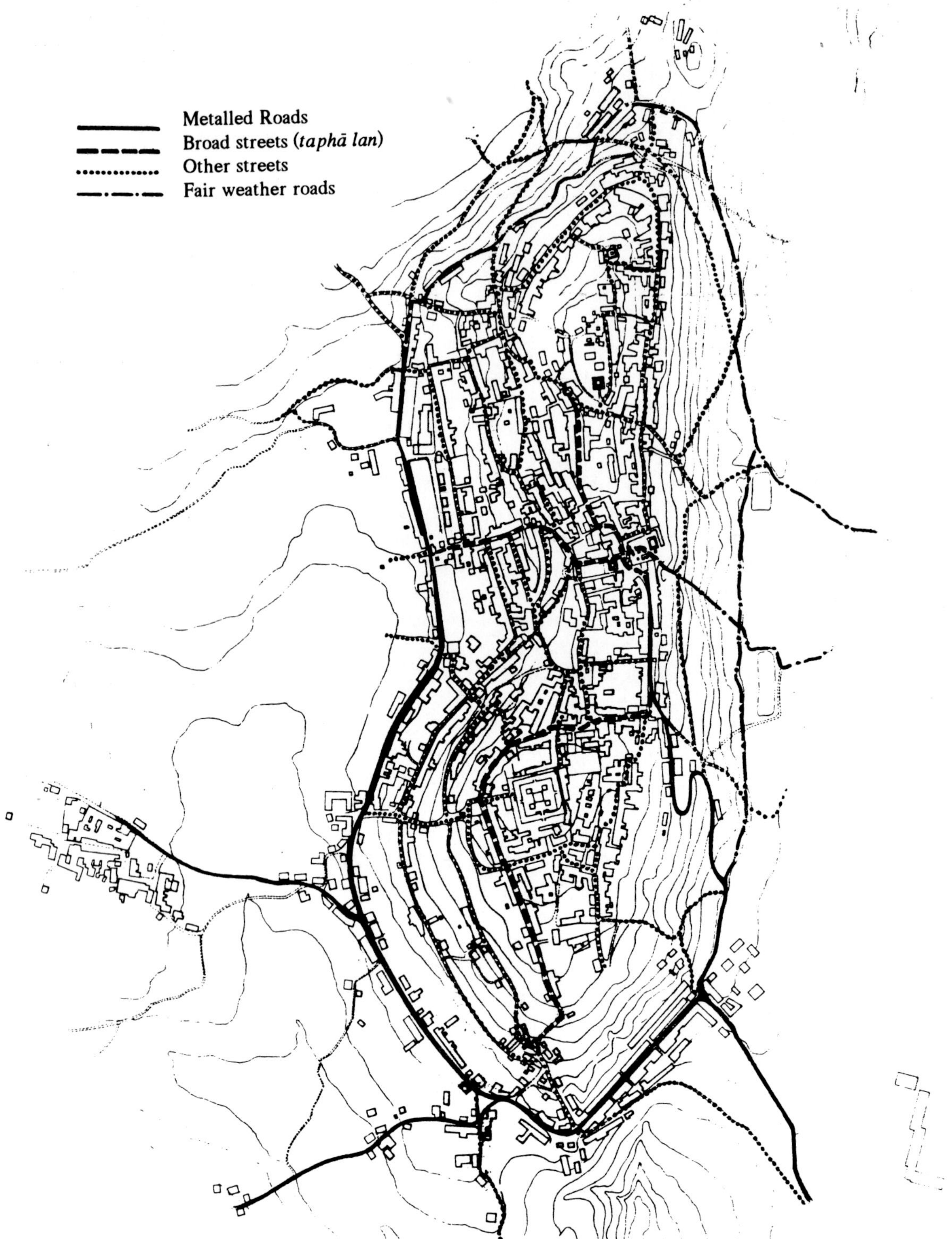


Figure 55 Map of Kirtipur showing roads and tracks.

Plate 114 View of the new development of Naya Bāzār to the south-east of the town, from the east, with four and five storeyed houses on either side of a metalled road.

steep paths are stepped. The streets are paved with brick or slabs of black basalt, or a combination of the two. A number of the old side streets are at present used as open latrines, and are not used for access and circulation, but the traditional routes for funeral processions still pass through them, and it appears that these are the ancient alleys of the historic town.

Another traditional division is between the streets used for festive processions, and those used for funerals. Festive routes are planned to take a clockwise direction, taking in the shrines of both the Hindu and Buddhist faiths. The festive routes and the funeral routes are distinct from each other.

Outside the town tracks connect Kirtipur with the villages of Chobhār, Pāṅgā, Nagāoṅ, Machhegāoṅ, Satuṅgal, Naikāp and Lhonkhā. For local religious rites Kirtipur is the foremost among this group of seven villages, and the *thakālī* or headman of Kirtipur has an important role in the annual festival of Indrāyaṇī in which all these villages participate. There is a considerable amount of intermarriage between the seven villages, and they are well connected to each other by a network of tracks.

## THE MODERN ROAD NETWORK

Until recently the Kathmandu Valley had no motorable road link with the outside world. The Tribhuvan highway was constructed in 1953, as a jeepable track, and in 1956-7 was improved so that lorries could reach Kathmandu. The few cars to be found in the capital before 1953 had been disassembled and carried up from the Indian border via Raxaul, Hetunda, Bhaise and Thankoṭ by the free labour system (*jhārā*) whereby relays of porters from the towns and villages on the route transported the crates along the tracks and high passes of Chisapani and Pānīghāṭ. When all the components arrived in Kathmandu the motor cars were reassembled. Once the Tribhuvan Highway was built the tracks linking the towns and villages were broadened and developed into motorable roads, but without any central planning.

With the establishment of Tribhuvan University Kirtipur was connected to the modern road system. The road built by the government from Tekusi Gate in the south-west of Kathmandu in the direction of Kirtipur in 1957 was extended as far as the University gate in 1961-2. More branches were provided within the Campus in 1963-4, and in 1965-6 the local people added a gravelled road along the line of the old canal to Khasi Bāzār, with a fork up to Bāgh Bhairav, and another along Naya Bāzār. The stretch from the University to Kirtipur was then metalled in 1983-4.

The first regular bus service to the vicinity of Kirtipur was established in 1967 for the University. The bus terminus was in the University

Plate 115 Recent buildings and workshops at the fork of the metalled road to Nagāoṅ.

campus, but some busses and minibusses now stop at the north and south ends of Naya Bāzār, and terminate at the west of Amalshi, near the tracks to Bhājangal and Pāṅgā. The bus service, though somewhat erratic, is the cheapest, and is used by the majority of commuters. The number of motor vehicles owned by people of Kirtipur while small, almost doubled in 1989, to a dozen taxis, ten minibuses, four private cars, and about 30 motorbikes. A number of middle class families own bicycles.

The roads, streets and lanes of the town take up an estimated area of about 27,900 sq.m. The measurements were taken by pacing the length of the roads and measuring the average widths. The lanes used as open latrines are not included in this figure. Of the roads leading into the town 2,380m. are asphalted, and 2,180m. of fair weather road is planned to be asphalted. Inside the town 2,240m. of the streets have stone paving, 3,400m. have sporadic stone paving, 1,160m. have brick paving, and 400m. have sporadic brick paving. In 1985 Taphālan, the broad street leading from Bāgh Bhairav to Lāyaku was paved with Chinese brick for 180m. of its length.

Until recently all goods and materials, even if transported by road, had to be carried by porters up the last stretch of the hill to Kirtipur itself. This had the effect of keeping the town safe from the ravages of motor vehicles, and also meant that building and development in general was restricted to what could be assembled from units of a size and weight that could be carried. The extension of the road to reach the town has been a crucial factor in the mushrooming of new building.

In the Kathmandu Valley, Kirtipur is exceptional for a town of its size and location in that the old street layout has been preserved, and its stepped lanes have prevented the invasion of motor vehicles into the old fabric of the town. The compact arrangement of Kirtipur also puts the outskirts within a short walking distance of the town centre. Within the town itself the streets and lanes, which connect the old town to the periphery, need to be improved. Most of these streets, particularly in the north and west of the town require re-paving and the provision of adequate drainage. These streets would then provide easy and comfortable access to the present motorable roads, which could be extended to form a ring road, keeping the old town free from motor traffic.

## COMMUTERS FROM KIRTIPUR

The development of transport and communications in Nepal in recent decades has made daily

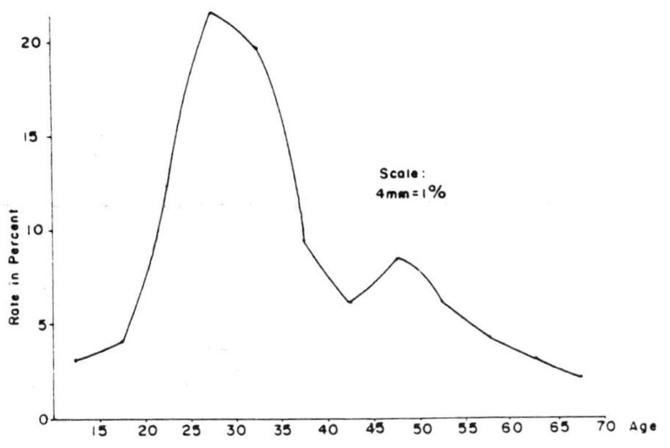


Figure 56 Graph showing the percentage of commuters according to age, indicating a relatively high proportion of employed people in their twenties and thirties (U. S. Shrestha).

commuting to work in the main cities an important part of the economy of village and small town communities. The concentration of commerce, administration, education, health care and other facilities in the municipalities of Kathmandu and Lalitpur (Patan) not only attracts migrant workers from distant parts of Nepal, but also commuters from the surrounding area of the Kathmandu Valley. The daily commuters mainly travel to the cities via the network of nine major metalled roads linked with the ring road surrounding Kathmandu and Lalitpur. Of these the Dakshiṇkālī road which branches to Tribhuvan University and Kirtipur, the Thankoṭ road, the Jitpurphedi road, the Buddhanīlkaṇṭha road via Bansbari, the Sāṅkhu road, and the Songa road via Bhaktapur radiate from Kathmandu; while the roads radiating from Lalitpur are the Lubhu road via Sanugāoṅ, the Chapagāoṅ road, and the Godāvarī road. In the past the people of Kirtipur and the villages around such as Pāṅgā, Nagāoṅ, Machhegāoṅ, Salyanthān and Bhājangal used the Kirtipur paths to commute to Kathmandu via Kalimati, and to Lalitpur via Javalakhel.

Our survey indicates that the population of Kirtipur in 1989 was close to 12,838, and according to the *paṅchāyat* records in 1988 the total population, including that of Naya Bāzār and other areas outside the historic town but under the *paṅchāyats*, was approximately 16,623. By the time of our survey in 1989, in Naya Bāzār 112 households accounted for a population of 401 people. It was estimated that the number of employed people in the town in 1989 was 3,676, and in a sample of households with a total population of 1,340 the number of employed people was 384 or 28.65%. The age distribution in the sample was as follows:

| Age | number | % | Age | number | % |
|---|---|---|---|---|---|
| 10-14 | 6 | 1.56 | 40-44 | 36 | 9.38 |
| 15-19 | 25 | 6.51 | 45-49 | 31 | 8.07 |
| 20-24 | 52 | 13.54 | 50-54 | 21 | 5.47 |
| 25-29 | 61 | 15.88 | 55-59 | 21 | 5.47 |
| 30-34 | 53 | 13.80 | 60-64 | 15 | 3.91 |
| 35-39 | 45 | 11.72 | 65-71 | 18 | 4.69 |
| **Total** | | | | **384** | **100%** |

The improvement in roads and transport, as well as changes in the occupations of the townspeople have greatly increased the number of commuters from Kirtipur. The town has to some extent become a satellite of Kathmandu and Lalitpur, with the economic and social life of the people closely related to the cities. In 1989 we carried out a survey to examine the number of people travelling and their means of transport via the main routes from Kirtipur. The traffic observed included not only residents of Kirtipur, but also people from other settlements including Pāṅgā and Nagāoṅ who use the Kirtipur routes as commuters or for social, recreational or other purposes. Figure 56 shows the age range of commuters. Working hours in Nepal for government offices, educational establishments and private companies are from 10 a.m. to 5 p.m., and Saturday is a holiday. The data used for the survey was collected on the week of Saturday 3rd - Saturday 10th June 1989 between 6.00 and 10.30 in the morning and 4.00 to 8.30 in the evening. People travelling outside these times were not counted, on the assumption that they would not be regular commuters in the strict sense of the term, and their numbers would be small.

It should be noted that the purpose of the survey was to record commuters from Kirtipur itself, rather than the area of the University campus. The survey took place during the University vacation when most of the campus was closed, and does not reflect the traffic of University employees. In addition, at the time of the survey many wage earners were unemployed because of the expiry of the trade and transit treaty between India and Nepal. Both these factors make the daily average number of commuters smaller than usual. The data was collected on all eight days at three observation points at Tyangla north of Kirtipur, Jhakya at the east, and the Tanlcha entry and exit to the University campus. At Naya Bāzār, where the

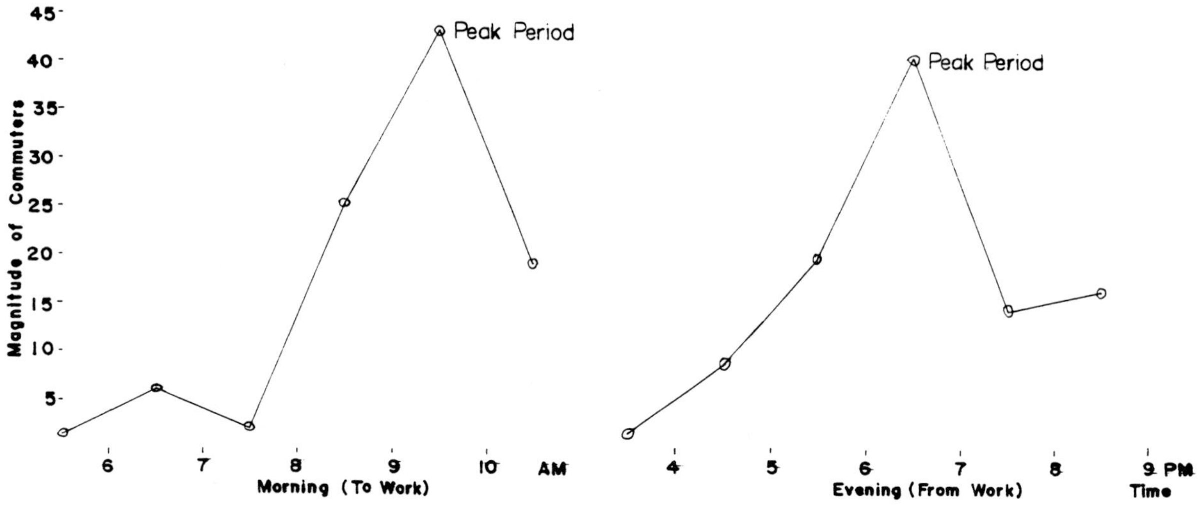


Figure 57 Graph showing the period of commuting, and the peak times between 9.00 and 9.30 in the mornings, and 5.30-6.30 in the evenings (U. S. Shrestha).

Pāṅgā, Nagāoṅ and Machhegāoṅ routes meet, the traffic was observed on only two days, a Tuesday and a Saturday. The graphs and diagrams show the volume of commuters from Kirtipur and the nearby villages, with their destinations. Figures are given separately for men and women, and for working days and Saturdays. The data indicates that the majority of commuters are male, and bound for Kathmandu. The number of people who commute to Kirtipur itself to teach in the schools, sell vegetables, or engage in small businesses is very small.

## COMMUTING ON WORKING DAYS

Our survey showed the average volume of commuters on working days as 3,455, of whom 58.35% (2,016 persons) were from Kirtipur, 25.33% (875 persons) were from Pāṅgā, and 16.32% (564 persons) from Nagāoṅ and Machhegāoṅ. Kirtipur, therefore, as might be expected provides more commuters to the cities than do the smaller neighbouring villages. The figures for Kirtipur represent 15.70% of the total population of the town, and show that one in six of the townspeople are in the habit of travelling to the cities.

The peak period for commuting (Figures 57 and 59) was observed to be between 9.00 and 9.30 a.m., when an average of 877.82 persons (22.43% of the male and 2.96% of the female commuters for the whole day) passed the observation points. In this period 10.93% (377.82 persons) set out from Kirtipur, 9.46% (327 persons) from Pāṅgā and 5.00% (173 persons) from Nagāoṅ and Machhegāoṅ. 25.40% of commuters travelled at this time in the morning, enabling them to reach their destinations by 10 a.m. The slack period for commuters in the morning was between 6.00 and 6.30 with only 1.86% of the traffic passing the observation points. Of the total numbers observed an average of 12.44% (429.83 persons) travelled to Kathmandu via the Tyangla route, and 7.06% (246.09 persons) commuted to Lalitpur (Patan) from the Jhakya route.

In the evening, the figure for commuters returning home was larger than for the morning traffic (Figure 58), with 3,566 persons (87.82% male and 12.12% female) observed. We may assume that the difference in numbers can be accounted for by those who travelled outside the times when observations were made. Kirtipur was the destination of 71% (2,532 persons), while 17.80% (635 persons) returned to Pāṅgā, and 11.18% (399 persons) to Nagāoṅ. The peak period in the evenings was between 5.30 and 6 p.m., when an average of 539.15 persons returned home. During this period 10.77% (384.15 persons) returned to Kirtipur, 2.43% (87 persons) to Pāṅgā and 1.90% (68 persons) to Nagāoṅ and Machhegāoṅ. In 1979-80 the Bristol team carried out a one day survey of the traffic returning to Kirtipur in the evening, in which 835 people were counted coming back to the town, 75% of whom had come from Kathmandu or Lalitpur. Taking the number of households at that time to

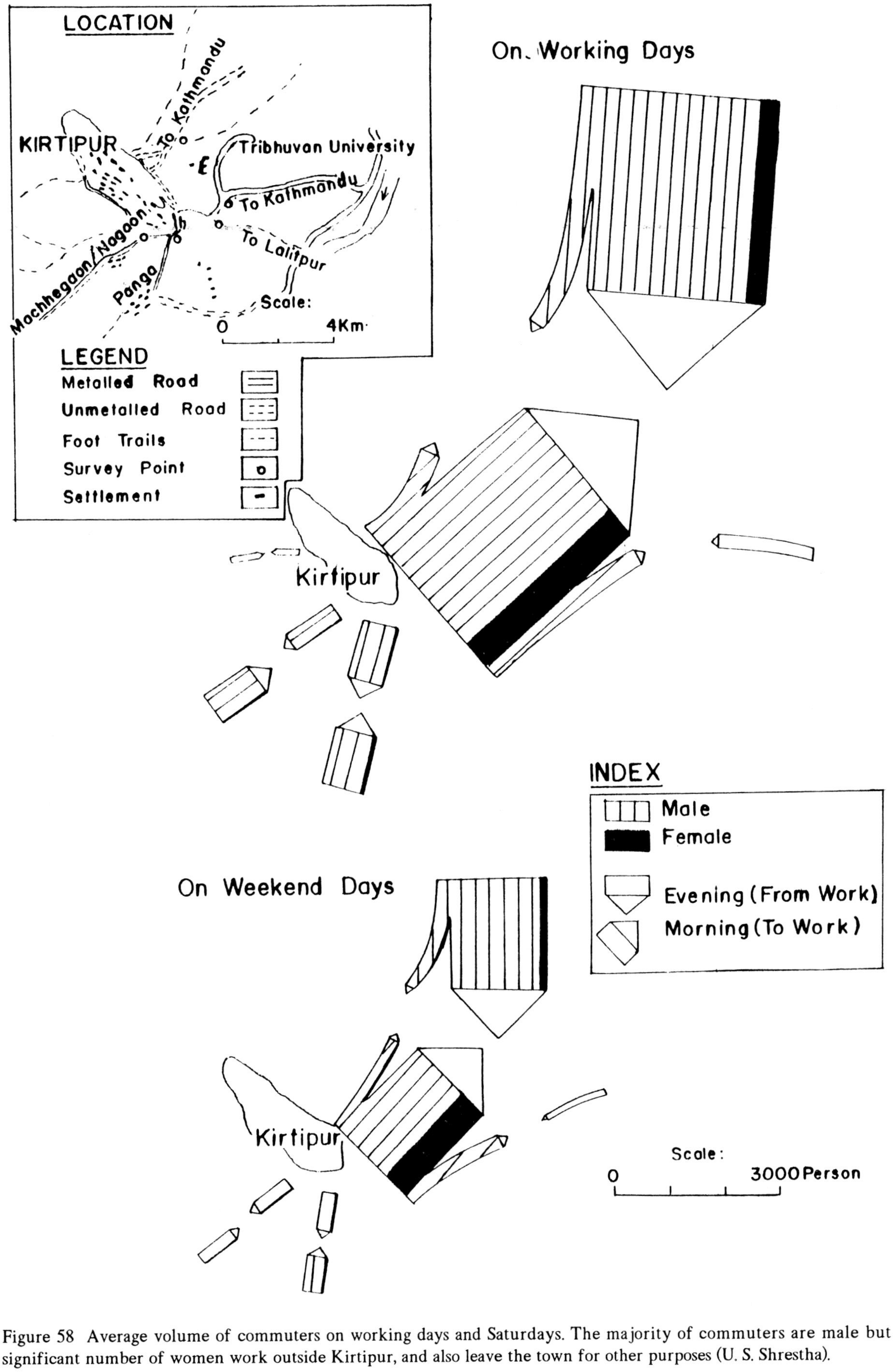


Figure 58 Average volume of commuters on working days and Saturdays. The majority of commuters are male but a significant number of women work outside Kirtipur, and also leave the town for other purposes (U. S. Shrestha).

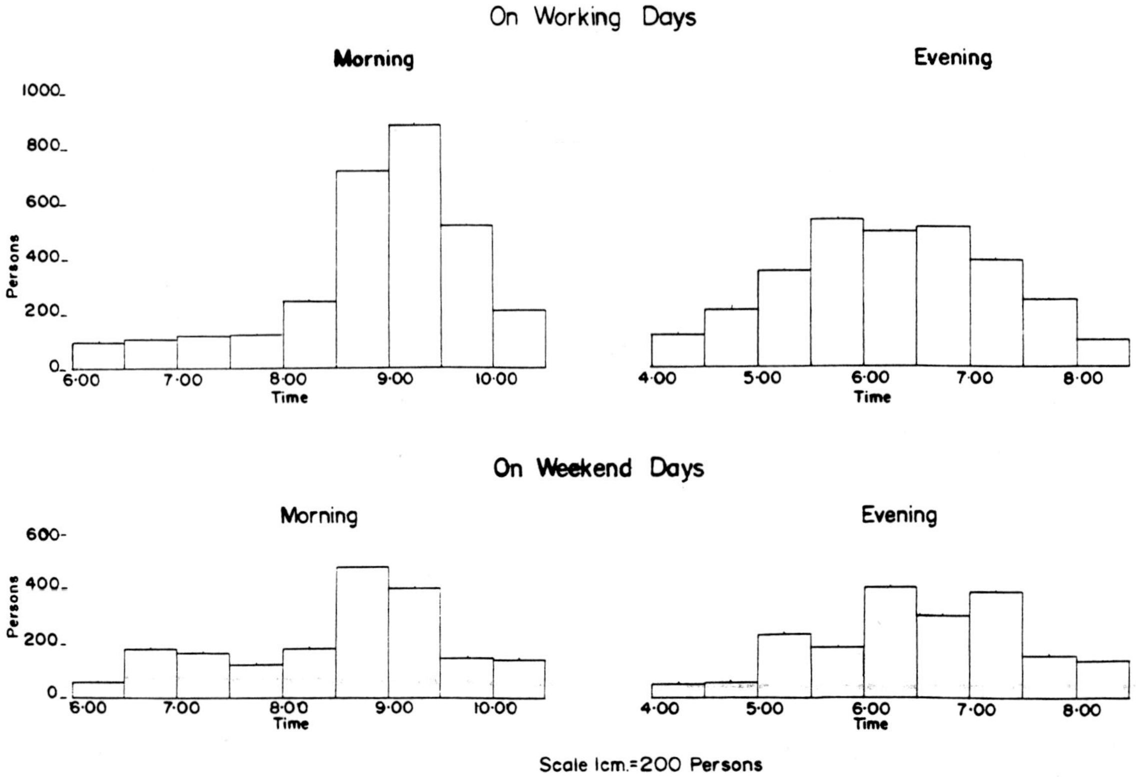


Figure 59 Graphs showing the average volume of commuters on working days and Saturdays. The volume is lower on Saturdays, when government offices, private companies and schools are closed, but as the shops and markets are open people involved in commercial activities commute (U. S. Shrestha).

be 1,300 they concluded that about one in five households in Kirtipur had one of their members working in an office.[7]

In our survey the slack period in the evening was between 4.00 to 4.30 p.m. when only 3.48% returned home. The proportion of commuters returning by the Tyangla route was about 7.73% (276 persons) and by the Jhakhya route 5.07% (181 persons).

## COMMUTING ON NON-WORKING DAYS

The volume of commuters on weekends (Saturdays) is shown in Figure 58. The average volume observed over two Saturdays was 2,182 persons (82.77% male and 17.23% female), among which 68.58% (1496 persons) came from Kirtipur, 20.43% (446 persons) came from Pāṅgā, and 10.99% (240 persons) from Nagāoṅ and Machhegāoṅ. The peak time in the morning was found to be between 9.00 and 9.30, when 18.83% (411 persons) passed the observation points. 11.64% (254 persons) of these were from Kirtipur, 5.54% (121 persons) from Pāṅgā, and 1.64% (36 persons) from Nagāoṅ and Machhegāoṅ.

The evening traffic on Saturdays showed a daily average volume of 1,935 persons (92.27% male and 7.73% female) returning to Kirtipur. The peak period was later than on weekdays and fell between 6.00 and 6.30, when 20.93% (405 persons) returned home. 14.00% (271 persons) were bound for Kirtipur, 3.97% (77 persons) for Pāṅgā, and 2.94% (57 persons) for Nagāoṅ and Machhegāoṅ. Only 2.86% returned during the slack period between 4.00 and 4.30. The proportion of people returning on Saturdays through Tyangla was 29.61% (573 persons) and through Jhakhya 13.48% (261 persons). The Saturday traffic is therefore about two thirds of the weekday traffic.

When the data for commuters to Lalitpur is analysed, it will be seen that on working days it follows the same pattern as that for Kathmandu. The data collected on Saturdays, however, showed a large number of people going to Lalitpur between 6.30 and 7.00 in the morning, with a particularly high proportion of women (16.48% more than men). The data was collected at the time of the annual festival of Rato Machindra Nath, and reflects the active role of women in the celebration of festivals and holidays.

## MEANS OF TRANSPORT

Changes in the socio-economic position and mobility of people tend to be closely related to the availability and frequency of public transport,

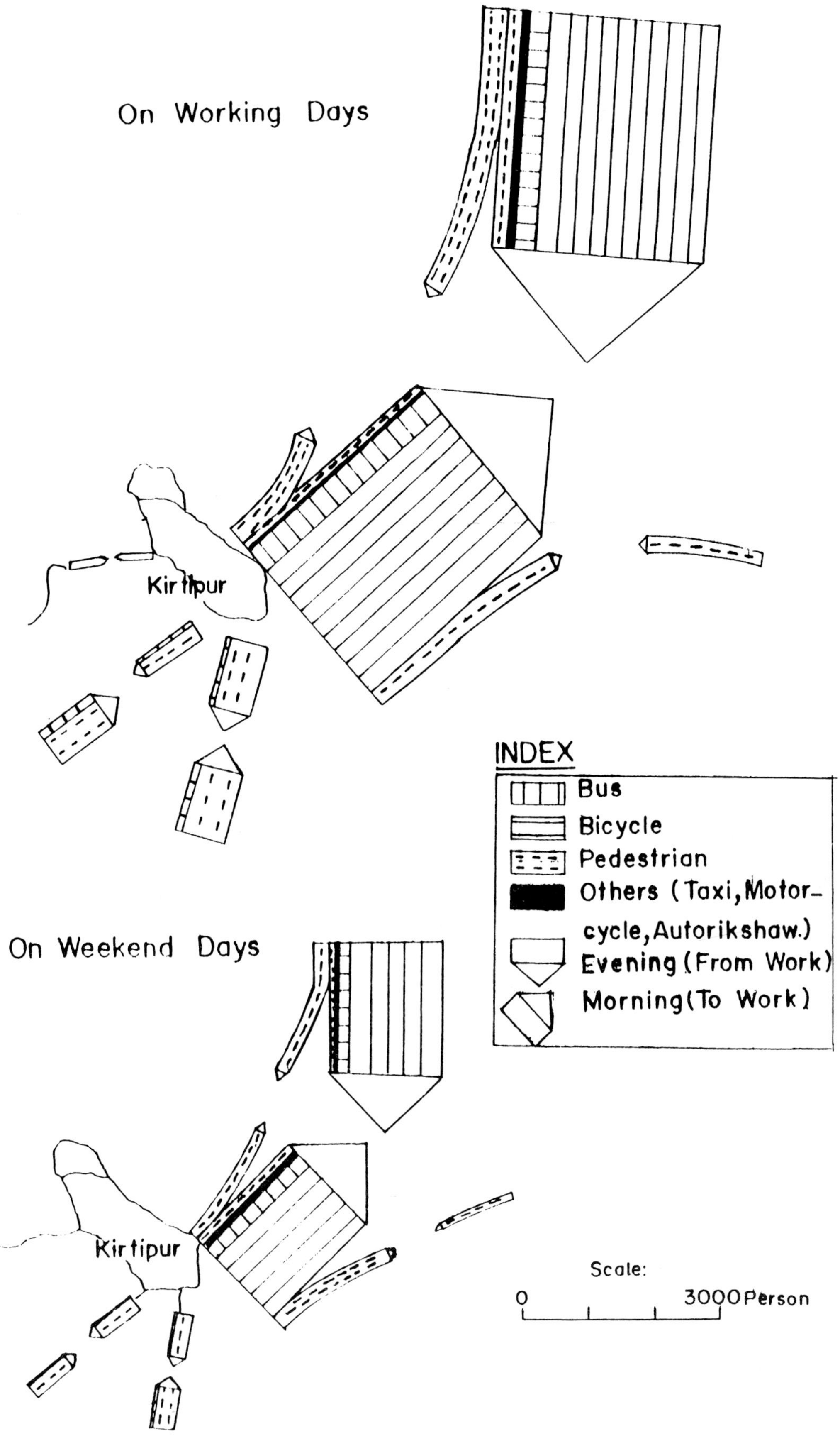


Figure 60 Means of transport used by commuters. Busses and minibusses are the principal vehicles used (U. S. Shrestha).

and in the case of Kirtipur the main means of transportation is the private and public sector busses and minibusses which ply the route from Ratna Park in Kathmandu to the Tribhuvan University campus. Of the 3,455 persons observed commuting to Kathmandu and Lalitpur on working days 73.15% used busses, 12.43 went on foot, 11.47 by bicycle, and a small proportion by motorbike, taxi, auto-rickshaw, and other vehicles such as lorries, tractors and carts (Figure 60). Cycle rickshaws are not used in these routes. The daily average number of people travelling home was found to be higher, 3,566 persons, with noticeable differences in the means of transport, 72.32% using busses, 16.31% going on foot, 8.57 by bicycle, and the rest travelling by other means. The pedestrians took the Tyangla route for Kathmandu and the Jhakhya route for Lalitpur. On Saturdays there was seen to be less traffic both to and from Kirtipur, with an average of 2,182 persons in the morning, of whom 72.57% went by bus, 12.64% on foot, 10.19% by bicycle, and the rest by other vehicles. A smaller number of people were observed returning in the evening, an average of 1,935 persons, with 73.59% using busses, 10.80% going on foot, and 12.17% by bicycle, with a small proportion using other means of transport.

The discrepancy between the data for outward and homeward journeys is partly due to the fact that data was collected for a total of only 9 hours each day, and the traffic was not observed outside these times. In addition more people travel by bus from Kirtipur than on the return journey because the bus route starts at the Campus and space is available, whereas, because of overcrowding, travellers returning from points along the route such as Tripureśvar, Teku, Kalimati, and Kuleśvar are sometimes obliged to walk. Another factor is that commuters who cycle to work often share a bicycle for the downward journey, but one of them walks back up the steep hill where the observations were made.

Taking the approximate figure for the population of Kirtipur as over 12,838, it appears that some 15.73% of the townspeople commute. If the number of adults of working age is assumed to be between 5,000 to 6,000, this indicates that over a third of the working population is employed in Kathmandu and Lalitpur, making a significant contribution to the Kirtipur economy. A comparison of our figures with those of the Bristol group in 1979-80 shows that there has been a significant increase in the number of commuters from Kirtipur within the last 10 years. The Bristol team pointed out that unless the retail trade and industry of Kirtipur was improved, the town was in danger of becoming a residential satellite of Kathmandu. This threat is now even more acute, and while the number of retail shops in Naya Bāzār has increased considerably, this has had little effect on the economy of Kirtipur. It is to be hoped that efforts will be made to use the human and physical resources of the town itself to generate income by the development of local industries and the creation of local employment, otherwise the people of Kirtipur, as well as those who have recently moved to the town will have no alternative but to seek employment in Kathmandu and Lalitpur. With future developments in public transport we should, in any case, be prepared to see an even greater increase in the number of commuters, and practical steps should be taken to make the best use of the transport facilities of the town both for the benefit of commuters and to increase its potential for producing sources of income.

The challenge now is to develop a simple and adequate system of roads to serve the town without adversely affecting its peaceful and safe environment. A ring road around Kirtipur would bring every corner of the town within reasonable access to transport, deliveries, and emergency services, while making it possible to retain an entirely traffic free environment in the old town itself. The ring road would need to have adequate car parks, loading and unloading areas, and taxi termini. The present bus route could then be extended to encircle the town with frequent stops where needed.

## NOTES

1 E. J. H. Mackay, *Further Excavations at Mohenjo-Daro*, 1927-31, Archaeological Survey of India (ASI), New Delhi, 1938, I, 25-36, 171; II, pls. 3, 6-7, 10-11.

2 Madho Sarup Vats, *Excavations at Harappa*, ASI, Delhi, 1940, I, 155; II, pl. 31.

3 *Encyclopaedia Britannica* (*Macropaedia*), XV, London, 1973-4, 893.

4 Mishra Tara Nand, *The Location of Kapilvastu and Archaeological Excavations 1967-1972*, The Lumbini Development Committee, HMG Nepal, Kathmandu, 1977, 12.

5 Bajracharya Dhana Bajra, *Lichchhavikalin Abhilekh*, CNAS Tribhuvan University, BS 2030/1973, 92, 356.

6 William Kirkpatrick, *An Account of the Kingdom of Nepaul*, London, 1811, reprinted New Delhi, 1986, 85, 286-327, Map of Nepaul, with the routes.

7 E. P. Davies *et al.*, *Kirtipur, a Newar Community in Nepal, Development in Debate*, Kirtipur Programme, Bristol, 1979-80, 88.

# WATER SUPPLY AND SANITATION

**ROBIN LALL CHITRAKAR**

The condition of the water supply and sanitation of a town are key factors in the health of the population. The mediaeval builders of Kirtipur and their successors constructed a city no less well planned and built than Kathmandu or the other major cities of the valley, incorporating systems for water supply and drainage conforming with the needs of the time, and what is equally important, provided for their upkeep. Here we are concerned with the present condition of the town, and the most appropriate ways of bringing these vital resources up to present day requirements.

## WATER SUPPLY

The traditional water sources in Kirtipur came from a combination of rivers, ponds, wells, springs (Plates 116-17) and rainwater. The Balkhu Khola river (Figure 2) flows to the north of the town, and ponds in and around the town collect rainwater during the monsoon. The ponds include De Pukhū (Plate 22) in the centre of the town, Mabhī Pukhū (Plate 113), now filled in, Bhī Pukhū (Plate 118) and Labha Pukhū (Plate 1) to the west, and several ponds around the town including Pale Pukhū to the east. Some of the ponds are designated locally as "clean" or "dirty". They provided and still do provide water for bathing, washing utensils, and laundry, as well as for the ritual dipping of children to cure them from diseases. Springs around the base of the hill were traditionally enclosed by stone structures and provided with water spouts, but with the loss of the surrounding woodland the springs now tend to run dry during the dry season. This is also the case with wells. During the rainy season, in addition to the water from springs and wells, rain water is collected from the roofs and used for washing.

The water supply to Kirtipur is now the responsibility of the Water Supply and Sewerage Corporation (WSSC). To supply more water for Kathmandu the Matta Thirtha spring source to the west of Kirtipur was tapped, and a supply via a 100mm. distribution main was provided for Kirtipur en route. Although originally planned to supply Kirtipur alone, in spite of the increase in habitation the pipe was subsequently tapped upstream of Kirtipur to supply another village en route, thus diminishing the supply to the town. To alleviate the problem a new reservoir was added to the north-west of Umā Maheśvara and new supply lines laid, but the supply is still inadequate. At present the water is supplied through 22 public stand-pipes (Plate 120) and about 10 private connections. The water runs only in the mornings and evenings, for a total of six hours a day. The traditional sources are therefore still used to supplement the supply. The townspeople have expressed a strong desire, and are willing to pay for private connections at a fixed rate of about Rs. 1,200 for a 1/2" connection, but so far additional private connections have not been made.

### *Future projections*

The demand for water in Kirtipur is increasing rapidly, both for domestic use and for small scale cottage industries such as handloom weaving and dying. To calculate future demand it is assumed

| | Private taps | Public Taps | Totals |
|---|---|---|---|
| 1 Population AD 2000 | 9,600 | 6,400 | 16,000 |
| 2 Water consumption (m 3/d) | 288 | 1,152 | 1,440 |
| 3 Leakage and gross wastage at 20% | 58 | 230 | 288 |
| Total domestic demand (2+3) | 346 | 1,382 | 1,728 |

Table 1 Water supply via private and public taps in 1988, and estimated future needs.

Plate 116 Spring with ancient water spout still in daily use east of the north circular road.

Plate 117 Women washing clothes and bathing at the continuous spring supply, with a reservoir and modern cover, on the road south of Bahirīgāoṅ.

Plate 118 Bhī Pukhū, one of the traditional water reservoirs at the west of the town.

that the population, estimated at 10,000 in 1983, will grow at the rate of 1.29% per year (the growth rate for the Kathmandu District) to about 16,000 by the year 2000. It is also estimated that about 60% of the population will be provided with private connections, and the remaining 40% by public stand-pipes, with domestic consumption from private taps at 120 litres per capita per day (lpcd), and from public taps at 45 lpcd. The present rate of consumption of piped water is between 12-15 lpdc. The estimated domestic demand is shown in Table 1.

As well as the estimated domestic demand of 1,728 m/d (20 litres per second) the requirements of cottage industries, public institutions and commercial centres have to be considered, and it is clear that the present supply from the 100mm. main will need to be augmented.

When considering the most appropriate way to provide an adequate water supply a number of cultural factors have to be taken into consideration. Water born diseases are common in the town, and a combination of contaminated water, filth and refuse in public places, and a poor understanding of general principals of hygiene all contribute to the spread of disease. Water is generally considered in Nepal to be an unlimited natural resource to be used freely. As long as it looks clean it is considered drinkable, and as the traditional supplies from springs flow unchecked the concept of conserving water, or even turning off taps, is little understood. In Kathmandu city in households where there are private connections it has been estimated that the rate of wastage and leakage is as much as 50%, mainly because of carelessness in the way water is used, and the traditional notion that water should be free.

In addition the distinction between pure drinking water and other water is not always made, so vessels used for carrying drinking water may be washed with, or used for contaminated water, and vegetables and utensils may be washed in pond water (Plate 119). Private taps are considered as a status symbol and this, as well as convenience are important factors in people's wish for a private supply. The water in the piped system is, however, unprocessed, and subject to contamination. For these reasons typhoid, acute dysentery and jaundice are common, as well as less serious complaints. An effective educational programme is therefore needed to make people aware of the dangers of contaminated water, and the steps they can take for their own safety and improved health.

Plate 119 Kitchen utensils being washed in pond water near the Health Centre in Deu Ḍhokā.

SANITATION AND DRAINAGE

The people of Kirtipur used to, and still to a lesser extent do practice open air defecation. Men used the surrounding woodland and fields, and particular lanes were set aside for the use of women and children. In spite of such practices the city was kept relatively clean because of the presence of the *poṛe* community, whose traditional occupation was the cleaning of streets and houses, and who made a living by scavenging waste and converting it to manure and selling it to the farmers. Pigs roamed freely, helping the scavengers by eating the waste. Until the takeover of much of the farm land of the town the majority of the townspeople practiced farming as well as their other occupations such as masonry, and were themselves accustomed to handling manure, including human excrement. The place below the staircase of a house was commonly used for dumping household waste, and in emergency for urination or defecation, and the waste was converted to manure. A few households had latrine pits dug in the kitchen garden, but on the whole the need for latrines in the houses was not felt, because the members of the family who were working the land could use the fields, and those at home could go to the designated public places.

The sanitary condition of the town had greatly deteriorated with the increase in density of the population, the change in lifestyle of the townspeople from farming to work in the towns, and the improved prospects for people of the so-called unclean castes who are also changing their traditional way of life and taking up other occupations, so that the number prepared to clean houses, let alone remove night soil, is diminishing. With the increase in the dirt and refuse in the streets the householders have also discontinued the traditional practice of keeping the courtyards and public places immediately around their houses clean and instead use the streets for dumping garbage.

Until recently under the *pañchāyat* regulations (Village and Town Panchayat Act) the local *pañchāyats* were required to take care of all local needs. The responsibilities of the *pañchāyats* are now transferred to the Village Development Committees or town Municipalities. These include the maintenance of drainage, public tanks, wells, stand-pipes, and the safeguarding of water supplies, the maintenance and cleaning of public latrines and urinals, and the removal of dirt and refuse from the streets. There are also provisions in the Act for the local authorities to make by-laws to safeguard the health and sanitary conditions of the community, and to impose

Plate 120 Water tank for the piped supply and stand pipe at Kuṭujhol.

Plate 121 One of the low cost pour seal latrines installed by a householder in Jochhe with the assistance of the Water Supply and Sewerage Corporation. Two litres of water are sufficient for flushing.

fines upon offenders. To alleviate the insanitary condition of the city HMG Nepal, Department of Water Supply and Sewerage (DWSS) launched a pilot low cost sanitation programme[1] in Kirtipur, which was the first programme of its kind in Nepal. Between 1976 and 1982 the project has constructed about 1000 pour-flush water seal twin pit latrines *sulav sauchalaya* (Figure 61, Plate 121), covering about 70% of the population.

The people of Kirtipur were already familiar with the design of the low cost latrines, as through the efforts of Dor Bahadur Bista, Professor of Anthropology at Tribhuvan University, the advantages of the system had been publicized, and some three dozen latrines had already been installed by householders with the help of funds donated by the Ambassador of the Federal Republic of Germany. The latrines were those designed for the United Nations Development Programme[2] for situations where no mains drainage existed, and where it was considered impractical to provide mains drainage, because of the unsuitability of the site, the cost of upkeep, or inevitable problems with maintenance and the ultimate disposal of the sewage.

The low cost water seal latrines have the advantage of being a self contained unit of the size appropriate to the household, and can be constructed and maintained by the owner. The latrines consist of a fibreglass or cement pan leading to a stone masonry drain, which forks to two leaching pits which are used alternately. Two litres of water are needed to flush the pan by hand, considerably less than with a conventional cistern. The walls of the pits are of brick or stone, but unlike a conventional septic tank, parts of the walls are set dry, without cement, and the floor is of earth, which allows water to seep away, and also means that the required capacity is smaller than that of a septic tank. The tops of the pits are closed by reinforced concrete slabs. When the first pit is full, the outlet to it is closed, and that to the second pit opened. After several months the contents of the fist pit break down to

Plate 122 Stone drainage channels of a stepped lane in Deu Ḍhokā.

form a fully composted manure ready to be shovelled away and used on the fields.

This type of latrine was considered most appropriate for Kirtipur, as the situation of the town on a rocky hill would have made the construction of a mains drainage system and sewage treatment plant complicated, costly, difficult to maintain, and likely to increase the level of pollution in the already overloaded Bagmati River. The low cost latrines, on the other hand, could be built by the householders or local labour, with supervision by the DWSS, using ordinary building materials available locally, and the cleaning and maintenance would be the responsibility of the householder, who would obviously wish to keep the latrine in good order as it was on his own property and for the use of his own family.

*Installation of sanitation*

As the low cost latrine project was the first public health programme of its kind to be carried out in Kirtipur, any future project will gain from a careful study of the way it was implemented. In the 18 months between the time the DWSS first suggested that such a project should be carried out, and decided on Kirtipur as the place for the first demonstration project, to the actual installation of the first latrines in the pilot scheme, the people had been mobilised, and were keen to build private latrines. The leaders of the two *pañchāyats* which then existed had been approached, and the *pañchāyat* leader of the Kirtipur Pañchāyat, which at that time covered the northern part of the town, was enthusiastic about the scheme. There was less initial interest in the Bāgh Bhairav Pañchāyat. Formal and informal meetings were held, in which the problems of health as well as the discomfort and inconvenience caused by the lack of private latrines were discussed, and negative propaganda and opposition was neutralised. Women, in particular, were addressed, as considerations of modesty and sensitivity to public criticism made them feel the disadvantages of the lack of private latrines most keenly. A number of latrines were installed with the help of funds raised by Professor Bista. The latrines to some extent become status symbols for those households, so the combination of this factor, and the mobilization of the women to support the project meant that by the time the DWSS was ready to start many householders in almost all areas of the town were keen to participate in the scheme.

It had been decided to concentrate the project in the old part of the town, where the houses are all owner occupied. The DWSS felt that in the case of the new buildings being constructed in the Naya Bāzār area the owners ought to be prepared to pay for the installation of sanitation themselves. It was also decided that only private latrines would be built at this stage, as the ultimate aim of the project was to have private sanitation for all households, and it was felt that the provision of public latrines would act as a disincentive, while by no means solving the problem.

The procedure adopted was for the individual householder to make a formal request to the DWSS for material through his *pañchāyat*. The DWSS overseer and supervisors of sanitation stationed in Kirtipur then made a site examination, and if the site chosen was suitable, instructions for the construction of the pits and the latrine were given to the householders. When the pit was dug the DWSS would distribute the materials: 3 bags of cement, 7 kg. of iron rods, and one fibreglass pan and syphon per family.

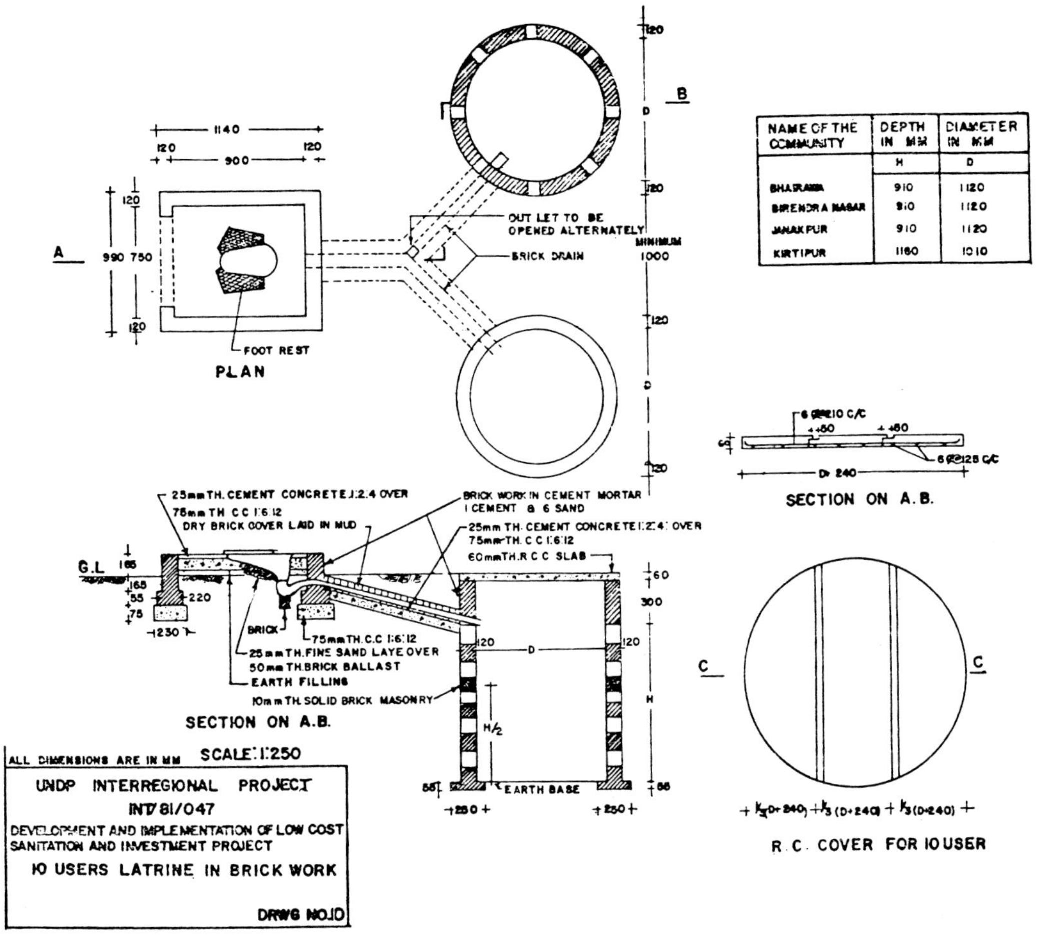


Figure 61 Plan and section of a low-cost waterseal pour flush twin pit latrine suitable for 10 users. One pit is used until filled with waste, which is left to break down into compost. The outlet is diverted to the other pit, until it in turn is full. Variations on the specification are available for different numbers of users, and other types of site (UNDP, 1985).

The householder's contribution was the bricks, sand, door and roof (if the latrine was installed outside the house) and labour. Three-quarters of the households carried out the labour themselves, the rest hiring labour or local contractors. It was found that after the first few latrines had been installed minimal supervision was needed as the installation procedure was quickly learnt. In particular, the syphon has to be set correctly for the water seal to be effective, and prevent a bad smell coming from the pit. The cost of labour varied between about Rs. 600 for a latrine inside the house, with no structure outside, to as much as Rs. 1,500 where rock had to be cleared to make the pits. The work was inspected on completion and an evaluation of the whole project was made.

The Evaluation Study carried out after the completion of the project in 1982 showed, however, that not all the latrines were used fully, and not all were kept clean. Although used by women, men and children still resorted to open air defecation. The men found going to an open space more agreeable, and the children were afraid to go into the dark latrines. However, in the opinion of the DWSS the results were promising as it was born in mind that it was to be expected that it would take a long time to establish a complete change in peoples' habits. With time and increased awareness the situation is changing, and the town has a much more sanitary appearance than before the introduction of the latrines. It is hoped that all the latrines will gradually be fully used by everyone as awareness grows.

*Drainage*

To dispose of storm water and domestic waste water, the traditional brick and stone paved streets were originally provided with channels on either side to give surface drainage (Plates 26 and 122), and carry storm water to ponds, leaving the streets free of water in the rainy season. Most of these channels have now deteriorated or are choked with refuse, and in some cases have been obstructed, for example by water pipes. Some households also have a pit in the vegetable garden, for waste water from the kitchen. There is a pressing need for the drainage channels in the streets to be reinstated, together with a general upgrading of the paving to make it possible for the streets to be kept clean and dry. With the planned improvements in the water supply, and the expected increase in water consumption, consideration also needs to be given to the best way of disposing of domestic waste water.

## FUTURE NEEDS

To bring the standard of sanitation and drainage up to an acceptable standard, as the pilot project has had a definite positive impact, an obvious objective is to have all the remaining households construct latrines. 30% of households still have no latrines, and there are none at all in the Poṛe Ṭol (Plate 29), as at the time of the pilot scheme the people of this area felt that the project was a threat to their livelihood. It is now the time to see if there has been any change in attitude in this community, and to encourage any efforts they may wish to make to improve their area. Consideration also needs to be given to the provision of communal latrines for locations such as schools. A further evaluation study of the installed latrines is vital to establish if the composting system is working, as it was too early to assess this in 1982. Every household should have guide-lines on safe composting methods, and an opportunity to solve any problems with expert advice.

The main problems which have arisen since the evaluation study are that the pits fill more quickly than was envisaged, partly because of the amount of water used for flushing and cleaning the pans. Rainwater can also cause the pits to flood. Seepage from the pits brings the risk of contamination of wells, and also the piped water supply via cracks and poorly made joints, and seepage may also cause weakening of the foundations of nearby buildings. In addition, a number of householders are not actually prepared to empty the pits themselves, and have found that the charges for this service by the local sweepers are prohibitively high. Saving on the cost of frequent emptying has been given as a reason for the men not using the latrines.

The importance of a structured and effective health education programme cannot be overstressed, as the factors of modesty and convenience only motivate part of the population, while the connection between faecal contamination and disease is not well understood. Thus the danger to public health in the form of faeces in the streets continues. The task of cleaning the streets is made even more difficult by the poor state of the paving and drainage channels, and upgrading the surface and the drainage should be seen not only in terms of making the streets more agreeable, but also as a matter of public health.

### *Health implications*

It is known that the combination of an improved water supply and sanitation can drastically improve the health of a community. The present water supply to the town is inadequate, and the people are in need of education in hygiene. Stomach complaints, typhoid, dysentery, diarrhoea and jaundice are common and can be attributed to the poor quality of the water supply. The sanitary condition of Kirtipur has improved after the introduction of the low cost sanitation programme, and there has been a marked improvement in the health of the people. The priority is therefore for an integrated programme to provide adequate water of good quality, combined with further sanitation and drainage, and a health education programme. At the same time systematic monitoring of the results of such a programme and of previous projects will show up the strengths and weaknesses of the methods employed, and give guide-lines for future programmes in Kirtipur or elsewhere. Attacking the problems on all fronts can be expected to have a far reaching impact on the improvement of the health of the townspeople.

## NOTES

1 Development Research and Communication Group, *Report on Evaluation Study of the Kirtipur Demonstration Project in Low-Cost Sanitation*, prepared for the Department of Water Supply and Sewerage, Ministry of Water Resources HMG Nepal, Kathmandu, 1982.

2 The Technology Advisory Group, *Nepal Master Plan Report on Low Cost Waterseal Latrine Project in 8 Urban and Semi-urban Communities in Nepal*, UNDP Inter-regional Project INT/81/047, June 1985.

# TOURISM AND ITS EFFECTS ON KIRTIPUR

MEHRDAD SHOKOOHY

One of the main sources of foreign currency in Nepal is its tourist industry.[1] The number of tourists visiting Nepal is rapidly increasing, and the statistics of the Ministry of Tourism[2] show that the number of foreign tourists grew from 6,179 in 1962 to 248,080 in 1987. During the same years[3] the revenue from tourism increased from $78,000 to nearly $56,000,000. Development of this important source of revenue has therefore been encouraged by the government, and it is expected that the number of tourists will continue to increase in the future. The effect of tourism is already being felt in the Kathmandu Valley towns, and particularly in Kathmandu where almost all foreign tourists tend to stay for a few days.

The average length of stay of the tourists in the years between 1962 and 1987, has, however, been similar, varying between 11 and 13 days.[4] In 1987 nearly 75% of the tourists visited the country for pleasure,[5] and spent most of their time in the Kathmandu Valley, and in Pokhara, the only other town with well known tourist attractions outside the valley. In addition to this number nearly another 5% of the visitors came to the country for business, and as Kathmandu is the main centre of commerce, almost all of them would have stayed there. Another important group of visitors are those whose main aim is trekking and mountaineering. In 1987 this group accounted for 17.6% of the total number of tourists, and although they do not generally spend their time in the valley, most of them spend at least one or two days in Kathmandu, and visit the main monuments of the capital as well as those of Patan and Bhaktapur.

## NUMBER OF VISITORS TO KIRTIPUR, AND METHOD OF TRAVEL

The impact of tourists visiting the Kathmandu Valley is now strongly felt in the three main towns of the valley, but so far the impact on Kirtipur has been very small. There has been little systematic study on the pattern of movement of tourists and the ways they spend their time, or the places they visit. However, apart from shopping, the main attractions in the valley are considered to be the historical and cultural sites. So far Kirtipur is not known to tourists in general, and the small number of foreign visitors who come to the town usually take a brief tour of the temples and the Chilañcho stupa, but perhaps what is of particular interest to these visitors is the quality of the unexploited urban environment of the town. A brief survey carried out for the purpose of the present study shows that of nearly 250,000 visitors to the Kathmandu Valley only 15,000 people come to Kirtipur.

Various reasons can be noted for the small number of tourists visiting Kirtipur. One of the main ones is perhaps a general lack of knowledge among ordinary tourists about the town. Those who visited the town mentioned that they became aware of it from tourist brochures, and, more importantly, from travel agency staff. However, a visit to the town is not strongly recommended in the guide books and brochures, and the importance of its cultural heritage and monuments is not stressed. With the improvement in road access tour organizers are including Kirtipur in more of their tours, and some of the commercial maps give a diagrammatic town plan of Kirtipur. Our survey revealed that almost 90% of the visitors came to the town in groups, most of them organized, and only about 10% of the visitors were on their own. This is an indication of the lack of awareness of Kirtipur among the great number of tourists who prefer to go sight seeing on their own. A more detailed introduction to Kirtipur in the brochures would no doubt encourage more people to visit the town, particularly those who visit sights independently.

Another reason for the lack of visitors has so far been the lack of good and regular transport between Kathmandu and Kirtipur. Although public transport is now improving, our survey showed that only about 5% of the visitors used

Plate 123 Adi Buddha Stupa and the surrounding paved square of Gutapau with *paṭīs*, houses and gardens, an example of an unspoilt Newar urban environment.

public transport to reach the town, and another 5% preferred private taxis. A similar percentage travelled on hired bicycles, a favourite method of transport among younger visitors. It should be noted that over 70% of foreign visitors to Nepal are below 45 years of age,[6] and many find bicycles a practical method of transport within Kathmandu and Patan. However, Bhaktapur and Kirtipur are slightly too far away for a bicycle ride, and it is likely that a more adequate public transport system, similar to that of Bhaktapur, would have an effect on the number of tourists visiting Kirtipur. At present nearly 65% of the visitors come by private coach, and another 20% in private cars, both mostly arranged by tour organizers.

## SEASON

The main season for visiting Kirtipur is the same as that of the rest of the country. From Autumn to Spring is generally preferred to the monsoon months in the Summer, and the favourite months are October, November and March respectively. However, the flow of tourists to the country as a whole is continuous, and even in July, the least popular month, the number of tourists does not fall much below half the number for October. The national statistics[7] show that in 1987 over 30,000 people visited Nepal in October, and over 27,000 in November, while in the so called off-season the number of tourists was over 15,000 and 14,000 for June and July respectively.

The effect of the fluctuation of the number of visitors to Nepal, and the Kathmandu Valley reflects directly on the daily number of visitors to Kirtipur. Our survey showed that during the season in average about 150 people visit Kirtipur on each Saturday and Tuesday, and about 75 people on these days during the off-season. These are the regular days for tours to be taken to Kirtipur, and on other days an average of only about 7 to 10 visitors come to the town.

## NATURE OF TOURIST VISITS

At present Kirtipur provides no facilities for tourists. The visitors usually arrive at De Pukhū and make a round tour, clockwise, around the north and centre of the town with halting points at Bāgh Bhairav, Umā Maheśvara and the Chilañcho stupa. In between they also see the old streets and houses of the town, particularly those of De Pukhū, Lāyaku, Mvāna Ṭol and Tananī Ṭol. Some of the smaller temples of the town, and particularly Loṅ Degaḥ also attract attention, but the monasteries are not usually visited. Not all follow this pattern in their visit of the town, and those who are on their own sometimes wander in the other parts of Kirtipur, but as a whole the three main monuments are always visited.

There is no formal tourist guide in Kirtipur. The tour operators sometimes have their own guides, and in most cases spend about an hour in the town. However, guiding the visitors is a favourite occupation of the young boys of Kirtipur, who race against each other to persuade visitors to follow them. Often more than one boy feels responsible, and expects to be paid as the guide. Almost all visitors do accept the guidance of one of the local boys, and only about 2% of the total number of the visitors insist on being left on their own during their tour. Following the boys, younger children also gather around the visitors asking for "one rupee", a habit encouraged by some grown ups, but as a whole regarded as unpleasant by most families of Kirtipur. It is not certain how often the children's request is met by the visitors, but many people of Kirtipur believe this habit has a negative effect on the tourists. A more organized system of tour guidance in the town, perhaps supervised by the Village Development Committees, could help remove the existing problems, and also stop the nuisance of begging children. It would also provide organized employment for young people with a good knowledge of their heritage.

Unlike in the other towns of the valley, in Kirtipur there are no cafes, restaurants or other facilities for tourists. Nor is there any lavatory suitable for visitors. These may be among the main reasons that the visitors do not spend more than an hour in the town. The few tea shops in Kirtipur cater mainly for the local people, and do not meet the standards favoured by tourists. Some stores sell soft drinks, "cold drinks" as they are known in Nepal, and on hot days some visitors halt for a soft drink, standing by the shop, but the number is small and on average no more than 5% of the visitors go to these stores.

Elsewhere in this report we have seen that Kirtipur is one of the main centres of weaving, and now carpet making. Hand made paper is also produced in the town, yet there are no outlets to sell the products to the visitors. These commodities are popular with tourists, who purchase them in the markets and shops in Kathmandu and other towns. At present a very few shawls and some cotton material are obtained by the tourists in Kirtipur, often bought directly from the workshops, and it is likely that establishing outlets to introduce and sell local products would be a significant addition to the attractions of the town, and contribute to reducing the dependence of the Kirtipur economy on Kathmandu.

## POSSIBILITIES AND PROBLEMS

Kirtipur, as the oldest town of the valley, with its unique town plan and some interesting temples, could reasonably be expected to attract more tourists than it does at present. We have already noted a number of suggestions, which not only include methods of raising the awareness of visitors to Nepal about Kirtipur, but also facilities which could be provided within the town. For the former a publicity campaign may be carried out with the production of free or inexpensive brochures and tourist literature to be provided for tourists in Kathmandu and elsewhere. Exhibitions in Kathmandu and other centres, and the publication of a guide book on Kirtipur may also be considered. In Kirtipur itself a tourist centre may also be set up, perhaps with a permanent exhibition area to introduce the historical and cultural heritage of the town. The centre might also publish and sell literature, guide books and brochures on Kirtipur. Authorized tourist guides from among the better informed people of the town could also work in conjunction with this centre.

However, it is more important to provide facilities and attractions in Kirtipur itself. Improvements such as the cleaning up of the town, repair of the streets and drainage, and restoration of the monuments would not only enhance the living environment for Kirtipur people, but also provide a more pleasant place for outside visitors. The establishment of other facilities such as cafes and restaurants will also have the effect of attracting more visitors, and encourage them to spend longer in the town, which will in turn bring revenue to the community. The local people can be encouraged to set up small businesses to provide these kinds of services and to upgrade some of the existing stores or tea shops. Further sources of revenue may be the establishment of shops selling local handicrafts, carpets and handloom material. All tourist facilities must be strategically located in the old town, and within sight of visitors; places with little interest to the general tourist such as Naya Bāzār are not suitable for the location of such services.

An increase in the number of visitors to the town would no doubt bring extra revenue to

Kirtipur, and could also increase local employment. However, it may be seen that in the long term the culture and habits of foreign tourists may have a negative effect on the townspeople. Although such factors should not be overlooked, in the case of Kirtipur this may not be a main consideration, as the town is close to Kathmandu and Patan, and most of the Kirtipur people, who work in these towns, have already been exposed to the exploitation that tourism can cause. Indeed, it may be argued that if tourists are not encouraged to come to Kirtipur, people from Kirtipur people will instead set themselves up in these towns to profit from the tourist trade.

Nevertheless, the development of tourism in Kirtipur must be planned and controlled from its infancy, to make sure that it does not have an adverse effect on the culture of the town, or the originality of the historic sights, something which unhappily has already happened not only in the Darbār squares of Kathmandu and Patan, but also in Bhaktapur which has been developed with these matters in mind. In Kirtipur one or two suitable locations should be designated for the development of services for tourists, and the rest of the town, and in particular the historic parts such as De Pukhū and Lāyaku should be kept free of intrusive structures and other features associated with the tourist trade. One of the suitable areas for tourist information and services may be the entry point to the old town at Chīthuṅ Ṭol, and another which can be considered is in Khasi Bāzār, if suitable parking spaces are provided for cars and coaches.

## NOTES

1 The author is indebted to Jagadish Man Amatya from the Ministry of Tourism, and to Sukra Sagar Shrestha for providing information.

2 HMG Nepal, Ministry of Tourism, Department of Tourism, *Annual Statistical Report 1987*, Kathmandu, 1987, 17, Table 1.

3 Ibid., 57, Table 27.

4 Ibid., 17, Table 1.

5 Ibid., 27-8, Tables 7-8.

6 Ibid., 23, Table 5.

7 Ibid., 19, Table 2.

# ART AND ANTIQUITIES

SUKRA SAGAR SHRESTHA

Kirtipur abounds in art objects of great antiquity. It cannot be established whether the earlier objects were made locally or brought from other centres, but it is known that in the mediaeval period icons were carved in Patan, and brought to Kirtipur for installation and worship. A number of the images in the Chilañcho complex were not only made in workshops in Patan, but were installed by people from that town, who must have regarded this early stupa with great respect. Since the time of a number of thefts of important images from Kirtipur, some icons are now kept in the collection of the National Museum (Apx. B and C).

One image known to have been made in Kirtipur is the un-baked clay image of Bāgh Bhairav kept inside the Bāgh Bhairav complex. As mentioned in the description of the temple, the icon is subject to damage by vermin, and has to be replaced every 15 or 20 years. This is done by the *bajrāchāryas* according to esoteric rituals, the clay having been collected from the shrine at Mhaipi and brought with a religious procession. The icon is covered with a cloth painted to imitate a tiger's coat, and also by a silver mask offered during the reign of Chandra Shumsher (1901-29).

The most common medium for the icons in the town is stone, but there are also examples in bronze, wood, and terra-cotta. The only extant wall paintings are those of the façades of the Bāgh Bhairav temple. We have already seen that Kirtipur stone has been used for images in the Kathmandu Valley from the earliest times to the present day. In Kirtipur itself there are images from the Lichhavi period (305-735 AD) of the Mātṛikās, Śiva, and Śiva-Pārvatī. Kirtipur is also rich in images which combine Buddhist and Hindu features. The tradition of carving these images has continued without a break up to modern times. The most recent addition to the town's icons is the Dhartī Mātā consecrated in 1979.

Wood carving is an important feature of both sacred and secular architecture in the town, and is also used for individual images. Among the earliest is a wooden image of Sambhara, originally from Kirtipur and now kept in the National Museum. The image is undated, but is considered to be of the 16th century, or perhaps earlier. Examples of wood carving of the 17th century are the Ashṭamātṛikās in the Umā Maheśvara temple façades, and the *toraṇa* (decorative arch) over the sacrificial altar in the Bāgh Bhairav temple.

The bronze sculpture of Kirtipur includes the 8th or 9th century Tārā Devī and the 16th century Sambhara from Chilañcho Mahāvihār, both now kept in the collection of the National Museum. These bronzes are gilded and studded with precious stones, a practice found from the 6th or 7th century AD. Several other fine bronzes from Chilañcho are also in the Museum collection. The Dīpankāra images in the Mahāvihār are also of interest. They are larger than life size, and have only heads and hands made out of copper, plated with gold. In this type of icon the body is not gilt, and to move the image from place to place a man goes inside the image and carries it. The people of Kirtipur call these images *koyampazu.*

The images are considered as the *thakālī* (pre-eminent) among many other images gathered during the Samyak festival at Nāg Bāhā in Patan every four years, and honoured in this way. There are more than 110 of such images gathered for the event, invited from all the *mahāvihārs* and their associated *bāhās* of Patan. The last festival was held in March 1988.

Apart from the clay image of Bāgh Bhairav there are said to be a number of terra-cotta images in the town, including a Chakra Sambhara in Chilañcho Mahāvihār. The Taleju Temple in Lāyaku is also said to have terra-cotta Ashṭamātṛikās. Entrance to these places is not permitted to the public, and further investigation is required for detailed study of these icons.

Plate 124 Bāgh Bhairav wall paintings, south-west façade, south side. The paintings which remain in the upper register are in a fair state of preservation.

Plate 125 Bāgh Bhairav wall paintings, south-west façade, south side, detail.

Plate 126 Ancient monolithic image of standing Śiva, known locally as Jhavā Dya, in the Gaṇeś Temple at Bāgh Bhairav (S. S. Shrestha).

WALL PAINTINGS

The surviving examples of wall painting in the town are found on a frieze around the façades of the ground level of the Bāgh Bhairav temple (Plates 124-5). The façades are divided horizontally into two registers by a course of timber, and the surviving paintings are in the upper register. They are executed on plaster, and depict a number of subjects including battles between gods and demons. The south-western façade has Ashṭabhairavas, Chandra and Sūrya on both sides of the main entrance, as well as other deities. The south-eastern wall has figures of the dancing Gaṇeś, Śiva in *tāndava nṛitya* the terrifying dance, and Mahishāsura Mardini, while on the north-eastern wall, though the colours are very faded, the Ashṭamāṭrikās and a Brahmāyaṇī can be seen. On the north-western side, where animals are sacrificed at the Nāsadya shrine, the wall used to be smeared with blood, and the paintings could not be seen. This wall has now been whitewashed (Plate 51), as has the wall behind the main sacrificial altar on the south-west side, and all trace of the paintings obliterated.

The dominant colour to be seen is red on a white ground. The blue of the outlines has faded to grey, and the other pigments are also faded. Dr Safalya Amatya[1] has suggested that these frescos are of the late Malla period. However, the colours in the late Malla examples in Shantipur of Svayaṃbhū, the Brahmāyaṇī temple at Panauti, the Kumārīghar in Kathmandu, and the Bhaktapur Darbār Square are all still shining and bright. On stylistic grounds, and the nature of the colours used the paintings can perhaps be ascribed to the early or middle Malla period. If this dating can be accepted, the Bāgh Bhairav paintings are among the earliest of their kind in Nepal.

Apart from the Bāgh Bhairav frescos there were some wall paintings inside the Chilañcho Mahāvihār, but, as mentioned before, the Mahāvihār is in a dilapidated state and its interior is not accessible. At present it is not known to what extent these rare examples of Nepalese wall painting are preserved.

STONE IMAGES

The most important stone images in Kirtipur are given below in approximate chronological order. The earliest stone examples appear to be the icons now housed in the 18th century Gaṇeś temple in the Bāgh Bhairav complex (Plates 56-7).

*Standing Śiva (Jhavā dya)*

The standing Śiva (Plate 126) now installed in the Gaṇeś temple of the Bāgh Bhairav complex is among the most ancient images extant in Kirtipur. The figure is carved out of a single block of stone, and is softly modelled, giving the impression of a shallow relief. The front of the image is carefully executed, while the back is left without detailed modelling, and some chisel marks remain. The image stands in the *samapāda* posture with the feet slightly apart on a small dais, and wears a *dhoti*, the hem of which is depicted. The erect phallus is shown, signifying the control over the senses of a perfect *brahmāchārya.*

The ornaments are restrained, and consist of large flat ear-rings and a beaded necklace. The facial features are serene, and the hair is tied up in the middle making two layers. The head has been eroded, leaving only traces of the locks of hair. Both hands are missing, so no details of the attributes can be given.

Plate 127 Śiva-Pārvatī Umā Maheśvara) image installed in the Gaṇeś Temple at Bāgh Bhairav. The plainness of the carving and iconographic details indicate that the image is late fourth century (S. S. Shrestha).

Plate 128 Gaṇeś image of the late fourth or early fifth century in the Gaṇeś Temple at Bāgh Bhairav (S. S. Shrestha).

The lack of a sacred thread (*yagyopavīt*), the absence of the bull vehicle, Nandī, and the sculpture being two armed are all indications of the antiquity of the figure. Bangdel[2] considers the image to be of the 4th century AD, and supports this view by comparison with the example in the Karle caves in India.[3] No parallel has as yet come to light in Nepal. The image appears to be the oldest icon in Kirtipur and the local people relate this image to the mythical origins of Bāgh Bhairav, considering it to be a herdsman, and the mother goddesses to be sheep. The image is also worshipped by sufferers from acute earache. The lack of adequate arrangements to keep the image safe has led to a number of unsuccessful attempts by antique smugglers to steal this outstanding figure. It should be a matter of priority for important images like this to be protected properly.

*Śiva-Pārvatī*

A noteworthy image of Śiva-Pārvatī (Umā Maheśvara) (Plate 127) is installed in the eastern wall of the Gaṇeś Temple. It is carved out of a single block of light coloured sandstone and has a tongue below the base which would have fitted into a stone slot in its original location. It is not known where the image came from. Like the standing Śiva, in this Śiva-Pārvatī the figure of Śiva stands in the *samapāda* posture, with the feet slightly apart, and the erect phallus shown. He holds a water pot in his front left hand, and what Bangdel[4] identifies as a bunch of flowers in his front right hand. The other two hands are worn away. The figure has broad shoulders, and the *dhoti* is arranged with the pleats in a decorative fold, and a diagonal sash around the thigh.

Plate 129 Vaishṇavī image in the row of ancient images of the divine mothers (Mātṛikās) installed in the Gaṇeś Temple at Bāgh Bhairav (S. S. Shrestha).

Plate 130 Brahmāyaṇī image in the Gaṇeś Temple at Bāgh Bhairav (S. S. Shrestha).

He again wears ear-rings and a necklace of large beads, but the face is damaged, the hair badly weathered, and the details of its carving lost. Behind the head is a broad halo.

The figure of Pārvatī has two hands, holding what Bangdel[5] identifies as a bunch of flowers in the left hand, and a mirror in the right. She wears large ear-rings, anklets (*kalli*), and bracelets. Her garment appears to be a single piece falling from the neck to the ankles, with pleats folded between the legs. This is similar to the garments described by Wang Hiuen-t'se[6] who visited the Kathmandu Valley during the reign of Narendra Deva (643-657 AD). The figure also has a diagonal sash across the thigh, and a halo behind the head, but like the Śiva, the face and hair are badly eroded.

Śiva's vehicle, the bull Nandī, stands on his master's right, but the image does not include Mount Kailāśa, an indication of the antiquity of the piece. The simple ornaments, and lack of flames round the halo also point to an early date, and Bangdel[7] dates the icon to the late 4th century AD, but no other image parallel in style and execution has come to light.

### *Gaṇeś*

The Gaṇeś (Plate 128) kept at the west end of the north-west wall of the Gaṇeś temple is another of the monolithic images carved in light coloured sandstone. Although the icon is very much worn and abraded the characteristics can be clearly recognised. The figure is sitting in the *sukhāsana* posture, with the right leg bent, and the left leg hanging down, and is pot bellied, with a snake tied round the stomach. There is no crown or other ornament visible. The trunk is bent towards the left hand, which might have been holding a ball of sweets (*modaka*), but this side of the

Plate 131 Kaumārī image in the Gaṇeś Temple at Bāgh Bhairav (S. S. Shrestha).

Plate 132 Śaivi (Maheśvarī) image in the Gaṇeś Temple at Bāgh Bhairav (S. S. Shrestha).

statue is eroded, and details cannot be seen. The right arm is bent at the elbow, with the hand resting palm upwards on the knee.

The lack of crown and ornaments make the image comparable with the Lichhavi examples at Chinamasta of Changu, and Majipat of Kathmandu. The stylistic features of the Kirtipur Gaṇeś indicate a late 4th or early 5th century AD date.

### *Mātṛikās*

Five figures of the Mātṛikās (divine mothers) are set in the south-west wall inside the Gaṇeś temple (Plate 57), arranged in a row with Vaishṇavī on the left, and then Brahmāyaṇī, Kaumārī, Śaivi, and Bārāhī. The figures have been cemented in place, and only the fronts can be seen.

### *Vaishṇavī*

The figure of Vaishṇavī (Plate 129) is seated in *sukhāsana* posture, with the right leg bent, and the left leg hanging down. The figure has a chubby face, short neck, heavy breasts, sturdy limbs, and broad shoulders, all indicating the antiquity of the piece. Her hands rest on the thighs, with a conch in the right hand and a lotus in the left. She is adorned with heavy ornaments such as thick ear-rings, a necklace of beads, armlets and anklets. A diagonal sash passes across the thigh, and the central folds are carved to show neat pleats below the right foot, an arrangement seen in early Nepalese sculpture.

Plate 133 Bārāhī (Vārāhī) image in the Gaṇeś Temple at Bāgh Bhairav (S. S. Shrestha).

Plate 134 Śiva torso in the Bāgh Bhairav complex. It is also regarded locally as a representation of the serpent king who holds up the universe (S. S. Shrestha).

*Brahmi*

The image of Brahmi (Brahmāyaṇī) (Plate 130) is seated in *padmasana* posture over a full blown double petalled lotus. The statue is severely abraded, but an ewer held in her left hand can be seen. The right hand is lost. Like the Vaishṇavī the figure has a round face, and a solid, sturdy looking body. Besides the usual ornaments she has a beaded necklace with a pendant in the centre.

*Kaumārī*

The figure of Kaumārī (Plate 131) is shown seated with her left leg bent and the right leg hanging in the *lalitāsana* posture. She holds a spear in the left hand, and in the right hand an object which may have been a full blown lotus[8] but which is now broken. The spear is decorated with a banner. The rendering of the body and ornaments resembles that of the other figures.

*Śaivi*

The figure of Śaivi, also known as Maheśvarī (Plate 132), is, like the Kaumārī, shown in the *lalitāsana* posture, and again has the spear or perhaps the more usual trident (now broken) in the left hand and the lotus in the right. The face, though eroded, still retains a serene appearance. The body and ornaments are again similar to the other figures, especially the Kaumārī.

*Bārāhī*

The last of this series of the divine mothers is a figure of Bārāhī (Plate 133), with the boar like face turned to the right. She is seated in *sukhāsana* posture, and is dressed and ornamented in a similar fashion to the other goddesses, but has a round belly. The attributes she holds in her hands can still be seen. While it is no longer clear exactly what they are, they are likely to be a fish

Plate 135 Images from Bishalnagar comparable to the Kirtipur examples, but later in date (S. S. Shrestha).

Plate 136 Nandī, the bull vehicle of Śiva, in the Bāgh Bhairav complex (S. S. Shrestha).

Plate 137 Small stone image of Śiva, possibly of the seventh or eighth century, excavated at Kvācho, the royal area of the town (S. S. Shrestha).

Plate 138 Inscription and image of Ārya Tārā dated 636/1516 in the Chilañcho complex (S. S. Shrestha).

and a cup, the usual attributes of Bārāhī, as already suggested by Bangdel.[9] Together with the other Mātṛikās the image is considered locally to represent the sheep connected with the mythical origin of Bāgh Bhairav.

*Śiva (torso)*

In the Bāgh Bhairav complex, outside the eastern corner of the Bhavānī Śaṅkar Temple, is the torso of an old stone image of Śiva (Plate 134). It is badly damaged and the head, arms, and lower parts of the legs are missing, but a pair of feet, possibly part of the same statue are kept by the image. The ewer (*kuṇḍika*) held in the left palm can still be discerned. The *dhoti* is arranged in the style seen in 4th century examples, and this is the date suggested for the image by Bangdel.[10] However, when the statue is compared with the Śiva-Pārvatī (Plate 127) in the Gaṇeś temple, the torso may be dated somewhat later, although it appears to precede another image found in Bishalnagar (Plate 135). The crude way the torso is carved, the texture and style of the *dhoti* pleated in the middle, and the position of the *kundika* held in the left hand are more characteristic of the late fifth or early sixth century, indicating that this work could be a century or two earlier than the Bishalnagar image. The local people regard the torso as a representation of Bāsuki (Vāsuki) Nāg, one of the eight serpent-kings (Nāgārāj).

*Nandī*

A stone image of Nandī (Plate 136), the bull vehicle of Śiva, is placed in the courtyard on the south-west of the Bāgh Bhairav Temple, facing towards the damaged Śiva torso. The image is eroded to the extent that the head has worn

Plate 139 Umā Maheśvara, the conjoint form of Śiva, the destroyer in the Hindu trinity, and his consort Parvatī, installed in the Umā Maheśvara temple in 775/1655 (S. S. Shrestha).

Plate 140 Mahishāsura Mardini Durgā, in the north-western façade of the Umā Maheśvara temple. The goddess slaying the buffalo demon (S. S. Shrestha).

away, but the simplicity of the carving of the body, and the texture of the stone is comparable with that of the torso of Śiva, and a similar date of the late fifth or early sixth century may be suggested for the Nandī.

*Śiva found near Kvācho*

A small image of Śiva (Plate 137), 15cm. high, was unearthed in 1981 from the debris produced by the excavation of the present water tank, just behind the Kvācho fort house near the Umā Maheśvara Temple. The site is part of the ancient palace complex at the highest point in Kirtipur. The excavation of the water tank was unfortunately carried out without consideration for the archaeological importance of the site, and when the image was found it had been damaged by the workmen's picks, which had partially destroyed the chest, right hand, the halo, the reclining support, and the base.

The image is seated in meditation. In spite of the recent damage, and the generally worn condition, some details of the head and ornaments remain which give us an indication of the date of the statue. The chubby face, the right eye of which can be faintly traced, is very similar to the faces of the Mātṛikā images in the Gaṇeś Temple. The long hair is elaborately arranged in the ascetic manner, with a tuft in the middle tied with a string of *rudrachhya* (*elaecarpus sphericus*), the praying fruit. The necklace appears to represent an iron torque, thicker in the middle and tapering towards the back of the neck. A torque of this kind is worn by the Pārvatī in the image of Ravaṇa lifting Mount Kailāśa in Cave 21 at Ellora.[11] The same type of necklace is also seen in an image of Śiva Naṭarāj at Badami, Karnataka.[12]

These images are dated to the 5th and 6th centuries respectively by Calambur Shivarama Krishnamurti.[13] By comparing the Kvācho Śiva with these examples we can suggest that the image is as least as early as the seventh or eighth century AD. The image is now kept near its find spot and close to the Umā Maheśvara temple.

### *Ārya Tārā*

An inscribed stone image of Tārā (Plate 139) attached to the wall of a house in Chilañcho complex is the earliest dated image known in Kirtipur. In the inscription (Apx. A, no. 2) the goddess is addressed as Ārya Tārā Bhattārika, and we are informed that the image was installed in 636/1516 by a noble, Suchhem Bharo of Libinchhen, Nakabihari, for the welfare of his deceased wife Bijaya Lakshmī.

The image is in a standing posture with its right hand in *abhāya mudrā*, the gesture of fearlessness, resting on a lotus, and its left hand in *varad mudrā* blessing or giving a boon, and holding a lotus. Her ornaments include ear-rings, a two stringed pearl necklace, armlets, bracelets, a waist band and anklets. The left leg is slightly bent, in the manner usually seen in Lichhavi works, but the body does not conform to the traditional proportions, and the breasts are small. The figure lacks the sense of mobility usually seen in Lichhavi images. The oblique eyes, the nose and the facial expression are similar to the Lakshmī of the Lakshmī Nārāyaṇ image[14] dated 537/1417 now kept in the archaeological garden in Patan.

### *Umā Maheśvara*

The most important image of Umā Maheśvara (Śiva and Pārvatī) (Plate 139) to the people of Kirtipur is that installed in 775/1655 (Apx. A, no. 7) in the Umā Maheśvara Temple. The icon is carved from a slab of black basalt, and shows Śiva and Umā standing on a full blown lotus with their vehicles, Nandī and the lion Siṅgh, on either side. The stem of the flower is carved to form a scrolling arabesque which ornaments the base.

Śiva is shown single headed with four arms, standing in *dvibhaṅga*, a posture bent at two points. The front right hand is in *abhāya mudrā*, with the palm facing forwards, and the left arm embraces Umā and holds a water pot. The rear hands hold a rosary and a trident. He wears a

Plate 141 Krodharāj, a guardian deity at the Chilañcho complex, carved in 788/1668.

crown, ear-rings and suitable ornaments for the wrists, arms and ankles, as well as a long garland of flowers. The waist is wrapped in a tiger skin.

The image of Umā (Pārvatī) stands in *tribhaṅga*, a posture with the body bent thrice, and with her right hand in *varad mudrā* and the left in *abhāya*, holding the stem of a water lily. She is decked with ear-rings and a crown and diadem. The folds of her garment and the draperies of both figures are carved to give an impression of being ruffled by the wind.

The heads of both figures are surrounded by an aureole of beads and flames and a further aureole of flames and floral patterns frames the pair, a popular way of representing Umā Maheśvara in mediaeval Nepal. This group, however, does not have the Śiva Gaṇa and other figures found in Lichhavi counterparts.

*Sarasvatī*

The Umā Maheśvara Temple has a monolithic image of Sarasvatī (Plate 66) installed in the north-east façade. The figure stands on a lotus and is unique in that above its right elbow is a Nāsapvā or aniconic representation of Nṛityeśvara, Śiva as Lord of the Dance. This takes the form of a sword and a small hole covered by a piece of white cloth painted with two eyes, and is the only example of its kind in the Kathmandu Valley. The main image stands in the *samnapāda* posture and has four hands. The two front hands are in *varad* and *abhāya mudrā*, and the hands behind hold a rosary in the right hand and a book in the left.

The icon is depicted with the facial expression and breasts of a adolescent girl. Behind the head is an aureole in three layers with a halo of flames around it. The garments consist of draperies passing around the arms and shoulders, and the type of dress known as *jāmā*, with a shawl, the traditional dress of mediaeval Nepal. It appears that the façades of the temple were made specifically to house images and it is likely that the Sarasvatī was installed at the time of the building of the temple.

*Mahishāsura Mardini Durgā*

The image of Mahishāsura Mardini Durgā (Plate 140) is set in the north-western façade of the Umā Maheśvara Temple, and may have been installed in about 775/1655, when the image of Umā Maheśvara was dedicated. The goddess is depicted slaying the buffalo demon, and is shown with her left leg pressing down on the buffalo, and her right leg bent at the knee, with the foot resting on her vehicle, the lion. She has eight arms; the attributes in the four right hands are the sword (*khadga*), wheel (*chakra*), arrow (*vāna*), and a long *triśūla* or trident, and those of the left hands are the shield (*dhāla*), the conch (*sankha*) and bow (*dhanusha*), while the lowest hand grasps the buffalo's tail. The lion is shown poised to attack the buffalo, and the whole group stands on a lotus flower and is framed by an aureole with scrolls of floral patterns.

The goddess is clothed in the typical costume of the time, with an intricately carved garment over the skirt. She is bedecked with a tiara, large finely carved ear-rings, a pendant, a necklace of small beads reaching to her naval, bracelets, and anklets (*tutibāgī*) for the feet. A garland of flowers hangs from the shoulders to the knees. The stone is exceptionally smooth and well polished.

*Sarasvatī of Nagacho*

An image of Sarasvatī (Plate 76) is kept in the temple dedicated to her at the north-west of the town. A long inscription in Sanskrit and Newari (Apx. A, no. 24) mentions that the temple was restored in 841, and describes the iconographic details of the goddess. The image is small, about 30 cm. high, and according to Lan Bahādur Maharjan who was responsible for the restoration of the temple in 1984 it was re-installed in the same position as it had been before.

The goddess is seated in *lalitāsana* posture on a double petalled lotus and is four armed. In her upper right hand she holds a rosary and in her upper left hand a manuscript. The other hands are engaged in playing a *vinā*, the Indian lute, with a *hitimāgaḥ* (dragon) design at the lower end. She has a halo of flames and her adornments include a five peaked crown, ear-rings, a three stringed necklace, armlets, and anklets, all finely carved.

Below her left leg, as is usual in images of Sarasvatī of the 16th and 17th century, is a four armed Gaṇeś in *sukhāsana* posture. The right foot of the goddess rests on a full blown lotus, as is the case in many mediaeval images of Sarasvatī in the Kathmandu Valley. From the artistic and iconographic point of view the figure can be compared with an icon of the same name in the Mahānkāla shrine at Kathmandu, but the modelling of the Nagacho Sarasvatī lacks the three dimensional quality of the Kathmandu example, and the hands rest on the lute without giving the impression of being engaged in playing the instrument.

Plate 142 Jarumanuchhya of 790/1670 on the Chilañcho stupa (S. S. Shrestha).

Plate 143 Vishṇu Nārāyaṇa born by his vehicle Garuḍa the mythical bird, dated 823/1703, in the rest house in Tuñjho (S. S. Shrestha).

*Krodharāj*

A striking pair of figures of Krodarāj (Plates 81 and 141) flanks the steps leading to the south-eastern side of the Chilañcho Stupa. An inscription (Apx. A, no. 13) on the back of the icon to the south informs us that both figures were carved in 788/1668, and they are referred to as Krodharāj. Oldfield[15] gives the names Kārak Vīr and Bajra Vīr, but he does not mention his source, and they are known locally as Karma Rāj and Janma Rāj. The figures appear to be manifestations of the Buddhist guardian deities known as Mahākāla which are traditionally installed in front of monasteries in India and Nepal. The figures are usually single headed and four armed and stand in *ālidhāsana*, a posture with the right knee advanced and left retracted, and *pratyālidhāsana*, a similar posture, but with the left knee forward.

The Krodharāj figures at Chilañcho are pot-bellied with terrifying faces. They stand on lotus flowers rather than on dead bodies, and are framed by flaming halos. They are decked with ear-rings, armlets and anklets in the form of snakes of various sizes, and have a garland of flowers and a garland of snakes (*nāgamālā*). The southern image holds the sword (*khadga*) and hook (*āṅkusa*) in the two right hands and the noose (*pasa*) and bell (*ghaṇṭa*) in the left hands, while the eastern image carries the thunderbolt (*bajra*) and arrow (*vāna*) in the right hands and the drum (*ḍamaru*) and bell in the left.

*Jarumanuchhyas*

Around the dome of the Chilañcho Stupa are four unusual figures placed to face the cardinal points. An inscription (Apx. A, no. 15) dated 790/1670 describes them as Jarumanuchhyas (Plate 142), meaning amphibious men. The figures have the head and body of a human being, and the feet of a swan. They are adorned with ear-rings, necklaces, and armlets and seated on lotus flowers. Our example facing south-east squats in *utkuṭukāsana*, the posture of a seated dog, and holds a conch from which he pours pearls, coral, and other precious products of the sea. It may be suggested that these figures represent the *jalatattva*, or watery element, but their iconography is as yet unstudied.

### *Śākyamuni Buddha*

Kirtipur has many images of Śākyamuni Buddha, the historic Buddha, mostly to be found in the south-eastern quarters of the town. They are either free-standing, or combined with images of the Buddhist trinity. The image under discussion is kept in the Śākyamuni Buddha Mandir in Sinaduvā Ṭol (Plates 93 and 144). According to the inscription (Apx. A, no. 6) of the foundation of the temple, the image was carved and established in 769/1649 by the *bajrāchārya* who built the temple, and also the nearby Chhve Bāhā.

The image is carved from a single piece of stone, and is seated in the *padmasana* posture on a double petalled lotus. The right hand touches the ground and the left is resting on the lap with the palm turned upward. He wears a light garment which leaves the right side of the chest bare, and has no ornaments. The image is surrounded by a simple frame and a carved arch (*toraṇa*) supported by a pair of celestial nymphs with fly whisks. Miniature figures of the Pañchā Dhyāni Buddhas and two more nymphs are carved round the arch. The Buddhas are shown seated on lotuses rather than on their respective vehicles, but they are in the usual postures, except for the Vairochana (known locally as Bairochana) in the centre whose palms are drawn up to the chest with the forefingers crossed, instead of being in the conventional *bodyāngrimudra*. The style of execution for the small figures is similar to that seen in the Tushahiti in the Darbār Square at Patan.

### *Garuḍ Narāyāṇa*

An interesting monolithic image of Garuḍ Nārāyaṇa (Plate 143) is kept in a small shrine behind a ruined rest house in Tuṅjho Ṭol south of Chilaṅcho. An inscription (Apx. A, no. 20) attached to the wall informs us that both the rest house and the image date from 823/1703.

Narāyāṇa is shown seated in *padmāsana* posture supported by the outspread wings of the flying Garuḍa. The four arms of Narāyāṇa hold the conch (*saṅkha*) and mace (*gadā*) in the upper hands, and the lotus flower (*padma*) in the lower right and the wheel (*chakra*) in the lower left. He wears a tall diadem in his head dress, and is decked with ear-rings of leaves (*patrakuṇḍala*), a necklace of the *tulasī* leaf, a long flower garland of the kind usually seen in metal images of the period, armlets and wrist bands. The facial features and garments are worn away. The image is flanked by two miniature female figures seated upon lotuses in *lalitāsana* posture and showing their hands in *abhāya* and *varad*. These figures may represent Lakshmī and Sarasvatī or Bhu Devī.

The Garuḍa is shown poised to take off. The upper part of the body is human, with the legs, claws and spread wings of a bird. The face is that of a boy, with a beaded cap covering the head and forehead. The human arms are shown with the palms of the hands stretched out beneath the outspread wings.

The Narāyāṇa and the female figures each have an aureole, and the whole group is surrounded by a further halo of flames. Only a few images depicted in this style together with the female figures have come to light. An example is in Deupatan.[16] The famous Garuḍa Narāyāṇa of Changu Narāyāṇa has no female figures. The Garuḍ Narāyāṇa painting of the year 1766 now in the collection of Bharat Kala Bhavan, Varanasi[17] indicates that there may have been a tradition of presenting Garuḍa Narāyāṇa along with Lakshmī and Bhu Devī in the 18th century.

### *Dhartī Mātā*

To the east of the Bāgh Bhairav temple, within the complex, is a shrine of Dhartī Mātā (Plate 145), installed in Vikrama Era 2036/1979 by Jitānanda Joshī of Kirtipur. The stone image, a cosmic representation of the universe, is exposed to the sky, and is in the form of a young woman in the act of giving birth to a child. She lies on a bed of waves, with the Hindu trinity disposed at her head, feet and right side. The body is naked, with the eyes wide open, the hair loose, the palms of the hands facing up in *varad mudrā*, and the legs apart. The infant is shown coming into the world with its hands together above the head. The only ornaments are the mother's ear-rings.

This is the first occasion on which an esoteric image of this kind has been displayed in public in Kirtipur, in a similar way to the Tunal of Yakseśvara Temple in the Darbār Square of Bhakta

Plate 144 Śākyamuni Buddha, the historical Buddha, surrounded by primordial Buddhas and celestial nymphs, carved and installed in 769/1649 in the Śākyamuni Buddha Mandir (S. S. Shrestha).

Plate 145 Dhartī Mātā a cosmic representation of the universe installed in VE 2036/1979 in the Bāgh Bhairav complex (S. S. Shrestha).

pur.[18] The image was formally worshipped only in an esoteric manner. When the author asked Jitānanda Joshī why the deity was now exposed he replied, "For the ignorant everything will remain esoteric; the image is exposed to let the laity know about the world."

The iconographic details were decided on by the *joshī* after study of a volume of manuscripts. The carver, the Jujukāji of Sundhara Patan, was instructed accordingly. The manuscript itself was then buried under the image, making it no longer accessible for study.

## WOODEN SCULPTURE

### *Sambhara*

A fine example of the wooden sculpture from the Chilañcho Mahāvihār is the Sambhara (Plate 146) now in the collection of the National Museum (Apx. B, no. 3). The image is carved according to the *sādhanā* or formula for a Sambhara described

Plate 146 Wooden image of Sambhara, the destructive form of Bhairav, from the Chilañcho Mahāvihār, and now in the National Museum (S. S. Shrestha).

Plate 147 Wooden *toraṇa* of 782/1662 above the sacrificial altar of Bāgh Bhairav, being prepared for a festival.

Figure 62 Bāgh Bairav, *toraṇa* over the sacrificial alter dated 782/1662 (S. S. Shrestha).

Key: 1 Maheśvari; 2 Kaumāri; 3 Vaishṇavī, 4 Brahmāyaṇi; 5 Bārāhī; 6 Indrāyaṇī; 7 Chāmuṇḍā; 8 Mahālakshmī; a Ruru Bhairav; b Chanda Bhairav; c Ashṭāng Bhairav; d Krodha Bhairav; e Unmatta Bhairav; f Karālā Bhairav; g Sambhara Bhairav; h Bhīshān Bhairav; r Siṅghnī; l Byanghini.

in the Buddhist text, *Nispanna yogāvali* of Abhayankara Gupta.[19] The icon is depicted in *ālidhāsana* posture, trampling Bhairav beneath his right foot, and Kalaratri beneath the left. Sambhara wears a tiger skin and a garland of severed heads (*muṇḍamālā*). He has three eyes, and the features appear Mongoloid, with oblique eyes and a prominent lower lip. The head is adorned with skulls, he wears large ear-rings and a two stringed necklace, perhaps representing pearls. His hands are crossed at the chest, his right hand holding the bell (*ghaṇṭa*) and the left the thunderbolt (*bajra*).

The image is surrounded by an aureole with a garland of leaves (*patramālā*), on the inside, then a row of skulls, and finally flames. The pedestal has turned down lotus petals. The body is shown as sturdy, with a vigorous, masculine character. The structure of the body and the style of carving is closely comparable with that of the stone image of Vishṇu probably of the 15th century, in the temple west of Indreśvara Mahādeva at Panauti. The Kirtipur image appears to date from the 15th or 16th century. It has been attacked by wood boring insects, and the toes are damaged. The piece is in need of immediate treatment to prevent further deterioration.

### *Wooden toraṇa, Bāgh Bhairav Temple*

The wooden *toraṇa*, or decorative arch, above of the sacrificial altar (*hi pha dyaḥ*) on the southwest side of the Bāgh Bhairav Temple is an exceptionally fine example of Newar craftsmanship (Figure 1, Plate 147). It was offered by a *gūṭhī*[20] in 782/1662. The *toraṇa* is built of six planks, carved after assembly. It stands on a pair of

Plate 148 Gilded bronze image of Tārā Devī from Chilancho Mahāvihār now in the National Museum. The image is studded with precious and semi-precious stones (S. S. Shrestha).

Plate 149 Gilded bronze Sambhara in *yab yum* posture from Chilancho Mahāvihār, now in the National Museum (S. S. Shrestha).

pillars, and is supported by a chain from behind. It has a central figure of Bāgh Bhairav flanked by Gaṇeś on the left and Kumāra on the right, with Narāyāṇa riding Garuḍa above and the eight divine mothers on either side. The divine mothers are carved in roundels, and their consorts the eight Bhairavas in smaller roundels forming an outer border to the arch.

The figure of Garuḍa holds a vessel (*kalāśā*) in his two front hands, and his other two arms are spread out under his flying wings. He holds in his claws two *nāgakanyā*, women in the form of a snake from the waist down, and they in turn hold two more *nāgakanyā*. Lord Narāyāṇa is seated on Garuḍa's shoulders in the *garuḍāsana* posture, commonly seen in 17th century images. A *mālā* (garland), seen by Tantrics during lightning, is shown below Gaṇeś and Kumāra, and there are two *hitimāgaḥ* at each end of the *toraṇa*, and two small flying griffins on each side of the intrados.

The characteristic feature of the *toraṇa* could be said to be the combination of images associated with Vaishnavism and Shaivism, displaying a degree of religious tolerance unusual between these two sects. In addition the high standard of execution and the intricacy of the carving make it a noteworthy example of its kind. As it has been the custom for the *toraṇa* to be sprinkled with the blood of sacrificial animals for the last three centuries, the images are covered with dried clots of blood, as well as layers of paint. The *toraṇa* requires immediate chemical treatment to prevent further damage to the wood. Behind this *toraṇa* are two other decorative arches, one of wood, of the 15th-16th century, and the other of stone, of the 16th-17th century.

## BRONZE IMAGES

### *Tārā Devī*

A gilded bronze image of Tārā (Plate 148) from Chilancho Mahāvihār is among the important images from Kirtipur which were removed to the National Museum by the priests and the Gūṭhī Saṃsthān in 1981 (Apx. B, no. 5). The image is studdded with precious and semi-precious stones, ten of which were in place when the icon was photographed by the author in 1983. The goddess stands on a pedestal, her right leg slightly bent.

She holds a lotus flower in her left hand, and her right hand is raised up to the breast in *abhāya mudrā* and holds a fruit. It is more usual for images of Tārā to show the lotus in the right and the fruit in the left hand, although a 10th century image[21] has the hands arranged in the same manner as the Tārā under discussion.

The garments of the goddess are shown as a dress of fine, transparent material on the upper part of the body, and a skirt of heavier material. She is crowned with a single peaked tiara showing off her elaborately arranged hair. She has large ear-rings, a studded necklace, armlets, bracelets and a waist band. There is also a rod kept with the image which may have supported a *prabhāmaṇḍala*, as is seen in a 15th century image.[22] There may also have been a halo attached to the *prabhāmaṇḍala*.

Individual female images of this kind are seen from the sixth to the eighteenth century, and are variously addressed as Tārā, Devī, Lakshmī, Gauri and Bhagavatī. Macdonald[23] has pointed out the difficulty of identifying these figures precisely from the information recorded in the local chronicles, because of the complexity of beliefs with regard to the particular members of the pantheon. Detailed study of the type is needed before a system for dating them can be established. However, some suggestions can be made by comparison with other examples. Von Schroeder[24] has shown that in bronze female figures of the 7th century AD the hips are broad, but after this period they become narrower, while the upper part of the body remains similar to the earlier type. The Tārā under discussion seems to fall into this category, and her skirt is shown as thicker than in 7th century figures. Furthermore, precious and semi-precious stones are used in figures of this kind from the 7th century onwards. Kramrisch[25] has shown that in the 10th century the images of Devi have parallels with the Pala sculpture of eastern India. This Tārā lacks these features and the writer is inclined to date it to the late 8th or early 9th century AD.

*Sambhara in yab yum posture*

Another fine gilded bronze image from Chilañcho Mahāvihār now kept in the National Museum is the Sambhara in *yab yum* posture (Apx. B, no. 2). The image is executed according to the iconology given in the *Nispanna yogāvali*.[26] The figures stand in *ālidhāsana* pose and Upayā, the male aspect, embraces the female aspect, his consort or *śaktī*, Bajrabārāhi (Plate 149).

Upayā has four faces, the main one to the front having a compassionate smiling expression. He is twelve armed; the front arms grasp his *śaktī*, while the back pair of hands each hold an elephant skin from which the blood trickles. The other right hands hold the axe, but the knife (*kartri*) and *triśūla* (trident) are missing. The skull cup filled with blood, and the severed heads of Brahmā are held in the left hands, but two of the emblems of the remaining left hands are also missing: the noose (*pāśa*) and the skull topped club (*khaṭvāṅga*). He wears an elaborate crown, with a small thunderbolt (*bajra*) signifying Achhyobhya his spiritual father. The female aspect has only two arms. Both figures are shown semi-naked, with ornaments around the waist, arms, wrists and ankles, and a garland of severed heads.

## NOTES

1 Safalya Amatya, "*Nepalka kehi mahattwapurna bhitte chitraharu*", *Ancient Nepal*, no. 28, 1974, 41.
2 Lain Simha Bangdel, *Early Sculptures of Nepal*, New Delhi, 1982, 98.
3 Ibid.
4 Ibid., 37.
5 Ibid., 57.
6 D. R. Regmi, *Ancient Nepal*, Calcutta, 1969, 177.
7 Bangdel, op. cit. 1.
8 Ibid., 28.
9 Ibid., 27-8.
10 Ibid., 55.
11 C. Shivarama Krishnamurti, *The Art of India*, New York, 1977, 88.
12 Ibid., 239.
13 Ibid., 11-12.
14 Ernst and Rose Leonore Waldschmidt, *Nepal, Art Treasures from the Himalayas*, tr. David Wilson, Calcutta, 1969, 62.
15 H. A. Oldfield, *Sketches from Nipal*, II, London 1880, reprinted New Delhi, 1974, 256.
16 Pratapaditya Pal, *Vaiṣṇava Iconology in Nepal: a study in art and religion*, Calcutta, 1970, 73.
17 Ibid., fig. 43.
18 Jurgen Winkler and Aryal Mukhand Raj, *Nepal*, first published Stuttgart, 1976, English ed. tr. F. A. Friedel and J. L. Lotnel Coeper, Tokyo 1977, 99-102.
19 Binayatosh Bhattacharya, *Indian Buddhist Iconography*, rev. ed. Calcutta, 1968, 160.
20 Sukra Sagar Shrestha, Three mediaeval inscriptions from Kathmandu, *Nepalese Culture*, IV, 1984, 57.
21 Stella Kramrisch, *The Art of Nepal*, (*catalogue of the first important exhibition of Nepalese art in New York*), New York, 1964, 131 no. 13.
22 Ibid., 136.
23 A. W. Macdonald and A. V. Stahl, *Newar Art*, New Delhi, 1979, 48.
24 Ulrich von Schroeder, *Indo-Tibetan Bronzes*, Hong Kong, 1981, 303, 308.
25 Kramrisch, op. cit. 2.
26 Binayatosh Bhattacharya, *Indian Buddhist Iconography*, rev. ed. Calcutta, 1968, 162.

# APPENDIX A

## INSCRIPTIONS OF KIRTIPUR

SUKRA SAGAR SHRESTHA

1. Bāgh Bhairav temple complex, inscription above the Māna Binayak image, 623/1503.

१. श्रीोस्तु सम्बत ६२३ माघ मासे शुक्ल पदाा पन्चमी प्र षाष्टम्यायान्तिथौ ।। उत्रभद्र
नदात्रः रिघप्रशिवयोग्यः अंगार वासरे

२. थूवदिनकुन्हु श्रीमत्र श्रीश्रीमनविनायकात्वं प्रतिष्ठा याङ०ा जजमान श्रीकीत्रिपुरी देश
वंथूवटोल नं(ते)छें हाकुभारीसन

३. श्व वदि मरिभरीसन ।। धर्म्म द्वयका अहोरात्र यज्ञ याङ० सम्पुर्ण ।। धर्म्म सस
गणाम्ह श ... थूवते दं ग्व (राज) देवत्वं

४. ... व छन्त श्वेदल्वि श्री गुंदि महास्थाने स्ठाप्ना याङ०ा दिन ।।

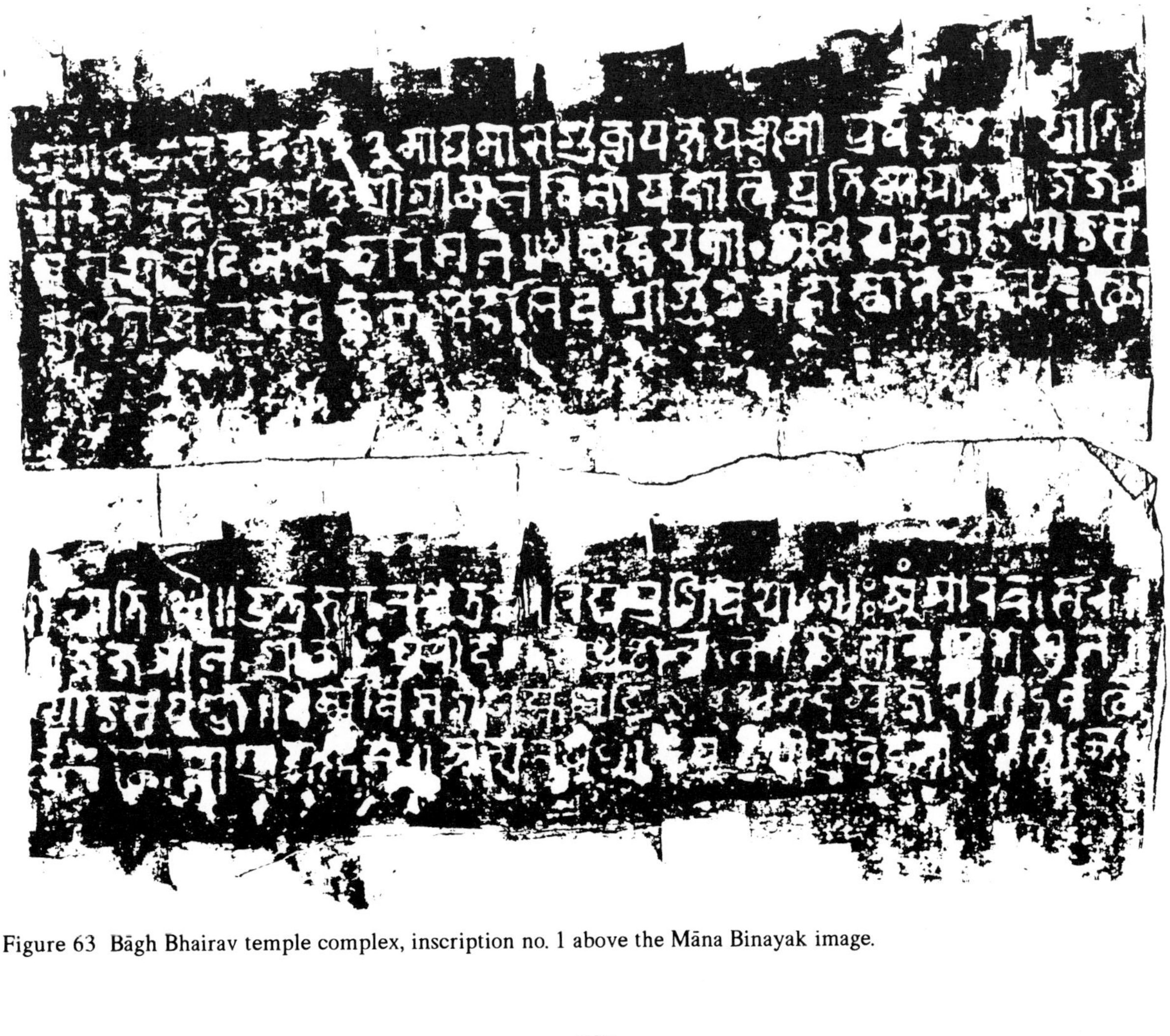

Figure 63 Bāgh Bhairav temple complex, inscription no. 1 above the Māna Binayak image.

2. Chilaṅcho complex, pedestal inscription of Ārya Tārā, 636/1516.

श्रीयोस्तु । सम्बत ६३६ जेष्ठ शुक्ल द्वितीयायांतिथौ रो
हिनि नक्षत्रे शुक्रम योगे शनैश्चर वासरे वृषाराशीगते स
वितरी सस्व राशीगते चन्द्रमासी दानपति श्री नकविकारिलिवि
हैं शुदोम भारी तस्य भार्या विजय लक्ष्मी नामनेन स्वप्रतिमा श्री आर्य
तारा भट्टारिका प्रतिस्था कृतं । पुन भाषा फले सह दम्म शिवका ४
थ्रवतेया वसानन कतिनि पुनिसि नकवल प्रतिप्वाथ ५ दिन प्रति प्वा
ठ १ मर्त, जवा २ धरी जवा २ फलै जवा २ ला जवा २ थ्रवं ... दमाविय
अनेन पुमेन सुख सम्पदं भवतु शुभ ।

3. Dabujho Ṭol, pedestal inscription of Nārāyaṇa, 650/1530.

श्रीयोस्तु । सम्वत ६५० वैशाख शुक्ल एकादस्यांतिथौ उत्र फल्गुने
प्र हस्त नक्षत्र वर्न प्र शुद्धि योगे शनेशचल वासरे ध्वकुन्हु हाकोयिदिशि
हात्वं दिवगत जुव दिन जुली । हेरभित्वं सहगामिनि सहितन श्रीश्रीश्री इन्द्रपु
त्वंग्व शुभ । शुभमस्तु सर्वदा भवतु जथा रस्तु शुभ ।।

4. Bāgh Bhairav complex, inscription on a stone slab above the entrance to Māna Binayak, 750/1630.

१. श्रीयोस्तु सम्वत ५० वैशाख मास्य शुक्र पक्ष षाष्टम्यायांतिथौ उत्राषाढ नक्षत्रे
२. ... जोग्य ।। वृहस्पति वासरे थ्रवकुन्हु श्री किर्तिपुरी देश्या वंथ्रव त्वाख्या
सत्र यन्ता गृ
३.(ह) भारोसन ।। श्रीमन्त श्रीश्रीमन विनायक देवस्त देवर दयका जुरो ।। शुभं ।।

5. Chhve Bāhā, copper plate inscription of the entrance, 762/1642.

ॐ नमो वुद्धाय ।। सम्बत ७६२ ज्रेष्ठ कृष्ण अष्टम्यांतिथौ उत्रभद्र
प्र रेवति नक्षत्रे शोभन योगे शुक्र वासरे । थ्रवकुन्हु श्रीशाक्य
वंश हाकु दानपतिनं ।। श्रीशाक्यमुनि ।। श्रीधर्मधातु वागिश्वर ।।
अहोरात्र यज्ञ याङ० स्थापना याना जुरो । तस्य भार्या मनिका
द्वितीय भार्या वनश ।। तृतीय जमुना पुत्र सहितनं (पुण्यं)जनध
न सन्तान लक्ष्मी आयु आरोग्यमस्तु ।।

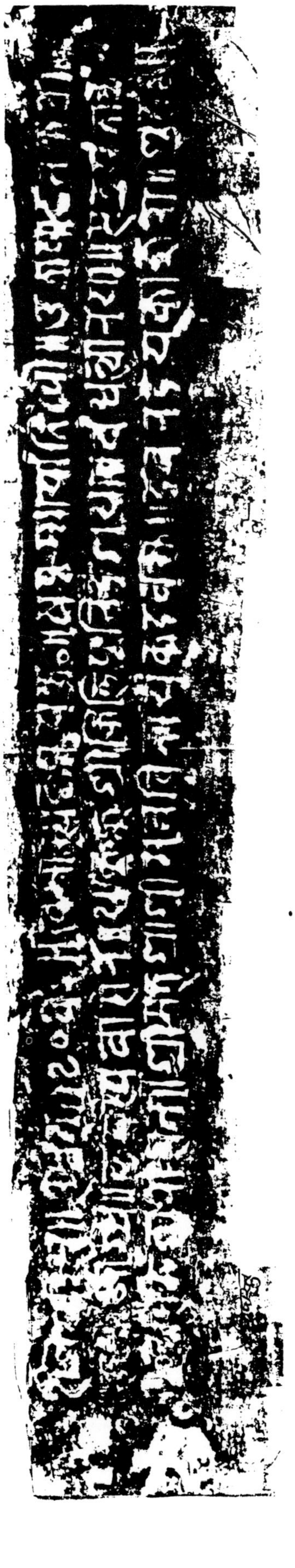

Figure 64 Inscription no. 4 above the entrance to Māna Binayak.

6. Śākyamuni Buddha Mandir, inscription inside the temple, 769/1649.

गुणेव लोकणास्तान, सवलंमार वलान्तकं देवदेवाधियंता
थं महावोधि नम्याम्यहं ।। मगधमनिशार्दुल, लोकेलोकानुच
भुकंसर्व्व देवास्तुम्र वंदे गुण सागर सागरं, श्रेयोस्तु सम्वत
७६९ माघमास्य शुक्र पदा ।। द्वादश्यांतिथौ।। मृगशिल नदात्रे स
वैधति जोगे, जथाकर्ण मुहुत्रे सोम वासरे मक्र रासि गते स
(वि) तरी वृषारासि गते चन्द्र मसि थ्रूवकुन्हु ल्दाहुति दादश्या
ग्निक्रिया आरंभ याङ०न ध्वजारोहन याङ०,पंन्च स्वर वाद्य धा
रा नृत्यपद साधन (भुजा ?) प्रकास याङ०नं देवास्य संजुक्ता
याङ०नं श्री श्रीमहावोधि शाक्यमुनि स्थापना याङ० दिवंगत दै
वकृतजुयातम्र स्वमाता लन्हाजु यात नेहलउभयस्त नामन द
यका दानपति श्रीशाक्यवंश हाकुजुन स्थापना याङ० तस्य भा
र्या मनिका द्वितीय भार्या वरूना तृतीय भार्या जमुना तस्य पु
त्र धर्मजोति द्वितीय पुत्र गुनजोति तृते दानपति(नं) जनध
न ल्दमी संप्राप्तवन्तु, आयु आरोग्य भुगुति मुगुति फलं
तथागत पदं प्राप्त वतु मूलाचार्य श्रीचैत्र रंङव्या जुगिदेव
उपाध्यायंथा श्रीवूवहार श्रीदेव कर्म्माचार्य श्री वूंग
या नायक गुन चन्द्र थ्रूवते जुरो । श्रीमानिगलाधिपति
श्रीश्रीश्रीसिद्धिनरसिंह मल्ल प्रभु , तस्यपुत्र श्री
श्रीश्रीनिवासमल्ल प्रभु, थ्रूव नेम्हस विजय राज्य
वेलस थ्रूव नेम्ह उभय विज्याकं ल्दाहुति
देव प्रतिष्ठा ध्वजा लोहन याना दिन जुरो ।।
तस्यपुण्यानुभावेन दानपति नाय यथा
फल प्राप्तमस्तु ।। शुभ मस्तु सर्व जगतां ।।

7. Umā Maheśvara Temple, copper plate inscription, 775/1655.

१. ऊँ नमः श्री भवानी शंकराभ्यां ।। अद्यश्वत वाराहकल्पे वैवश्वत म(त्वं) तरेकायु... चरणे
जम्बुद्विपे भरतखण्डे आर्यावर्त पुण्यदेशे हिमवत्या दे (शे)प

२. शुपति सन्निधाने वासुकिदोत्रे वाम्हाभ्यां ददिाणकुले नेपाल देशोन्तर्गत ललितपट्ने इहैव
पुण्य भूमै। श्रोस्तु सम्बत ७७५ वैशाष मासे शुक्ल पदा स्काद

३. श्यांतिथौ हस्त नदात्रे सुद्धियोगे आदित्यवासरे स्तस्मिन दिवसे पद्मकाष्ठगिरिस्ठाने तेवं
वाहाया पात्रवंश राउत विश्वनाथ वावुसन स्वष्ठ देवताप्रितिनं

४. भवानी शंकर मूर्ति स्ठापना याङठा दिन जुरो । थूवयात अर्थन बुं दुंता रोव सान्ह १०
लगलाअफल ।वि गु ६ पांगक्व रोव १५ क्वाथदोको कर्षा षु ६ चोवाहार

५. क्वथेल छि १ चोगल व्यंजन वार्किा थूवते वुया वरसाननवुसाधन आदिन मालको हने
जुरो ।। पुजा जो १ चेतस्वान, अला नसि २ जाकि निस्ला वजि नसि २ माथेता नसि २

६. मतयात चेकन कुडछि १ रस प्र छि थूवते न्हिनयात जाकेफं पियडठा ४५ देवपुजायाक व्राह्मण
जुस्तं वजी फं वु ६ घेल कुड स्व ३ साषार स्व ३ थूवते वंशगोपाल

७. यात ददिाना तोचके जुरो ।। देवया निश्ला व वजी जोको जोनस्यिा घरिसह पुजावारि
ब्राह्मण यात जुरो ।। माथेजुको देवयात वछि काय जुरो । देवया कोश माथूयता नसि

८. २ श्री वावुजुयात, ता नसि २ यजमान यात ता नसि २ वेश्यात थूवते माथे वेशतन सछिस
विय मार, पुनशेष लंक्रामोधि म्यिाव देवयात तय जुरो । पुनः भाषा

९. इन्द्रजात्रा पेन्हु ४ तो न्हिन फछिन चावथूय श्रीश्रीश्रीभवानी शंकर देव देवरस चाक्रमत छोयेके
माल वलषु मण्डल्यात चायातकुन्हु चाक्रमत छोयके माल मत

१०. प्वान डठापोरन प्वाठ चयङठ ८५ दयकं छोयके जुरो ।। भुयशिव षु ६ ल्वला अफल्य थूव
वुया वरसानन अंवालृसिस दयका मण्डप जल्धेनुस दान विय मेष सं

११. क्रान्ति कुन्हु जुरो ।। भुय शंवश्व...... थूवया वरसानन वोसाधनकुहु चाक्रमत प्वात चयछि
८१ श्री ३ धुंवाहारस्के छोयेके कितकि स्वान (सूण्ड) किछि

१२. ..... जुरो ।। थूवया चिन्ता याक गोष्ठी मधुराज भारो वैकुण्ठ राम भारो तेकुलसिंह भारो
(रामस्कृष्ण भारो रामकृष्ण क्वाठनायक भवानी दाश थूवते गुथि (भोदे)

१३. न चोस्यतको अविछिन्न निस्त्रप्यंजुयमाल ।। मनिस्त्रपंरोपारोप्याकार पन्चमहापातकी ...निस्त्रपं
हंतार उर्वरतं ।। थूवतेया साछि १ सनिहश्री विश्वनाथ

१४ उपाध्याय शर्मा जुरो ।। थूवते हस्यनसि मोट सान्ह १० रेनके मार सेल्हायात ।। स्वदत्तं पर
दत्तं वा योहरेत्सुविप्र्यो ।। वृर्विसजायते विष्णुकूलषां मुदातायु

१५. तै ।। द्वेषाण लोभर पसङ० ल्यात कोटी शिवलिंग मोचकाया पाप राक जुरो ।। भुयक्रसङठ ५
सुदोलपाखा ।। पुनभाषा षुत्वाल्या त्वाल्नायक पनि प्रजा

१६. सुधाप्रषा जगात सेल्हा मारक्व याये मार जाक्य फं सतछि १०० व्याहान
गुथिनं विय माल थूव जाक्य दशपति ६ त्वार न न्ये सेल्हा मा...

१७. न याय (षुत्वा)ल्या त्वाल्नायकन ल्होने सेनकसं फसप्रति चिन्तामार तवधङ० सेल्हास
देवर या माल ... जगतिया... .... ।।

**8. Bāgh Bhairav complex, Śridhara Temple, inscription, 778/1658. Reading from a rubbing kept in the National Archive of Nepal.**

ॐ नमो भगवते नारायनाय ।। नमः कमल नेत्राय कमला
प्रीतिदायिनी शंखचक्रगदापद्मधारिणीजलशायिने ।। ।
नः करोतुकल्यानं व्याघ्ररूपो महावलथ्युधिष्ठिरानुजोक
री भक्तानाम् भयःप्रदेःयत्कीर्तिपुर्यान्च विभातिदेवो भीमो
महाभीषाण व्याघ्ररूप। अनेकपापार्तिविनाश हेतुःकरो
तुनित्यं सुखदः सुमङ्गलं ।।कीर्तिपुर्योमहावासीष्ठ त्र्योध
निकास्यहः ।। धनीघो धर्म्मशीलश्च पूरितः ।। परमार्थतः ।। त
स्या धनाघोधर्म्मज्ञः धनेनधन दीपनः ।। दातादमन शीलो
सोप्रष्ठितोरूप्यांतिच ।। तत्पुत्रोभुत्सुशीलश्च सुखद सर्व्वदेही
नांच अनेक गुण सम्पन्नोकीर्तिमात्कुल नायकः ख्याते नाराय
ण सिंह नारायण परायण नानाधर्म्म कलाभिज्ञो द्विजपा
दाब्जसेवितः ।। तस्यपुत्र द्वयंजर्ज्ञ सर्व्वधर्म्मार्थ कोविदो । यथा
नामात्मजोधन्यो तथैवगुण सागरो ।। तेकनसिंहो धर्म्मदीपः
मुल्नानास्ति तत्समः ।। तत्भ्राता रामहरिर्भ्रातृवाक्यपरायण ।। एषा
धन्यो रामहरि ।। भातुराज्ञा किरिटक सर्व्वर्ध विमोदाय हरेह
र्म्यं कृतोमतिधा ।। अव्देनेपालीकाकं जमुनितुरगें फाल्गुने शु
क्ल पदो यश्यांपावि तिथ्यां शशधर तनुजेष्टषादेवदा शुक्रे ध
न्य ।। भौकन्नसिंहो मजकुलरियोर्म्मन्दिरं सच्चकारस्वर्ण्णकु
.. ख्य चित्रं द्विजवरपद ।। शोभ्यामासहम्यां ।। सम्वत ७७८ फा
ल्गुन शुक्ल तृतीया रेवती नक्षत्र शुक्रयोग वुधवार थ्वकुन्हु सत्को
तोठ सिवराम हरिभारो निम्हफु किजुसेन गुदिश श्री ३ नाराय
णस देवर दयकं थव नामन वंश गोपाल स्ठापना अहोत्र यज्ञ
याङ०ान गजुरी क्षाया जुरो ।। रोव ८ वंवु दुका जुरो शुभ ।।

9. Indrāyaṇī Temple, pedestal inscriptions of the two guardian lions, both 781/1661.

ॐ सम्वत ७८(१) जेष्ठ मासि शुक्र पदो ... ... नक्षत्र शुक्रवार थ्वकुन्हु तया
थान वाहार (परम जिवि) प्रमुखन दयका जुरो पुत्र जुगीदेव (भारो)
पुत्र वावुदेव भावो

ॐ श्र्योस्तु ।। सम्वत ७८(१) जेष्ठ मास्य शुक्लपक्ष षाष्ठम्यांतिथौ मेघ नक्षत्रे... न्हुमन...जुरो ।।
प्रभु...विजय भावो पत्र दप्कुरसिं भाव पुत्र...भाव...चिन्ता याक प्रमुखनं मनिसिंङ० भाव ।।
थान वाहार

10. Chilaṅcho Stupa, inscription of the installation of the *gajū* (pinnacle), 781/1661.

ओं नमः श्रीधर्म्मधातवे ।। (त्रि)कोणो निर्म्मलीभूत्वा
निश्प्रपन्चगुणाश्रया । पन्चस्कन्ध मनशान्ता त
स्मै मुपात्मने नमः ।। स्वस्ति सम्बत ७८१ वै
शाष शुक्र सप्तम्यांतिथौ वृहस्पति वासरे
थ्र्वकुन्हु श्रीपद्मकाष्ठगिरि महाविहारे श्री
धर्म धातु वागीश्वर भट्टारकस्के ध्वजा
रो हन गजुार छाया दिन जुरो ।।०।।
थुतिया दानपति जेष्ट श्रीजकेसिंहजुस
.. लाकि ।। श्री म..पाल्जु समोटं २
श्री ...ल्जु समोटं १० श्रीरासिं देवजु
समोटं ५।। श्रीमंजु समोटं १। श्रीमनिथ
... समोटं ४। श्रीदेवजु समोटं १।
...षानाजु समोटं १। थुति थव गोस्ति
समुहनं याङगा जुरो । थुतिया पुण्यया
प्रभावन धन सन्तान वृद्धिरस्तु ।। शुभ ।।

11 a. Umā Maheśvara Temple, inscription on the wall of the elephant, Kisi, 839/1719.

सम्वत ८३९ फाल्गुण कृष्ण त्र्योदशि शनिश्चल वार
थ्र्वगरि देव गुथिन देवस्या भगिलि, धरोल स्वत ल्होङगा
जुरो ।। ० ।। शुभ ।।

b. Umā Maheśvara Temple, inscription below the right foot of Kisi, 782/1662.

संवत ७८२

c. Umā Maheśvara Temple, inscription above the gateway to the courtyard, 835/1715.

ओं सम्वत ८३५ आश्विनि शुक्र
तृतृया श्वमवार थ्र्वकुन्हु
जायका दिन जुरो । शुभं ।

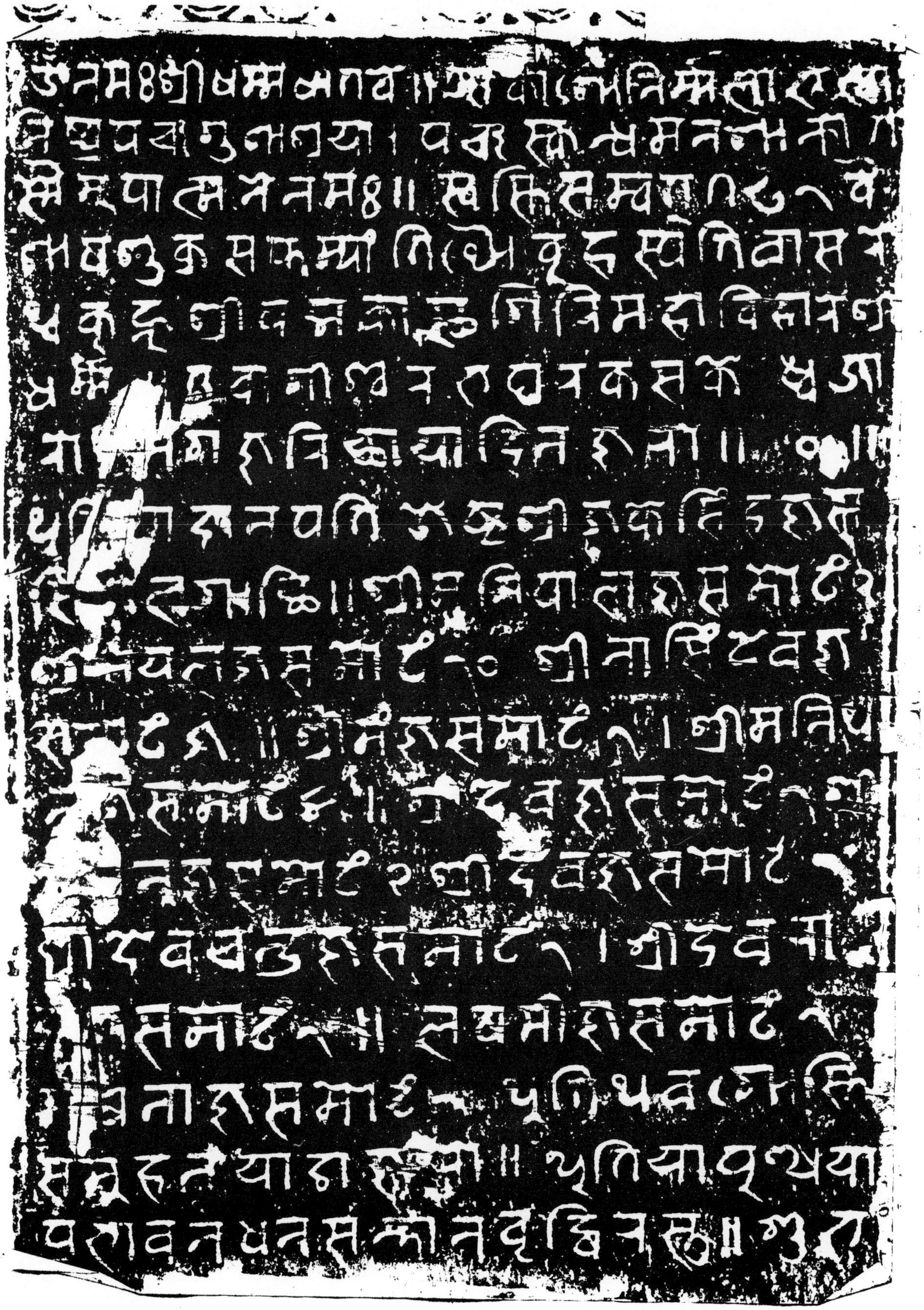

Figure 65 Inscription no. 10 recording the installation of the pinnacle of the Chilancho Stupa.

12. Chilaṅcho complex, inscription of the offering of a *ghaṇṭa* (bell) and a *suvarṇa chakra* (golden disc), 788/1668.

ॐ नमः श्रीधर्म धातु वागीश्वराय ।। आकाशो निर्म्मलीभूत
निष्प्रपन्च गुणाश्रयः ।। पन्चस्कन्ध मनशान्तस्तस्मैस्तु पापात्मने न
मः ।। श्रेयोस्तु सम्वत ७८८अश्विनी शुक्र पूर्णमास्यांतिथौ
रेवति नदौत्रे, हर्षनियोगे, शुक्र वासरे ।। थूवकुन्हु श्रीचैत्य
रड० धर्मधातु भट्टारकस्के, लोहोन मणिारि दयकं प्रति
स्ठा याड०ा दिन जुरो । दानपति चैत्य रड० पछिं गृहाधिवासित
श्रीवज्राचार्य गुनचन्द्र प्रमुखन, श्रीदेवजोति, श्रीग्याखु, श्री
सुनादेव श्रीजयजोति श्रीगुरुदेव श्रीजयमुनि श्रीहृद
यपार श्रीदेवजोति, श्रीरत्न, श्रीदेवजोति, श्रीधनपति
थुति वुद्धगीत गोष्ठि समुहन दयका जुरो । थुय थुतिसे
नं घण्ठ गोत्र १ दोहरपा जुरो । थुयमशिरिया देवस सूव
र्ण चक्र तयाया विन्ता याक, श्रीजयदेव श्रीगुनचन्द्र श्री
धनदेवया, सिजर जुक्व जुरो ।। वुद्धगीतया गुरू श्रीपुन
देव जुरो।। शुभ ।। श्रीश्रीश्रीनिवास मल्ल देवस्य विजय रा
ज्ये समय वेल्स दयका जुरो । थुति पृण्यया प्रभाव
नं शास्त्रीक्त फल प्राप्त मस्तु । शुभमस्तु सर्वदा ।।

13. Chilaṅcho complex, inscription on the back of the Krodharāj image, 788/1668.

श्रेयोस्तु ।। सम्वत ७८८ आश्विन मा
से कृष्ण पदी चतुर्थी प्र पन्चम्यां
तिथौ, मृगशील नचत्रि, परिध
योगे, वुधवासरे, पद्मकाष्ठग्री
स्ठाने थूवकुनु दानपति माथन दा
ल नानि गृह ।। शाक्यवंश सतमुनि
जु ग्यनजसजु अमृत चन्द्रजु, वे
षा भारो मानसिंहभारो, विश्व दे
व भारो व राम भारो थूवते समुह
न वुधगीत धर्म्म ।। ।।श्रीश्रीश्री
धर्मधातु भट्टारकस्य द्वार दजि वा
मे क्रोध राज प्रतिमा नेस द्वयकं
प्रतिष्ठा याड० स्थापना याड०ा दिन
जुरो शुभ ।। थूवतेया पुण्यया प्रभा
वनं शास्त्रीक्त फल प्राप्त मस्तु ।।

Plate 150 Inscription no. 13 on the back of the image of Krodharāj at Chilaṅcho (see Plates 81 and 141).

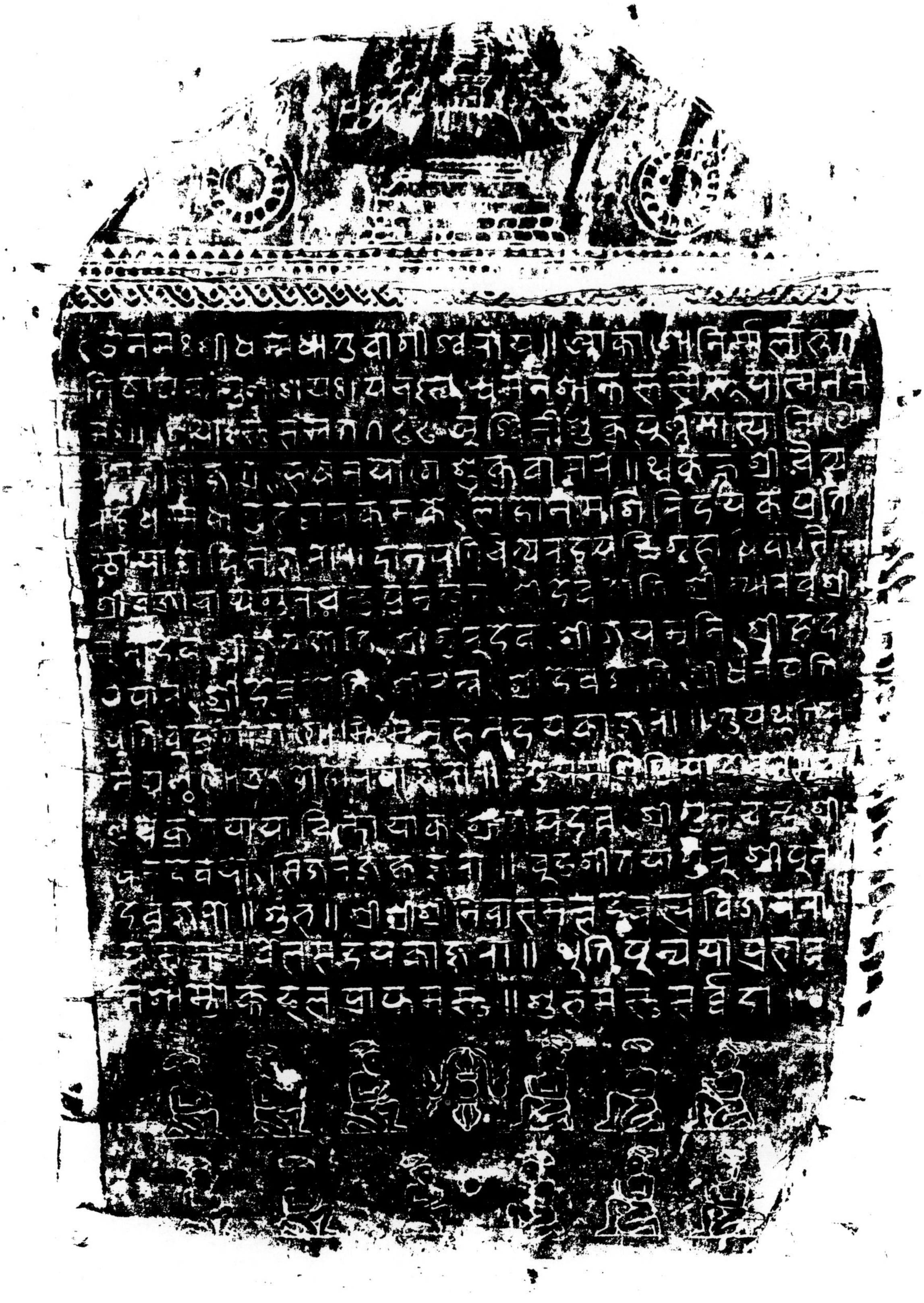

Figure 66 Inscription no. 12 recording the offering of a bell and a golden disc at Chilaṅcho.

14. Chilaṅcho complex, inscription on a stone slab below the right foot of an elephant, 789/1669.

श्रेयोस्तु सम्वत ७८९ अश्विनी शुक्र पन्चम्यातिथौ अनुराध ... ... नक्षत्रे

आयुष्मान योगे सोम वासरे थ्वकुन्हु धर्म्म धातु वागीश्वर भट्टार

कसके लोहोन जवखव किसि नेह्ल प्रतिष्ठा याङा तया दिन जुरो ।।०।।

... ...राम भारो ..राम भारो रस ...भारो सुष्टुरसिंह भारो थुति समोहन

तया जुरो ।। शुभमस्तु सर्व्वदा ।।

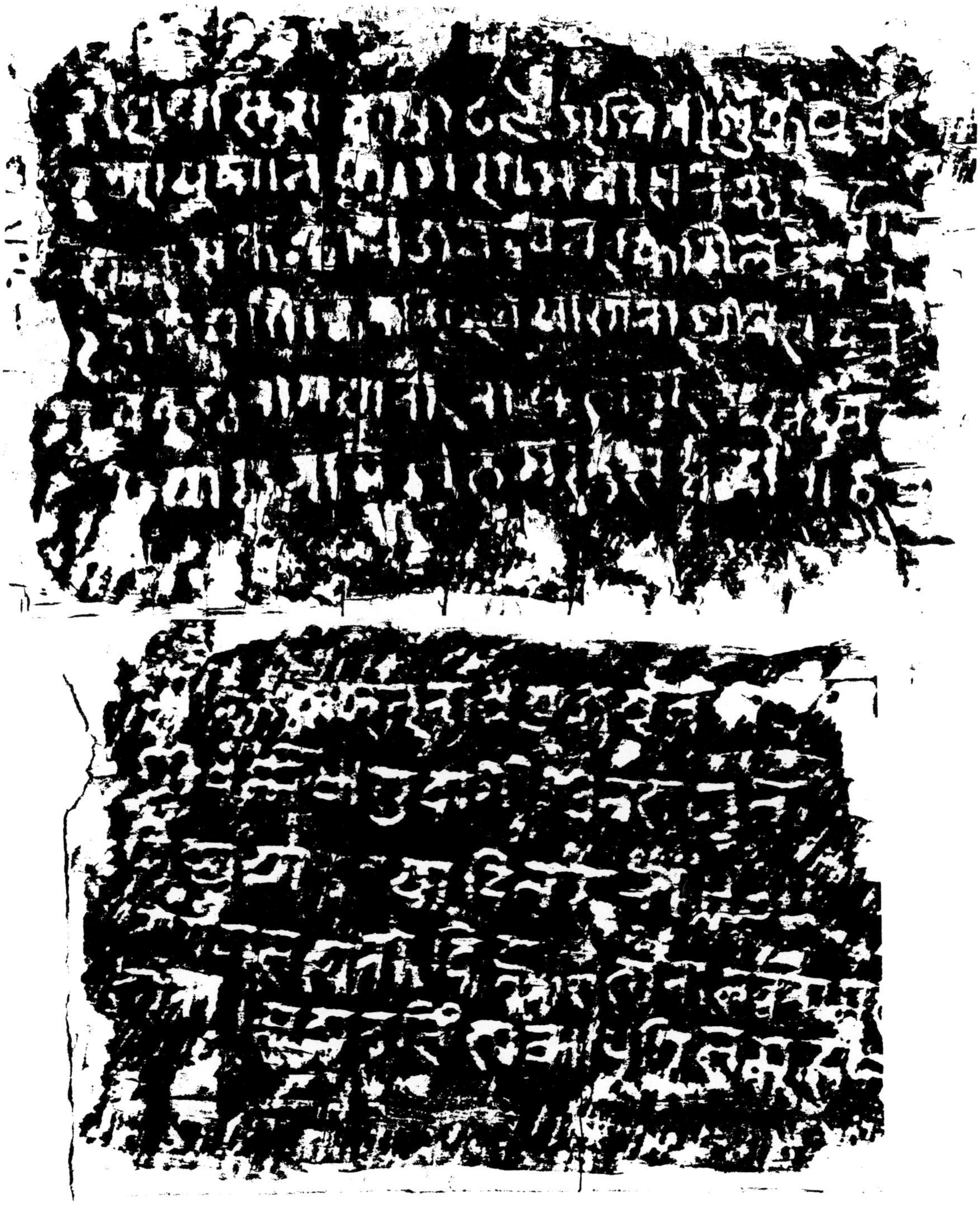

Figure 67 Inscription no. 14 below the foot of an elephant at Chilaṅcho. Above: left side of the inscription; below: right side.

15. Chilancho complex, inscription of the installation of Jarumanuchhya icons, 790/1670.

ॐ नम वुद्धाय श्रेयोस्तु सम्वत ७९० अशुणि मास्य
शुक्लपक्षा। पुर्णमास्यातिथौ । उत्रभद्र नक्षत्रे ...व
जोगे, साम्वासले ।। थ्वकुन्हु श्री ३ धर्मधातु भट्टारकस
के, दोहोन जरमनुछा पीकुनसं तयाव पर्दिष्ठा याडा० जु
रो, दानपति क..ष्टि कसिक्व नरसिंह भारो गोपाल सिं
ह० भारो वज्राचार्य श्रीचन्द्रजु वुद्धगितया गुरू श्रीअम
जु हाकु देव भारो ।। विश्वदेव भारो ।। फछिराम भा
रो ।। विश्वसिंह० भारो ।। गंगाराम भारो ।। सिधुराम
भारो ।। थ्वति समोहन देयका जुरो ।। चिंता याक राघ (व) सिंह भारो
वुधगिष्टि जुयाव ।। चैत्यरड०स तया जुरो, पद्म
काष्ठगिरि स्थाने श्री ३ निवास मल देव, समय
विजय राज्यस दयका जुरो ।।०।। शुभ ।।

16. Chilancho complex, inscription of the installation of the Tri-ratna images, 793/1673.

ॐ नमो रत्न त्रयाय ।। त्रिभ्योपिसततं नमः सर्व वुद्धं
नमस्यामि ।। धर्मन्जजिन भाषितं संघंच शील...म्यन्नर
त्न त्रय मनोस्तुते ।। श्रेयोस्तु सम्वत ७९३ ... मासे शुक्र
पक्षा सप्तम्यां ... अशु ...नक्षत्रे ...योग यथाक
र्ण मुहुर्त्रके, वुधवासरे ... राशि ...सवितरि मे
षा राशिगते चन्द्रमसि ।। (तस्मि)न्दिने, महाराजाधिरा
ज श्रीश्रीनिवास मल्लस्य (विजय राज्य) समये ।। श्रीचै
त्य रड० न्ह्यु जवस ।। श्री ३ वुध धर्म संघ प्रतिमा दयकं
प्रतिष्ठा याड०ा दिन जुरो ।। दानपति श्रीचैत्यरड० पच्छिम (य)
तागृहाधिवासित ।। शाक्यवंश श्री (ज्ञान)जोति तस्या भार्या ल
यिता तस्य भातृ श्रीज्ञारवु द्वितिय भातृ श्री रूबु तृतीय भा
तृ श्री रत्नसिंह ।। पुत्र श्री रत्नजोति, श्रीधर्मजोति ।। थुति
समुहन, दिवंगत पिता श्रीज्ञानचन्द्रजु माता रमनी
जुं पुत्र गुणाजोतिजु । थ्व स्वहस्त नामन थ्व वुद्ध धर्म्म
संघ प्रतिमा स्थापना याड०ा जुरो ।। शुभ ।। थुति पुण्यया
प्रभावन शास्त्रोक्त फल प्राप्त मस्तु । जनधन सन्तान
लक्ष्मी वृद्धिरस्तु । त्रान्ते सुखावती प्राप्त मस्तु
गोह्लनं थ्व देव खोन याड० सेनकरसा पन्च महापातक
राक जुरो ।।०।। गोह्लनं भिनक निदान यातसा पुजाया
तसा पुने राक जुरो, शुभमस्तु सर्व्वजगतां ।।०।।
कथिनियात कुन्हु पुजा यायनिसरा १ जुछि १ मत
प्वात छि १ छोयके, दानविया सिफरुकी कु
दन सि २ रा पर छि १ थ्वते वच्छि ।। थुति याय
माल जुरो ।। ० ।। शुभ ।।

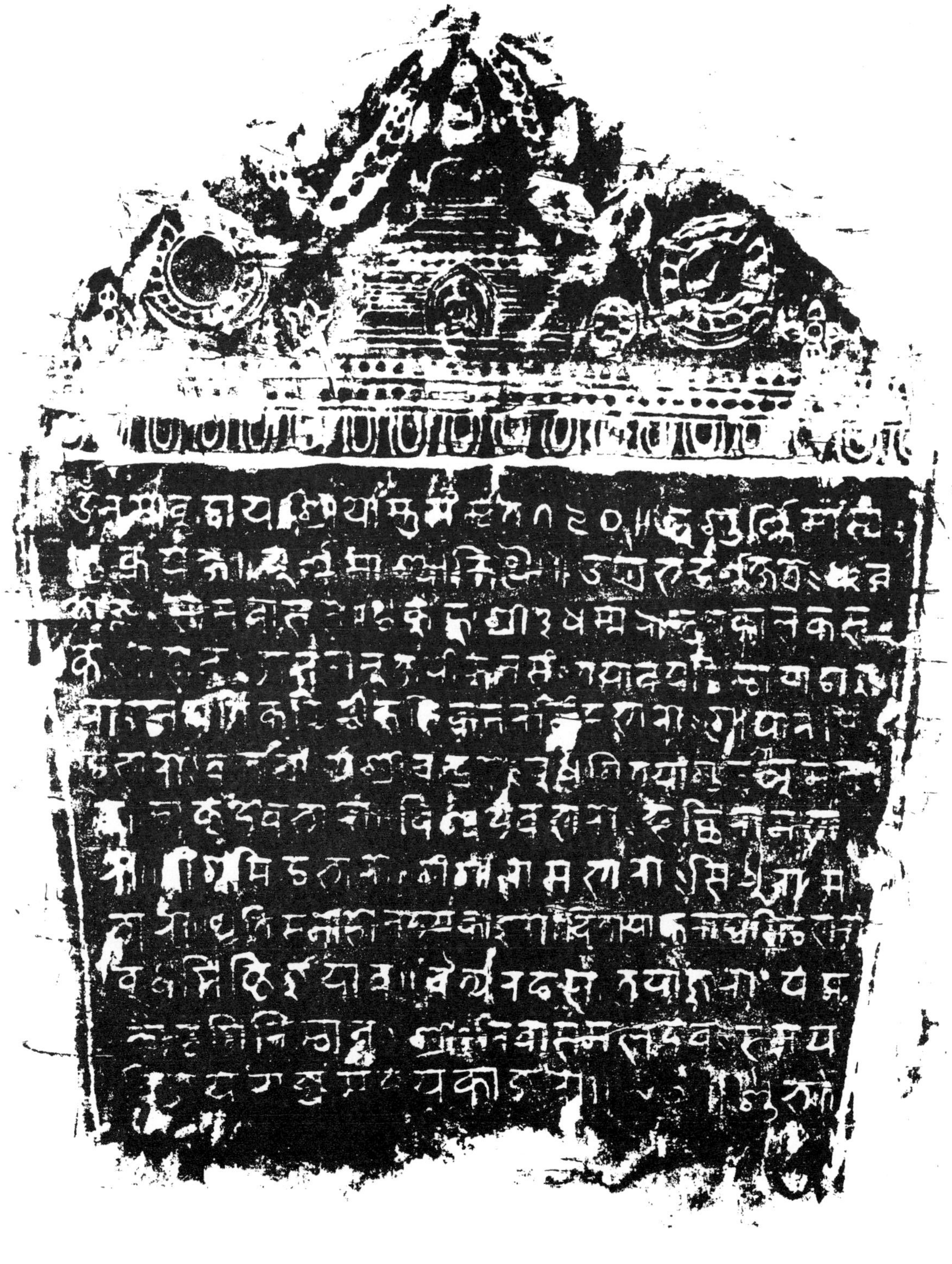

Figure 68 Inscription no. 15 recording the installation of the Jarumanuchhya icons at Chilañcho in 790/1670.

17. Bāgh Bhairav complex, Tulasī Degaḥ, inscription of 796/1676.

ॐ नमो नारायणाये ।। नारायणं गरूड वाहनंमम्बिकेशं, नस्वासरस्वति पदं
मुरलीधरंच श्रीमाधवं सुखरं कमलाधवन्च स्वत्यमठं तुलशिकाननंकं
तं तेत ।। वन्दे ताज्यांसिन दसवं, लक्ष्मी नारायाणं पुन भवानिशंकरंचैव सा
पाल गायियुते ।। माधवं सारदादेवी तुलसाचाति पुण्यं दा ...
विनोदाय लोकव्यसखायच ।। मायोन्चारं कतेयस्या प्रीणातिस्वलु दे
भ्यदा, पापानि यान्ति वल्यं पुण्यां भवति च ...मसाकथं तुलसीलोके
पुजिता वन्दिता नहि, दशने नास्यित्योतुफले कोटी ... दैत गोलनं
तुलसी नाम मात्र कायन दैत्यं फुतकाव चोड० नारायण प्रितिजु...
पाप समस्त फु यिव जुयिया थथिड०म्ह तुलसी लोकस
गथे पुजा मयाय गथे नमस्कार मयाय, गोलन तुलसीया हर मा
त्र दर्शन याड०न गोकोटी सादान वियाया फल वियिव, श्रेयस्तु ।।स
म्बत ७९६ जेष्ठ शुक्ल द्वितीयांतिथौ मृगशिर नदात्र शूल्योगे आदि
त्य वार थ्रवकुन्हु किविपुरिया श्री(अ)जाजु व्याघ्रश्वरया प्रसादन, गुदेश
श्रीगरूड नारायण, श्रीलक्ष्मी नारायण, भवानी शंकर, वंश गोपाल, माधव
सरस्वती तयाव... स्वान तुलसी फल देवलवा दयकं प्रतिष्ठा याड०ा दिन
यजमान फक्किराम भारो, हरिनारायण भारो, शिवकृष्ण भारो, स्वलस
मुहन जुरो ।। पुनः थ्रव तुलसी फलस गोलनं धर्म्म भारपं तुलशी .. यमा
र ।। शुभ मंगलं सर्व्वदा ।।

18. Lokeśvar Temple, Bhariyan Pukhū, inscription of 807/1687.

ॐ नमो रत्न त्रयाय श्रेयोस्तु सम्बत ८०७ श्रावन मासे शुक्र पदो अष्टम्यांतिथौ शुक्रवा
सरे थ्रवकुन्हु स्काशि पुजा याड० स्थाप याड०ा दिन जुरो । थ्रवनलि माघ मासे शुक्रप
दो पन्चयांतिथौ रेवती नक्षत्रे शुभ योगे यथाकरणं मुहुर्त्के वृहस्पति वासरे
रे कुम्भ राशिगते सवितरि मेष रासि गते चन्द्रमसि ।। थ्रवकुन्हु रत्न न्यास जुरो
श्रीमत श्री ललितापुरी श्रीमानिगलाधिपति, महाराजाधिराज श्रीश्रीजय
श्रीनिवास मल्लदेव तत्पुत्र सकल नीति शास्त्र काव्य व्याकरण कोषाल काल संगी
तादि कुशल राज राजेन्द्र श्रीश्री योग नरेन्द्र मल्ल देव प्रभु छत्रधारि ।। तस्मिन्स
मय ।। दानपति श्रीकिविपुरी देश हर्षकिवि महाविहाराधिवासित: श्री
शाक्यवंश श्रीगुणाज्योति, तस्य भार्या चंपावती तत्प्रथम पुत्र श्री सर्वजोति द्विती
यपुत्र श्रीलक्ष्मी जोति तृतीय पुत्र श्रीरदा जोति चतुर्थ पुत्र श्री गुण श्रीपुत्री गुण
वती द्वितीय पुत्री जमूनावती ।। थ्रवति समूहन स्वपिता हाकुजु स्वमाता सह
गामी जमूना ... थ्रव नेहस्त नामन ।। थ्रव देवल दयकं ।। श्री ३ लोकेश्वर भट्टारकस
तारा सहितन प्रतिमा दयकं थापना याड०ा जुरो ।। ० ।। भाषा थो देवर वुसाधनया
त योदोर वु वाज मदुल्व २ संकल्प याड० दुन्ता जुरो ।। ०।।

Figure 69 Inscription no. 17 dated 796/1676 at the Tulasī Degaḥ in the Bāgh Bhairav complex.

Figure 70 Inscription no. 18 dated 807/1687 at the Lokeśvar Temple, Bhariyan Pukhū.

19. Bāgh Bhairav complex, inscription on a stone frame for a missing bell, 811/1691.

१. श्रीस्तु ।। सम्वत ८११पौष कृष्ण चतुर्दश्यां तिथौ ...नक्षत्र वज्र
जोगे शनिश्चल वासरे थ्रवकुन्हु ... ...
२. त थान वाहारया डक्कुलसिंह भावो ... चतुर्दशी पुजा समूहन
श्रीश्रीश्री व्याघ्रश्वल भट्टारकासके घंठ
३. गोदार दोहोरपा जुरो ।। गुथि चायि भावो ...व भावो सिंह भावो
... सिंह भावो ... सिंह भावो विष्णुसिं भावो
४. दातिम्ह भावो, कक्कुसिं भावो मुणुरि भवावो... ग्व सिंह भावो, वावुदेव भावो
गोपिराम भावो ...त्यापा
५. सिं भावा, मानदेव भावो, मुणुरिचा वाभो, वैकुराम भावो भाविनसिं
भावो भागीनाथ मावो थ्रवते समूहन दोहोरपा जुरो ।। शुभ ।।

20. Tuṅjho Ṭol, inscription of the installation of Garuḍ Nārāyaṇa, 823/1703.

ॐ नमो नारायणाय ।। नमामी मिस्ततंभक्त्या गरूडाशन केशवं शंख
चक्र गदा पद्मधारि सवनमालिनं । नद्रम कंव नामासी ब्रह्मणोवेद वि
दामोदरमुत्यत्रो वृन्दावस्य प्रियासती ।। तयो पुत्रो विष्णुधरो वेद क
सतत्वा वितृपन्चाग्नि होतीतत्परी भुवनाब्राह्मणी सती अनन्तधरो त
त्पुत्रो वेद गीत मृदंगविना पितु... म्य भुक्त्यार्थ संचक्रे विष्णु मन्दिरं ।। तत्रैक
तोधर्मशालां लोक विश्राम हेतव ।। स्वगृह दक्षोणभागे नृपामा... मिसं
मते । यातेव्दे गुण नेत्र गगनिते मासंच जेष्टशिते पंचम्यां शशि वासरे
तिमस्वैहोस्कैच पुष्पयतेन विप्नोनत्त धरः स्वयंमुनया मात्रा संमभक्ति
ते संचक्रे गरूड ध्वजस्य विधिना ... प्राण प्रतिष्ठा महा ।। अथ नेपारभाषा
श्रीजय योग नरेन्द्र मल्ल महाराजस्य विजयराज्यस सं ८२३ जे
ष्ठ शुक्ल पंचमी पुष्य नक्षत्रे वृद्धि योगे सोमवार थ्रवकुन्हु विष्णुधर स्वर्ग
प्राप्ति कामनान फले देव गृह दयकाओ श्री गरूडनारायण स्थाप
ना याडoा दिन । थ्रवयात वर्षं वन्ध याय निमित्तिन ...दीपन स्वहस्तेन
ओ वुरोवर जव २ संप्रदत्ता भवति... ... ... तेन दोत्र
या वरसानन ... वोसाधन याय होम जो श्र विधि माल्को द्रयक
प्रसि गुथिन रोया ।। गुथि भारोन अविच्छिन्नि दान याय मार ।
शुभ सर्व्वदा ।।

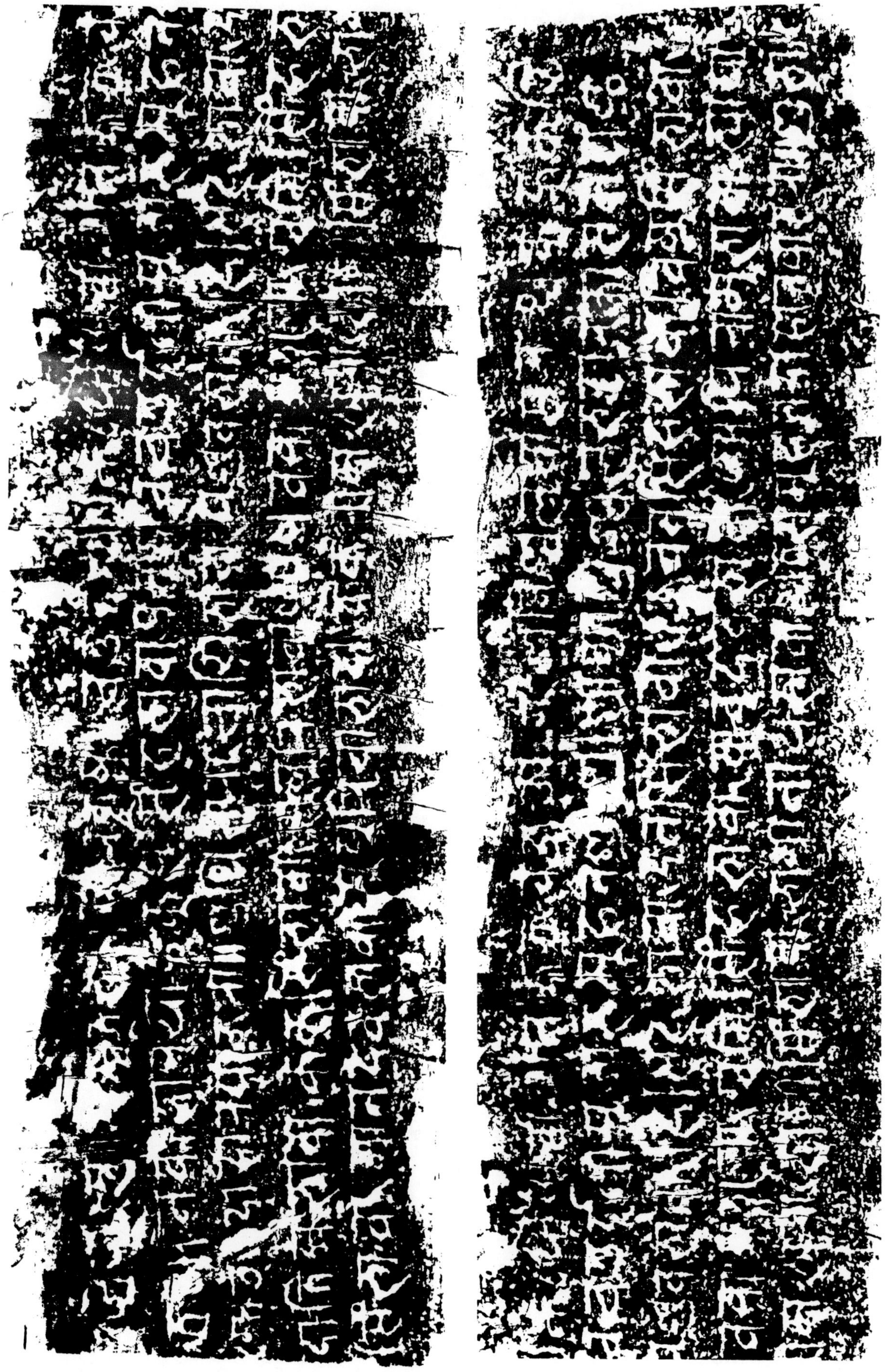

Figure 71 Inscription no. 19 dated 811/1691 and carved on a stone frame of a missing bell at Bāgh Bhairav. Above: left side; below: right side.

Figure 72 Inscription no. 20 recording the installation of Garuḍ Nārāyaṇa at Tuṅjho Ṭol in 823/1703.

21. Bāgh Bhairav complex, Gaṇeś Temple, inscription recording the offering of the *suvarna gajū* (golden pinnacle), 824/1704.

श्रीगणेशायनमः वंथ्रव त्वार सव्यन्तागृह रामहरि भारो ।। सस्वसवर वन्तागृह मनो
हरसिंह भारो ।। सस्व सवर यन्ता गृह मिरम्ह भारो ।। सस्व त्वार कुसिक्वगृह हरिकृष्ण
भारो ।। सस्व त्वाख्या कातछेन यिता गृह चिकुटि भारो । थ्रवल समोहस्न, ड०कुडिध
र्म दयकं प्रासाद ध्यका जुरो ।। ।।स्वस्ति ।। अद्य श्वेत वराह कल्पादि ।। श्रेयास्तु ।।
सम्वत ८२४ माघ मास्य शुक्ल पक्षा। त्रयोदश्यांतिथौ ।। पुष्य नक्षत्रे ।। सौभाग्ययोगे
सोमवासरे ।। काल्वकरणे ।। तथा मुहुर्ते कुम्भरासिगते सविवरि, ककटरासिग
ते चन्द्रमसि ।। अस्मिन्दिने श्रीमच्छ्री श्रीविघ्नेश्वर भट्टारकास्के प्रासादोवलो सुवर्ण क
लश ध्वजावरोहन सहप्राऩ्हूति यज्ञ याड० प्रतिष्ठा याड०न दिन जुरो । शुभं ।।

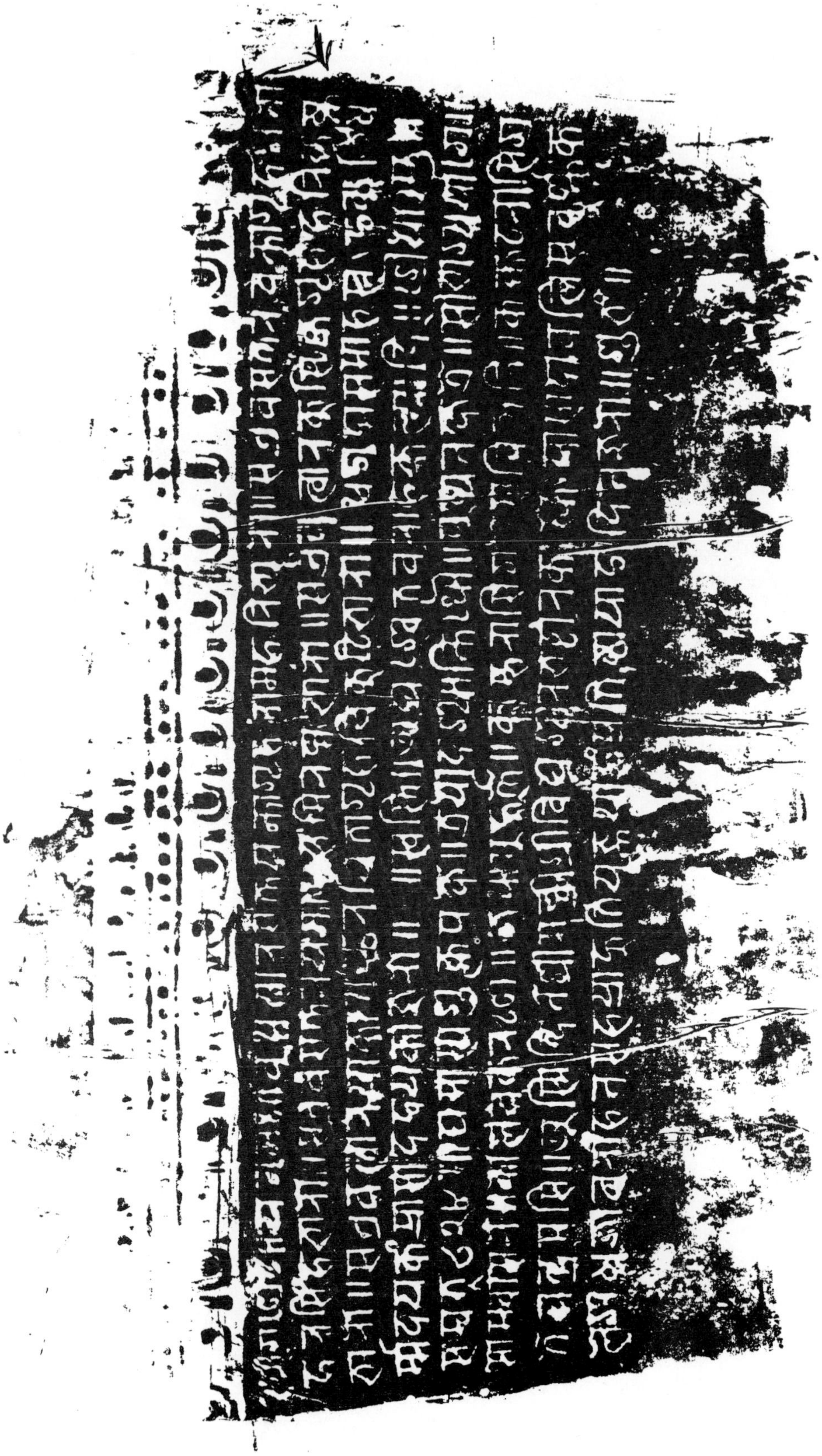

Figure 73 Inscription no. 21 at the Gaṇeś Temple in the Bāgh Bhairav complex recording the offering of a golden pinnacle in 824/1704.

22. Chilañcho complex, inscription of the renovation of the stupa, also recording the offering of four silver flowers and the installation of the lions in the *āgam chhen*, 836/1716.

ॐ नमः श्रीशाक्यमुनि नमः ।।
श्रेयोस्तु सम्वत ८३६ फाल्गुण शुक्र पंचमि ।। वृहस्पति वारे थ्वकुन्हु
चत्रे ल्ददा ल्होनाव यज्ञ याङ०न क्वाचपारस पुजा, आगमस पुजा याङ०
ओहोया परेस्वान फोर पि ४ स्वभिमं क्षास्यं ज्रोङ वाहाख्या क्षत्रधारि
वंगया सूयमि भव सर्व संग इष्टमित्र दक्व पुजन याङ०न सिंह तस्यं धू
नकाया, दानपति चुस्थलि त्वार वाहार गृह श्री वज्राचार्य शिल
जोति भाज्यां ल्दाना पुत्र शिमुन्त देव तस्य भाज्यां कमरावति
थ्वते समूहन देवस्के भक्त याङ०न प्रतिस्ठा याङ०ा दिन जुरो ।। शुभ ।।

23. Bāgh Bhairav complex, Bhavānī Śaṅkar Temple, inscription dated 838/1718 on the north-western façade.

१. ॐ स्वस्ति ।। ॐ नमः ।। श्रीश्रीश्री भवाणी शंकलाभ्यांस्फुरद्रत्न माल्लोल्ल
सत्पदृवेन्तभु
२. जंशाधिपे ... व्याघ्रवम्मांविर्यं सिरस्थुल्ल सच्चंद्र सांदुर व्यागेवायुक्त सिंहास
३. न स्ठानिशंमां ।। स्वस्ति ।। नेपालेव्दे व्यतीते वसुणी वस्यनै संयुतेवाष्ट संख्यमा
४. सोण्डव्दे शुचौ वैसूलव्ति सम्य, पन्चमी कृष्णपक्षे ।। वैधृम्याखेसुयोगे वसु
५. वअधिपतौ, रिदादैत्यज्यवारे, शुद्धा रूपं शंकलस्य सयेतत्कलासाथे स्ठाप
६. येत्सिधिरा।।०।। श्रेयोस्तु ।। सम्वत ८३८ जेष्ट कृष्ण चतुर्थं पर पन्चम्या
७. न्तिथौ ।। श्रवणा नदोत्रे ।। वैष्टति प्रविस्कम्भयोगे ।। शुक्र वासरे ।। थ्वकुन्हु
श्रीकीर्तिपुरी देश वं
८. थ्वव त्वार कुसिर्व गृह, सिद्धिाम भारो, स्वभ्यां गंगामयि भद्र्यो उतेसन गुधेश, ळोहो
९. या देवल दयकं दुसंधियज्ञ सुवर्ण कोण ध्वजावरोहरिन, श्रीमच्छी श्रीभवाणी शंकल प्र
१०. तिमा प्रतिष्ठा याङ०ा दिन जुरो ।। थ्वते यात आय दुंता, फ यिढल वुरोव
स्व ३ वंपिफुल्वु
११. रोवनसि २ थ्वते वुया वर्षं प्रतिं वल्सानन कुसंधि यज्ञ देशवलि
१२. देव पुजा याङ० व्राह्मण, जोसि, आचार्य भाग्यकं वर्षं प्रति विभिन्न वुसाधन
याङ० निस्त
१३. पं हने मार ।।०।। नित्य पुजा यात, स्वानके, देकन्हाके, फं ६ नैवेदेयात वजिफं
६ घेर प्र २
१४. साषार प्र २ नित्य मत वियुयात चेक्त कूड ३ श्री पुजावारि व्राह्मणाजुयात जाक्य
फं ४५ पुनपुनि
१५. राया संक्रान्तिकुन्हुप्र २ घेरन चावथे मत क्षोयेके, जु १ पुजामंडि दयकं देवपुजा याय
१६. मार पुन वुसाधन कुन्हु जु १ पुजा मण्डि दं १ ददािणा दयकं श्रीमच्छी
श्रीव्याघ्रमूर्ति भीमिश्वर
१७. भट्टारकास्के पुजा याय मार ।। थ्वतेया चिन्ता याक ग्वष्ठि भारो सस्व दानपति
सिद्धिराम भारो
१८. मन्दयको गृह ध्वकल दुवार भारो, दथ्वत्वार गृह भण्डारी दातिह्म आरो थ्वतेसन

... प्रति अविच्छि

१९. न्न चिन्ता याड० निस्त पहने मार जुरो, चिन्ता म्याकारे गोव्राह्मणादि
पंचमहापातक राक ।। चिन्ता

२०. याकारे उवोवल जुरो ।। ग्वह्म देवार स्यनकंसनकारे महापातक राक जुरो थ्वतेया

२१. साक्षी श्रीश्री चन्द्र सूर्यत्वं जुरो ।। लिखितं दैवज्ञ सैसिन ।। शुभमस्तु ।। ०।।

24. Nagacho Sarasvatī Temple, inscription dated 841/1721 on the south-western façade.

१. नम श्री सरस्वत्यै ।। सरस्वती शरदवन्द्र वक्त्र्या विद्यादामालावरं यन्त्रहस्ता पद्मस्थिता
पंकज पत्र नेत्रात्कविन्द्रवध्याध्वनुहंश

२. पुत्रा आसित्क्षमन्ति सत्वदेवनामाय पद्मकाष्ठागिरो शुदेशो सुमन्त्र तुत्योवरवुद्धियुक्तौ
दीनोपकारिनि जमुपसे

३. वि ।। तदात्मजे कीर्त्तिं कीर्ति वृन्दो वभूव भूमी पतितुनि मान्यः ।। धरातले
धन्य तमोति धर्मा, धीरोवृथपि मान्यरली धरारन्य

४. तस्यप्रियासीत्सुंदरी सतिसा गंगावनाम्ना प्रथितापृथिव्यां ।। सदा ..तावारवति
सुचिन्ता लक्ष्मी निवासो पतिपाद भक्त्या ।। तस्यै

५. व भार्यां प्यपराभूव, सिद्धेश्वरीति प्रथिता जगभ्यां पतिप्रताचार वतिवलिष्ठा
गुणेशनिष्ठा पतिधर्मनिष्ठा तदात्मजोसौगुण

६. वाश्चलक्ष्मी सिंहामिध्यानः सचिवोधसिंहः वभूवमंत्रि सुजनोपकारि सेवा प्रसन्नीकृत
भूपसिंह ।। तस्यप्रियासीत्सुमुखीसु

७. शीला विश्वेश्वरो सविदिताहि लोके ।। पतिव्रताधर्म धरातिधन्या गुणैस्त
यास्मिन सदृशी हिनान्य ।। कन्यावतिनाम वभूव भार्या

८. तस्यापरासो सुमुखी सतीच ।। लज्जाभियुक्ता पतिधर्म रक्ता गृह समाचार विचार
चिन्ता ।। याते नेपाल वर्षा विधुच तुरूगे कृष्ण प

९. दीच पौष षाष्ट्र्यां हस्तारव्य भूदो दिनकर दिवसे मूर्त्तिमन्यांच देव्या ।। स्ठाप्य
प्रसाद मेतं व्र्युपरिसुद्रिषादाष्णियित्व सविप्रान, कत्वाम्द्रा

१०. दिदानैः सुकनककल शंस्ठापयामास सम्यत ।। रराजराजि वसुकुम्भलाभं सरस्वतीसद्म
मनोहरयेत् ।। व्यतविकंलीकंकल

११. शतहेम्ना, हिमाद्रि श्रृंगा, दृदयोरविकिं ।। अतपरं देशभाषा ।। श्र्योस्तु सम्वत
८४१ पौष कृष्ण षाष्टयांतिथौ हस्ता नदात्रे

१२. सुकर्म योगे, आदित्य वासरे ।। थ्वकुन्हु श्री किर्तिपुरि देश दथ्व त्वार, राजकूल
लाछि यंतागृह लक्ष्मी सिंह क्वाठ नायक भारोसन, न

१३. ग्ल्वोस श्रीसरस्वती जिर्णोद्धार याडव्न लीहो देवाल्यं दयकं सूवर्ण कलश
ध्वजावरोहण यास्यं श्रीमच्छ्री श्रीसरस्वती दे

१४. वी प्रतिष्ठा याडव्न दिन जुरो ।। थ्वते यात प्रत्याय वु दुन्ताया भाषा थ्वते ।।
फुर वु रोवनसित्या २।। म्यवु रोवनसि २ जवस्व रुने

१५. ... तरण ।। पुनः ।। दुलापोखु रोवन सि २ जवनसित्या २।। जाखा वु रोवन
सि २ सोयल वु रोवन छि १ जवस्यं भाषा थ्वते वुया व

१६. र्षं प्रति वरसानन, शुक्र पदाया द्वादशी प्रति देवपुजा यात ददिाण कि जोक
प्र १ अष्टा १ चेत स्वान यात शुद्धा, नैवेद्य यात वजि प्र २

१७. दं १ घेर दं १ शाखर थ्रुवते दयकं मासप्रति श्री सरस्वती पुजा यायमार , देव
पुजा याक ब्रालण यात जाके फं ४ वर्षप्रति विय मार

१८. वर्षवर्द्धन कुन्हुयात पुजा भादंजु ३ निश्रावी देवयात ददिणा दं ४ पंचामृत दयकं
देवपुजा याय मार ।। यज्ञजोर शामा

१९. एको दयकं यज्ञ याङ्ग वाहान लं १ दयकं देश वली विय मार ।। श्रीप्रोहित
ब्रालण जुलं १ ब्रालणी लं १ श्रीचन्द्रपति ब्रालण लं १ श्री

२०. पाठकजु ल १ काशीनन्द जोशि लं १ मीरदाति जोशी ल १ वलभद्र जोशी ल १
आचार्य ल १ थ्रुवतेयात जज्ञ याङ० देव ददिणा दं ६ श्री प्रोहि

२१. त यात दं ८ पशेष लतिं दं ४ ददिणा विस्यं भदा भोजन याके मार ।।
श्रीपंचमिकुन्हु षोडशोपचार दयकं देव पुजा याय मार

२२. निश्ला वजि १ देव ददिणा दं ४ पुजावारि वाने ददिणा विर समस्तं
वर्षवर्द्धनकुन्हु याथ्रुयं जुरो ।। आचार्य जुक्व मुमार ।। शियाफठकि फं

२३. २ दं ८ ला पालुम्वात मुति, थ्रुवते दान विय मार पुनर्भाषा शश्यया मुल
जुकोस्यल्हायात मुने मार ।। सख्वार न पाय मार वर्षवर्द्धन

२४. कुन्हु ।। पशेस गुथि भारोपनि सेन भदा भोजन याय मार जुरो ।। पुनर्भाषा
श्राद्ध गुथि दाफा गुथि, थ्रुवन गरिमत ।। मिखाळ

२५. क्वगलसि वुरोव पि ४ भ्यु दोल्वु रोवछि १ वाजीव भाषा थ्रुवते कुया वर्षप्रति
वल्सानन भाद्र पद कृष्ण द्वितीयाकुन्हु ....

२६. यया जोरण दयकं पिण्ड थय मार ।। गुरू वाहार ल १ मात्राजु ल १ श्रीब्रालण
जुल १ ब्रालणीजु ल १ श्रीइन्द्रपति ब्रालणजु ल १ जो

२७. शि जुल १ थ्रुवतेवोस्यं पिण्ड्यात ददिणा दं २ क्वति दं २ ददिणा विस्यं
पूजन याङ०व भदा भोजन यातके मार भ्योभाषा दान

२८. पतिया वंश दतोले पिण्ड थय, वंश मदयाव वंकाले ग्रोग्रास पुजा याय जुरो ।।०।।
दाफा गुथिया ।ि श्रावण कृष्ण प्रतिपदा

२९. कुन्हु श्रीमच्छी श्रीव्याघ्रेश्वल भट्टारक पुजा यास्यं देव ददिणा दं २ वाहान
लं १ दुथ्रुय थोते दयकं देव पुजा याङ०व भदा भो

३०. जन यातके मार ।। पशेष गुथि भारो पनि सेन भदा भोजन याय मार जुरो ।।
थ्रुवतेया चिन्ता याक दानपति लं १ फों

३१. गाया अमलसिंह वावु, मंदपक्व दातिल दुवार भारो, कोथ्रुव वाहार जशवन्त सिंह
वावु गुव वन्ता जयभद्रा सिंह भा।ो को

३२. थ्रुव फोल दातिल मंदिरि भारो ।। थ्रुवते सेन थ्रुव चास्यं ... क वर्ष प्रति
अविछिन्न याङ० चिन्ता याय मार जुर ।।

Figure 74 Inscription no. 22 at the Chilancho complex recording the renovation of the stupa in 836/1716.

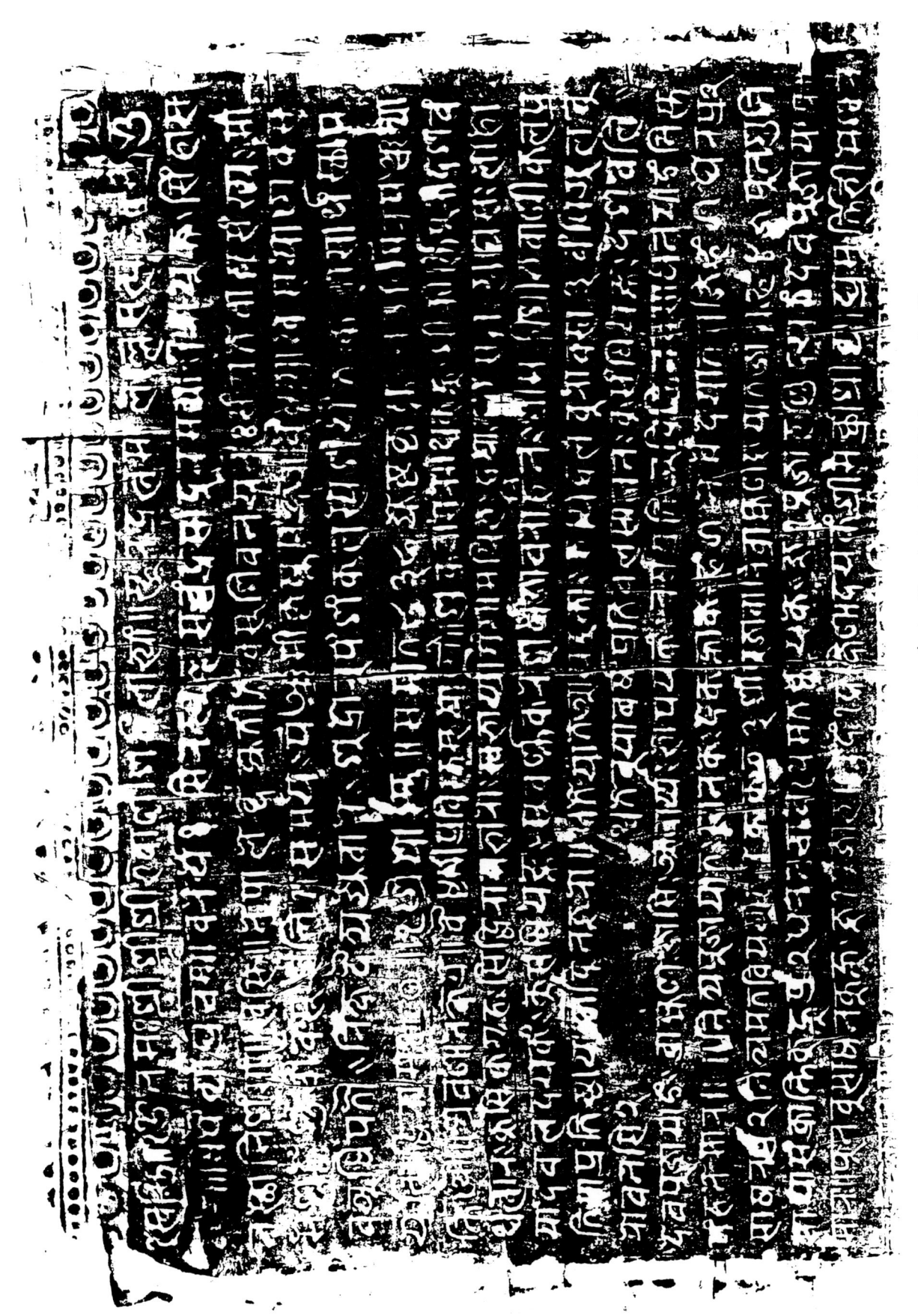

Figure 75 Inscription no. 23 dated 838/1718 at the Bhavānī Śaṅkar Temple in the Bāgh Bhairav complex. Upper part.

Figure 76 Inscription no. 23 dated 838/1718 at the Bhavānī Śaṅkar Temple in the Bāgh Bhairav complex. Lower part.

25. Indrāyaṇī Temple, Pīgāṅ, inscription at the foot of a tree, 849/1729.

श्रेयोस्तु सम्वत ८४९ भा

द्र पद कृष्ण ।। तृतियान्तिथौ

थ्रवकुन्हु श्रीचौव्रष्णुया सियु

चात र ग्रह्ले त्वास्या ...धुकु

त त्वार समुहन चिडण ।।शुभ।।

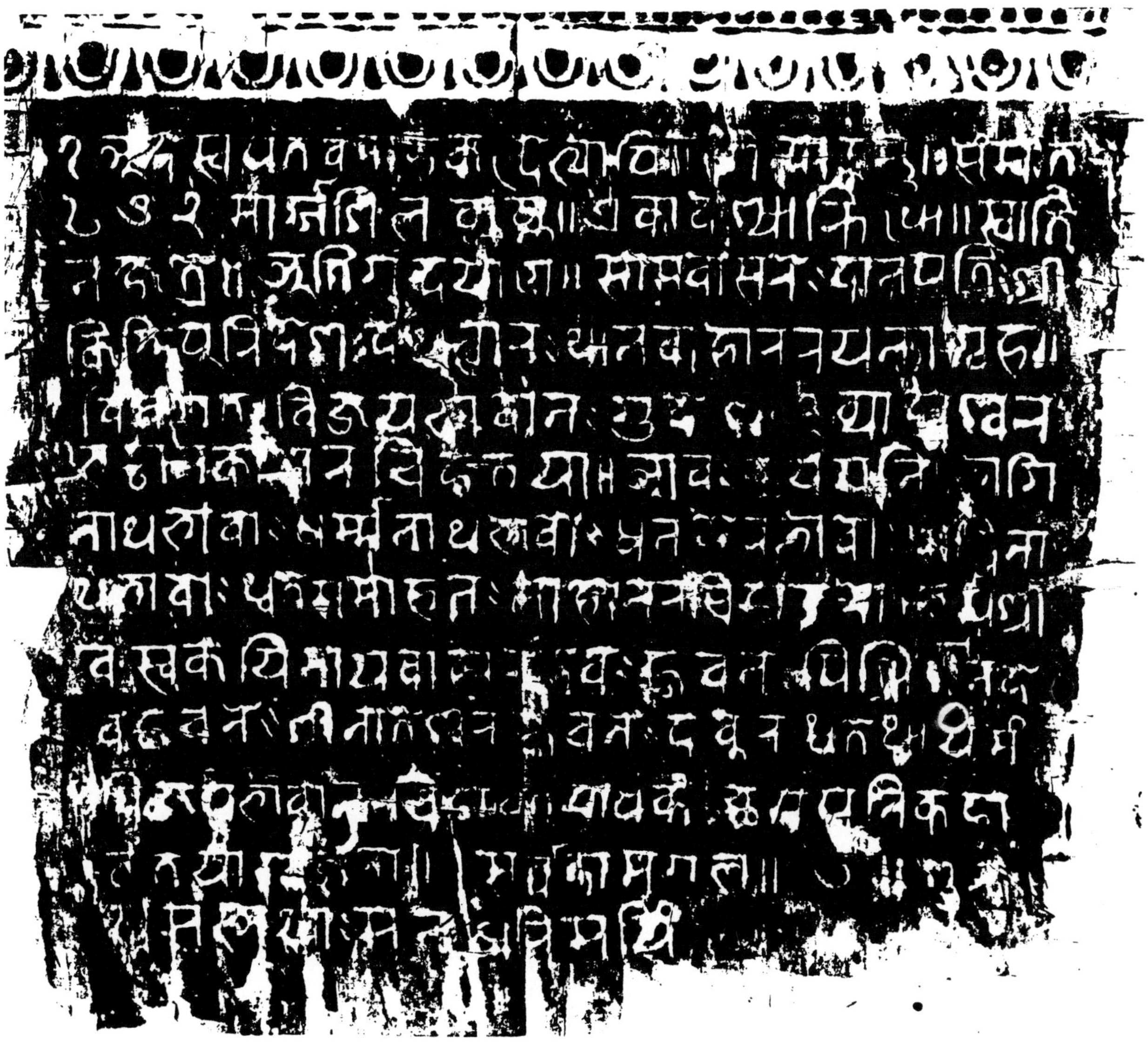

Figure 77 Inscription no. 26 below the lion at the entrance of Bāgh Bhairav.

26. Bāgh Bhairav Temple, inscription below the lion at the entrance, 682/1742.

अब्देस्वयत्र वराह कल्पेभ्यापि श्रेयोस्तु ।। सम्वत
८६२ मार्ग्गशिल कृष्ण ।। स्कादश्यान्तिथौ ।। स्वाति
नदोत्रे ।। अतिगन्द योगे ।। सोमवासरे, दानपति श्री
किर्तिपुरि देश्या दथ्रुव त्वार थान वाहार यन्तागृह
दिवंगत, विजय भावो न गुदे श्री ३ व्याघ्रेश्वर
भट्टारकास र चिड० तया ।। आव क्ष्यपनि ।। भागि
नाथ भावो, धर्म्मनाथ भावो, धनदेव भावो, सिद्धि ना
थ भावो, थ्रुवते समोहन, ठोहोन र चिड०ा जुरो ।। भूय श्री
व स्वकेयिनाथ वाहार देव न्ह्यवने विथिगन दे
व न्ह्यवने, श्री नातेश्वर न्ह्यवने, देवुर थ्रुवते थाय मं
विजय भावो न चिड०ावतया यकं क्ष्यपनि काड०ा
व तयाव जुरो ।। सर्व्वथा मंगल ।। शुभं ।।
पुन भाषा मतध्धरिमसिं

27. Chilancho complex, inscription mentioning the installation of a bell, and the lamps for festive days (*godāramata*), 877/1757.

१. ॐ नमः ।। श्रीधर्मधातु वागिराय नमः ।। नमस्ते पन्चवुद्धोनामात्यादि कुलत्रयमध्यवेलोच
२. ननकर्थ पंचवुद्धं नमोस्तुते ।। स्वस्ति ।। अलसुवेत वाराह्कारपुण्यादि श्रेयोस्तु सम्वत ८७६
वैशाख
३. मास्य शुक्लपदा।। षाष्ट्र्यांतिथौ ।। पुनवसु नदात्रे ।। शुल्योगे वुधवासरे ।। मेषरासि
गतेस
४. वितरि ।। क्रकट रासिकते चन्द्रमसि।। तस्मिंपर्वदिने घण्ठ ग्वदाल पतिष्ठा याड०ा
दिन जुरो ।।०।।
५. भूय ।। सम्वत ८७७ श्रावणमास्य शुक्लपदा ।। चतुदसि पर पूर्णमास्यांतिथौ ।।
उत्राषाढाय
६. यर । श्रवण नदात्रे प्रीतिप्र आयुष्मान योगेशनिश्चर वासरे ।। क्रकटरासि कते
सवितरि
७. मक्र रासिकते चन्द्रमसि ।। अस्मिंचन्द्रग्रास पर्व्वदिने ।। दानप्रति श्रीकिर्तिपुरि
देश भुतिगा
८. र त्वाल ।। चाफरे यता टोर गृह ।। वज्राचार्य श्री त्रैलोक्रजुसव ।। भाज्या
धनलक्ष्मी मात्राजुसव
९. द्विभार्या चिकति मात्राजुसव ।। मातुलसिंह दुवाल, रासियुत गृह वज्राचार्य
श्री भागिसिंहजुसव भाज्या
१०. चिकति मात्रा जुसव त्राते श्रीजयसिंह जुसव भाज्या चिकधिक मात्राजुसव ।। थ्रुवते
समोहन
११ स्वहस्तेन ।। चैत्रराड०स ।। घंठग्वदाल दुन्ता जुलो ... घण्ठस प्वात मत
सि १२ मत ग्वदारस मतप्वा ।।
१२. त १४ २ भूय थव थव क्षेया चैत्र वहारस ।। नतकात १ क्षोयेके ।। श्रीव्याघ्रश्वलस्के
प्वात १ मतग्व १ क
१३. रत्री चकंयने जुरो ।। आश्विनी शुक्ल्या पुर्णमासिकुन्हु घंठ ग्वादार वोसाधन
यास्यं जजमान ।। वोसाधन

१४. यातवस्य जोरन थ्रुवते ।। जु १ पुजाभरि दिन जजयात अष्टविहिरि मालक्व कुड
२ च्याविह्य २ सा

१५. दुदु।। अष्ठा १ साघेर जज्ञ १ क्वछि मारक्व शुक्रियाओषाधि जारेडणय
देवददिाना दुंथसहरिस

१६. दं २ गुरुवाहाकन कमुरिज दं ४ ल्दाना ।। उपाध्या महिपातिजु, दं ४ ददाना
वासके कुडा तिन

१७. वियै ।। घंठ पुजा याय जु १ पुजाभरि ।।कुड १ संख्वार पाय । केफं १ जुस्यं
मथिरय । जु १ निस

१८. रा दं २ ददाना।। चैत्रस दं १ ददाना।। जुन निस्ला ।। क्व ... दानयात
दं १ ददाना । जु १निसरादि गीस

१९. जु ।। पुजाभरि ।। वोकादि सिमाथ्रुवन पुजा याय जुरो ।। दं २ ददाना
वुरुवाहा उपाध्याउपिनं ।। पन्थ

२०. थोरिनायक पनि स्यन चौजाहारि मार ।। पुत्रे २ ददाना जुरो ।। यात
२ स्वकंधरि, ग्वत्र २ व्य

२१. अष्टा २ डण फं १ वजि सल्लिव ।। थ्रुवते धुनका ...नायकल १४ नकिं ल
४ पंचथोरिया । गु

२२. स्वाहा, उपाध्या थ्रुवसजावथ्रुय जुरो ।।म्हं १ त्रजु गुरुवाहाया ।। हं १
देव पाराक हं १ भिक्षुजु ।।

२३. थ्रुवते क्षेस विज्याकं पुजन याय जुरो ।। थ १ ददाना विय भोजन याकं यंजमाल
श्रीभिक्षुसु

२४. यंमुनिजु व वर्षा प्रति ग्वदार स्वाय ल्होने ।। विज्याय मार ।। थ्रुवते
धुनकाव, पुजन यास्यं दं १ ददाना

२५. विस्यं भोय यके जुरो ।। वेकन फं ६ वर्षापतिं थ्रुवते न वाछि जुरो ।। थ्रुवतेयात
आय स्वहस्तेन दुत्ता

२६. ओपिभुर वु रोव षा ६ सधु वु रोवनि सित्या २।। थ्रुवते वुंस प्रदुत्ताभवति
थ्रुवतेवुया वासान

२७. न वर्षाप्रतिं आश्विन शुक्ल्या पुर्णमासिकुन्हु वन्हिस मत क्षोयकं, दानपिते फं
४ सि

२८. यावजि ।। के फं १ षापनादि ।। कुड २ ।। कु १ म्वा ।। ता १ सरा
धारा ।। थ्रुवते दानपितानरिपुस्य

२९. षान गुथि महपनि स्यन भदा भोजन जुरो ।। थ्रुवतेया चिन्ता या जजमान
श्रीत्रैलोक्यजु श्रीभागी

३०. सिंहजु थुथि भाद श्रीधर्मसिरिजु ।। मतकुर धगुमि ल्दमीसिंह भावी, रहदेव
भावी, हाकुदेव भावी देसिंहर भावी

३१. राम भावी थ्रुवते ग्वदार चिन्ता याक जुरो, थ्रुवतेया चिन्ता याकम्ह माफर
ल्दमीसिंह भावी जुरो ।। थ्रुवते चिन्ताया

३२. क जजमान गुथि वाहस्न वर्षापतिं निस्त ...यजमान

३३. कनिष्ठ पहंकाल ग्व प्रहनादि पन्च महापातक

३४. राक जुरो निस्तपहंतार जुर धनलदिम संतुति संतान वृद्धिलस्तु थ्रुवतेया साछि

३६. ... ... चन्द्र सूर्यतुं जुरो ।। शुभं ।।

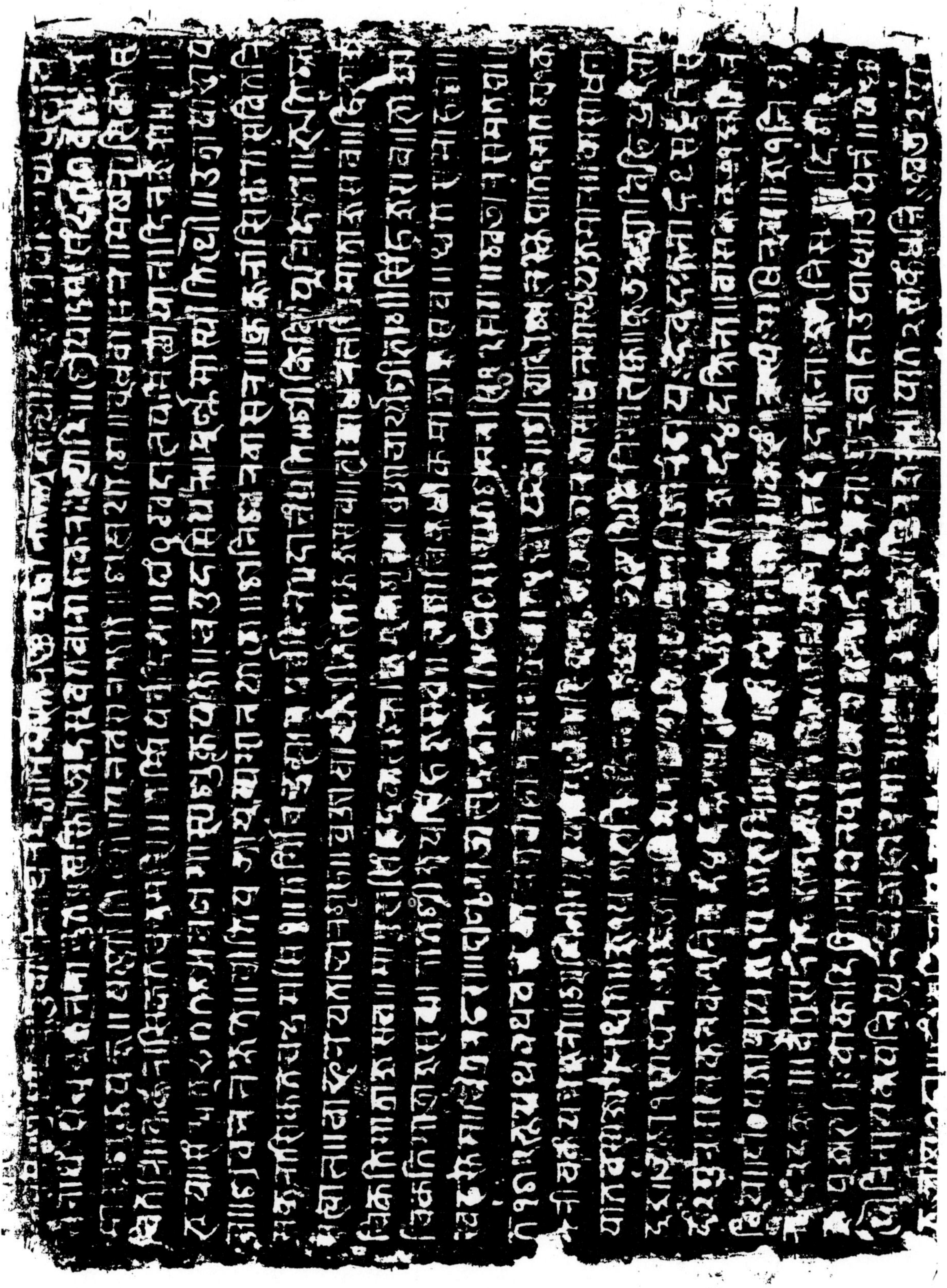

Figure 78 Inscription no. 27 at the Chilancho complex recording the installation of lamps and a bell in 877/1757. Upper lines.

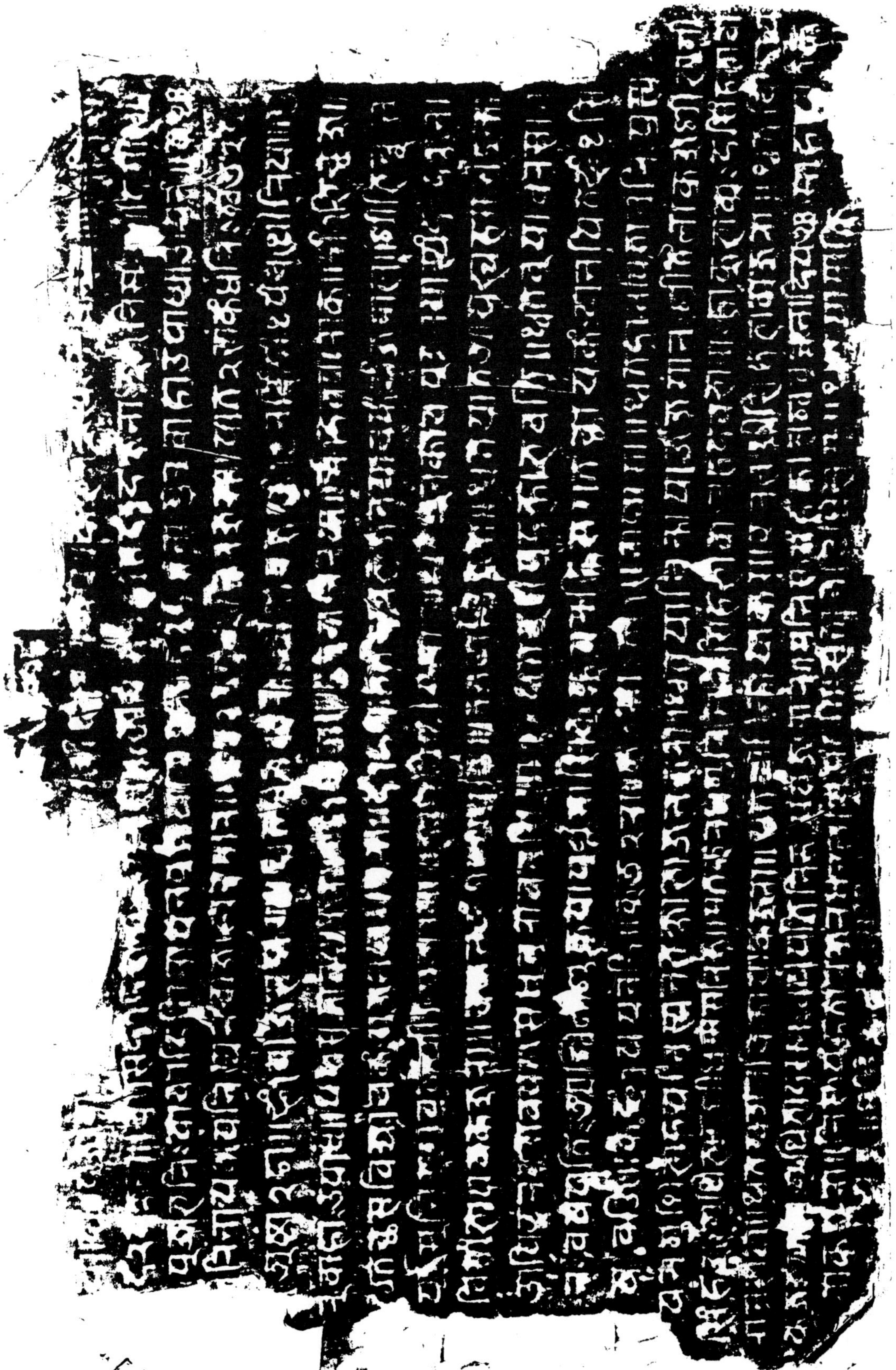

Figure 79 Inscription no. 27 at the Chilañcho complex recording the installation of lamps and a bell in 877/1757. Lower lines.

28. Chilańcho complex, inscription mentioning the reactivation of the *gūṭhī* of *godāramata*, 1099/1979.

श्रीगणेशायनम ।। सनातनधर्म न्हापांनिसें चलेजुया च्वंगु श्री श्रीचीलं
चो भगवानया जात्रा कौलाथ्व कतिपुन्हिया वहनि गोडामत च्याकेत आ
यस्ता वइगु वुंतया गुठि वल्येयाना गुठि संस्थान अड्डा दर्ता जुया च्वंगु वुं
श्री त्रिभुवन विश्वविद्यालय स्थापनाया थासे लाना अधिकर्ण याना काल
वुंयास्ता भर्ना मव्यु वुंज्यानातपिं म्ह्यतयेके विश्वविद्यालयन कुत काल कु
तया आयस्ता मदया नेपाल संवत १०८६ या कति पुन्हिनिस्यें
नेपाल सम्वत १०९८ या कतिपुन्हि तक भि निदं वन्ड जुयाचोंगु
लोप मयासे चेल्यायेत चन्दा फोना तप्सील्या चन्दादाता
महानुभावपीनीसं तया व्युगु जम्मा डां ६०००।- खुडो डां राष्ट्र वा
णिज्य वैंक कीर्तिपुर शाखाया मुदति खाताय् जम्मा याना वगु व्या
ज्या डाम जग थ्वहे नेपाल सम्वत १०९९ या कति पुन्हिया वहनि
न्हापाया गाडाले जम्मा मतप्वा १३३ सछि व सुइसोप्वा मत च्याके
गु गोसा चिना संचालक समिति निर्णय जुया थ्व सिलापत्र चो
का स्वानागु जुल व्याज वाहेक मा सैकि मदु ।

<u>चन्दादाताया ना</u>

१. श्रीसाहिला महरजनया जहान श्रीभुयुमै समल डां डोछि ------------ १०००।-
२. श्री मंगल मानंधर कुतुसा ----------------------------------- १०००।-
३. श्रीव्रम्हु महरजन खासी ------------------------------------ १०००।-
४. श्री पृथि नारायण मानन्धर थक्वा पानीघाट ----------------- १०००।-
५. श्री भाइ महरजन भरिगां पुखुसि डां न्यास ------------------- ५००।-
६. श्रीमाहिला महरजन कुलाछें ------------------------------- ५००।-
७. श्री किसलाल महरजन कोछें -------------------------------- ५००।-
८. श्री नीलकंठ अमात्यया मां श्रीरामप्यारी अमात्य साग: -----------५००।-
९. श्री पुजारी जुरु प्रोहित थप्पाजु चन्द्र नारायण ---------------- २००।-
१०. श्री कालीगड भुयु महरजन तुंफो नीलवन ----------------------- १०५।-
११. श्री ज्यामि शर्णं महरजन भरियां पुखु मान कृष्ण --------------- १०५।-
१२. ज्यामि श्रीकाजिलाल महरजन तनी -------------------------
१३. श्रीवुलाल महरजन ध्वाकासी -------------------------------
१४. श्रीसंचालक सदस्य विचा याइपिं द्वारिका महरजनतनी -----------
१५. संचालक गोपाल अमात्य साग:ब्रुसु तनि -----------------------

29. Indrāyaṇī Temple, Pīgaṅ, inscription on a stone slab below the lion.

श्रीोस्तु ।। सम्वत ..२ मार्ग्गशिल कृष्ण ।।
स्कादश्यांतिथौ...नदात्रे ।। अतिगन्द
योगे सोमवासरे दानपति श्री किज्ञिपुरि
देश दथ्रूव त्वार थान वाहार गृह दिवंगत
विजय भारोनं चिड० तया र आव क्ष्य प
नि भागिनाथ भावो धर्म्म नाथ भावो धन दे
व भावो ।। सिद्धिनाथ भावो ।। थ्रूवते समोहन ल्वहो
न ठ ल्होडणव प्रतिष्ठा याडण दिन जुरो
भुयश्री चोशिदेवया न्ह्र्यवने दथ्रूव वलषु दे
व न्ह्र्यवने चिथ्रूव वरषु देव न्ह्र्यवने थ्रूवते विजय
भारोन चिडणव तया धर्कं क्ष्यपनि कडण
व तथर जुरो ।। शुभ मंगल ।। शुभ
पुन भाषा म... ... ।।।

30. Loṅ Dega (Buddha Dharma Saṅgha), inscriptional *slokas* (stanzas) above the entablature of the north-east façade.

१. ॐ नमो वुद्धाय ।। वन्दे श्रीआदिवुद्धं प्रवर गुणनिधिं देवदेवाधि देवं
वुद्धं ज्ञान मुनिन्द्रं परम पद परम मोदादं वुद्ध ना
२. थं संसारे सार मतं भव भय हरणं सस्व संसार तार भावा भावस्वरूपं
सकल भय हरं शाक्यसिंह नमामि ।। प्रज्ञादे
३. वी पवित्री परम पद करो विश्वमाया धरित्तां सत्वानी मातभूतां
भवभय हरणी मुक्ति मार्ग प्रदेयां विश्वेषांवि
४. श्वर पिठगण समगति भावना भावरूपिण्ड न्यांगीण्डन्यरूपीं
सुखकर प्रवरां वुद्धमाता नमामि ।। लोकशं
५. लोक नांति पिर मल हरं सर्व्व लोकानु कंपं सत्वानां मोदा हेतुं प्रवर
वल्धरं पद्म हस्तं सुण्डदं शुद्धं सव्वार्थिका ।।
६. मं समपद गमनं मुक्ति मार्ग प्रदाता सर्वदेवा सुरान्तं प्रणमत चरणं
लोकनाथं नमामि ।।०।। शुभं ।।

# APPENDIX B

## IMAGES FROM CHILAṄCHO VIHĀR KEPT IN THE NATIONAL MUSEUM, KATHMANDU

SUKRA SAGAR SHRESTHA

The following list of images was prepared by the National Museum in 1981 when the images were removed to the Museum for safekeeping. Image number 1 is still kept in the Mahāvihār as it is difficult to move, and numbers 18 and 19 are in the possession of the Gūṭhī Saṃsthān of HMG Nepal. Measurements are approximate and given in centimetres, and the dates are given by the archaeology staff of the Museum. The list was made available by Pushpa Bajracharya.

| NO. | IMAGE | MATERIAL | SIZE(CMS.) | DATE (AD) |
|---|---|---|---|---|
| 1 | Chakra Sambhara | Terracotta | 62x49 | 16th cent. |
| 2 | Chakra Sambhara | Gilt | 35x27 | 17th cent. |
| 3 | Two handed Sambhara | Wooden | 70x40 | 17th cent. |
| 4 | Bajrabārāhī | Terracotta | 69x65 | 17th cent. |
| 5 | Ārya Tārā | Cast metal | 69x65 | 17th cent. |
| 6 | " " | Gilt | 57x23 | 16th cent. |
| 7 | " " | Gilt | 57x23 | 16th cent. |
| 8 | Amoghasiddhi | Gilt | 64x47 | 16th cent. |
| 9 | Gaṇeś | Brass | 62x40 | 20th cent. |
| 10 | Amitābha Buddha | Gilt copper | 47x64 | 17th cent. |
| 11 | Ratna Sambhava | Gilt copper | 68x47 | 20th cent. |
| 12 | Bairochana Buddha | Cast metal | 51x33 | 20th cent. |
| 13. | Ārya Tārā (four peices) | Brass | 48x35 | 20th cent. |
| 14. | Padmapāṇi Lokeśvara | Cast metal | 74x42 | 20th cent. |
| 15. | Heruka | Cast metal | 13x7 | 20th cent. |
| 16. | Heruka | Cast metal | 9x7 | 20th cent. |
| 17. | Bhūmisparśa Buddha | White stone | 8x4.5 | 16th cent. |
| 18. | Svayaṃbhū Chaitya | Cast metal | 15x9 | 15th cent. |
| 19. | Padma Chaitya | Cast metal | 20x21 | 20th cent. |

# APPENDIX C

## OBJECTS FROM MŪL BHAGVĀNSTHĀN, CHILAṄCHO MAHĀVIHĀR KEPT IN THE NATIONAL MUSEUM, KATHMANDU

SUKRA SAGAR SHRESTHA

The following images and objects were removed to the National Museum in 1981. Measurements are approximate and given in centimetres, and the dates are given by the archaeology staff of the Museum. The list was made available by Pushpa Bajracharya.

| NO. | IMAGE | MATERIAL | SIZE(CMS.) | DATE (AD) |
|---|---|---|---|---|
| 1 | Śākyamuni Buddha | Stone, head covered with gilt copper | 52x25 | 17th cent. |
| 2 | Padmapāṇi Lokeśvar | Stone | 56x26 | 17th cent. |
| 3 | Vāsudharā | Stone | 14x18 | 17th cent. |
| 4 | Dīpankāra Buddha (Phūdyacha) | Wood | 14x78 | 17th cent. |
| 5 | Bhūmisparśa Buddha | Stone | 34x21 | 20th cent. |
| 6 | Chandramāha Roshani | Stone | 19x22 | 19th cent. |
| 7 | Dīpankāra (Phūdyacha) | Wood | 18x78 | 17th cent. |
| 8 | Gaṇeś | Stone | 18x22 | 19th cent. |
| 9 | Bhūmisparśa Buddha | Stone | 15x22 | 19th cent. |
| 10 | Bhūmisparśa Buddha | Terracotta | 12x15 | 18th cent. |
| 11 | Maitreya Buddha (mutilated) | Stone | 8x12 | 17th cent. |
| 12 | Palcha Kalaśā (lamp) | Iron | 38x9 | 16th cent. |
| 13 | Inscription dated NS 903 (referring to establishment of Dīpankāra Buddha) | Stone | 25x35 | 20th cent. |
| 14 | Dīpankāra Buddha | Terracotta | 68x40 | 16th cent. |
| 15 | Devotee | Cast metal | 7x11 | 19th cent. |

# GLOSSARY
## NEWARI, NEPALI AND SANSKRIT WORDS

*abhāya mudrā* - gesture of fearlessness
Adi Buddha - Buddha, the supreme spirit
*āgam* - Sanskrit treatise on sacred science
*āgam* - specific room for Tantric deities in *āgam chhen*
*āgam chhen* - private shrine for Tantric deities of *saṅgha*
*agniśālā* - a sacrificial altar for fire
*agnisthāpanā* - the establishment of a ditch where fire sacrifices are performed
Akshobhya (Achhyobya) - the second of the five transcendent Buddhas
*ālidha* - posture with right knee advanced and left retracted
*ālidhāsana* - *alidha* posture
*āmalaka* - the fruit of the emblic myrobalan
Amitābha - name of the Buddha who presides over the western paradise
Amoghasiddhi - name of the fifth of the transcendent Buddhas
*āṃypā* - (see *jhingati*) small clay roof tile used in Newar houses
*āṅkusa* - goad
*apā* - brick
*āsana* - posture

*bāapā* - moulded brick
Bāgh Bhairav - tiger incarnation of Śiva, and guardian deity of Kirtipur
*bāhā* - Buddhist monastery of *bajracharya saṅgha*
*bahī* - Buddhist monastery of *śākya saṅgha*
*baigaḥ* - top floor of a Newar house
Bairochana - (Vairochana) the name of the first of the five transcendent Buddhas
Baiśākh - first month of Hindu solar calendar
Baiśākh Sūkṛa Dvitiyā - second day of bright moon of Baiśākh
*bajra* (*vajra*) - diamond, Indra's weapon the thunderbolt, indescribably strong, and the main emblem of *bajrayāna* Buddhism
*bajrayāna* (*vajrayāna*) - Buddhist sect prevalent in the Kathmandu Valley, a Tantric form of *mahāyāna*
Bāmana - dwarf, the fifth or dwarf-incarnation of Vishṇu
*bā-phuki* - collective term for Newar extended family from third to seventh generation (lit. half-*phuki*)
Bārāhī (Vārāhī) - a form of mother goddess with a sow's face
Bhādra - fifth month of Hindu solar calendar
Bhagavatī - the goddess Durgā or Lakshmī
*bhājan* - ritual song, hymn or sung prayer
*bhāju* - a brahman rank
*bhāro* - old term of address mainly for a *śreshṭha*, *pradhān* or *amātya*
*bhaupvāḥ* - outlet for smoke in roof of a Newar house
*bhikshu* - initiated
*bhūmisparśa mudra* - posture of the Buddha touching the ground while seated
*biyegu* - to offer, to give
Bodhisattva - a being on the way to highest enlightenment
Brahmā - the creator in the Hindu triad
*brahmacharya* - one who remains celibate
Buddha - enlightened, awakened, honorific applied to Siddhārtha, also known by his clan name Gotama, the sage of the Śakya tribe (Śakyamuni)
Buddha Dharma Saṅgha - Buddhist trinity, see Tri-ratna
*buinga* - attic
*bungāchā* -a small well with a spring

*chā* - clay
*chaitya* - commemorative monument in the form of a stupa
*chakra* - wheel, circle, disc,
Chakra Sambhara - a form of terrifying god in the *bajrayāna* pantheon
Chāmuṇḍā - Ashṭamātṛikā with emaciated body, form of Durgā
*chauk* - courtyard, square
*chhapa* - five
*chhapa jhyāḥ* - monastery window with five openings
*chhatra* - (or *chatra*, *chhattra*) umbrella
*chhe* or *chhen* - house
*chheli* - ground floor of a Newar house
*chhiḍi* - (or *chhi-ḍi* or *chhe-ḍi*) see *chheli*
*chhvāsa ajīmālo* - unhewn stone symbol
*chibhāḥ* - miniature stupa
*chikā apā* - brick polished with oil before firing, sometimes glazed
*chisī* (or *chisiṅ*) - floor board, rafter, binding wood
*chūrā* - powder, bruised grain
*chvatā* - second floor of a Newar house

*dalā* - open space in ground floor
*ḍamaru* - small drum shaped like an hour glass played with one hand
*dāphā* - a group of musicians who sing ancient ritual songs
*darbār* - royal court
Daśamī Tithi - tenth day of new moon or full moon
*dathu* - middle
*de* - town, city or country
*de dhvākhā* - defensive gate
*de gūṭhī* - the main *gūṭhī* of the town, supervises cremation performed by other *gūṭhīs*
De Pukhū - town pond
*degaḥ* (*degā*) - temple
*deo pvāḥ* - hole of the god, a small window

Deu Ḍhokā - defence gate (corrupt form of *de dhvākā)*
*deva* - deity, god
Devagala - spiritual term for the eastern half of Kirtipur
*devī* - female deity
*dhala* - shield
*dhalī* - beam, joist, *dhalina* - joists
*dhanusha* - bow
*dharma* - religious law (lit. that which is to be held fast or kept)
*dharmadhātu* - primary *dharma*
*dharmadhātu maṇḍala* - subsidiary monument beside a *chaitya*, with a *maṇḍala* drawn on the top of it
*dhārni* - weight equivalent to 2.5 kg.
Dhartī Mātā - Mother earth
*dhatu* - (lit. erected platform) relic, stupa, small sacred structure
*dhime* - drum used by *dāphā*, for mediaeval ritual songs
*ḍhoka* - gate, city gate (corrupt form of *dhvākā*)
*dhoti* - loin cloth, drapery worn by men and women
*dhukū* - treasure room
*dhvākā* - city gate, main road through a village
*dhyānī* - contemplating, meditating
Dhyānī Buddha - transcendental Buddha (mostly the five Dhyāni Buddhas)
*digi* - meeting room for elders in a monastery *āgam chhen*
*din* - day
Divālī - Hindu festival in honour of Kārttikeya, when houses and streets are illuminated
Durgā - consort of Śiva, "the inaccessible goddess"
*dvādaśa tīrtha* - (lit. twelve shrines) a hole on the south of Chilañcho Stupa representing all twelve Buddhist pilgrimage centres in Kathmandu
*dvāra (duāra)* - gate
*dvārapāla* - watchman at a gate, representation of a guardian
*dvarāsthāpana* - placing the gate
*dvāre* - local administrator (see also *sāmanta* and *kvathanāyaka*), a village mayor often appointed by the government
*dya, dyaḥ, dyo (deo)* - variations of *deva* - god
*dyo pvāḥ* - see *deo pvaḥ*

*gā* - defence forest or woodland
*gadā* - mace
*gahjhyāḥ* - blind window, niche
*gajū* - pinnacle
*gaṇa* - flock, troup, group, class (e.g. Śivagaṇa - followers of Śiva)
*gāoṅ* - village
Garuḍ Nārāyaṇa - form of Vishṇu, riding Garuḍa
*ghaṇṭa* - bell
*ghaṇṭa stambha* - bell frame
*ghāt* - washing and bathing platform, ascent
*godāramata* - group of lamps burnt in front of important shrines on certain festive days
Guṅ De - (or Guna) forest town (old name for Kirtipur)
Guṅdesthanadhipāṭi - name for Bāgh Bhairav Temple in inscriptions (lit. rest house placed or erected in the forest town)
*guru* - teacher, religious instructor
Gutapau - nine storied, now name of a locality in Kirtipur
*gūṭhī* - organisation devoted to the cult of a deity, and concerned with the regulation of religious and social life in the community
Gūṭhī Saṃsthān - government organisation concerned with temple authorities

*hāku* - black
*hāku loṅ* - black stone
*hākuvā* - fermented rice
*harmikā* - tower
*hi pha dyaḥ* - sacrificial altar (*hi* - blood, *pha* or *phaḥ* - platform)
*hiti* - tap, water spout, spring
*hitigaḥ* - bathing place
*hitimāgaḥ* - tip of a spout carved with the head of a dragon

*jā* - boiled rice
*jag* - foundations
*jala tattva* - watery element
*jāmā* - mediaeval drapery worn by male dancers
*jarū hiti* - drinking water tank
*jarumanuchhya* - aquatic beings in human form
*jātrā* - (*yātrā*) processional festival
*java vaha* - lioness
Jestha - second month of Hindu solar calendar
Jhavā Dya - shepherd god
*jhingati* - (or *āṃypā*) small clay roof tile
*jhyāḥ* - window

Kālarātri - form of Mahālakshmī personifying time destroying the world at the end of each age
*kalaśā* - vase shaped finial, special sacred vessel, one of the eight auspicious symbols
Kālī - black, epithet of goddess Durgā, consort of Śiva
*kalli* - anklets
*karbujha* - funerary musician
*kartri* - knife, an attribute of Mahākāla
Kārttik - seventh month in Hindu solar calendar (Oct-Nov)
*khaḍga* - sword, horn of a rhino
*khagu vaha* - tigress
*khālapā* - cornice brick with rounded mouldings
*khalu* - sill, threshold
*khāpā* - door leaf, shutter
*khapyākhaṅ* - staged ritual drama
*khaṭvāṅga* - a club with a skull at the top, attribute held by Mahākāla, having sown the human skulls
*khebā* - kitchen garden
*kisi* - elephant
*koṭ* - fort
Kṛishṇa Janmāshṭamī - birth anniversary of Kṛishṇa
*kula devatā* - household gods associated with a particular family, house or neighbourhood
*kuldevata* - principal deity (epithet of Durgā)
Kumāra - adolescent, youth, or son of Śiva other than Gaṇeś
*kuṅ (kū)* - corner
*kuṅ phale* - rest house built in a right angled corner
*kūṅdika* - pitcher
*kuret* - linear measure 140mm.
*kuti* - cottage or hut
*kuthi* - room
Kuṭujhol - a locality in Kirtipur (lit. a row of houses)
*kuṭumb* - family, household
*kvāpā dya* - main non-Tantric deity in ground floor shrine of a *bāhā* (lit. lower god, guard)

Kvātha Nāyaka - head of the *kvātha* (fort), village mayor appointed by the government, local administrator (see *dvāre*)

*lalitāsana* - seated posture, with left leg bent and right leg hanging down (lit. ever-graceful)
*lan* - lane, street, route
*lavarju* - rank of *brāhmans*
*lāyaku* - old term for royal palace in Newari
*lhāhkā* (*lhāhpā*) - palm of hand, hand shaped cornice brick, temple corner
*lhāhphvah* - back of hand (lit. hand flower)
*lidhan* - leaning against wall
*lidhan phale* - type of rest house built resting on a house wall
*liṅga* - phallic icon, symbol of Śiva
*loṅ* - stone
Lukama Dyo - a form of Śiva

*mahādīp* - numerous lamps
Mahālakshmī - one of the Ashṭamātṛikās in Nepalese tradition. In India there are seven mother goddesses (Saptamātṛikā) and Mahālakshmī is not included
*mahāvihār* - principal monastery
Mahishāsura Mardini Durgā - terrifying incarnation of the goddess Durgā, killing the demon Mahishāsur (lit. the great demon crusher Durgā)
Maitreya - (lit. friendly, benevolant) name of a Bodhisattva and future Buddha, the fifth of the present age
*makaḥ* - portable clay brazier
*makara* - sea monster
*mālā* - garland, necklace
*man* - maund, weight about 80 lbs
*man* - mind
*maṇḍala* - sacred diagram
*mandir* - temple
*mārakhyo* (*mārakhyaḥ*) open space, playground
*mārga* - road, way, doctrine, creed, belief
*mātā* - first floor (second level) of a Newar house
*mata* - lamp
*mata biyegu* - to light a lamp
*metha* - capital
*mhutaḥ* - eaves fascia
*modaka, mudaka* - sweetmeat ball
*mohara* - mohur coin, value of half a rupee
*mū* - main
*mūbāhā* - principal monastery
*mudrā* - gesture of hands of a deity, and of priests during rituals (lit. a signet, seal, form of entwining the fingers)
*mūl* - root, beginning, origin, source
*mūl chhe* - house of the ancestors
*muṇḍamālā* - garland of severed human heads
*murali* - flute
*mushyā* - soya bean
*musī* - rafter
*mvaḥapā* - brick with moulded end

*nāga* - serpent
*naga* - rock
Nagacho - lit. rock temple, temple of Sarasvatī in Kirtipur
*nāgakanyā* - serpent girl (lower half serpent, upper half human)
*nāgamālā* - serpent garland
*nāgapāsa* - serpent noose, noose used to capture enemy in wars
*nagara* - town or city
*nāḥ* - one bay of a house
*nāla* - unit of space in a house
*nanī* - courtyard
*nani* - beam
Nāsadya - Śiva manifested as Lord of the dance, Naṭarāj or Nṛityeśvara
Nāsapvā - aniconic form of Nāsadya
*nātā* - relation
*naṭa* - dancer, actor
*nāyakhin* - drum played by *nay*
Nepālī Saṃvat - (NS) Nepali era beginning 880 AD (October 20th 879)
*nhāykhan* - nose, split of a door leaf
*nidalā* - main beam
*nināḥ* - beam (lit. two bays)
NS - see Nepālī Saṃvat

*pā* - brick, tile
*pāda* - foot, measure, quarter; metre in prosody
*padma* - lotus
Padmapāṇi - Lokeśvara holding *padma* (lit. lotus handed), name of the Bodhisattva Avalokiteśvara
*paisā* - smallest unit of Nepalese monetary system, 1/100th of a rupee, money
*pākhā* - eaves of a house
Pañchā Dhyāni Buddha - five transcendental Buddhas or primordial Buddhas
*pañchāyat* - administrative system in Nepal
*paryanta* - boundary, limit, edge
*pāśa* - noose
Paśupatināth - epithet of Śiva, Lord of the animals, temple outside Kathmandu, north of Kirtipur
*pāṭi* - (*phalechā*) public rest house
*patra* - leaf
*patrakuṇḍala* - ear ornament of leaves
*pau* - roof, also wayside shelter
Paush - ninth month in Hindu solar calendar
*phale* or *phalechā* - public rest house (see *pāṭi*)
Phālguna - eleventh month of Hindu solar calendar
*phaṛ* - podium, a place where goods are displayed
*phaṛī* - slab, block of stone
*phuki* - brothers, clan, collective term for Newar extended family up to three generations (also see *bā-phuki*)
*pīgāṅ* - temple, usually an open shrine (lit. seat of gods)
*pikhā lākhi* (or *lukhā, lakhu*) - front plinth of a house
*pīṭh* - temple
*prabhā* - light, splendour
*prabhāmaṇḍala* - halo or aureole behind a divine head
*pramāṇ* - local administrative post during Malla period, old term for *pradhān* (lit. magnitude, extent, authority)
*pramānsūtra* - written testimony
*pratyālidha āsana* - posture similar to *ālidha*, but with the left knee advanced and the right retracted (lit. witholding, relinquishing, resigning (of the world), renouncing)
*pucha loṅ* - surface stone
*pūjā* - worship
*pūjādevī* - goddess in worshipping posture
*pūjārī* - temple keeper, also worshipper

*pūjita* - the honoured ones, worshipped ones, i.e. religious leaders
*pukhū* - pond
*puṇya* - religious merit
*pūra* - town (lit. strong wall, walled town, fort, rampart)
*purāṇa* - past, old times
*pvaḥ* - window, opening, hole
*pyākhan* - dance

*ratna* - jewel, pearl, treasure
Ratna Sambhava - one of the five Dhyānī Buddhas, represented as sitting on the south of a stupa
*ropani* - measure of land, 72 square feet (21.96 square metres)
Rudra - god of tempest, epithet of Śiva
Rudrāyaṇī - local form of Rudrānī, consort of Rudra, name for Maheśvarī

Sā - Tibet
Sā Pāru - see Gāī Jātrā
Sadāchhyari Lokeśvara - master of *om mani padmi hum*
*sādhanā* - meditation, formula for an icon; the act of accomplishing, observance, performance
*sādhu* - mendicant or hermit (lit. perfect, excellent)
*sahaprānhuti yagya* - sacrifice of male and female birds or animals together
*Śaiva* - (Shaivite) relating to Śiva, name of one of the three divisions of Hindus
*śakti* - energy or active power of a deity personified as his consort
*śākya* - high Buddhist caste (derived or descended from the Śakya); name of the tribe, family of the Buddha, the Buddha himself
Śākyamuni - the sage of the Śākyas, name for the historic Gotama Buddha
*śāl* - saul tree (*shorea robusta)*
*sālā* - apartment, house, abode
*sāmanta* - administrator, chief of a district (see *dvāre)*
Sambhara - destructive form of Bhairav (lit. one who brings together)
*samyak* - in Buddhism, right action or occupation (one division of the *āryashṭaṅga mārga* - holy eightfold path)
*sān jhyāḥ* (*sā jhyāḥ*) - ornate window (lit. Tibetan window)
*saṅgha* - community of Buddhist monks, in Nepal *gūthī* responsible for monasteries
*saṅkha* - conch
Sarasvatī - consort of Brahmā, goddess of speach and eloquence, patroness of music and the arts
*śastra* - code of law, rule
*sattal* - public rest house, space for a feast or a shelter
*satungāchā* - stone tub for mixing lime at Chilaṅcho, called after ditches used for mixing lime for stupas in the Kathmandu Valley
Shridhara Vishṇu - Vishṇu with Lakshmī on the right and Garuḍa on the left
*sikhāli pyākhan* - ritual dance from Khokana
*śikhara* - temple tower, a form of temple
*śilpa śastra* - book on any mechanical or fine art (e.g. architecture)
*silpī* - relating to any mechanical art or profession; an artist, artisan
*sīṃhamvaḥ* - lion face
*siṅgh* - lion
Siṅgha Saṅkrānti - first of the month of Bhadra, passing of the sun or planets to the sign of Leo, a Hindu festival
Sītā - wife of Rāma (also a name of Lakshmī, of the consort of Indra, and many others)
*siu* - prescribed parts of a sacrificial animal or chicken
Śiva - the destroyer in the Hindu trinity
*sorahkuṭṭe* - (*solah kuṭṭi*) or *manda phalecha, pāṭī* with sixteen king posts, sixteen sided or circular
Śrāvaṇ - fourth month of Hindu solar calendar, July-August
*stambha* - frame, post, column, pillar
*stupa* - Buddhist monument in the form of a solid dome erected over a relic
Sukhāvati Lokeśvara - Lokeśvara residing in the western paradise of Amitābha
*sukū* - straw mat
*sukūdā* - special oil vessel with a lamp and icon of Gaṇeś for rituals and worship
*sukumbāsi* - landless
*śula* - spear, pike, dart
*sūtra* - rules or aphorisms in religion and morals (lit. thread)
*suvarṇa* (*subarṇa*) *gajū* - golden pinnacle
*svāne* - stairs
Svayaṃbhūnāth - the "self existent" stupa

*tāhā phale* - long rest house
*tāndava* - striking with fire
*tāndava nṛitya* - terrifying dance performed by Śiva
*taṅgāya* - lintel
*taphālan* - broad street
*thā* - pillar, post ( see *thaṅ*)
*thakālī* - (lit. eldest) head or elder of family, community
*ṭhakur* - a deity, lord, master, chief of a tribe or village
*thakur thāṅ* - column
*thakurāḥ* - pine tree, *sāl* wood
*thāṅ* - column, pillar, post
*tiki jhyāḥ* - latticed window
*tīrtha* - shrine, sacred place
*tithi* - a lunar day
*ṭol* (*tvaḥ*) - a neighbourhood in a Newar town
*toraṇa* - (lit. arch, archway) decorative arch over entrance to a temple, portraying the main icon of the temple and many other decorative elements
*trayodaś bhūmi* - the thirteen stages of existence or perfection in Buddhism
*tribaṅgha* (*trivaṅgha*) - posture with the body bent twice (lit. tree movement)
*tribhuvan* (*tribhuvana*) - three worlds (heaven, earth, hell), master of the three worlds, i.e. Śiva
Tri-ratna - three jewels, in Buddhism the trinity (Buddha, Dharma, Saṅgha)
*triśūla* - trident
*tulasī* - vulg. *tulsī*, basil, holy shrub produced from the hair of the goddess Tulasī, fragrant leaf on the head of an idol
Tulasī Dega - temple with a basil plant
*tunāḥ* - strut, eave strut, lower end of a corner strut
*tutibāgī* - mediaeval anklet, see *kalli*
*tva devāra* - style of temple with two layers of core walls

*tvāḥ* - see *ṭol*

*utkuṭuka* - sitting upon the hams
*utkuṭukāsana* - posture of a seated dog

*vajra* see *bajra*
Vaṃśa Gopāla - name for Vishṇu or Krishnā (lit. the flute playing cowheard)
*vaṃśāvālī* - chronicle
*vāna* - arrow
*varad mudrā* - gesture of the palm, blessing, giving boon
Vārāhī - see Bārāhī
*vasigā* - small ditch where remains of offerings are thrown (*va* - ditch)
*vāsta* - site and foundation of a building
*vāstu śastra* - treaties on architecture
*vihār, vihāra* - Buddhist monastery
Vikrama Era - (VE) (Vikram or Bikram Saṃvat) era beginning 57 BC, established by Hindu king Vikrama
*vīṇā* - Indian lute, instrument held by Sarasvatī
Vishṇu - (Nārāyaṇa) the preserver in the Hindu trinity
Viśvakarman - architect and artist of gods

*yab yum* - in Nepalese Buddhism equivalent of the concept of *yin yang* in China and Śiva Śaktī in Hinduism
*yagyopavīt* - sacred thread
*yaḥnaḥchhe* - extension to a house
*yākaḥ* - alone, single
*yākaḥ phale* - free standing pāṭī
*yantra* - sacred diagram
*yogapaṭṭāsana* - squatting crosslegged posture, tied by a belt (*yogapaṭṭa* - the cloth thrown over the back and knees of a devotee during meditation)
*yogīnī* - female spirit, attending on Durgā

# BIBLIOGRAPHY

## HISTORY, ANTHROPOLOGY AND GENERAL ACCOUNTS


Acharyā, Bābu Rām, *Prithvī Nārāyan Shāhko jīvani*, Part III

Amatya, Safalya, "*Nepalka kehi mahattwapurna bhitte chitraharu*", *Ancient Nepal*, no. 28, 1974

Auden, J. B. and Ghosh, A. M. N., Preliminary account of the earthquake of the 15th January, 1934, in Bihar and Nepal, *Records of the Geological Survey of India*, LXVIII, ii, 1934, 177-239

Bajracharia, Dhana Bajra, *Lichchhavikalin Abhilekh*, CNAS, Tribhuvan University, VS 2030/1973

Bajracharia, Dhana Bajra, "*Mallakalka ek prakhyat Rājā Siva Deva*", *Contributions to Nepalese Studies*, VII, i, December 1980

Ball, Warwick, *Archaeological Gazetteer of Afghanistan*, Paris, 2 vols., 1982

Bendall, Cecil, *Journey of Literary and Archaeological Research in Nepal and India in the Winter of 1884-5*, Cambridge, 1886, (reprinted in Bibliotheca Himalayica Series no. 3, Kathmandu, 1974)

Bhattacharya, Binayatosh, *Indian Buddhist Iconography*, rev. ed. Calcutta, 1968

Chattopadhyay, K. P., An essay on the history of Newar culture; social organisation of the Newars, *Journal of the Asiatic Society of Bengal*, XIX, 1923, 465-560

Doherty, V. S., Notes on the origins of the Newars of the Kathmandu Valley of Nepal, *Himalayan Anthropology, the Indo-Tibetan interface*, ed. J. F. Fisher, La Haye, Paris, 1978, 433-45

Führer-Haimendorf, C. von, Elements of Newar Social Structure, *Journal of the Royal Anthropological Institute of Great Britain and Northern Ireland*, LXXXV, ii, 1956, 15-38

Giuseppe (Father), Account of the Kingdom of Nepal by Father Giuseppe, prefect of the Roman Mission, communicated by John Shore Esq., *Asiatick Researches*, II, London, 1807, 307-322

Greenwold, S. M., Newar castes again, *Archives Européennes de Sociologie*, XVIII, i, 1977, 194-197

Hamilton Buchanan, Francis, *An Account of the Kingdom of Nepal, and of the Territories Annexed to this Dominion by the House of Gorkha*, Edinburgh, 1819

Hasrat, Bikrama Jit, *History of Nepal as Told by its Own and Contemporary Chronicles*, Hoshiapur (Punjab, India), 1970

HMG Nepal, Ministry of Tourism, Department of Tourism, *Annual Statistical Report 1987*, Kathmandu, 1987

Hofer, A., *The Caste Hierarchy and the State in Nepal, a Study of the Muluki Ain of 1854*, Innsbruck, 1979

Jista, D. B., Nepalis in Tibet, *Himalayan Anthropology, the Indo-Tibetan interface*, ed. J. F. Fisher, La Haye, Paris, 1978, 187-204

Kirkpatrick, William, *An Account of the Kingdom of Nepaul, being the Substance of Observations Made During a Mission to that Country in the Year 1793*, London, 1811, reprinted New Delhi, 1986

Kramrisch, Stella, *The Art of Nepal (Catalogue of the first important exhibition of Nepalese art in New York)*, New York, 1964

Krishnamurti, Calambur Shivarama, *The Art of India*, New York, 1977

Landon, Perceval, *Nepal*, 2 vols., London, 1928

Lévi, Sylvain, *Le Népal, étude historique d'un royaume Hindou*, 3 vols., Annales du Musée Guimet, Bibliothèque d'études XVII-XIX, Paris, 1905-8

Mackay, E. J. H., *Further Excavations at Mohenjo-Daro, 1927-31*, Archaeological Survey of India, New Delhi, 1938

Nand, Mishra Tara, *The Location of Kapilvastu and Archaeological Excavations 1967-72*, The Lumbini Development Committee, HMG Nepal, Kathmandu, 1977

Nepali, G. S., *The Newars, an Ethno-Sociological Study of a Himalayan Community*, Bombay, 1965

Oldfield, Henry Ambrose, *Sketches from Nepal*, 2 vols., London 1880, reprinted New Delhi, 1974, 1981

Pal, Pratapaditya, *Vaiṣṇava Iconology in Nepal: a Study in Art and Religion*, Calcutta, 1970
Regmi, Dilli Raman, *Mediaeval Nepal*, 4 parts, Calcutta and Patna, 1965-6
Regmi, Dilli Raman, *Ancient Nepal*, 3rd ed., Calcutta, 1969
Sakya, Hem Naj, *Nepal sanakritiya mulukha*, Lalitpur, 1089/1969
Satyal, Yajna Raj, *Tourism in Nepal — a profile*, Varanasi, 1988
Schroeder, Ulrich von, *Indo-Tibetan Bronzes*, Hong Kong, 1981
Toffin, Gérard, *Société et religion chez les néwar du Népal*, Paris, 1984
Vats, Madho Sarup, *Excavations at Harappa*, Archaeological Survey of India, Delhi, 1940
Waldschmidt, Ernst and Rose Leonore, *Nepal, Art Treasures from the Himalayas*, tr. David Wilson, Calcutta, 1969
Winkler, Jurgen and Raj, Aryal Mukhand, *Nepal*, (First published Stuttgart, 1976) English ed. tr. F. A. Friedel and J. L. Lotnel Coeper, Tokyo, 1977
Wright, Daniel, *History of Nepal, translated from the Parbatiyā by Munshī Shew Shunker Singh and Pandit Shrī Gunānand*, Cambridge, 1877
Yaqūt Hamawī, *Geographisches Woerterbuch (Mu'jam al-buldān)*, ed. Ferdinand Wustenfeld, Leipzig, 1869

## ARCHITECTURE AND PLANNING

Acharya, Parasanna Kumar, *Architecture of Mānasāra*, IV, New Delhi, 1980, 63-98
Agrawala, V. S., *Sarnath*, Archaeological Survey of India, New Delhi, 1956, 4th ed. 1984
Ananthalwar, M. A. and Rea, Alexander (eds.), Thiagaraja Iyer, A. V. (compiler), *Indian Architecture*, I, 1980
Auer, Gerhard and Gutschow, Niels, Domestic architecture of Nepal, *Art and Archaeology Research Papers* (*AARP*), XII, December 1977, 64-9
Bangdel, Lain Simha, *Early Sculpture of Nepal*, New Delhi, 1982
Bernier, Ronald M., *The Temples of Nepal, an introductory survey*, Kathmandu, 1970, 2nd rev. ed. New Delhi, 1978
Bernier, Ronald M., *The Nepalese Pagoda, origins and style*, New Delhi, 1979
Bhaktapur Development Project, *Bhaktapur Town Development Plan*, 3rd revision, Heidelberg, 1979
Boner, Alice and Sarmā, Sadāsiva Rath, (trs.) *Silpa Prakāsa, Medieval Orissan Sanskrit Text on Temple Architecture by Rāmacandra Kaulācāra*, Leiden, 1966
Brown, Percy, *Picturesque Nepal*, London, 1912.
Fergusson, James and Burgess, James, *The Cave Temples of India*, 1880, (repr. Delhi, 1969)
Ghosh, A., *Nalanda*, Archaeological Survey of India, New Delhi, 1939, 6th ed., 1986
Gutschow, Niels and Kölver, Bernhard, *Ordered space concepts and functions in a town of Nepal*, (Nepal Research Centre publication no. 1) Wiesbaden, 1975
Gutschow, Niels, The Pujahari Math: a survey of Newar building techniques and restoration methods in the valley of Kathmandu, *East and West*, XXVI, 1976, 191-204, figs. 7-30
Gutschow, Niels, *Urban space and ritual: proceedings of an international symposium on urban History of South and East Asia, 2-4 June 1977*, ed. N. Gutschow and T. Sieverts, 2nd ed. *AARP*, 1978.
Gutschow, Niels, Functions of Squares in Bhaktapur, *AARP*, XVII, March 1980, 57-64.
Gutschow, Niels and Shakya, Hemraj, The monasteries (*bāha* and *bahī*) of Patan, *Journal of the Nepal Research Centre*, IV, 1980, 161-174
Gutschow, Niels, Kölver, Bernhard and Shresthacarya, Iswaranand, *Newar Towns and Buildings, an Ilustrated Dictionary, Newārī-English*, Sankt Augustin, 1987
Gutschow, Niels and Hagmuller, Gotz, The reconstruction of the eight-cornered pavilion (Cyasilin Mandap) on Darbar Square in Bhaktapur, Nepal, *Ancient Nepal, Journal of the Department of Archaeology*, no. 123-125, April-September 1991, Kathmandu, 1-9
Hamid, M., *Excavations at Sanchi*, Archaeological Survey of India Annual Report, 1936-37, Delhi, 1949, 84-87
HMG Nepal, *The Physical Development Plan for the Kathmandu Valley*, Kathmandu, 1969
Hosken, Fran P., *The Kathmandu Valley Towns, A record of life and change in Nepal*, New York, Tokyo, 1974
Khanna, Madhu, *Yantra, the Tantric Symbol of Cosmic Unity*, London, 1979

Korn, Wolfgang, *The Traditional Architecture of the Kathmandu Valley*, Kathmandu, 1979
Künzle, Alex and Scheibler, Giovanni, *Bhaktapur: mittelalterliche Stadt in Nepal*, Zurich, 1977
Levy, Robert I., *Mesocosm: Hinduism and the Organisation of a Traditional Newar City in Nepal*, (University of California Press) Berkeley - Los Angeles - Oxford, 1990
Locke, John K., S. J., *Buddhist Monasteries of Nepal: a Survey of the Bāhās and Bahīs of the Kathmandu Valley*, Kathmandu, 1985
Macdonald, Alexander W. and Stahl, Anne Vergati, *Newar Art: Nepalese Art during the Malla Period*, New Delhi, 1979
Marshall, John, *Archaeological Survey of India Annual Reports*, 1912-13, Calcutta, 1915, pt. i, 17-24, pls. 6-9; 1913-14, Calcutta, 1915, pt. i, 20-23, pls. 19-21: pt. ii, 1-39, pls. 1-24
Marshall, John and Foucher, Alfred, *The Monuments of Sāñchī*, Delhi, (not dated) c. 1944
Müller, Ute, *Land Aquisition for Public Purposes in Nepal*, Town Implementation Office (KVTDC), Bhaktapur, September 1981
Pruscha, Carl, *A Protective Inventory*, Anton Schroll & Co. for HMG Nepal, 2 vols., Vienna, 1975
Sanday, John, The Hanuman Dhoka Royal Palace Kathmandu, Building Conservation and Local Traditional Crafts, *AARP*, London, 1974
Sanday, John, *Les monuments de la valée de Katmandou*, (UNESCO) Paris, 1980
Sanday, John, *Kathmandu Valley: Nepalese Historic Monuments in need of Preservation*, (UNESCO) Paris, 1982
Slusser, Mary Shepherd and Vajracarya, Gautamavajara, Two mediaeval Nepalese buildings, an architectural and cultural study, *Artibus Asiae*, XXXVI, iii, 1970, 169-218
Snellgrove, D. L., Shrines and temples of Nepal, *Arts asiatiques*, VIII, 1961, i, 3-10; ii, 93-120
Tiwari, Sudarshan Raj, The non-conformist temples, *The Rising Nepal*, 30th November 1973
Tiwari, Sudarshan Raj, The tiered temples, a cosmological overview, *Tribhuvan University Journal*, XI, no i, 1980, 16-24
Toffin, Gérard, *Pyangaon, une communauté néwar de la vallée de Kathmandu*, Paris, 1977
United Nations Development Programme, *Master Plan for the Cultural Heritage of the Kathmandu Valley*, Serial no. FMR/CC/CH/77/216 (UNDP) NEP/74/003, UNESCO, Paris, 1977
Wiesner, Ulrich, *Nepalese Temple Architecture: its characteristics and its relations to Indian development*, (Brill) Leiden-Cologne, 1978

## KIRTIPUR

1962 Shrestha, Shyam Man, "Kirtipur, Population Settlement and Communication", MA Geography Dissertation, Tribhuvan University, November
1972 Joshi, Hari Ram, "*Kirtipur Umā Mahesvara mandirstit Sarasvatī ek adhyayana*", *Prachin Nepal*, no. 21, (Kartik VE 2029)
1976 Joshi, Hari Ram, "*Kirtipurko stapana*", *Madhuparka*, VIII, no. x
1979 Bista, Hari Bahadur, "A study of handloom industry of Kirtipur village", MSc Thesis, Commerce and Business Administration, Tribhuvan University
1979 Bristol University Kirtipur Team, A keen eyed idyll in Nepal, *Bristol University Newsletter*, 8th March, p. 9
1979 Ranjit, Mana Mohan, "A study of agricultural production function of Kirtipur village", Tribhuvan University MSc. Statistics Dissertation
1980 (VE 2037) Bajracharia, Dhana Bajra, *Shahkalin Abhilekh*, Kirtipur
1980 Davies, E. P., Davis, R. W., Finn, W. R., Miers, C. J. P., Park, M. and Robertson, G. V. L., *Kirtipur, a Newar Community in Nepal, Development in Debate*, Kirtipur Programme 1979-80, Bristol
1980 Nepal Red Cross, *Community Basic Service*, Kirtipur Survey
1980 (VE 2037) Vaidya, Shanta Ram, "An analysis of farm efficiency between large and small farms in Kirtipur panchayat of Nepal in 1980", MSc Statistics Dissertation, Tribhuvan University
1981 Shrestha, Sanu Kaji, "A general study of handloom industry in Kirtipur", MA Economics Thesis, Tribhuvan University
1982 Development Research and Communication Group, *Report on Evaluation Study of the Kirtipur Demonstration Project in Low-cost Sanitation, prepared for the Department of Water Supply and Sewerage*, Ministry of Water Resources, HMG Nepal, Kathmandu
1982 *Expatriate Assisted Community Development as a Possibility in Kirtipur*, Kirtipur Programme,

December 1982, Kathmandu

1982 Linguistic Society, *Household Survey of the Use of Nepali in Kirtipur*, Tribhuvan University

1984 Devkota, Padam Lal, Illness interpretation and modes of treatment in Kirtipur, *Contributions to Nepalese Studies, Journal of the Tribhuvan University*, Kirtipur, XI, ii, pp. 11-20

1984 Shrestha, Sukra Sagar, "Art and architecture of Kirtipur" MA Dissertation in Nepalese History, Culture and Archaeology, Tribhuvan University

1984 Shrestha, Sukra Sagar, Three mediaeval inscriptions from Kathmandu, *Nepalese Culture*, IV, no. iv, p. 57

1985 Galdieri, Eugenio, Nepal, Campaign held between November 1985 and January 1986, Report of Centro di Studi Storici e per la Conservazione dei Monumenti, *East and West*, XXXV, vi, pp. 493-503

1985 Herdick, Reinhard, Urban residential quarters of the Newar in Nepal — a symbolic and spatial social unit, in A. L. Dallapiccola, ed., *Vijayanagara — city and Empire: New currents of Research*, I, Beiträge zur Südasienforschung, Südasien-Institut, Universität Heidelberg, Band 100, Stuttgart, pp. 380-398

1985 The Technology Advisory Group, Nepal, *Master Plan Report on Low Cost Waterseal Latrine Project in Eight Urban and Semi-Urban Communities in Nepal*, UNDP Interregional Project INT/81/047, June

1988 Herdick, Reinhard, *Kirtipur Stadtgestalt, Prinzipien der Raumordnung und gesellschaftliche Funktionen einer Newar-Stadt*, (Weltforum Verlag) Munich-Cologne-London

1992 Herdick, Reinhard, Kosmisch, sozial, leiblich: Gestalt-Ordnungen in Nepal und Marokko, *Daidolos, Architektur, Kunst, Kultur*, Körper und Bauwerk/Body and Building, XLV, pp. 26-9

1992 Shokoohy, Mehrdad and Natalie H., History and architecture of Kirtipur, Nepal, *South Asia Library Group Newsletter*, London, no. 39, January, pp. 25-9

# INDEX


Abhayankara Gupta 204.
*āchārya*, (*achar*) caste of religious instructors 22, 26.
Acharyā, Bābu Rām 19.
Acharya, Parasanna Kumar 48.
Achhyobhya at Chilañcho 105, 107, 206, also see Akshobhya
Adi Buddha Stupa see Gutapau Chaitya.
Afghanistan 131-2, 146.
Āgam (sacred Hindu text) 9.
Agni (god of fire) 79.
Agrawala, V. S. 146.
Ājaju Byaghreśvara, a name of Bāgh Bhairav deity 79.
Ajanta 132.
Ājudyaḥ, a name of Bāgh Bhairav deity 79.
Akshobhya 138, also see Achhyobhya.
*ālama* caste 22.
Amalshi (area of Naya Bāzār) 121, 153, 155-9, 167, 170, also see Naya Bāzār.
Amaramalla (Rāja of Kathmandu) 15.
*āmātya*, (or *śarma* or *mahāju*) caste of ministers 22, 27.
Amatya, Safalya 191, 206.
Amitābha images, Chilañcho 105, 107, 240.
Amoghasiddhi image, Chilañcho 105, 107, 240.
Ananthalwar, M. A. 48, 74.
Ārya Tārā (a form of Tārā) 197, 199, 208, 240.
Aryal, Mukhand Raj 206.
Association for Comparative Alpine Research 7.
Aśoka 13-14, 43, 108, 167.
Aśoka Chaitya 113.
Ashṭabhairava (eight divine fathers, consorts of Ashṭamātṛikā) 64-5, 78, 97, 191, 205.
Ashṭamaṅgala (eight auspicious symbols) 96.
Ashṭamātṛikā (eight divine mothers) 34, 64-65, 77, 87, 96, 101, 189, 191 also see Mātṛikā.
Ashṭa Nāgā Rāj (eight divine serpent-kings) 65 also see Nāgā Rāj.
Ashṭāng Bhairav (one of the Ashṭabhairavas) 204.
Asia 131.
Auden, J. B. 20.
Auer, Gerhard 74
Aurangabad 132.
Avalokiteśvara (the first Bodhisattva) 116.

Bābu, Rāṭhaura Bisva Nāth 91.
Badami 198.
Badaregāoṅ village 35.
*badī* or *badīkar* or *dhom*, castes of musicians 22, 27.
Bāgh Bhairav (guardian deity of Kirtipur) 75, 79-80, 189, 197, 205.
Bāgh Bhairav Jātrā (festival) 30, 32.
Bāgh Bhairav Temple (Kirtipur) 3, 10, 16-8, 43, 57, 75-86, 88, 98, 101, 121, 123, 128-30, 142, 151, 167, 169, 189, 190-7, 202-4, 207-8, 212, 220-1, 223-7, 231-3.
Bāgh Bhairav Pañchāyat, 157, 182.
Bāgh Bhairav (*ṭol* in Kirtipur) 153.
*bagho shashu*, *śūdra* sub-caste 26.
Bagkumārī Temple (Patan) 130.
Bagmati River 30, 182.
Bahādur Shāh (Rānā) 82.
Bahirīgāoṅ (*ṭol* in Kirtipur) 46, 48, 50-1, 152-4, 158, 167, 178.
Bairochana (Vairochana) 105, 107, 116, 202, 240.
Bajrabārāhi (deity) 206, 240.
*bajrāchārya* (or *gubhājū*), Buddhist priestly caste 26-7, 30, 80, 108, 115, 135, 142, 189, 202.
Bajrāchāria, Badri Ratna 108.
Bajracharia, Bahādur 100.
Bajracharia, Buddha Ratna 63.
Bajracharia, Dhana Bajra 19, 122, 176.
Bajracharia, Pushpa 240-1.
Bajra Vīr (Janma Rāj) image at Chilañcho 201.
Baku Nanī (Kirtipur) 115.
Bālāju (Kathmandu) 80.
Balkhu Gorge 30, 159.
Balkhu River 30, 157, 163-4, 177.
Ball, Warwick 146.
Bāmana 79.
*bandya*, Buddhist caste 26.
Banepā village 29.
Bangdel, Lain Simha 83, 122, 192-3, 197, 206.
*bangra* caste 26.
Bansbari 171.
Bārāhī (a *mātṛikā*) 76, 84, 86, 96, 194-5, 197, 204.
*baṛāju* (goldsmiths), *śākya* sub-caste 26.
Barriteau, Richard 7.
Basantpur 35.
Bāsuki Nāg (a serpent-king) 76, 197.
*bāthahom* caste 22.
Benares (Varanasi) 167, 202.
Bengal 45.
Bernier, Ronald M. 8, 91, 122, 130.
Betāla 65.
Bhadgaon or Bhatgaon (names of Bhaktapur) 1.
Bhagavatī image at Chilañcho 206.
Bhagavatī Temple (Nālā village) 126, 128, 130.
Bhagvānī Śaṅkar (deity) 84.
Bhairav (Bhairava) (form of Śiva) 75, 79, 113, 123, 130, 203-5.
Bhairavsthan Temple (Bhaktapur) 130.
Bhaise 169.
Bhājangal (in Kirtipur vicinity) 162, 170-1.
Bhājan Pāṭi at Bāgh Bhairav Complex 76.
Bhājunanda, Śrī of Chhve Bāhā 64.
Bhaktapur (Bhadgaon or Bhatgaon) 1, 8, 15-17, 29, 57, 98, 126, 130, 147, 171, 191, 202-3.
Bhaktapur Art Gallery 94.

*bhansāli*, caste of custom collectors 121.
Bhansāli, Satya Lal 121.
Bharat Kala Bhavan (Varanasi) 202.
*bhārika*, caste of porters 22.
Bhariyan Pukhū (Kirtipur) 220, 222
*bhāṭ*, dyers, *jyāpu* sub-cast 26.
Bhattacharya, Binayatosh 206.
Bhattārika (Ārya Tārā) 199.
Bhavānī Śaṅkar (Umā Maheśvara) 84, 86, 96, 126.
Bhavānī Śaṅkar Temple at Bāgh Bhairav Complex 76, 83-85, 90, 197, 227, 231-2.
*bhāyalāchanchu* caste 22.
Bhī Pukhū 177, 179.
Bhīmasena 16 also see Bhīmsen
Bhīmsen Bhaṭṭāraka, a name of Bāgh Bhairav deity 79.
Bhīmeśvara, a name of Bāgh Bhairav deity 79.
Bhīmsen (deity) 94, 130.
Bhīm Shumsher Rānā 123.
Bhīshān Bhairav (one of the Ashṭabhairavas) 204.
Bhojdeva 63.
Bhubaneśvar 130.
Bhubaneśvari Temple (Deupatan) 130.
Bhu Devī (deity) 202.
Bhumangat (a name of Gopāla) 13.
Bhūmisparśa Buddha images, Jagat Pāl Bāhā 240-1.
*bhūpa* (*chhatrī*) caste 22.
Bibakhādeva (deity) 108.
Bidyādhana, Byāpāri 82.
Bighnaraj 63.
Bijaya Lakshmī 199.
*bimārī* caste 22.
*bipra* (*brāhman*) caste 22.
Bishalnagar 196-7.
Bisheśvara Temple (Patan) 94.
Bista, Dor Bahadur 181-2.
Biśvakarmā see Viśvakarmā.
Bisva Nāth Bābu, Rāṭhaura 91.
Boner, Alice 122.
Brahmā (the creator in the Hindu triad) 64, 79, 96, 206.
Brahmācharya Bhikshu Śri Deva Ratna 146.
*brahmāchārya* 191.
*brāhman* (the Hindu priestly caste) 13, 22, 24, 26.
Brahmāyaṇī (Brahmi) (a *mātṛikā, consort of Brahmā*) 76, 79, 84, 86, 96, 191, 194-5, 204.
Brahmāyaṇī Temple at Panauti 191.
Bristol University Team 6-7, 122, 172, 176.
British Government's Overseas Development Administration 6.
Brown, Percy 8.
Buchanan (later Hamilton), Francis 26-8, 48.
Buddha 23, 32, 48, 65, 107-8, 110, 112-14, 132-3, 138, 146, 167, 202-3, 240-1.
Buddha Dharma Saṅgha Temple see Loṅ Degaḥ.
Buddha Jayantī (festival) 30, 32.
Buddhamārga (Buddhists) 24, 26.
Buddhanīlkaṇṭha Road 171.
Burgess, James 146.
Burma 21.
Byanghini (deity) 204.
Byaghreśvara, a name of Bāgh Bhairav deity 79.
*byanjanakāra*, caste of cooks 22.
Byāpāri Bidyādhana 82.

Capuchin friars 167.
Chakra Sambhara images, Chilaṅcho 110, 189, 240.
Chakra Vartendra Malla 33.
*chamakhallak* or *kuchikāra*, caste of sweepers 27.
Chāmuṇḍā (a Mātṛikā, a form of Durgā) 76, 79, 204, 241.
Chanda Bhairav (one of the Ashtabhairavas) 204.
Chandagiri, Mount 35.
Chandra (moon, deity) 96, 191.
Chandramāha Roshanī 64, 241.
Chandra Sumsher 80, 189.
Changu 194.
Changu Nārāyaṇa 202.
Chapagāoṅ Road 171.
Chapagāoṅ village 29.
Chaphal (*ṭol* in Kirtipur) 153.
*charmakāra*, caste of leather workers 24.
Chattopadhyay, K. P. 27.
*chhatrī* (or *chhattrī*) military caste 22.
Chhve Bāhā (Harshakīrti Mahāvihār) (Kirtipur) 64, 72, 75, 117, 120, 131, 135-6, 138-40, 142, 144, 146, 202, 208.
*chichhaka* caste 22.
Chilaṅcho Stupa and complex (Kirtipur) 13-14, 22-23, 26, 35, 42-3, 70, 72, 73, 80, 97-8, 101, 103-11, 113, 115, 117, 132-5, 142, 144, 146, 189, 191, 197, 199, 201, 208, 213-19, 227, 230, 234, 236-8.
Chilaṅcho Mahāvihār see Jagat Pāl Mahāvihār.
Chilaṅcho (*ṭol* in Kirtipur) 153.
Chillaṅdeo see Chilaṅcho.
China 15, 21, 131.
Chinamasta (Changu) 194.
*chipi*, dyers, *jyāpu* sub-cast 26.
Chisapani 167, 169.
Chīthuṅ Bahī (Chīthu Bahī) (Kirtipur) 43, 75, 113, 131, 145-6.
Chīthuṅ Bihār Paṅchāyat (Kirtipur) 152, 155, 158, 163.
Chīthuṅ (*ṭol* in Kirtipur) 146, 153.
Chitlang 167.
*chitrākāra*, painters, *jyāpu* sub-cast 22, 26.
Chobhār village 29, 35, 48, 169.
Croydon 98.

Dabujho (*ṭol* in Kirtipur) 96, 98, 121, 123, 208.
*daivagya*, caste of astrologers 22.
Dakshiṇkālī Road 171.
Dakshiṇkālī, shrine 100.
Dānapati Śākyavamsa Hākuju 117 also see Hākuju.
*danghu* (land surveyors), *jyāpu* sub-cast 26.
*dāphā phalechā* 76.
Darbār Square (Bhaktapur) 8, 191, 202.
Darbār Square (Kathmandu) 8, 100.
Darbār Square (Patan) 8, 202.
*dārukāra*, caste of wood carvers 22.
Dasaī (festival) 34.
Dathu Balkhu (middle Balkhu) 30.
Dathu Lan (street in Kirtipur) 167.
Dathu Tajhya Ṭol (Patan) 91.
Davies, E. P. 8, 27, 122, 146, 176.
De Paḥkhāḥ (defensive town wall, Kirtipur) 155.
Department of Archaeology (HMG Nepal) 103, 130.
Department of Cottage Industries (HMG Nepal) 155.
Department of Forestry (HMG Nepal) 155.
Department of Housing and Physical Planning (HMG Nepal) 7, 147, 149.
Department of Water Supply and Sewerage (HMG Nepal)

6, 181-3.
De Pukhū Square (Kirtipur) 30-1, 33, 43-44, 46, 57, 60, 98, 153-4, 177.
Deu Ḍhokā (north-east gate of Kirtipur) 36, 38-40, 122.
Deu Ḍhokā (*ṭol* in Kirtipur) 153, 180, 182.
Deupatan 130, 202.
*devachinta*, caste of priests 22.
Devapāli 13.
Devī (female deity) 96, 130, 202, 206.
Dhalpāḥ (in Sāgāl Ṭol, Kirtipur) 158.
*dhānyamārī*, caste of rice liquor makers 22.
*dharma stambha* at Bāgh Bhairav 76.
*dharma stambha* at Chilaṅcho 105, 107.
Dhartī Mātā shrine or image at Bāgh Bhairav 75-76, 83, 90, 189, 202-3.
*dhobī*, caste of launderers 24, 27.
*dhom* see *badī*.
Dhupa (Tīn Thana) 157.
Dhyānī Buddha images 108, 110, 113-14, 116-17, 202.
Dīpankāra images, Jagat Pal Bāhā 189, 241.
Divālī festival 29.
Doherty, V. S. 27.
Dopacha (*ṭol* in Kirtipur) 153.
Dristi Rāj, Kvātha Nāyaka 100.
Dukuchhap 100.
Durgā image at Umā Maheśvara 96, 198, 200, also see Mahishāsura Mardini.
Dvāre Jātrā (festival) 34.
*dvija* (*brāhman*) caste 22.
Dyaḥ Chhen see Indrāyaṇī shrine, Bāgh Bhairav.
*dyola* see *poṛe*.

Ellora caves 132, 198.
England 98.

Fergusson, James 146.
Fisher, J. F. 27.
Foucher, Alfred 146.
Friedel, F. A. 206.
Führer-Haimendorf, C. von 27.

Gachhen (*ṭol* in Kirtipur) 40, 153.
Gahirigāoṅ village 35.
Gāi Jātrā (festival) 30-3.
Galdieri, Eugenio 122.
*gamsabarhi* (woodworkers), *śākya* sub-caste 26.
Gaṇeś (elephant headed god, son of Pārvatī) 34, 63, 98, 103, 117, 121, 123, 191, 200, 240-1.
Gaṇeś images at Bāgh Bhairav 76, 79-80, 83-4, 86, 90, 192-4, 205.
Gaṇeś image from Umā Maheśvara 41, 96.
Gaṇeś Jātrā (festival) 33-4.
Gaṇeś *phalechā* at Lāyaku 41, 96.
Gaṇeś shrine at Chilaṅcho 22, 72.
Gaṇeś shrine at Tuṅjho 97-8.
Gaṇeś Temple at Bāgh Bhairav complex 76, 80, 83-7, 191-5, 197-8, 225-6.
Gaṇeś Temple at Dabujho (Kirtipur) 96, 98, 123, 125.
*gaṇika*, caste of mathematicians 22.
*garhtho* (*gāthu*), caste of gardners 27.
Garuḍa (mythical bird vehicle of Vishṇu) 56, 201-2, 205.
Garuḍ Nārāyaṇa 84, 202, 223, 225.
*gāthu* caste 27.
Gāthu Pyākhāṅ (festival) 33.
Gauri image at Chilaṅcho 206.
*gāyine* (*gāyana*), caste of musicians 22, 24, 43, 55.
Gāyine Ṭol or Settlement (Kirtipur) 153.
Germany 8, 181.
Ghaṇṭaghar clock tower (Kathmandu) 98.
Ghaṇṭākarṇa festival 13, 34.
Gharelau Udhyog (Department of Cottage Industries, HMG Nepal) 155.
Ghosh, A 146.
Ghosh, A. M. N. 20.
Gillet and Johnston Founders 98.
Giuseppe (Father) 20.
Giva see Gvā.
Godāvarī Road 171.
*gopāla* (*gopaka*), caste of cowherds, 13, 22.
Gopāla (legendary founder of Kirtipur) 13.
Gopāla dynasty 13.
Gopāla (Vaṃsa) see Vaṃsa Gopāla.
Gopālarāja Vaṃśāvālī 16.
Gopura (Kirtipur) 13.
Gorakh Nath 103.
Gorkha town 8.
Greenwich, University of 7.
Greenwold, S. M. 27.
*grahachintaka*, caste of astrologers 22.
*gubhājū* (Buddhist pristly caste, also see *bajrāchārya*) 26, 72.
Gul Darra (Afghanistan) 132.
Guna (old fort of Kirtipur) 16.
Gunajyoti Śākya 120.
Gunānand (Pandit Shrī) 19.
Guṅ De Kvātha (old name for Kirtipur) 16, 128.
Guṅdesthanadhipāṭi 16.
Gupta dynasty 15.
Gurkha dynasty or period 16-18, 20, 24, 35-6, 78, 82, 131.
Gurkha Nath School (Kirtipur) 159.
Gutapau (*ṭol* in Kirtipur) 112, 113, 123, 153.
Gutapau Chaitya (Adi Buddha Stupa) 112-13.
Gūṭhī Saṃsthān (HMG Nepal) 82, 113, 136, 142, 205, 240.
Gutschow, Niels 28, 74.
*gvā*, caste 13.
Gvā Pukhū (Kirtipur) 13.

Hadda (Afghanistan) 132.
Hadigāoṅ Bhīmsensthan (Kathmandu) 130.
Hākuju 117, 120.
Hamid, M 146
Hamilton Buchanan, Francis 26-8, 48.
Hanumān (monkey god, devotee of Rama) 77, 82, 90, 105.
Hanumān stambha at Bāgh Bhairav 76.
*harahuru* or *saṅghar*, caste of sweepers 27.
Harappa 167.
Harisiddhi Bhavānī Temple (Harisiddhi village) 126, 128.
Harshakīrti Mahāvihār (Kirtipur) 117, 142, also see Chhve Bāhā.
Hastikā, wet-nurse of Bahādur Shāh 82, 87.
Hasrat, Bikrama Jit 19-20.
Herdick, Reinhard 8, 27, 39-40, 48, 74, 130, 146.
Heruka images, Jagat Pāl Bāhā 240.
Hetunda 169.
Himalayas 2, 18 146, 167.
Hindu Kush 146.
Hitigaḥ (*ṭol* in Kirtipur) 153.
Hofer, A. 28.

Horticultural Research Station (Kirtipur) 155-6, 158, 160, 164.
Hosken, Fran P. 8.
Hva Kuncha (*ṭol* inKirtipur) 53, 55, 57, 59-60, 66, 68, 153.

Ikhā Bāhā (Kirtipur) 72, 131, 133-6, 138-9, 146, 163.
India 21, 40, 45, 61, 75, 113, 121, 131-2, 167, 169, 171, 192, 201, 206.
Indian Subcontinent 36, 132.
Indra (deity, king of heaven) 96.
Indra Than, Mount 35.
Indrāyaṇī (a Mātṛikā, consort of Indra) 30, 32, 75, 96, 101, 204.
Indrāyaṇī images at Bāgh Bhairav 76, 79.
Indrāyaṇī Jātrā (festival) 30, 32, 169.
Indrāyaṇī shrine (Dyaḥ Chhen) at Bāgh Bhairav 76.
Indrāyaṇī Temple (Kirtipur) 38, 101, 212, 233, 239.
Indreśvara Mahādeva Temple (Panauti) 204.
Ishtachoni Mahākāra see Manjuśrī shrine.
Iṭāchhen (*ṭol* in Kirtipur) 57, 153.
Iyer, Thiagaraja A. V. 48, 74.

Jagannāth Temple (Tvā Dvāra) at Kathmandu 100.
Jagat Bahādur Pradhān 98.
Jagat Pāl Mahāvihār (Chilaṅcho Vihār) (Kirtipur) 19, 32, 75, 103, 105, 108, 110, 131-5, 138, 142, 146, 189, 191, 203, 205-6, 240-1.
Jagat Pāl Varmā (a member of one of the seven ruling families of Patan) 80, 108.
Jaifal (Jaiphal), son of Hastikā 82, 87.
Janma Rāj (Bajra Vīr) image at Chilaṅcho 201.
Jarumanuchhya images at Chilaṅcho 201, 218-19.
*jauśī* see *joshī*.
Javalakhel 171.
Jayabhageśvari Temple (Deupatan) 130.
Jaya Prakāśa (Malla Rāja) 16-17.
Jayasthiti (Mala Rāja) 22, 24.
Jhakya (in Kirtipur vicinity) 171-2, 174, 176.
Jhavā Dya (standing Śiva) at Bāgh Bhairav 86, 128, 191.
*jiāpu* see *jyāpu*.
Jista, D. B. 27.
Jivadharma Vihāra 144, also see Yāka Bāhā.
Jochhe (*ṭol* in Kirtipur) 42, 58, 153.
*jogī* see *kusle*.
Johnston see Gillet and Johnston Founders.
*joshī*, caste of astronomers 22, 26-7, 203.
Joshi, Birananda 122.
Joshi, Hari Ram 91, 122.
Joshī, Jitānanda 202-3.
Joshīnanī (Kirtipur) 57, 65.
Juddha Shumsher 98.
Jujukāji 203.
*jyāpu*, caste of farmers 24, 26, 27, 29-30, 43, 70, 72, 142, also see *maharjan*.
*jyotisha* see *joshī*.

Kailāśa (legendary mountain in Tibet, abode of Śiva) 193, 198.
Kāji Gūṭhī houses (Kirtipur) 63.
Kalaratri 204.
Kālī era 13.
Kalimati 171, 176.
Kālū Pandey (Gurkha commander) 16, 82.
Kanheri 132.
*kāṅjīkāra*, caste of brewers 22.
*kānsyakāra*, caste of brass workers 22.
Kantipur (old name of Kathmandu) 1.
*kapalī* see *kusle*.
Kapilvastu 167.
Kapu (old name of Kathmandu) 1.
Kāprankā (deity) 79.
Kārak Vīr (Karma Rāj) image at Chilaṅcho 201.
Karālā Bhairav (one of the Ashṭabhairavas) 204.
Karle 132, 192.
Karnataka (India) 198.
Karṇātaka Mahāvihāra 135, also see Kve Bāhā.
*karṇikā*, caste of weavers 22.
*kasāī* (or *nāy*), caste of butchers, 27, 36, 43.
Kathmandu 1-3, 7-9, 15-16, 24, 27, 29, 54, 98, 100, 127, 130, 147, 151-2, 154, 157, 160-1, 165, 167, 169, 171-2, 174, 176-7, 191, 194, 200, 240.
Kathmandu Valley 1-3, 5, 7-10, 13, 21, 24, 26, 32, 35-6, 40, 45, 48, 56-7, 75, 83-4, 90, 105, 108, 113, 121, 126, 130-1, 133, 139, 142, 147, 149, 151, 157, 161, 163-4, 167, 169-72, 177, 179, 189, 193, 200.
Kathmandu Valley Town Development Board 147, 149.
*kaua* (or *nekarmi*), caste of blacksmiths 27.
Kaumārī (a Mātṛikā) 76, 79, 84, 86, 96, 194-5, 204.
*kāyasth*, caste of scribes 22.
Khanna, Madhu 130.
Khasi Bāzār (Kirtipur) 45-6, 153-5, 157-9, 164, 167.
Khauma Ṭol (Bhaktapur) 126.
Khoyanala (in Kirtipur vicinity) 161, 163.
*khusal* (or *tandukāra*), caste of weavers 22, 27
Kipu (old name of Kirtipur) 1.
*kirāta*, caste of singers 22.
Kirāta dynasty 21.
Kirkpatrick, William 18, 20, 35, 48, 176.
Kisi (at Umā Maheśvara Temple) 213.
Kitapāla (Raja) 16.
Kochhen (*ṭol* in Kirtipur) 153.
Kodari Pass (Kuti Pass) 167.
Kölver, Bernhard 28, 74.
Korn, Wolfgang 48, 125, 130, 146.
Kramrisch, Stella 206.
Kṛishṇa (deity) 33, 84.
Kṛishṇa Janmāshṭamī (festival) 30, 33.
Krishnamurti, Calambur Shivarama 199, 206.
Krodha Bhairav (one of the Ashṭabhairavas) 204.
Krodharāj images at Chilaṅcho 105, 107, 199, 201, 215.
*kshaṭrikāra*, caste of carvers and potters 24.
*kshatriya* caste (also see *chhatrī*), 22, 24, 26.
*kshetrakāra*, caste of land measurers 22.
Kubara (deity, king of wealth) 94, 123.
*kuchikāra* see *chamakhallak*.
Kulajoti, Śri of Saka Bāhā 64.
Kuleśvar 176.
*kulū*, caste of musicians 27.
Kumāra (deity) 50, 79, 205.
Kumārīghar (Kathmandu) 191.
*kumbhakāra* (*kumhār*), potters, *jyāpu* sub-cast 22, 26.
*kundakāra*, caste of bone and ivory carvers 24.
Künzle, Alex 8.
Kusi Bāhā (Kirtipur) 131, 141-3.
Kusicha (ṭol in Kirtipur) 142.
*kusle* (or *jogī* or *kāpalī*) caste of tailors and temple keepers 27, 30, 55, 76, 122.
Kuti Pass (Kodari Pass) 167.

Kuṭujhol (*ṭol* in Kirtipur) 66, 153, 181.
Kvā Bāhā (Patan) 146.
Kvācho (*ṭol* in Kirtipur) 36, 153, 197-9.
Kvācho Degaḥ (a name for Umā Maheśvara temple) 90.
Kvātha Nāyaka Dristi Rāj 100.
Kvātha Nāyaka Lakshminārāyaṇ Bharo 100.
Kvātha Nāyaka Lakshmi Singh Bharo 101.
Kve Bāhā (Kirtipur) 72, 75, 131, 134-8.
Kyapu (old name of Kirtipur) 1, 135.
Kyapu Bāhā (a name of Jagat Pāl Vihār) 135.

Labhā Pukhū (Kirtipur) 6, 46, 158, 177.
*lakhipar, śūdra* sub-caste 26.
Lakshmaṇ (deity) 90.
Lakshmī (goddess of fotune, consort of Vishṇu) 65, 87, 97, 199, 202, 206, also see Mahālakshmī.
Lakshmī Nārāyaṇ 199.
Lakshminārāyaṇ Bharo (Kvātha Nāyaka) 100.
Lakshmi Singh Bharo (Kvātha Nāyaka) 101.
Lalitpatan or Lalitpur (names of Patan) 1, 171-2, 174, 176.
*lamu*, caste of royal palanquin bearers 24.
Landon, Perceval 19-20, 27, 108.
Lāyaku (Kirtipur) 26-27, 33, 41-3, 52, 94, 96, 115, 152-3, 167, 189.
Lāyaku Pañchāyat 94, 103, 152, 155, 158, 162-3.
Leissi, Bahram 7.
*lekhaka*, caste of writers 22.
*lepika*, caste of stucco carvers 22.
Lévi, Sylvain 7, 13, 18-20, 27.
Lhasa 21, 167.
Lhonkhā village 30, 169.
Libichhen 199.
Lichhavi (dynasty or period) 21, 128, 194, 199-200.
Lochani image at Chilañcho 108.
Locke, John K., S. J. 131, 146.
*lohakāra*, caste of blacksmiths 24.
Lokeśvar (Lokeśvara) (a name of Buddha, a form of Bodhisattva, lit. Lord of the world) 103, 105, 107, 117, 120.
Lokeśvar platform, Sinaduvā (Kirtipur) 72.
Lokeśvar Temple (Kirtipur) 43, 75, 120, 220, 222.
Loṅ Degaḥ (Buddha Dharma Saṅgha Temple) (Kirtipur) 43 75, 114-17, 120, 143, 239.
Loṅ Degaḥ (*ṭol* in Kirtipur) 153.
London 7.
Lotnel Coeper, J. L. 206.
Lubhu 171.
Lumbini 32, 167.

Mabhī Pukhū (Kirtipur) 155, 164, 177.
Macdonald, Alexander W. 114, 122, 206.
Machhegāoṅ village 30, 169, 171-2, 174.
Mackay, E. J. H. 176.
Mādhaveśvara (a form of Śiva) 84.
Madhyamik Vidyalaya School (Kirtipur) 158-9.
Māghe Jātrā (festival) 34.
Mahābharat, Mount 35.
Mahālakshmī (a Mātṛikā) 76, 79, 97, 204, also see Lakshmī.
Mahādeva (Mahā Deo) (epithet of Śiva) 35, 64-5.
Mahākāla (lit. Lord of time, guardian deity of a monastery) 105, 117, 201.
Mahānkala shrine (Kathmandu) 200.
Mahāpātra (prime minister or governor) 80.
*maharjan*, caste of farmers (see *jyāpu*).
Maharjan, Lan Bahādur 200.
Maharjan, Tuyu Bahādur 122.
Maheśvara (lit. Great Lord, epithet of Śiva) 79.
Maheśvarī (epithet of Durgā) 64, 194-5, 204, also see Śaivi.
Mahishāsura Mardini Durgā 191, 198, 200.
Maitreya Buddha image, Jagat Pāl Bāhā 241.
Majā Degaḥ (Kirtipur) 110.
Majipat (Kathmandu) 194.
*makhi*, śūdra sub-caste 26.
*mālī*, caste of gardners 22.
Malla dynasty or period 15-16, 21, 24, 27, 42, 45-6, 75, 96, 123, 131, 191.
Māmaki image at Chilañcho 108.
Māna Binayak temple or image (Bāgh Bhairav complex) 75-76, 83, 207-9.
*mānandhar*, caste of oil pressers 27, 43, 82.
*māndhura* caste 22.
Mangal Bāzār (Patan) 91.
Manjuśrī, (Bodhisattva) 21.
Manjuśrī shrine (Kirtipur) 103.
*mānsabikrī*, caste of butchers 22.
*mantrī*, caste of state officials 22.
Mārakhyo (ṭol in Kirtipur) 153.
*marīkāra* caste 22.
Marshall, John 146.
*mātangī*, caste of leather workers 24.
Māṭrikā (Divine mothers) 80, 84, 86, 189, 193-4, 197-8, also see Ashṭamātṛikā.
Matsyapurāṇa 127.
Matta Thirtha spring 177.
Mhaipi shrine (Kathmandu) 80, 189.
Ministry of Housing (HMG Nepal) 7.
Ministry of Water Resources and Power (HMG Nepal) 7, 8, 184.
Ministry of Tourism (HMG Nepal) 188
Moddha 65.
Mohenjo Daro 167.
Mṛityusamskara Gūṭhī 30.
Mughal 61.
Mūl Bhagvānsthān, Jagat Pāl Bāhā 241.
Müller, Ute 8.
Mvana (*ṭol* in Kirtipur) 44, 57, 143, 153.

*nādīchhedi*, caste of midwives 22.
Nagacho (Sarasvatī image at Sarasvatī Temple) 101, 200.
Nagacho (*ṭol* in Kirtipur) 40, 153, 200, 228.
Nagāoṅ (Naugam) village 29-30, 48-9, 154, 169-72, 174.
Nāgā Rāj (serpent-king) 65, 197.
Nāg Bāhā (Patan) 189.
Naikāp village 29-30, 35, 169.
Nakabihari 199.
Nālā village 126, 128, 130.
Nalanda 132.
Nand, Mishra Tara 176.
Nandī (bull vehicle of Śiva) 76, 192-3, 196-7, 199.
Nandurgā festival (associated with Durgā) 15.
*nāpika (nau)*, caste of barbers and surgeons 22, 27, 70.
Narasiṃha (Malla Rāja) 131, 133.
Naravocha (in Kirtipur vicinity) 161-2.
Nārāyaṇa (Vishṇu Nārāyaṇa) 201-2, 205, 208.
Nārāyaṇ Degaḥ (Kathmandu) 125, 127.
Nārāyaṇ (Nārāyaṇa) images at Bāgh Bhairav 79, 84, 87.
Nārāyaṇ (Nārāyaṇa) image at Nārāyaṇ Temple 100.
Nārāyaṇ (Nārāyaṇa) images at Umā Maheśvara 96.

Nārāyaṇ Temple at Bāgh Bhairav Complex 76, 83, 87-9.
Nārāyaṇ Temple (Kirtipur) 30, 75, 98-100, 123, 130.
*narendra* (*chhatrī*) caste 22.
Narendra Deva (Rāja) 193.
Nāsadya (Nṛityeśvara) shrine at Bāgh Bhairav 76-7, 80, 191.
Nāsapvā (Śiva as Lord of the dance) 200.
Naṭarāj 80, 198.
National Archive of Nepal 84, 212.
*natebaruda* caste 22.
*naṭījīva*, caste of actors, dancers and prostitutes 22.
National Museum of Nepal 135, 189, 203, 205-6, 240-1.
National Planning Commission (HMG Nepal) 7.
*nau* see *nāpika*.
Naudvan Bāhā (Patan) 82.
*nāy* (or *kasāī*), caste of butchers, 27.
Naya Bāzār (Kirtipur) 1-2, 24, 27, 45-9, 62, 121, 148-9, 152-4, 157, 161-2, 169-72, 176, 182, also see Amalshi.
Nāya Deva (legendary king of the Newars) 21.
Nayakoṭ 24.
*nekarmi* (or *kaua*), caste of blacksmiths 27.
Ne Muni the Sage 13.
Nepal 1-3, 7-9, 13, 15-16, 20-1, 24, 26-7, 32, 36, 40, 42-3, 45, 75, 82, 94, 110, 127, 131, 133, 135, 147, 151, 164, 167, 171, 181, 191-2, 200-1, 212, 240.
Nepali (*Nepālī*) language 21.
Nepali, G. S. 27.
Newari (*Nevārī*) language 21, 200.
Newars (Newar community) 1, 21-2, 24, 26-7, 30, 32, 34-5, 45, 49, 57-8, 63-5, 68, 70, 72, 120, 131, 135, 204.
Neyara (legendary homeland of the Newars) 21.
Nhaykaṅ Bahī (Patan) 146.
*nibharbari* (bronze workers), *śākya* sub-caste 26.
*nikhu*, *kshatriya* sub-caste 26.
*Nispanna yogāvali* 204.
*niyogī* caste 24.
Nṛityeśvara (Śiva as Lord of Dance) 200, also see Nāsadya.
Nṛityeśvara shrine at Bāgh Bhairav see Nāsadya shrine.
Nuvakoṭ 100.

Oldfield. H. Ambrose 8, 18-20, 27, 35-6, 40, 42, 48, 82, 87, 94, 98, 122-3, 125, 201, 206.

Padma Chaitya, Jagat Pāl Bāhā 240.
*Padmagiri Chronicle* 13.
Padmakīrtigīri Mahāvihār 146, also see Chīthuṅ Bahī.
Padmapāṇi Lokeśvar (deity) 103, 105, 107, 109, 240-1.
Padmapāṇi Avalokiteśvara 116.
Padmochcha Bāhā 131, 133, 144.
Pakanājol (Kathmandu) 80.
Pal, Pratapaditya 206.
Pala 206.
Pale Pukhū (lit. lotus pond) 177.
Pāliphal Ḍhokā (west gate of Kirtipur) 36, 38-40.
Pāliphal (*ṭol* in Kirtipur) 36, 52, 121, 152-3.
*pamā*, traders, a *śresṭha* sub-caste 70, 72.
Panauti village 29, 191, 204.
Paṅchā Dhyānī Buddha see Dhyānī Buddha.
Paṅchamī see Śrī Paṅchamī.
Paṅchamukha Brahmā (Brahmā with five faces) 79.
Paṅchā Tathagata 65.
Pāṇḍurā image at Chilaṅcho 108.
Pāṅgā (or Saṅkhapur) village 29-30, 48-9, 162, 169-72, 174.
Pānīghāṭ 167, 169.
*Pārbatiya* 22, 131.
Pārvatī (Parbati) (consort of Śiva) 35, 64-5, 84, 86, 96, 100, 189, 192-3, 197-200, also see Maheśvarī.
Paśupatināth 13, 100.
Patan 1, 8, 13, 15-16, 24, 27, 29, 40, 54, 57, 80, 82, 91, 94, 98, 108, 115, 117, 126, 130-1, 135, 146-7, 151, 167, 171-2, 189, 199 202, also see Lalitpatan or Lalitpur.
Patna 167.
Peking 167.
Persian (language) 146.
Pharping village 29, 167.
Phūdyacha images, Jagat Pāl Bāhā 241.
Pīgāṅ (Kirtipur) 38, 48, 101, 157-8, 233, 239.
Piṇḍa Bāhā (Patan) 80, 108.
Poole, Allen 7.
*poṛe* or *dyola*, caste of sweepers 27, 36, 43, 51, 55, 180.
Poṛe Ṭol or settlement (Kirtipur) 15, 38, 40, 49, 51, 153, 167, 184.
*pradhān* (*pramāṇ* in mediaeval Nepal), Hindu caste of administrators 27, 91, 142.
Pradhān, Jagat Bahādur 98.
Pradhān, Kaziman 98.
Pradhān, Lakshmaṇ 98, 100.
Pradhān Paṅcha of Kirtipur 71, 158.
Pragya Devī 116.
Pratap Malla (Rāja) 33.
Pṛithvī Nārāyaṇ (Gurkha King) 16-17, 24.
Pruscha, Carl 19, 122, 146.
Pūjādevī at Chilaṅcho 105, 107.
*pūjita* caste 22.

Rādhā Kṛishṇa images at Bāgh Bhairav 84.
Raj, Aryal Mukhand 206
Rāghava Bharo 108.
*rāja* (*chhatrī*) caste 22.
*rājaka*, caste of dyers and sweepers 24.
*rājbandari*, Hindu caste 27.
Rāma (deity) 90.
Rāmachandra Kaulācāra 122.
Rām Chandra (deity) 105.
Rām Chandra Temple at Bāgh Bhairav Complex 76, 83, 90.
Rām Malla (Rāja) 110.
Rām Navami (festival) 34.
Rānā family 9.
Rānā Malla (Rāja) 108.
Ranjit Malla (Bhaktapur Rāja) 16.
Rāṭhaura Bishva Nāth Bābu 91.
Ratna Malla (Rāja) 108.
Ratna Park (Kathmandu) 174.
Ratna Sambhava, Chilaṅcho 105, 108, 240.
Rato Machindra Nath (festival) 174.
Ravaṇa (deity) 198.
Raxaul 169.
Rea, Alexander 48, 74.
Red Cross 158.
Regmi, Dilli Raman 16, 19, 21, 27, 122, 206.
Rudrāyaṇī 79, 96.
Ruru Bhairav (one of the Ashṭabhairavas) 204.

*sachiva*, caste of men of arms 22.
Sadāchhyari Lokeśvar image at Chilaṅcho 105, 108.
Sadāśivadeva (Rāja) 13, 43, 123.

Sāgāl Ṭol (Sā Gā Tvāḥ) (Kirtipur) 13, 53, 121, 153, 158, 167.
Śaivi (a Mātṛikā) 76, 84, 86, 194-5, also see Maheśvarī.
*sajakāra* caste 22.
Saka Bāhā 64.
Śaktī (deity) 123, 125.
*śākya*, Buddhist caste, 26-27, 30, 142-3, 146.
Śākya, Gunajyoti 120.
Sakya, Hem Naj 122.
Śākyamuni Buddha image 115-17, 202-3, 241.
Śākyamuni Buddha Temple (Kirtipur) 72-3, 75, 117-20, 202-3, 210.
Sakya, Suresh 63.
Salayanch (in Kirtipur vicinity) 162.
Salichhen (*ṭol* in Kirtipur) 122, 153.
Salyanthān village 162, 171.
Samal (*ṭol* in Kirtipur) 36, 153.
Sambhara (deity) 189, 203-6.
Sambhara Bhairav (one of the Ashṭabhairavas) 204.
Saṃsthān, Gūṭhī, HMG Nepal 82, 113, 136, 142, 205, 240.
Samyak (festival) 189.
Sāñchī 132.
Sanday, John 8.
Śaṅkar (epithet of Śiva) 84, 86, 96, 126.
Saṅkhapur (or Pāṅgā) village 29-30, 48-9.
Sāṅkhu Road 171.
Sāṅkhu village 29.
Sanskrit 131, 142, 143, 146, 200.
*saṅghar* see *harahuru*.
Sanugāoṅ 171.
Sāpāru (second day of Gāi Jātrā) 33.
Sapta Ṛishi (seven hermits) 65.
Sarasvatī (deity) 103, 200, 202.
Sarasvatī images at Bāgh Bhairav 84, 87, 90.
Sarasvatī images at Sarasvatī Temple 101-3, 200.
Sarasvatī images at Umā Maheśvara 93, 96, 200.
Sarasvatī Temple (Kirtipur) 101-3, 200, 228.
Sarmā, Sadāsiva Rath 122
Sarnath 132.
Sarup Vats, Madho 176.
Satako (*ṭol* in Kirtipur) 34, 153.
Sat Tale Darbār at Nuvakoṭ 100.
Satuṅgal village 30, 169.
Sāyami (*ṭol* in Kirtipur) 46-7, 61, 153, 167.
Scheibler, Giovanni 8.
Schroeder, Ulrich von 206.
Shaivism 205.
Shantipur 191.
Shew Shunker Singh (Munshī) 19.
*shiyashu*, *kshatriya* sub-caste 26.
Shresthacarya, Ishwaranand 74
Siddhi Narasiṃha Malla (Rāja of Patan) 117, 144.
Sieverts, T. 74
*śilpakāra*, caste of craftsmen 22.
*Śilpa Prakāśa* 130.
Sinaduvā (*ṭol* in Kirtipur) 57, 70, 72-4, 117, 120, 138-9, 202.
Siṅghnī 204.
Sipāhī Bājyā see Jagat Bahādur Pradhān.
Sirsha, Mount (China) 21.
Śiśu Nag, the king of snakes, 64-5.
Sītā (deity) 90.
Śiva (deity) 87, 93-4, 96, 100, 123, 125, 128, 189, 191, 196-200.
Śiva Deva (Rāja) 80.
Śivadeva II see Sadāśivadeva.
Śiva images at Bāgh Bhairav 76, 80, 84, 86, 191-2, 195, 197-8.
Śiva *liṅga* (phallic emblem of Śiva) 87, 94.
*Śivamārga* (Hindus) 24, 26.
Śiva Śakti 65.
Śiva Temple at Bāgh Bhairav Complex 76-7, 83, 86-8.
Slekhamavti jungle (near Kathmandu) 13.
Snellgrove, D. L., 8.
Songa Road 171.
South Asia 2.
South-East Asia 131.
South India 21.
*śreshṭha*, *kshatriya* sub-caste 26-7, 29-30, 70.
*srichānte* caste 22.
Śrīdhara Vishṇu Temple at Bāgh Bhairav complex 76, 83, 86, 212.
Śrinivās Malla (Rāja of Patan) 115, 117.
*śriṅkharī* caste 22.
Śrī Pañchamī (festival) 34, 103.
Stahl, Anne Vergati 114, 122, 206.
Stanford's Geographical Establishment 7.
Stokes, Mark 7.
Suchhem Bharo 199.
*śūdra* caste 26.
Sukhāvati Lokeśvara (deity) 103, 105.
Sundarighāṭ 167.
Sundhara Patan 203.
*sūpika* caste 22.
*surābīja* caste 22.
Sūrya (sun god) 96, 98, 100, 191.
*sūrpakāra*, caste of cooks 22.
*suvarnakāra*, caste of goldsmiths 22.
Svayaṃbhū 191.
Svayaṃbhū Chaitya, Jagat Pāl Bāhā 240.

Ta Dhang Ga (Kirtipur) 158-9.
*takshaka*, caste of carpenters 22.
Taleju (clan goddess of the Mallas) 123.
Taleju Chhe 123.
Taleju Temple (Lāyaku) 189.
Taleju Temple (Patan) 98.
*tāmrakāra*, caste of coppersmiths 22.
Tananī (Taninī) (*ṭol* in Kirtipur) 43, 57, 69-74, 121, 153.
Tananī stupa 70, 111, 113.
*tandukāra* (or *khusal*), caste of weavers 22, 27.
Tang dynasty 15.
*tankādhārī* caste 22.
Tanlcha (in Kirtipur vicinity) 172.
Taphālan (street in Kirtipur) 170.
Tārā (Tārā Devī) (deity, lit. star) 103, 105, 107-8, 189, 197, 199, 205-6, 208, also see Ārya Tārā, Pāṇḍurā, Māmaki and Lochani.
*tayoruta* caste 22.
Tekusi Gate (Kathmandu) 169, 176.
*ṭhakur*, *kshatriya* sub-caste 24.
Thankoṭ 169.
Thames Polytechnic (University of Greenwich) 7.
Thimi town 40.
Thomson, Ian 7.
Tibet 21, 26, 103, 121, 131.
Tibetan monastry at Naya Bāzār 48.
Tibetan monastry at Pīgāṅ 48.

Tihār (festival) 34, 50.
Tika Bhairav Temple (Patan) 130.
Tīn Thana village 157.
Toffin, Gérard 27.
Town Plan Implementation Committee, Nepal 147, 149.
Trasisāngha Bibakhādeva (deity) 108.
Tribhuvan Highway 169.
Tribhuvan image at Bāgh Bhairav 79.
Tribhuvan University 1-2, 131, 136, 142, 147-8, 155-8, 160-1, 164, 169, 171-2, 174, 176, 181.
Tripureśvar (Kathmandu) 127, 176.
Tri-ratna shrine at Chilaṅcho 105, 107-8, 218.
Tri-ratna Temple (Buddha, Dharma, Saṅgha Temple) see Loṅ Degaḥ.
*triśūla* (trident of Śiva) at Umā Maheśvara 93-4.
*tulādhara*, caste of weighers 22.
Tulasī Degaḥ at Bāgh Bhairav 76, 83-4, 220-1.
Tuṅjalayachvaṅgu Bāhā 144, also see Padmochcha Bāhā.
Tuṅjho (*ṭol* in Kirtipur) 97-8, 144, 153, 201-2, 223, 225.
Tushahiti (Patan) 202.
Tvā Dvāra (Jagannāth Temple) at Kathmandu 100.
Tyangla (Kirtipur vicinity) 162, 171-2, 174, 176.

*uda*, Buddhist caste of metalworkers and traders 26.
Umā Maheśvara (Śiva Pārvatī) images at Bāgh Bhairav 84, 86, 90, 192.
Umā Maheśvara (Śiva Pārvatī) image at Nārāyaṇ Temple, 100.
Umā Maheśvara (Śiva Pārvatī) image at Umā Maheśvara Temple 96, 199-201, 211, 213.
Umā Maheśvara Temple (Bhaktapur) 126.
Umā Maheśvara Temple (Kirtipur) 10, 16, 19-20, 36,40-2, 75, 80, 90-6, 98, 101, 122-4, 126-7, 177, 189, 198-200, 213.
UNDP 8, 183-4
UNESCO 5-6, 8.
United Nations 2, 5-8, 147, 181.
Unmatta Bhairav (one of the Ashṭabhairavas) 204.
*upadhyāyā*, *brāhman* caste, spritual preceptor 24.
Upayā 206.
*urhay*, Buddhist caste 27.

Vairochana Buddha 202, also see Bairochana.
Vaishṇavī (a Mātṛikā) 76, 84, 86, 96, 193-5, 204.
Vaishnavism 205.
*vaiśya*, third Hindu caste, farmers and traders 26.
Vaitāl Deul (Bhubaneśvar) 130.
Valley see Kathmandu Valley.
Vaṃśa Gopāla (deity) 84.
Vārāhī see Bārāhī.
Varanasi (Benares) 167, 202.
Vasigā at Chilaṅcho 105.
Vāsudharā image, Jagat Pāl Bāhā 241.
Vāsuki see Basūki Nāg.
Vats, Madho Sarup 176.
*Vedas* 9.
Viradeva (Rāja) 15.
Vishow Rastriya School (Kirtipur) 158.
Vishṇu (deity) 64, 79, 83, 96, 123, 201, 204.
Vishṇu Narāyāṇa 201-2.
Vishṇu Temple see Śrīdhara Vishṇu.
Viśvakarmā or Viśvakarman (deity) 63-64, 90.
Viśvakarman Shrine at Bagh Bhairav 76, 83, 90.

Waldschmidt, Ernst and Rose Leonore 206.
Wang Hiuen-t'se 15, 167, 193.
Water Supply and Sewerage Corporation (HMG Nepal) 177, 181.
Winkler, Jurgen 206.
Wright, Daniel, 19-20, 27, 146.
Wustenfeld, Ferdinand 146.

Yāka Bāhā 131, 142-4.
Yakseśvara Temple (Bhaktapur) 202.
Yāqūt Hamawī 146.
Yoginī 65.